The Marion Experiment

The Elmer H. Johnson and Carol Holmes Johnson Series in Criminology

The Elmer H. Johnson and Carol Holmes Johnson
Series in Criminology

Survived by One: The Life and Mind of a Family Mass Murderer
Robert E. Hanlon with Thomas V. Odle

Negotiating Responsibility in the Criminal Justice System
Edited by Jack Kamerman
Foreword by Gilbert Geis

The Gambler King of Clark Street: Michael C. McDonald and the Rise of Chicago's Democratic Machine *Richard C. Lindberg*

Shattered Sense of Innocence: The 1955 Murders of Three Chicago Children *Richard C. Lindberg and Gloria Jean Sykes*
Foreword by Larry G. Axelrod

The Man Who Emptied Death Row: Governor George Ryan and the Politics of Crime *James L. Merriner*

The Marion Experiment: Long-Term Solitary Confinement and the Supermax Movement *Edited by Stephen C. Richards*

The Marion Experiment

Long-Term Solitary Confinement and the Supermax Movement

Edited by Stephen C. Richards

Southern Illinois University Press
Carbondale

Printed in the United States of America

18 17 16 15 4 3 2 1

Publication of this book has been underwritten by The Elmer H. Johnson and Carol Holmes Johnson Series in Criminology fund.

Cover illustration: Perimeter of an Israeli maximum-security facility. Courtesy of the Israel Prison Service

Library of Congress Cataloging-in-Publication Data
The Marion experiment : long-term solitary confinement and the supermax movement / edited by Stephen C. Richards ; foreword by Greg Newbold.
pages cm. — (The Elmer H. Johnson and Carol Holmes Johnson series in criminology)
Includes bibliographical references and index.
ISBN 978-0-8093-3376-9 (paperback)
ISBN 0-8093-3376-7 (paperback)
ISBN 978-0-8093-3377-6 (ebook)
1. Prisons—Law and legislation—United States. 2. Imprisonment—United States. 3. Solitary confinement—United States. I. Richards, Stephen C., editor.
KF9730.M37 2015
365'.33—dc23 2014015460

Printed on recycled paper. ♻

The paper used in this publication meets the minimum requirements of American National Standard for Information Sciences—Permanence of Paper for Printed Library Materials, ANSI Z39.48-1992. ♾

Contents

Foreword:
The Phenomenon of USP Marion

It was a fine, chilly November morning when United States Penitentiary (USP) Marion came into sight. Set on the flat, forested plains of southern Illinois, the low-profile buildings and razor wire–topped perimeter fences were as featureless as the landscape. An area around the prison had been cleared of trees, no doubt to remove cover for escapees, but otherwise the environment was pristine, pretty, and rustically silent. In contrast, the prison was forbidding and gray, and it reminded me of a place where, a couple of decades before, I'd spent most of my 20s.

Steve Richards and I have been mates for many years. In 2002, we hooked up at the American Society of Criminology conference in Chicago, and knowing my interest in Marion, he'd invited me to stay afterward at his home in Cincinnati. After a few days at Steve's and a couple of guest lectures at Northern Kentucky University, I drove west with him along I-64, across Indiana and into southern Illinois, reaching the small city of Carbondale. We spent the day meeting with criminologists at Southern Illinois University, who then treated us to dinner.

At the time, Marion, Illinois, was a small city of around 16,000 people with a fairly large mall, several businesses that together employed more than 500 people, and a modest number of local and chain restaurants and motels. Just outside of town is USP Marion. It's only a small pen by American standards; in fact, originally built for just 350 men, it's the smallest penitentiary in the federal system. Constructed with the same "telegraph pole" design used at the famous 19th-century prison of Wormwood Scrubs in England, USP Marion first opened in 1964. Originally run on liberal humanitarian lines, the place became famous when, in 1979, the Federal Bureau of Prisons decided to concentrate all the worst offenders in the federal system at a single institution and picked Marion as the location. A new level of security was created on top of the five levels then in existence. Thus in 1979, Marion became the nation's first level-six penitentiary, making it the first "supermax" of the modern era. From the 1980s onward, rising levels of violence led to even greater security, and in 1983, the prison went into permanent lockdown. This is one reason why the institution was of particular interest to Steve and me.

With the sun rising low in the autumn sky, the next morning Steve and I drove out to the prison. After establishing our credentials to the armed guard on the perimeter gate and having our vehicle searched, we were met at the institution by the executive assistant, Kevin Murphy. We had a brief discussion in his office, and then he showed us around the place, through the general population units, the intermediate and pretransfer units, and the special housing unit for disciplinary segregation units, or segs. Now over 40 years old, and with added accommodations providing housing for up to 483 men, Marion was looking shabby and run-down. It was hard to imagine that it had once been one of the most advanced, secure, and sophisticated prisons in the Western world.

All this certainly made the place interesting. But there was another reason why Marion was fascinating to me. In 1965, following a destructive riot at New Zealand's archaic 19th-century maximum-security prison at Mount Eden, the country had searched the world for modern ideas in high-security construction. Although it was impressed by new facilities at Blundeston in the United Kingdom and Kumla in Sweden, Marion had by far the greatest impact. So when a new prison at Paremoremo, New Zealand, finally opened in 1968, the influence of Marion was unmistakable. The prison was built on the same telegraph pole model as Marion, and the bars on the cells and sally ports used the same toughened manganese steel. The door-opening mechanisms were made upstate from Marion at Joliet, and the whole institution was linked by state-of-the-art intercommunications and closed-circuit television. Paremoremo, built to hold 240 men, was a modernized version of its big sister in Illinois.

In 1975, when I got sentenced to seven and a half years' imprisonment in New Zealand for selling an ounce of A-grade smack, they sent me to Paremoremo. Over the next few years, I became intimately familiar with the smells of floor wax and disinfectant and the echoing of whirring electronics and crashing grilles that characterized maximum-security prisons of the era.

Like Marion, Paremoremo started off with a liberal regime that encouraged education and other programs. But as occurred at Marion, it soon became corrupted by gangs and escalating violence. A brawl between the Mongrel Mob and the Head Hunters in 1984 caused segregation of the cellblocks and the end of many programs. Violence continued, and in 1998, influenced by what they knew about Marion, the managers at Paremoremo also put the prison into permanent lockdown. Thus it remains today.

Paremoremo is significant because it illustrates how substantially American social trends have become an international phenomenon and how, more particularly, American modes of criminal justice have been adopted in other parts of the world. Not only New Zealand but also Australia, Britain, and parts of Europe have followed the United States in establishing private prisons, supermaximum-security prisons, hair-trigger parole regimes, and sentencing policies like "three strikes and you're out." Punitive isolation practices are a part of this phenomenon.

I was one of the lucky ones. I served time in maximum security during the liberal era, before the advent of the gangs, the endemic violence, and the lockdown that followed. The research I did inside became the substance for the master's thesis I completed while still in Paremoremo Prison and provided the foundation for the doctoral dissertation I did when I got out. I am what I am now, a well-established university professor, because of the opportunities that were then available.

Prisoners who wind up in today's supermaximums have no such freedoms. Theirs are lives of highly controlled drudgery, boredom, and irrelevance. Days, months, and often years go by with little purpose or progress. When a man or woman is released from such a vacuum, with nothing to show but years of blankness, his or her chances of successful readjustment diminish. Thus a person who is a victim of a crime control problem may easily become a part of it. It is in the interest of awakening the public to the ramifications of this situation, and to the alleviation of it, that this book is dedicated.

Professor Greg Newbold
University of Canterbury
Christchurch, New Zealand

Preface

I have been thinking about writing this book for nearly 30 years. In 1984, I began my own Orwellian journey through the Federal Bureau of Prisons (BOP).[1] The authors in this book will take you to prison, inside and beyond into the segregation units where prisoners suffer the terror of solitary confinement. Once you open this book, there is no turning back. We are headed over the edge into the abyss. I warned you.

Although today I am a professor of criminal justice and criminology, my first introduction to the study of jails and prisoners was as a federal prisoner. Like many convicts, I learned about prisons the hard way. My writing in this book and other publications is both predicated on and prejudiced by this experience.[2] As a federal prisoner, I saw riots, murder, and suicide, and I spent my share of time in the "hole." I have seen men cut, beaten to death, take swan dives off of cellblock tiers, and end their lives through "suicide by gun tower." I have few illusions about the horror of prison.

Research Questions

Although I am now a tenured professor living a comfortable life, I cannot shake the past. A bad night is when I close my eyes to sleep and drift off into nightmare. I find myself back on the tier, walking the range, or locked in a cage.

I can see the faces and hear the voices of the penitentiary. Even today, many years after I got out of prison, I cannot forget.

As a former prisoner, I know long-term imprisonment is a traumatic, life-altering experience for many men and women. Most prisoners suffer significant damage, and some never recover.[3] In general, I hypothesize that the longer people spend in prison, the higher the security level of their confinement, and the more time they spend in solitary confinement, the more likely they will return to prison after release to parole or community supervision.

The fact is that the psychological adjustment required to survive doing time in high-security confinement is radical and bizarre. People enter prison as inmates, and over time, usually three years or more, depending on the individuals and the conditions they encounter in different prisons, they become full-fledged "convicts." Once they become convicts and learn the ways of the penitentiary, they acquire an edge and a hard shell that they may never entirely shed.

This Book Attempts to Answer the Following Questions

Part One

- Why is USP Marion historically significant for the construction and operation of supermax prisons in the United States and other developed nations?
- What do prisoners write about their own experiences with long-term solitary confinement?

Part Two

- How did USP Marion contribute to the supermax movement in the United States?
- What do we know about women and children locked up in solitary confinement cells?
- What happens to prisoners after many years of solitary confinement?
- How does solitary confinement affect prisoners that are vulnerable to mental illness?

Part Three

- What can we learn from international perspectives on the imprisonment of prisoners?

Conclusion

- Finally, what policy recommendations might we suggest to limit the damage done?

Plan for This Book

The questions above open a conversation that requires more than one author. There are many witnesses: Tens of thousands of prisoners have suffered long-term confinement in harsh conditions. In the introduction, I begin by offering my own argument and observations on the problem under study, and then add the voices and perspectives of convicts and fellow academic scholars.

The main body of this volume is divided into three parts. Part one, "Convict Experience With Solitary Confinement," includes five chapters written by the most authoritative authors on the subject. These authors have endured many years incarcerated in high-security penitentiaries. They write vivid accounts of what they have survived in some of the roughest prisons in the Western world. As some of these authors are still in prison, we should recognize the considerable courage required to share their critical accounts of solitary confinement.

Chapter 1, "The Politicization of the Hole in Indiana and Missouri," was written by Jon Marc Taylor, an accomplished convict author who has done over 30 years in maximum and medium security. Chapter 2, "The Realities of Special Housing Units in the Federal Bureau of Prisons," was written by Seth Ferranti while doing time in solitary confinement at a federal correctional institution in New Jersey. Chapter 3, "Going to the Hole in California: Cauldron of Solitude," was authored by Eugene Dey, a prisoner serving a "three strikes" life sentence for drug-related offenses in California. In Chapter 4, "The Boy Scout in Solitary at USP Lompoc," Brian Edward Malnes provides an intimate portrait of his experience in solitary confinement at a maximum-security federal penitentiary in California. In Chapter 5, "Long-Term Solitary Segregation in the United States and Canada," Gregory J. McMaster, a convict in Canada, takes the reader into the "hole" for an extended stay.

Part two, "The Effects of Solitary Confinement," includes four chapters written by prison scholars based on their personal observations of the use of solitary confinement. Each of these chapters demonstrates how USP Marion has served as a model for construction and operation of other prison systems. They also show how solitary confinement is used to punish and control women and children as well as men.

In chapter 6, "Theorizing Marionization and the Supermax Prison Movement," Kevin I. Minor and Marisa M. Baumgardner use the theoretical literature on punishment and society to better understand "Marionization" as a movement. Chapter 7, "Female Prisoners and Solitary Confinement," by Dennis J. Stevens, looks at girls and women doing time in segregation cells. In chapter 8, Christopher Bickel reports on "The Scene of the Crime: Children in Solitary Confinement." Chapter 9, by Russ Immarigeon, discusses the "Colorado Supermax Study: What the Critics Say and the Future Holds." In chapter 10, "Revisiting the Mental Health Effects of Solitary Confinement on Prisoners in Supermax Units: A Psychological Jurisprudence Perspective," Bruce A. Arrigo and Heather Y. Bersot explore how solitary confinement threatens the mental health of prisoners.

Part three, "International Perspectives on Solitary Confinement," begins with one more chapter written by a convict. In chapter 11, "Doing Hard Time in the United Kingdom," David Honeywell tells his tale about doing time in England's famous old Durham Prison. Chapter 12, "Solitary Confinement and Convict Segregation in French Prisons," Martine Herzog-Evans, examines the history of legislation and administrative rulings concerning high-security confinement in France. In Chapter 13, "Israeli Maximum-Security Prisons," Lior Gideon, Dror Walk, and Tomer Carmel discuss the innovative way the Israel Prison Service uses both the carrot and the stick to manage prisoners in maximum-security prisons.

Finally, in the conclusion, "Rethinking Prisons in the 21st Century," I suggest several policy recommendations to better manage prisoners without the use of long-term or supermax confinement.

I hope the reader will use this book to better understand the history of supermax imprisonment and how the Marion model has been adopted by a wide array of prison systems. Maybe when the public understands the failure of long-term solitary and supermax confinement as a correctional practice, and realizes the exorbitant cost in lives, we will see it outlawed in civilized society.

Stephen C. Richards
University of Wisconsin–Oshkosh
United States

Notes

1. For a similar story, see Raine, 1993.
2. See Richards, 1990, 1995a, 1998, 2003, 2005a, 2005b, 2008, 2009a; Richards & Ross, 2001, 2003a, 2003b, 2003c; Ross & Richards 2002, 2003, 2009.
3. See Ross & Richards, 2002, 2009.

Acknowledgments

I thank my wife, Donna, and son, Andre, and hope they forgive me for the many years we missed together. Also, I acknowledge the support received from my Convict Criminology colleagues and friends, including Tracy Andrus, Andy Aresti, Bruce Arrigo, Greg Barak, Thomas Bernard, Karen Bond, Mary Bosworth, Bud Brown, James Burnett, Todd Clear, Angela Crews, G. David Curry, Walter DeKeseredy, Chris Eskridge, Preston Elrod, Karen Evans, Bill Farrell, Jeff Ferrell, John Frana, Marianne Fisher-Giorlando, Bob Grigsby, Mark Hamm, Keith Hayward, Stuart Henry, Michael Hirsch, Richard Hogan, Veronica Horowitz, Matti Hytönen, Ekunwe Ikponwosa, Russ Immarigeon, Mark Israel, Robert Johnson, Annette Kuhlman, Michael Larsen, Tom LeBel, Paul Leighton, Michael Lenza, Shadd Maruna, Marc Mauer, Von Nebbitt, Daniel O'Connell, Brian Oliver, Bernie Olson, Barbara Owen, Stephen Parsons, Justin Piche, Richard Quinney, Matthew Robinson, Richard Rosenfeld, Julia Scott, Donna Selman, Randall Shelden, Matthew Sheridan, Charlie Sullivan, Nate Terrell, Chuck Terry, Jim Thomas, Grant Tietjen, William Tregea, Edward Tromanhauser, Kevin Walsh, Denise Woodall, K. C. Wong, Matthew Yeager, and Barbara Zaitzow. I especially need to thank Jim Austin, John Irwin, Rick Jones, Alan Mobley, Dan Murphy, Greg Newbold, and Jeffrey Ian Ross for their friendship and support building the Convict Criminology Group.

Earlier versions of three convict chapters were originally published in the *Journal of Prisoners on Prisons*. These articles have been revised and updated to focus on solitary confinement. Jon Marc Taylor's "The Politicization of the Hole in Indiana and Missouri," Gregory J. McMaster's "Long-Term Solitary Segregation in the United States and Canada," and Eugene Dey's "Going to the Hole in California: Cauldron of Solitude" appear in this volume with the express permission of the authors and managing editors at the *Journal of Prisoners on Prisons*. I wish to thank Editor-in-Chief Bob Gaucher and Managing Editors Justin Piché and Mike Larsen for their assistance in this regard.

I also wish to thank Kate Black, Eric Cadora, Eddie Ellis, Helena Huang, Miriam Porter, and especially Susan Tucker of the Soros Foundation. This publication was supported by a grant from Criminal Justice Initiatives of the Open Society Institute. The Soros Foundation Grant provided the funds to conduct on-site collection of data and observations at USP Marion and other federal prisons and to begin the book. Without the award of a Soros Justice Senior Fellowship, this book would not have been possible.

This book is supported by a grant from Elmer H. Johnson and Carol Holmes Johnson. The University of Wisconsin–Oshkosh approved a sabbatical semester so I could complete the final manuscript. Finally, I wish to thank Barbara Martin, Karl Kageff, and Wayne Larsen at Southern Illinois University Press, as well as copyeditor Joyce Bond.

The Soros Foundation, Open Society Institute, University of Wisconsin, Prisoner Visitation and Support, and FedCURE are not responsible for anything I write in this or any other publication.

The Marion Experiment

Introduction

Stephen C. Richards

This book tells how the experiment with long-term solitary confinement at USP Marion became the model for many states and other countries. The Federal Bureau of Prisons, each state, and the other countries discussed in this volume (Canada, United Kingdom, France, and Israel) all use different terminology to name the housing units or cell blocks where convicts are confined. For example, SHU may refer to special, secure, or segregated housing unit, depending on the prison system. While the official names may differ, the terms are interchangeable for both guards and inmates. In fact, over the years, different prison systems may change the names to conform to new law or correctional fashion. Regardless of how cellblocks are named, the experiment involves testing how long-term isolation affects the convict.

Most textbooks on prisons begin with a discussion of historical eras explained by reforms or advances in correctional philosophy. The historical eras are usually tied to new architectural ideas or ways to separate people into different institutions. The correctional philosophies are the socially accepted assumptions about how to punish people. A discussion of historical eras in the 20th century might start with descriptions of the various types of penal institutions: penitentiary, a maximum-security prison for older men, surrounded by a wall; reformatory, a medium-security prison for juveniles or young men, surrounded by a wall or fence; correctional institution, a medium-security facility for adult men, surrounded by a fence; and farm or camp, a minimum-security facility for short-term prisoners.

In contrast, the entire focus of this book is on long-term solitary confinement and supermax prisons. Solitary confinement is not new. Historically, most jails and every prison for juveniles, men, and women had a few segregation cells. It has been common practice in nearly every federal and state penitentiary, reformatory, and correctional institution in the United States to use solitary confinement to punish prisoners. What's new is the growth and expansion in the use of this practice; more cellblocks and entire prisons are filled with prisoners in long-term isolation. I submit that the Supermax Prison Era began in 1983, when the Federal Bureau of Prisons (BOP) built the first control units at United States Penitentiary (USP) Marion. This book is about how prisoners survive high-security cellblocks and supermax prisons. The reading will take you into the darkness, where prisoners struggle to cope with time alone in segregation cells.

Strange Worlds

Prisons are the distant country of this 21st century, strange worlds where people live in cages, doing time confined behind the walls and fences of security perimeters. Since 1970, the jail and prison population of the United States has increased tenfold, from approximately 200,000 to over 2.4 million today (Rose, Beck, & Richards, 2010).

Today, unbeknownst to most people, the United States is being transformed into a convict nation. The American landscape is littered with jails, prisons, and correctional facilities of various configurations, built here and there over the last 40 years. We have special prisons for men, women, juveniles, even drug offenders, traffic offenders, and sex offenders. There are so many prisons now that a pilot can navigate a plane at low altitude across the country at night guided by the high-security lighting of correctional institutions and penitentiaries.

Even the typical motorist can easily spot the high-security prisons in many states. Most facilities have tall gun towers and massive security perimeters. They are virtually impossible to miss as you drive along the interstate highways. Still, the public knows little about what happens behind the fences, inside the walls, where men and women live in absolute peril and quiet desperation.

This volume does not focus on the historical evolution of punishment and sentencing of criminals. There are already detailed accounts of how prisoners were brutally tortured and killed as punishments for their crimes,[1] as well as histories of legal theories that support these practices.[2] We would like to think that modern democratic societies no longer torture prisoners. Unfortunately, although we no longer use crucifixion, the rack, or drawing and quartering of prisoners, I would argue that modern long-term solitary confinement is another form of torture. Further, some of the modern practices, such as reduced rations, "hog-tying," forced administration of "chemical restraints," and the use of cattle prods, attack dogs, and gassing prisoners in their cells, while technologically different, are not far removed from the punishments meted out by the Romans two millennia ago, the aristocracy in the European Middle Ages, or sadistic guards in early 20th-century American prisons. Today prison control units are well equipped with an arsenal of torture devices routinely deployed to punish rebellious convicts. In fact, the hoods, leather straps, and clubs used today in many prisons are rather reminiscent of the medieval tools of the torture trade.

Long-term solitary confinement is slow torture, simply a bit less morally repugnant than tortures like stretching a man out on the rack or pouring hot lead down his throat, which might result in immediate death. Modern correctional authorities don't want to be charged with murder. Better to lock incorrigibles in concrete boxes, feed them as little as possible, restrict their communication, and force them to commit suicide or go crazy.

Solitary confinement cells have been a part of most, if not all, prisons in the United States since the opening of maximum-security "big house" penitentiaries in the 19th century. Today modern prison systems receive many prisoners that have received extremely long sentences. Because the criminal courts in large countries that are backward in their approach to dealing with criminals, like the United States, Russia, and China, still hand down death sentences, life without parole, and sentences of many decades, they are forced to build high-security cellblocks and supermax prisons where they confine tens of thousands of prisoners. In comparison, some of the more advanced Nordic, Scandinavian, and European countries, as well as New Zealand and Israel (discussed in this volume), have much shorter sentences and have developed more humane correctional practices.

Still, even the most progressive prison systems have classification procedures that decide if men or women prisoners are dangerous, a security threat, mentally ill, or unmanageable, as well as a disciplinary process that punishes or withdraws privileges when a prisoner violates institutional rules or policies, usually after a review or hearing. Nearly all national prison systems must segregate prisoners, such as during investigations or for a short time to give them an opportunity to regain composure and control of their own behavior. Unfortunately, many people with problems—social, economic, behavioral, or chemical—find themselves for a time confined in prison.

Concentration and Displacement

Given the difficulty of doing prison time, it is not surprising that prison systems have struggled with how to maintain order. In response, they use two practices to address misbehavior: "concentration" and "displacement." In the United States, both the federal and many state prison systems use concentration and displacement in an attempt to reduce prisoner attraction to gang affiliation or political ideologies. In every large prison, there are charismatic or predatory prisoners that are especially disruptive or dangerous because of their leadership abilities. These are the prisoners most prison systems attempt to neutralize through concentration or displacement.

The federal prison system first used USP Alcatraz, then USP Marion, and now Administrative Maximum Facility (ADX) Florence to concentrate the most difficult or dangerous prisoners. The construction of new supermax prisons in many state prison systems, based on the Marion model, is the most recent example of using concentration as a method of managing problem prisoners.

In comparison, displacement is an opposite idea that distributes problem prisoners to numerous prisons, and then transfers them again every few years as a means to isolate them and manage their influence on other prisoners. It may be a way for a prisoner to make a fresh start at another prison, to separate a prisoner from enemies or predators, or remove a prisoner from a prison where he or she has serious difficulties with other prisoners or staff. But distributing hard-core problem prisoners has its drawbacks. First, it may be responsible for spreading gangs or political ideas to more prisons. Second, it may simply be a way for wardens to unload their problem convicts on other wardens. And finally, distribution is usually done without consulting the prisoner. Male and female prisoners may have good reasons for requesting or resisting transfer to another prison; for example, they may want to be closer to family, the other site may have programs they want (e.g., prison work assignments or education), or they may have social relationships with prisoners at the other location. Unfortunately, maximum-security prisoners are not likely to be consulted before they are routinely transferred to another prison. In the federal prison system, they may be transferred across this vast country.

The reality is that prisoners do not do time passively. Imprisonment creates artificial worlds where resistance to authority grows, and is even honored. Some prisoners become Marxists or find religion, while other join gangs based on racial, ethic, or regional affinity. The point is that despite the efforts of prison administrators to control prisoners through concentration, displacement, or total isolation, their efforts are only marginally successful. The chapters in this volume written by convicts are testimony to the fact that whatever name prisons give to solitary confinement, and whichever way prison administrators try to break the will of prisoners, the convicts resist as they know they must to survive.

The Literature on High-Security Prisons

While the academic literature on prisons is large, the research on high-security prisons is limited in both depth and breath. Few authors have narrowed their focus to look exclusively at high-security penitentiaries and how prisoners survive long-term solitary confinement. Understanding the literature requires dividing the writers into five groups. The first group consists of prison administrators, staff, and archivists.[3] The second group is academic scholars, with some of their work officially sanctioned by prison administrators.[4] The third includes journalists and freelance writers who have authored reports and books.[5] The fourth consists of prison reform activists.[6] The fifth is prisoners that did or are doing time in federal or state high-security prisons, writing from a "convict or ex-convict perspective."[7] The authors of chapters 1–5 and 11 in this book are examples of educated convicts writing for an academic audience.

The five groups write very different accounts of penitentiaries. The prison administrators and staff tend to write noncritical articles and books that highlight their own achievements and discuss how prisons have improved over the decades. The academics, while more distant from the subject, provide a more varied approach. Much of their work attempts to penetrate the reality of high-security punishment through research and critical discourse. Nevertheless, few academic authors fully understand the horrors of prison. The journalists and freelance authors are an eclectic group of individuals that write from diverse perspectives. The prison reform activists include persons concerned with social justice, convicts, ex-convicts, and their family or friends. Their writing may also include pamphlets and websites designed to organize and encourage prison reform. The convicts and ex-convicts write from direct experience, from the "belly of the beast" (Abbott, 1981; Abbott & Zack, 1987).

A Convict Criminology Perspective

While I borrow from all five groups above, my account, and this book, is written from a Convict Criminology perspective. This perspective began with Frank Tannenbaum (1893–1969), a professor at Columbia University best known for his contributions to labeling theory. In 1914, Tannenbaum was a labor activist with the International Workers of the World when he was sentenced to one year in prison for unlawful assembly. He later used his personal experience with prison to write numerous magazine stories, journal articles, and books, including one of the best-known criminology textbooks of the 1930s, *Crime and the Community* (1938). Matthew Yeager (2011) tells the story of his career as a convict and then a professor in his journal article "Frank Tannenbaum: The Making of a Convict Criminologist."

The most famous Convict Criminologist is John Irwin (1929–2010). After being convicted for armed robbery and serving a five-year sentence in California's prison system, he received his doctorate in sociology from the University of California–Berkeley in 1968. Irwin taught sociology and criminology at San Francisco State University for 27 years. In prison, he discovered that convicts were mostly ordinary human beings. This insight, not entirely appreciated by many academics that study crime and criminals, guided all of his academic and political activities. His considerable research on prisons included six books: *The Felon*, *Prisons in Turmoil*, *The Jail*, *It's About Time* (with James Austin), *The Warehouse Prison*, and *Lifer*. He was also one of the contributing authors to the American Friends Service Committee's influential report *Struggle for Justice*.[8]

Stephen Richards and Jeffrey Ian Ross (2001) coined the term "Convict Criminology" in their first article introducing "The New School of Convict Criminology," published in the journal *Social Justice*. In 2003, Ross and Richards published the edited book *Convict Criminology*, with chapters written by the founders of the movement, which included eight autobiographical chapters by ex-convict criminologists, as well as a number of supporting chapters by "non-con" academics. This was the first time the writings of professors with prison records appeared in a book together, in which they discussed their own criminal convictions, time in prison, and transition from prisoner to professor.

In 2009, a paper titled "The First Dime: A Decade of Convict Criminology," by Richard Jones, Jeffrey Ian Ross, Stephen Richards, and Daniel Murphy, was published in *The Prison Journal*. In 2012, Stephen Richards and Mike Lenza edited a special double issue of the *Journal of Prisoners on Prisons* celebrating the 15th anniversary of the Convict Criminology perspective, group, and movement.

The Convict Criminology perspective is predicated on both convict memory and academic research, as illustrated in a long list of publications.[9] Most of the authors and coauthors writing from this perspective are ex-convicts that have become professors of criminology, criminal justice, or other related disciplines. We refer to some of the authors and coauthors as "non-cons." These are persons without felony convictions or prison records that have chosen to associate with our group and write from our perspective. Convict Criminology is a theoretical perspective that uses direct observation, face-to-face interviews, autoethnography, and retrospective analysis to penetrate the reality of distant social worlds.[10]

A Research Note

I have conducted research and written about prisons for more than 25 years. As a convict, I served a nine-year sentence beginning in 1984, completing parole in 1992. Three of these years I spent being transferred from prison to prison, doing time in minimum-, medium-, and maximum-security institutions, including USP Atlanta, USP Terre Haute, USP Leavenworth, and the first federal supermax, USP Marion. In total, I was incarcerated in nine different federal prisons in six different states. So I got a pretty good tour, or "forced passage,"[11] through the various convict worlds that exist at different levels of custody within the BOP. My research for this book began with those years I spent in cellblocks and dormitories collecting observations through both firsthand experience and conversation with hundreds of convicts. Through these conversations, I learned about conditions of confinement in many prisons, besides the nine institutions I had spent time in as a prisoner. This also helped me better understand how the federal system has grown and hardened over the years.

After getting out of federal prison in 1987, I went to graduate school, became a professor, and progressed through the ranks of the academy. I have devoted most of my academic career to the study of prisons and related subjects.[12] This has included mastering the voluminous literature on the subject. I have also carried on years of correspondence by mail and phone with many prisoners that have become authors of prison literature.[13] As the years pass, the number of prisoners continues to increase. Because of my publications and the Convict Criminology website, every month I receive numerous letters, emails, and phone calls from prisoners or their families from all over the United States and other countries asking for assistance, relating their own experiences with incarceration, or simply reaching out for understanding.

Upon becoming a professor, despite the research visits and correspondence with prisoners, I knew I would need to find new ways to get back inside, to spend more time close to my academic subject, if I were to comprehend the changes happening in the social worlds unique to prison. So, beginning in 1994, I served 10 years as a volunteer coordinator for Prisoner Visitation and Support (PVS). My volunteer group visited with prisoners at the Federal Medical Center, Lexington, a federal prison hospital facility in Kentucky. Every month, the group I coordinated visited family-style with more than a dozen different male prisoners.[14]

I also helped found (with Karen Bond) and still serve on the board of directors of the Federal Chapter of Citizens United for Rehabilitation of Errants (FedCURE). We welcome the public to our website with these words:

> FedCURE is the world's leading advocate for America's, ever growing, federal inmate population. On behalf of the Board of Directors, we would like to extend an invitation to each of you to join us in our efforts to reform the federal criminal justice system in the United States. Federal CURE, Incorporated is a nonprofit organization that, inter alia, deals largely with the issues faced by federal inmates and their loved ones.

The FedCURE Mission Statement reads as follows:

> Advocacy on behalf of the federal inmate population is the central focus of Federal CURE, Inc. (FedCURE). Realizing that successful advocacy can only occur when society has been enlightened about federal prison reality, FedCURE seeks to create a paradigm where elected officials and American society have a clear understanding of the issues confronted by the federal inmate population. Reducing crime in our communities requires society's involvement so that the federal criminal justice system can effectively address escalating crime rates through the adoption of alternative sentencing options in the federal court system; facilitate transitional services during reintegration into the community; and, reintroduce effective rehabilitative programming into the federal prison system thus engendering positive changes in the lives of those incarcerated within.

Today we have chapters in many states. Still, I deserve no credit for the growth of the organization. Nearly all the hard work was done by two former federal prisoners, Kenny Linn and Mark Varca, who have devoted nearly 20 years to organizing, managing, and building the group. The FedCURE website is an important resource for federal prisoners and their families.

As a result of serving as a contact person for both the Convict Criminology group and FedCURE websites, I am often asked to advise or informally counsel federal prisoners or their families. I receive requests for assistance from a diverse group of people, including men and women doing time for street, white-collar, and corporate crimes. I even receive mail from judges, lawyers, and law enforcement personnel serving time in federal prisons.

All of these activities over the last 25 years have allowed me to visit and converse with hundreds of federal prisoners, conducting nearly 300 formal and informal extended interviews of male and female convicts and ex-convicts. Most of these interviews were face-to-face, some by phone, a few by correspondence. I have also visited many state and federal prisons, managed education prison programs, served as invited speaker, conducted trainings, and toured numerous prisons across this country and other countries.

In summary, this book is based on my prior experience as a federal prisoner, years of visits with both state and federal prisoners, tours of prisons, and an exhaustive review of government, prison reform activist, and scholarly literature on federal penitentiaries and high-security segregation.

The Supermax Movement: "Marionization" of U.S. Prisons

As the U.S. prison population expanded from the 1970s until today, sentences got longer, and federal prisons became the standard for the states, more Marion-type prisons were built. USP Marion represents the blueprint for building supersecure state and federal facilities. Based on our observations and interviews of prisoners and prison staff, our research demonstrates a trend or movement in correctional policy to build more segregation cellblocks and supermax prisons. In addition, many medium-security federal correctional institutions (FCIs) have recently built new administrative segregation cells for solitary confinement to suppress the resistance of prisoners serving longer sentences.

States have recently turned to the use of supermax units or institutions to control the most disruptive or potentially troublesome prisoners. A survey conducted by the National Institute of Corrections in 1997 found at least 57 supermax facilities with more than 13,500 beds in the United States, and 10 jurisdictions were developing 3,000 additional supermax beds. In 1999, King updated this to nearly 20,000 cells in 34 states. Abramsky wrote in 2002:

> All told, more than 8,000 prisoners in California and at least 42,000 around the country, by the conservative estimate of the *Corrections Yearbook*, are currently held in similar conditions of extreme confinement. As of 2000, Texas alone boasted 16 supermax prisons and supermax units, housing some 10,000 inmates. In Florida, more than 7,000 inmates were double-bunked in such facilities and the corrections department was lobbying to build another one (at an estimated cost of nearly $50 million dollars) to house an additional 1,000 offenders. (p. 26)

Still, the figures are only estimates, as supermax is defined differently by many prison systems. At the very least, we know that across the country, a growing number of prisoners are being confined in high-security cellblocks, control units, segregated housing units, and supermax penitentiaries. In 2013, more than 2.3 million persons were incarcerated in jails and prison. Assuming 10 percent of prisoners are in disciplinary detention, including those persons locked in solitary confinement in local jails, there may be as many as 200,000 prisoners at this moment locked in high-security confinement.

"Marionization" refers to the spreading of design features and operational procedures from USP Marion in the redesign of existing prisons and construction of new ones. Since 1983, Marion has been closely studied by correctional experts all over the world. Abramsky (2002) reported:

> First, prison authorities developed procedures to minimize inmate-staff contact; then they took to "locking down" entire prisons for indefinite periods, keeping inmates in their cells all day and closing down communal dining rooms and exercise yards. Eventually, they began to explore the idea of making the general population safer by creating entirely separate high-tech super max prisons in which "the worst of the worst" gang leaders and sociopaths would be incarcerated in permanent lockdown conditions. (p. 27)

Prison administrators adopted high-security detention as a means to control dangerous prisoners, protect prison staff from violent assaults, frighten "mainline" prisoners, isolate politically active convicts that spread revolutionary ideas, and segregate gang leaders.

Isolating prisoners for many months in segregation cellblocks or for years in new stand-alone disciplinary prisons became the trend in the United States. Harrington (1997) wrote that "Marion was the model for programs adopted in prisons at McAlester, Oklahoma, in 1985, at Pelican Bay, California, in 1989, at Southport, New York, in 1991, and at Walpole, Massachusetts, in 1992" (p. 16).

Prison administrators argued that to isolate and segregate was cost-effective. This was predicated on the idea that prisoners confined in solitary confinement would require fewer amenities, services, and programs. This has not proven to be the case. Abramsky estimated in 2002 that it cost $50,000 a year to lock down one convict in a supermax compared with $20,000 to $30,000 a year in a lower-security prison (p. 28). Much of the expense is a result of the number of prison staff needed to patrol, service, and maintain the high-security regime in these institutions. The $50,000 a year does not even include the cost of constructing the supermax facility. High-security prisons are much more expensive to build, as they require extra gun towers, heavy security fences, sophisticated electronic surveillance equipment, and steel and concrete cellblocks comprising single cells. Their construction and operational costs will only escalate in the future.

Conditions of Confinement in Federal and State Supermax Penitentiaries

The new-generation supermax state prisons modeled after USP Marion are built like massive factories enclosed by heavy security fences and gun towers. They usually have double fences spaced 10 to 30 yards apart, with rolls of razor wire in between that may carry an electric current, and include remote sensors and video cameras to alert the guards of attempted escapes. Inside, these correctional institutions have limited space designated for convict employment in prison industries, recreation, or education. The housing units are pods with single-bed cells, each with a metal door and a combination toilet and sink. Communal showers are at the end of each tier.[15]

Virtually every state medium- and maximum-security prison has an isolation unit or disciplinary cellblock in which disruptive, difficult-to-manage, aggressive or escape-risk prisoners are kept, sometimes for months or years. Many of these convicts are men who have served long stretches in prison. Typically, this represents less than 10% of the total population, many of them prisoners serving long sentences, but can have a major impact on the prison system in general. Within this population is a small subset of prisoners that are the most violent, and difficult to manage, even in the confinement of a secure segregation unit. The management of this relatively small number of prisoners has consumed a tremendous amount of resources and effort because of their serious potential threat to staff and other prisoners. Although each jurisdiction developed its own unique approaches to the issue, states have recently turned to the use of supermax units or institutions to control the most disruptive or potentially troublesome prisoners.

The conditions of confinement in these supermax prisons are more restrictive than those on death row. For example, the typical death row in a state prison is composed of cells with bars. Even USP Marion, although the cells have concrete walls, was originally designed with open cell fronts. These were later changed to closed fronts, as all the housing units were converted to control units. Then in 1994, ADX Florence was designed with entirely closed-off cells, consisting of concrete walls and a solid steel door with a service slot.

The Marion Experiment

I met Victor Bono in 1998, just after he was released from federal prison. We talked for a few hours. I asked him about his time at Marion. Bono was a biker, caught attempting to smuggle 800 pounds of pot across the Mexican border. In 1967, at the age of 26, Bono pled guilty to two counts of murder and two counts of robbery in connection with the deaths of two U.S. Border Patrol agents. He spent nearly 31 years in federal prison for his crime, including many years at USP Marion. Bono wrote about his time at USP Marion, "Having spent a total of two and a half years in this experimental behavior laboratory-type fortress, I have witnessed atrocities that are on the same par as Pinochet's concentration camps in Chile and that of Hitler's Auschwitz" (Griffin, 1993, p. 17).

The Marion experiment began in the 1960s and continues on as the Marion model for prisons all over the world. According to Perkinson (1994):

> The Marion model for control-unit prisons originated within the Bureau of Prisons some 30 years ago. At a 1963 conference in Puerto Rico, prison administrators sought to cope with the closure of Alcatraz by dispersing "problem prisoners" throughout the federal system and experimenting with psychological rehabilitation programs (Ward and Carlson, 1994, p. 3). With the rise of national liberation movements, however, and especially after the Attica uprising of 1971, U.S. power brokers soon missed the ability of Alcatraz to isolate and rigidly control those who most articulately and effectively opposed their role. In an era of increasing economic stratification and civil disorder, they moved to create embryonic institutions of social control for whatever perilous conditions the future might hold. (p. 120)

The Marion experiment gradually evolved over a 20-year period, from 1963 to 1983. The Marion wardens operated the prison as a model "behavior modification laboratory."[16] Perkinson (1994) wrote:

> With this behavior modification experiment underway, Marion became the "end of the line" for federal prisoners. By the dawn of the Reagan era, when Warden Harold Miller assumed the helm, Bureau of Prisons' plans were already underway to convert Marion into a permanent isolation facility (Dunne, 1993, p. 40). It was a gradual transformation, and as prisoners resisted the erosion of their already limited civil rights, prison administrators justified each new step. After a long 1980 work strike, for example, the Bureau of Prisons permanently closed Marion's prison factory. The atmosphere became increasingly coercive and as guard violence, religious persecution, and other maladies increased, Warden Miller began the final crackdown. (p. 121)

The wardens used numerous pseudonyms and correctional rhetoric to disguise their "programs." Behavior modification at Marion consisted of Dr. Edgar H. Schein's brainwashing methodology, Skinnerian operant conditioning, Dr. Robert B. Levinson's sensory deprivation design, and chemotherapy and drug therapy (Griffin, 1993, p. 17). The prisoners were treated like lab rats.

Two chapters in Jessica Mitford's seminal book, *Kind and Usual Punishment: The Prison Business* (1973), should be required reading for social scientists interested in the abuse of prisoners. In chapter 9, titled "Cheaper than Chimpanzees," she told about how American universities used convicts as research subjects in drug trials. The prisoners were paid cigarettes for participating in studies conducted by pharmaceutical companies. Mitford wrote, "One of the nicest American scientists I know was heard to say, 'Criminals in our penitentiaries are fine experimental material—and much cheaper than chimpanzees'" (p. 139). Tens of thousands of prisoners were subjected to serious medical injury at prisons in Michigan, Iowa, Maryland, and California, to name just a few.

It was, she said, "the ultimate exploitation of the prisoner: systematically impoverished by his keepers, denied a decent wage, he is reduced to bartering his body for cigarette and candy money" (p. 163). According to Mitford, the academic researchers knew the experiments were not safe or ethical, and they could not conduct these studies on students or "free world" subjects because the universities would never permit it (p. 166). They set up shop in the prisons because they regarded the prisoners as less than human.

In chapter 8, "Clockwork Orange," Mitford discussed the Marion experiment at length and in chilling detail. Beginning in 1968, Dr. Martin Groder, the prison psychiatrist at Marion, implemented Dr. Schein's ideas about brainwashing prisoners. This included severing the inmate's ties with family, complete isolation, character invalidation, and thought reform. If the prisoner resisted, he would do many years in the control units or, worse, he would be forced to become a chemical zombie. As Griffin (1993) described it:

> Chemotherapy is administered four times daily at Marion. The loudspeaker announces: "Control medication in the hospital . . . pill line." Valium, Librium, Thorazine and other "chemical billy-clubs" are handed out like gumdrops. Sometimes the drugs mysteriously make their way into the food. For example, the strange month of December, 1974, recorded five unrelated, inexplicable stabbings. During the same time, eight prisoners suffered from hallucinations in the "hole" and had to be treated (with Thorazine injections). Drugs are often prescribed for minor ailments and are often suggested to prisoners as a panacea for all the psychological ill-effects of incarceration. Some drugs such as Prolixin make prisoners want to commit suicide. Some attempt it; some succeed. (p. 22)

After nearly 20 years of behavior modification experimentation on prisoners, Marion became a battleground.

Failure of the Control Cell Blocks

The experiments backfired. The behavior modification schemes did not work to turn the convicts into docile inmates, compliant subjects that would cooperate by testifying against each other. Instead, the result was work strikes, hunger strikes, assaults on staff and other inmates, and resistance to Groder's schemes. The convicts resisted the experiment at every turn, refused to share information with prison staff, and even organized escapes. The toughest convicts became the spiritual leaders of the resistance. By 1983, federal prison administrators knew the game was over. They wanted an excuse to end the "program" and convert all the housing units to total isolation control units. Perkinson (1994) explained:

> The immediate pretense was a series of murders inside. On October 22, 1980, prisoners in the control unit separately stabbed two guards to death. Four days later, a prisoner was found murdered in his cell (Dowker & Good, 1993, p. 3). Although two perpetrators were brought to trial and convicted of murder, [Warden Harold] Miller placed the entire prison under a state of emergency on October 28. The Bureau of [P]risons transferred riot squads with names like the "A-Team" and "Blue Thunder" from other prisons and a comprehensive shakedown began on November 2 (Dunne, 1993, p. 52). With every prisoner locked 24 hours a day in solitary cells, guards began a veritable reign of terror more violent than anything since the Attica rebellion. Guards in full riot gear removed their nametags and moved cell by cell through the prison, extracting and beating inmates and confiscating their property (Amnesty International, 1987, p. 1). (p. 122)

From the prisoners' perspective, after 1983, with all the medical pretenses long gone, the real experiment began. They knew now for sure that there was no way to "program out" of Marion. The struggle became staying alive, surviving the madness of long-term isolation. Perkinson (1994) wrote:

> After several weeks of total lockdown, Marion settled into its present conditions. It has served as the cutting-edge model for control-unit prisons ever since, dispensing entirely with the seemingly anachronistic rhetoric of rehabilitation and linking punishment to every aspect of prisoners' lives. Today, Marion prisoners spend 23 hours each day in their cells alone. There are limited educational and religious services, no central library, and no job-training program. In the most controlled cell block, inmates are allowed only one 10-minute phone call each month, three showers per week, and they can never move from their cells without shackles and handcuffs. At any sign of resistance, the prison's Special Operations Response Team (SORT) uses "whatever force is necessary" to restore order, including chaining prisoners to their beds for days at a time (*ABC's "20/20,"* 1988). All this is at the cost of $40,000 per prisoner every year. "Marion is an experiment," Chicago Lawyer Jan Susler comments, "to see how much a prisoner can take before he breaks, to see how far they can dehumanize somebody before they completely lose their sanity" (*The Washington Post*, May 28, 1991). (p. 123)

The Marion experiment resulted in the destructive use of sensory deprivation, deterioration of prisoners, suicides, murders, and senseless damage of human life by an institution set up to bend, break, and destroy men. Those that were not broken got even stronger and more dangerous. Thus Marion and other supermax penitentiaries are systematically socializing prisoners to be serial violent offenders. Conversely, research may also conclude that only a small number of federal prisoners require the close supervision provided by USP Marion's control unit design.

An International Model

Information is power. Today we live in an age where governments require intelligence information to conduct military operations around the world. At the same time, the use of supermax confinement to "debrief" prisoners has spread from correctional institutions to intelligence agencies and the military. *Debrief* is the official term federal law enforcement uses for interrogating or "interviewing" suspects and prisoners. For example, if a prisoner shares information about prison gang activity, he or she may be released from a control unit or "experimental group." Today many suspected terrorists are confined in supermax prisons until they debrief.

The War on Terrorism dates back to the 1980s. The term refers to the global war waged by the United States, United Kingdom, and the North Atlantic Treaty Organization (NATO) against Islamic terrorism, especially in Iraq, Afghanistan, Pakistan, Syria, and other nations.

On November 7, 2007, on *The Washington Post* online chat, Stephen Grey, an investigative reporter for *Frontline/World*, discussed his investigative report "Extraordinary Rendition" and his book *Ghost Plane: The True Story of the CIA Rendition and Torture Program*. In his *Frontline* video program, Grey documented stories of hundreds of people, many them innocent civilians, being abducted in numerous foreign countries on suspicion that they have knowledge of terrorist activities. He asserted that the U.S. Central Intelligence Agency (CIA) and military orchestrate these kidnappings.

In *Ghost Plane*, Grey referenced CIA flight records and interviewed dozens of sources, from the most senior levels of the National Security Council to the CIA, to tell the true story of the CIA's program of torture, known by the euphemism "extraordinary rendition." Since the 1990s, thousands of people have been "rendered" expendable. Begun during the Clinton administration and expanded after Al-Qaeda's September 11, 2001, terrorist attacks in the United States, the rendition system includes secret prisons stretching from Guantanamo to Syria, Kabul, Bangkok, and Eastern Europe. Among these "dark prisons" were Abu Ghraib prison (also known as Baghdad Correctional Facility) in Iraq and the Bagram Theater Internment Facility (also known as Bagram Collection Point or BCP) in Afghanistan, operated by the U.S. military. Numerous military personnel at these prisons have been convicted of torturing prisoners. The CIA later set up dark or secret interrogation prisons in Romania and on an airbase in Poland.

The lessons learned in the Marion experiment are now being applied on a global scale, as the U.S. military and CIA are operating control units at Guantanamo Bay and Abu Ghraib and countless "rendition prisons" across the globe.

Although reported tortures include "waterboarding," sleep deprivation, bright lights, and loud noise, these are necessary only when the interrogators require information quickly, such as about imminent terrorist attacks. The vast majority of prisoners are broken by long-term solitary confinement, degradation, and humiliation. Ultimately, after months or years in isolation, they "voluntarily" submit to "debriefing" to protect their sanity and defend against madness.

The Marion experiment began the supermax movement, which encouraged prison systems all over the world to build long-term solitary cellblocks. Today, in the information age, the U.S. military and intelligence agencies have adopted the same model in their War on Terrorism. Thus a failed experiment is now being replicated on an international scale. As in the Inquisition that began in France in the 12th century, torture is again in vogue, as the Marion experiment and supermax movement are visited upon the 21st century.

Jacob's Ladder

Alone in his cell at USP Marion, a man talks to himself and all the imaginary figures that come and go. The description of Jacob's ladder appears in the book of *Genesis* (28:10–19 English Standard Version):

> Jacob left Beersheba, and went toward Haran. He came to the place and stayed there that night, because the sun had set. Taking one of the stones of the place, he put it under his head and lay down in that place to sleep. And he dreamed that there was a ladder set up on the earth, and the top of it reached to heaven; and behold, the angels of God were ascending and descending on it!

The prisoner welcomes the angels to his cell, he converses with them, and when he closes his eyes, they are gone. They return at will, as they decide, each with a different face, somehow familiar.

After a few years in solitary confinement, deterioration sets in. The convict's routine of study, exercise, and prayer cannot completely overcome the loneliness of isolation. Slowly, over time, he slips into the abyss. When his memory fails, he is lost. Like the prisoners at Eastern State Penitentiary in the 19th century, the Marion convicts struggle every day to remain sane. Griffin (1993) wrote about what he experienced at USP Marion:

The cell itself contains a flat steel slab jutting from the wall. Overlaying the slab is a one-inch piece of foam wrapped in coarse plastic. This is supposed to be a bed. Yet it cuts so deeply into the body when one lays on it, that the body literally reeks with pain. After a few days, you are totally numb. Feelings become indistinct, emotions unpredictable. The monotony makes thoughts hard to separate and capsulate. The eyes grow weary of the scene, and shadows appear around the periphery, causing sudden reflexive action. Essentially, the content of a man's mind is the only means to defend his sanity.

Besides these methods of torture (and they are torture), there is also extreme cold conditioning in the winter, and a lack of ventilation in the summer. Hot and cold water manipulation is carried out in the showers. Shock waves are administered to the brain when guards bang a rubber mallet against the steel bars. Then there is outright brutality, usually in the form of beatings. The suicide rate in the Control Unit is five times the rate in the general population at Marion.

At the root of the Control Unit's behavior modification program, though, is indefinite confinement. This is perhaps the most difficult aspect of the Control Unit to communicate to the public. Yet a testament to this policy was a man named Hiller "Red" Hayes. After thirteen years in solitary confinement (nearly six in the Control Unit), he became the "boogie man" of the prison system—the living/dying example of what can happen to any prisoner. The more he deteriorated in his own skeleton, the more prisoners could expect to wane in his likeness. He died in the Unit in August, 1977. In essence, the Unit is a Death Row for the living. And the silent implications of behavior modification speak their sharpest and clearest ultimatum: *conform or die*! (p. 23)

Notes

1. See, e.g., Foucault, 1975/1979.
2. See Duff & Garland, 1995; Morris & Rothman, 1995.
3. E.g., Henman, 1988; Corrothers, Alexander, Carlson, & Quinlan, 1994; Roberts, 1994; Carlson, Hess, & Orthmann, 1999; Neal, 2003.
4. E.g., Lockwood, 1980; Fleisher, 1989; Hamm, 1991, 1995, 1997; Keve, 1991; Hamm, Coupez, Hoze, & Weinstein, 1994; Ward, 1987, 1994; Silberman, 1995; Bosworth, 2002; Briggs, Sundt, & Castellano, 2003; Rodriguez, 2006; Sundt, Castellano, & Briggs, 2008.
5. E.g., Mitford, 1973; Earley, 1993; Harrington, 1997; Annin, 1998; Parenti, 1999; Abramsky, 2002.
6. E.g., American Friends Service Committee, 1985/1993, as well as various publications of Amnesty International, the Committee to End the Marion Lockdown, and Human Rights Watch.

7. E.g., Abbott, 1981; Abbott & Zack, 1987; Richards, 1990, 1995a, 1995b, 1998, 2003, 2004a, 2004b, 2005a, 2005b, 2008, 2009a, 2009b; Dowker & Good, 1993; Dunne, 1993; Griffin, 1993; Raine, 1993; Wilson, 1993; Richards & Jones, 1997, 2004; Levasseur, 1998; Levasseur & Burton-Rose, 1998; Pens, 1998; Peltier, 1999; Richards & Ross, 2001, 2003a, 2003b, 2003c; Ross & Richards, 2002, 2003, 2009; Murphy, 2003; Mobley 2003; Hassine, 2011.

8. See Richards, 2009b; Richards, Austin, Owen, & Ross, 2010a, 2010b, 2010c.

9. E.g., Irwin & Cressey, 1962; Irwin, 1970, 1980, 1985a, 1985b, 2005, 2009; Richards, 1990, 1995a, 1995b, 1998, 2003, 2004a, 2004b, 2005a, 2005b, 2008, 2009a, 2009b; Austin, Bruce, Carroll, McCall, & Richards, 2001; Austin & Irwin, 2001; Richards & Ross, 2001, 2003a, 2003b, 2003c, 2004, 2005, 2009; Richards, Terry, & Murphy, 2002; Ross & Richards, 2002, 2003, 2009; Mobley, 2003; Murphy, 2003; Terry, 1997, 2003; Richards, Ross, & Jones, 2008; Jones, Ross, Richards, & Murphy, 2009; Ross et al., 2010; Richards et al., 2011; Richards & Lenza, 2012: Ross, Richards, Newbold, Lenza, & Grigsby, 2012; Richards, 2013a, 2013b.

10. See Richards & Ross, 2001; Ross & Richards, 2003; Murphy, Fuleihan, Richards, & Jones, 2010; Lenza, 2011; Richards et al., 2010; Richards et al., 2011; Newbold, Ross, Jones, Richards, & Lenza, 2014.

11. See Rodriguez, 2006.

12. See, e.g., Richards, 1990, 1995a, 1995b, 1998, 2003, 2004a, 2004b, 2005a, 2005b, 2008, 2009a, 2009b.

13. See, e.g., the writings of K. C. Carceral, Seth Ferranti, Victor Hassine, Wilbert Rideau, Jon Marc Taylor, Ron Wikberg, and many others.

14. See Beck, Richards, & Elrod, 2008.

15. For more details, see Austin et al., 2001.

16. See Griffin, 1993. This is an amazing article written by Eddie Griffin, a former civil rights activist and Black Panther, that lays out the details of the Marion experiment, including all the chemical and psychological torture visited upon the prisoners.

PART I

Convict Experience With Solitary Confinement

> We must destroy the prison, root and branch. That will not solve our problem, but it will be a good beginning. . . . Let us substitute something. Almost anything will be an improvement. It cannot be worse. It cannot be more brutal and more useless.
>
> —Frank Tannenbaum, *Crime and the Community*

| 1 |

The Politicization of the Hole in Indiana and Missouri

Jon Marc Taylor

As McMaster (1999b) wrote, "Placing a writer in segregation is probably the most efficient form of censorship employed by corrections" (p. 49). It definitely complicates the situation and frustrates the victim, although it is not entirely successful in quashing the voice. For the past 32 continuous years, I have been doing (not serving) time in maximum-security midwestern state penitentiaries. During this tenure of Convict Criminology (Richards & Ross, 2001, 2003), I have experienced or witnessed about everything that occurs behind bars, from riots to rapes, robberies to roughhousing, assaults to escapes, and mayhem to murder. I have known some gentler aspects as well, such as the enlightenment of education, the friendship of good men, and the forgiveness of understanding.

Dominating every aspect of every minute of this existence has been the absolute, totalitarian, controlling presence of the state penal apparatus. Short of death row culminating in execution, solitary confinement, also known as the "hole," is the worst form of imprisonment. Many euphemisms have been created to obscure the dire circumstances of this reality—administrative segregation (Ad Seg), maximum restraint unit (MRU), security housing unit (SHU)—all obfuscating the elemental horror to the human spirit that such places may provide.

I am the first to acknowledge that restraint units (i.e., jails within the prison) are necessary, but to be true to their identification with jails, a person should only be confined in these holes for a relatively short time. Very few prisoners are violent predators that require long-term isolation for the "safety and security of the institution." However, that is another matter altogether and not the subject of this commentary.

The hole may be used as an internal political gulag (Solzhenitsyn 1973, 1975, 1978; Richards, 1990) to punish the prisoner activist and author. While at the Indiana State Reformatory during the 1980s and early 1990s, I only indirectly experienced the influence of the lockup units.[1] After being transferred to the Missouri Department of Corrections, as a result of consecutive sentencing, my contact with the hole became more personal. All encounters, though, were politically motivated. In this chapter, I discuss my time in Indiana and Missouri prisons, focusing on how my political activism resulted in my long-term confinement in the hole.

The Indiana Department of Corrections

During the thirteen and a half years I did time at the Indiana State Reformatory (ISR), I never saw the inside of the hole. Still, most prisoners understand how the growing use of solitary confinement is used to abuse and punish. A federal court's finding of fact cited that prisoners were routinely stripped naked and fastened to four-point restraints on slat metal bed frames in the dead of winter, with the windows left open, in the maximum restraint unit.[2]

By 1986, the organized beatings of convicts by the guard "goon squad" became so routine in this prison's MRU and Ad Seg unit that it led to the bloodiest riot and hostage takeover in the reformatory's six-decade history. The violence included the stabbing of seven guards, the taking of three hostages, and the seizure of a cellhouse by prisoners. The entire Department of Corrections (DOC) was locked down, meaning all the Indiana state prisons; the National Guard was activated; and representatives from the state legislature came to the penitentiary to negotiate a peaceful resolution. A few years later, various correctional officers were convicted of federal civil rights violations and officially blamed for instigating the riot.

As a result of this event, and in conjunction with the emerging national trend, the state built the 200-bed Maximum Control Complex (MCC) at Westville, Indiana. Still, by the end of the second year of operation, the supermax prison was only one-third occupied. Conditions in this new high-security penitentiary were so desperate that two prisoners self-amputated fingers and attempted to mail them to the state's U.S. senators in protest. Amnesty International eventually condemned the facility, along with California's Pelican Bay, for violation of the prisoners' basic human rights.

In 1991, in a move perceived by the prison population to be a smoke screen, the ISR administration announced while the "hole" at the reformatory was remodeled, the 100 men in the lockup units, MRU and Ad Seg, would be "temporarily" transferred to the Westville MCC. The general consensus was that once the men were transferred, doubling the population of MCC—though still not filling it—those men so exiled would not be transferred back. The move was viewed as an excuse for the DOC to circumvent its own transfer and admittance regulations and to camouflage the waste of tens of millions of construction dollars for the unnecessary supermax prison.

Prisoner Protest and Administrative Reaction

In October 1991, a unique prisoner protest began.[3] It was surreptitiously organized by the older and better-educated convict leaders, most of whom had lived through the turbulent 1980s and were keen observers of the DOC's response to violent altercations. They persuaded the younger prisoners to adopt a different strategy of peaceful protest. If the alternative strategy failed, the hotheads were told, they could always "go to war." Instead of a costly riot that they knew would be ultimately futile, the men executed a nonviolent, nondisruptive demonstration of silent solidarity. At the conclusion of the early evening recreation period, 200 to 300 men quietly marched around the large drill field. There were no threatening or militant gestures, just a formation four abreast, displaying a unity unseen at the prison in anyone's memory.

No manifestos were issued. No leaders were apparent by actions. None of the prison staff was entirely cognizant as to what was transpiring and why the peaceful demonstration was being conducted.[4] With such near universal participation and no immediate rules having been broken, the guards returned the men to their respective housing units. In response to the "unity walks," each participating housing unit was placed on lockdown status. Over the next two days the protest continued, as additional housing units marched, eventually involving all of the "mainline" (general) population. The ragged formations would have made any drill sergeant apoplectic, but the intent of unity was apparent for all to see. The supportive cohesion surprised even the organizers and, more importantly, prevented violence.

On Monday morning, the lockdown was lifted with no further administrative action, such as shakedown or isolation of instigators. Then at lunch the next day, on orders from the central office, the entire prison was returned to lockdown.[5] This time it lasted seven months, becoming what was then the longest lockdown in the state's history. Thus the "Marionization" of the Indiana State Reformatory was ordered by the administration, even though not a drop of blood had been shed nor an angry word said.

The prison administration went through a litany of rationales for the punitive action.[6] The entire Indiana State Reformatory became a prison hole. This meant there would be no hot meals, family visits, phone calls, recreation, or work activities, with only one shower every three days. All of this created extreme psychological trauma, and there was a large increase in the number of successful suicides during this period.

Also in response, one entire cellhouse was designated as Ad Seg, with the old MRU being closed. One-quarter of the 300 cells in the three-tiered building were caged in, more than doubling the prison's maximum restraint capacity, while the rest of the cellhouses were used as general-purpose "non-punitive" isolation units. Prisoners were allowed to go to scheduled meals in the mess hall, and they were allowed time on the yard, although their recreation line was kept separate from the mainline population, but no education or work assignments were permitted. The end result of this overreaction by the DOC was that one-quarter of the prisoners were held in segregation or control units. In hindsight, might the "unity walks" simply have been used as justification for the ratcheting up of further system-wide control?

New Maximum-Security Prison

In 1993, the state opened its newest maximum-security prison, the Wabash Valley Correctional Center. To facilitate transfer of prisoners to the new prison, the Indiana State Reformatory was redesignated as a level-four medium-security institution, necessitating the transfer of all level-five prisoners to the new prison. This lowering of custody level of the prison, from level-five max to level-four medium, did not negate the use of the previously created control units. Thus a medium-security prison had more than 400 prisoners in 24-hour lockup.

Once the new prison was filled, the correctional fairy waved his hand again, and "abracadabra," ISR was redefined as a level-five prison. All of the remaining pre-1993 prisoners who had not been transferred and reclassified as medium-security custody level were, by default, re-reclassified as maximum-security hooligans.

The Missouri Department of Corrections

My experience with the hole became much more personal a few years after my arrival in Missouri. For years, even before my transfer to this system, I have been a community activist, social lobbyist, writer, and researcher.[7] After being cited in the *Congressional Record* and criticized by name by members of the U.S. Congress for my support of Pell Grants for prisoners,[8] writing multiple editorials rebutting fallacies or illuminating opportunity costs of the criminal justice system (Taylor 1996a, 1996b, 1997b, 1997d, 1997f, 1997g, 1997h), and even eventually crafting the introduction of positive correctional education bills in the state legislature,[9] I learned firsthand about long-term hole time.

In 1996, while at the Jefferson City Correctional Center (JCCC), I wondered, why not use the multi-million-dollar rebate from the Inmate Collect Call Phone System contract to refinance post-secondary correctional education (PSCE) opportunities in Missouri? This was only one of three states with rebates from their prison phone contracts that were not used to support prisoner education and welfare funds. Instead of being deposited directly into the state's general fund, I suggested, the $3 million could be used to pay for college courses for prisoners.

Writing a white paper on the concept (Taylor, 1997a), working with outside and inside activists, I had compatible bipartisan enabling legislation introduced in the Missouri House (H.B. 424) and Senate (S.B. 336). Using an analogous article from *U.S. Catholic* magazine (Leder, 1996) as a segue educational piece, I wrote to all the legislators of the Catholic faith (approximately one-third of the 160 seats), urging them to support their chambers' respective bills. Moreover, I wrote similar letters to some 60 college professors and university presidents across the state, seeking their political support in expanding higher-education opportunities for prisoners.[10]

Political Punishment

During this period of active lobbying, three seemingly inconsequential, though in hindsight revealing, events transpired. Shortly after posting approximately 50 sealed letters to the aforementioned legislators,[11] while returning to the housing unit from my work assignment, I crossed paths with one of the prison's investigators. Never having had an occasion to interact with him, I was surprised, as we waited for a security gate to open, when he offhandedly commented about my "interesting mass mailing to the legislature." Walking away, I wondered, how did he know who I was?

Next, a "free world" activist related to me an encounter she and one of the legislative sponsors of a bill had had with a high-ranking DOC official immediately after a hearing on the legislation. According to the state representative, the DOC official had cryptically quipped over her shoulder, "It's too much money." Curious as to what the official had meant, and acting on a hunch, the representative retrieved the new phone contract from the Public Services Commission, learning the rebate had increased (along with the overall rates) more than threefold to a guaranteed $10 million per annum. This essentially hidden program then became $10 million in non-tax-induced revenue, a politician's dream come true. Moreover, this was a substantial sum, making one curious as to why the DOC did not advocate for its direct use.

As a member of the executive board of the JCCC's Charitable Campaign Committee, I organized several publicity events about the prisoners' donations that were covered in the local newspapers and newscasts. By default, as the other prisoners on the committee were camera shy, I became the spokesman. At one multimedia-covered presentation of three $1,000 checks donated to local charities, the third curious incident occurred. I asked the DOC's public relations director if the commissioner of corrections would support our efforts to start a blood donation drive. As we were standing together, watching a news crew conducting sound bite interviews, I sketched a picture of two prisoners side by side on gurneys, one white, the other black, donating the 999th and 1,000th pints of blood "from the men of the Jefferson City Correctional Center." He laughed, turned, and called me "a dangerous man."

Shortly thereafter, the state's latest maximum-security prison, Crossroads Correctional Center, came online. For the next 90 days, a couple of busloads a week left the old prison to fill the new one. Volunteers were requested from among the convicts for immediate transfer, to be followed by "disciplinary" prisoners (i.e., those prone to conduct violations). While several hundred prisoners did volunteer for transfer to the northeastern corner of the state, most sweated out the selection process. By June, the new joint was pretty much filled.

One week after I assumed the directorship of the Center for Braille and Narration Production, the most responsible inmate job in the Missouri Department of Corrections, I received a phone call in my fifth-floor office. As I stood, looking out the window over the prison wall at the golden dome of the state capitol, where my correctional education legislation had recently been defeated, the officer on the line ordered me to report back to my housing unit and pack my personal property. I was being sent to the new prison on the last bus.

In my three years at the state prison, I'd had only one violation for the most minor offense possible. I had just earned my dream job of my prison experience and was well involved in contributing to community affairs. I placed a call to the assistant superintendent with whom I had consulted on many prison programs, seeking his intervention to cancel the transfer, but was told that the order had come from the DOC Central Office. By way of explanation, he attributed it to my editorial and legislative activism, which he privately applauded. "You have disturbed the status quo of the powers that be"—he really spoke like this—"and they want you as far away from the state capitol as possible. Crossroads," he quipped, "is about as far as you can get." One week later, I was in the hole on charges of guard assault and drug possession.

The Setup

At the bewitching hour, the solid steel door was yanked open. The white-shirted sergeant charged in, screaming, "What's that smell?" Sitting at the small metal desk, watching TV with the headphones on as my cellie slept, I had extinguished a tobacco cigar moments before.

Startled, I asked, "Huh?"

Yelling in my face, the sergeant ordered me to my feet. "Give it up."

"What?" I asked.

Standing less than 3 feet from me in the cramped space of the cell, he ordered, "Strip."

Understanding the command after more than two decades in prison, I removed my clothing, spread my fingers and palms forward, lifted my scrotum, turned around, and then lifted my feet and exposed their soles. The next thing I knew, before the final humiliation of the bend over and spread 'em anal check, I was slammed against the cell wall, with the sergeant screaming that I had tried to kick him.

Eight Months in the Hole

According to the inmate violation report, the sergeant had ordered me to submit to a strip search.[12] Spying a "package" on the floor next to the removed clothing, the officer bent over to retrieve it, and the prisoner attempted to kick him in the head. The sergeant reported that the inmate was not belligerent, complied with orders, and offered no resistance. The package, weighing less than a gram, was field-tested positive as marijuana. I was "cuffed up" and "frog-marched" across the prison to the hole.

A week later, the single female caseworker found me guilty of assault on staff, sanctioning me to a series of punishments and referring me for prosecution and to the Administrative Segregation (Ad Seg) Committee for isolation determination. Appearing before this three-person committee, I explained what had really happened. As expected, the committee upheld the charge as written by the officer. Stating that they had no choice but to follow directives, they sentenced me to the hole for 30 days until my next review. In parting, the Ad Seg Committee chairman urged me to appeal the violation, handing my escort officer the form.

The next morning, I filed the first four stages of the grievance process. Prison policy stated that a response would be rendered in 30 days.[13] With one jumpsuit, a change of underclothes, minimal toiletries, and a pair of laceless tennis shoes, I began my monthlong wait, to be released either by the committee or when the violation was reversed. Why, after all those years of surviving prison, I still adhered to the notion that being right would set one free, I cannot fathom for the life of me.

The committee reviewed my case the next month, consigning me to the hole for a second month, with still no response to my written appeal. Three months later, the committee then reassigned me to segregation for another 90 days. My grievance was returned officially denied. "The offender was afforded due process" was the justification for affirming the violation.

By now, my delusions had faded enough that I realized I was in the hole for the long haul. I stayed engaged by reading everything I could. Initially, there was a paucity of materials, with a few romance novels the only books provided. The lack of mental stimulation may be the greatest threat to a person in an isolation cell. To maximize my reading materials and maintain a "beyond-the-wire" focus, I subscribed to five newspapers, *The Kansas City Star*, *New York Times*, *USA Today*, *Wall Street Journal,* and *Washington Post*, investing my days in extensive current affairs reading and correspondence. During this period in the hole, I still managed to write and have work published (Taylor, 1997i, 1998b, 1998c). I also got my legislation introduced again (H.B. 1372), but this time, by happenstance or design, I was in no position to support it through lobbying the measure, as I had been able to while at JCCC.

The greatest strain in these circumstances is being locked up with another person in an 8-by-10-foot space with out-of-cell recreation a couple of times a week and showers every three days. Until this "new" prison, I had never heard of a double-celled hole. The intensity of isolation is great enough, but to couple that by locking two angry individuals together is a recipe for heightened levels of conflict. Fights are common among cellmates in the hole.

A few days before Christmas, I was shackled and transported to the county court, where I was officially charged with a Class B felony assault on a correctional officer and Class C felony drug possession. My arraignment was in January, during which the uniformed sergeant testified as to the facts of the case. When the officer testified that I did not strike him, as the charging papers stated, the prosecutor looked surprised and befuddled. The judge eventually had to amend the statement to read "attempted to strike," a matter of semantics that carried the same penalty as if I had bashed the officer's brains in. Trial was set for that spring.

By this date, the second stage of my grievance appeal had been denied ("afforded due process" and so forth), and the Ad Seg Committee had reassigned me for another 30 days. As it became more apparent that I was going to be in the hole for many more months on this phony, trumped-up violation, I began a letter-writing campaign to the network of "free-world" friends I had accumulated over two decades. My correspondence intensified when the local prosecutor decided to charge me with assault on an officer, which carried a 20-year consecutive sentence, if convicted, to begin after the completion of my present sentence. My "free-world" friends contacted the commissioner's office regarding my case, and various published articles reported on my situation, generating more support (Editor 1998a, 1998b; Chambers 1998).

The Ad Seg Committee assigned me another 30 days in the hole. When my February review rolled around, the superintendent was on vacation and the committee released me back into the general population, four months earlier than standard practices dictated for prisoner assault on a guard. The third stage of the grievance was denied, and I filed the final appeal.

I began to gather information about the notorious reputation of this sergeant. Through the discovery process and a few hints from other sympathetic prison staff, I learned at the arraignment that the charging officer had his own legal problems. He was out on bond for felony fraud charges from two different counties, was suspended from duty for investigation of sexual harassment, and was eventually demoted to officer grade and "encouraged" to resign. The public defender felt this had no bearing on my case. Moreover, she believed that a motion to review the officer's personnel file would be summarily denied and urged me to take a plea bargain.

After firing the public defender, I began filing pro se motions for continuance, additional discovery, and appointment for new counsel. Shortly thereafter, it became apparent the state was going to railroad me and give me 20 more years. I decided to hire private counsel. I made ready to access my mutual fund, which had been invested over a dozen years for "gate money," jargon for money saved for release from prison, to pay the lawyer fees. (With the money accumulated from writing awards and fees invested since 1997, my fund had grown to $5,600.) Then Missouri's attorney general, acting on information provided by the institution, sued me for incarceration reimbursement expenses. Employing a statute (RSMo 217.825) enacted eight years after my original conviction in court, the attorney general had my assets frozen. Stunned and infuriated, I regrouped and sought contributions from family and friends.

The DOC finally reversed the assault violation and instead found me guilty of the marijuana possession charge. In the commissioner's decision, it was noted that the offender had said, "The marijuana is mine." (Huh?) Thus, after I had served eight months in the hole for an assault violation I did not commit, the pot violation was added to my institutional record.

Shortly thereafter, the felony assault charge was dropped in Missouri state court, but the possession offense was retained. The prosecutor now offered a plea bargain for seven consecutive years. Enough funds had been raised to retain a prominent attorney.[14] Additional discovery was granted, in which we learned three important things. First, the court could not find the 0.18 gram of marijuana evidence. Second, the copy of the conduct violation had been altered. The standard form used is a two-page carbonless copy set, with the second page going to the offender. The photocopy of the original top page noted in the "Offender's Remarks" section that I had said, "The marijuana is mine." (At least now I knew where the commissioner's reference had come from.) The only problem was that I had never made that statement. The really interesting point of this "evidence" is that on my now dog-eared, year-old carbonless copy, that statement did not exist. Even though the two forms were exactly the same in all other respects, including signatures, the incriminating statement was not on my offender's copy. The only way that statement could have gotten on the top cover page of the form is if it had been written after the copy or second page had been removed and given to me. Thus the incriminating statement had been added after I had read and signed the violation. Third, we learned that the now former correctional officer had been denied employment by the Kansas DOC and was under arrest in another state.

By this time, a new election cycle had transpired, and a new county prosecutor had taken over. Between the mess the DOC had handed him and the bulldoglike tenacity of the private attorney, the marijuana charge was dropped in state court. Still, the violation for possession of pot remains on my prison record. I had no way to challenge the prison's Ad Seg Committee's decision.

The only option open was to file a federal section 1983 civil rights action, which required a $150 filing fee,[15] as well as retention of counsel or pro se litigation in a whole new area of the law. Honestly, I was afraid to continue my legal battles with the DOC. To prevail in court, I would have to prove fraud and possibly conspiracy, and if the involved officers gave sworn testimony as to the validity of the statement (something that would be unbelievably stupid, considering their own documentation, but not an unheard-of action in an obstinate and obtuse, if not arrogant, system), the potential existed for perjury charges against those officers. Finally, to conduct such a campaign while in custody of the DOC and exposed to their mercies would have placed me in danger of ending up back in the hole, this time with a better-constructed frame-up. Discretion, I decided, was definitely the better part of valor in this case. Besides, I was exhausted. Even with all the great support and care I had received from so many people beyond the walls, it is a lonely and frightening struggle against the Goliath of the state from inside the keep of the kept.[16]

The End Game

I negotiated an armistice of sorts between the DOC and myself. I have managed to remain out of the hole for the past four years, although the imminent threat of such gives me the willies from time to time. Spending long stretches in isolation, even with the stimulation of reading materials, is a progressively disturbing and upsetting experience. Great rage accumulates. Unhealthy thoughts and paranoia manifest, making the transition back to the general population problematic as one "depressurizes" from the bowels of the penitentiary.

And now I am a marked man. Recently, during my annual review, the caseworker asked me about "this guard assault." When I pointed out that the commissioner had dismissed the violation, the caseworker had to flip through several pages before locating that notation. "Okay," he said. "What about this serious contraband violation?" The DOC, I fear, not only succeeded in removing me from active legislative advocacy and community building at the state prison in the capitol, but also has bureaucratically marked me for the parole board to deny early release. The bottom line is that the prison administration punished me for attempting to promote college courses for prisoners. I spent eight months in the hole but beat the "screws" (guards) in court.

Control units are used to punish prisoners for attempting to lobby legislators, influence legislation, and improve prison conditions. Stalin is dead and the Soviet Union has passed into history, but the gulag is alive and well, thriving in the American prison-industrial complex.[17]

Postscript 2014

Twelve years after the events in this chapter, I am still in prison, and not much has changed in relation to how the hole is used in Missouri. If anything, it's employed as a disciplinary sanction more often. At varying times, there is a virtual parade of convicts being escorted to the hole. At the same time, orange-suited men are recycled back to the housing units, constantly churning the scarce bed space within the prisons.

The DOC has created its own structural monster by converting cellblocks originally designed as general population housing units (280 beds) into Ad Seg housing units. With its penal system functioning at overcapacity, all bed space must be employed. Thus the hole always remains full, even if those so sanctioned are there for the most inconsequential offense, such as possessing minor contraband, being "out of bounds," or literally walking on the grass.

Doing time, prisoners witness men being cuffed up and dragged to the hole every day. The decision to punish convicts by locking them down in segregation cells has become so predictable that most prisoners expect some hole time during their incarceration. The expectation is that it is your turn this week or next to be busted for breaking some petty regulation. For persistent rule violators, a trip to the hole has become routine, just considered another day in the joint, a day off work with room service. The sanction for many convicts has become a minor hassle to be endured, until rotating back into the mainline population to anticipate the next trip to the hole.

The structural Frankenstein of wholesale conversion of entire general population cellblocks into Ad Seg units has resulted in court-ordered changes at the Crossroads Correctional Center, a maximum-security penitentiary with 1,500 male prisoners. For years, men served their sanctioned periods in the hole and then waited for bed space in the mainline population for 30, 60, even 90 or more days, until such became available. Even with minor infractions receiving segregation sanctions, the waiting period the men endured routinely became longer, doubling or even tripling the original sanction time.

As a result, a civil suit was filed and adjudicated for years, costing an untold sum of taxpayer dollars, inevitably resulting in a court order to move hundreds of prisoners to transitional housing units. To accommodate the order, one wing of a converted Ad Seg unit was reconverted back to a mainline housing area. The more things change, the more they remain the same.

Marionization meant the Indiana Department of Corrections built a stand-alone supermax it calls the Maximum Control Facility (MCF) in Westville, along with the secure housing unit (SHU) at the Wabash Valley Correctional Facility in Carlisle. In comparison, the Missouri Department of Corrections has never constructed a stand-alone supermax institution. Instead, it built high-security control units in all of its maximum-security penitentiaries.

These new control units have produced a host of unnecessary but not unforeseen problems for the mental health of prisoners. These problems have to be dealt with somewhere down the line. In reflection, during the eight months I served in the hole in Indiana and Missouri, I was able to remain intellectually engaged, although I was cognizant of the psychological pathologies of such isolation. While I usually shared space with another human being, I was still negatively affected by the experience. This included intense irrational anger, obsessive-compulsive behaviors, and problems with focusing for prolonged periods.

I dread to think what damage is done to the men that are forced to endure many years alone in single cells. It is difficult to predict what long-term irreversible effects will manifest after years of time alone in isolation. Although every man is different, some can handle long stretches in solitary, while others cannot, but each has a point of no return. On a daily basis, I routinely encounter prisoners with systematically induced disturbances and pathologies that are haphazardly managed. Pathetically, I see men returned to the hole, sometimes with tragic consequences, as they are forced to go back into the very environment that aggravated if not produced their disorders in the first place.

Notes

1. The Indiana State Reformatory opened in the late 1920s and was magically rechristened the Pendleton Correctional Center in the late 1990s.

2. At that time, ISR had three lockup units: the "Bullpen," which was used for informal sanction of a few hours of isolation from "mainline" activities; Ad Seg, a small cellhouse of 90 lockdown cells allowing minimal possessions and no activities, with incarceration periods averaging from one month to one year; and MRU, with 8 complete strip cells of intense isolation and supervision. All three units were separate, though in the same building complex.

3. For a more detailed account of the event, refer to "The Unity Walk" (Taylor, 1998a).

4. The communication strategy of the demonstrators relied on the ubiquitous snitches to convey the purpose of the demonstration, along with a few well-placed judicious comments to particular administrators. That the demonstrations were apparently a complete surprise to the staff is a testament to the careful planning of the organizers.

5. A few years afterward, the commissioner of this period received an award from a national association for his decisiveness in instituting the longest lock-downs in departmental history at the state's maximum-security prisons. A year after the ISR lockdown, the Indiana State Prison in Michigan City was locked down in similar fashion for many months.

6. See Ivan Denisovitch, 1992a, 1992b, 1992c, 1992d.

7. While at ISR, I was involved in Christian Outreach, the Jaycees, and Red Cross community programs, among others, and organized a temporarily successful grassroots lobbying campaign in opposition to Pell Grant restrictions on prisoners. My writings have been published in academic journals, magazines, and newspaper op-eds, receiving numerous academic and journalistic recognitions, including *The Nation*, I. F. Stone, and Robert F. Kennedy student journalism awards.

8. Illinois senator Paul Simon read my *New York Times* op-ed piece "There Ought to Be a Law (but Not This Crime Bill)" (Taylor, 1994) into the *Congressional Record* (September 12, 1994) during the chamber's debate over the amendment excluding prisoners' Pell Grant eligibility. In rebuttal to my piece in *The World & I* (Taylor, 1995a) magazine, Tennessee representative Bart Gordon (1995) misapplied my academic example in criticism of prisoners' Pell Grant eligibility.

9. 89th General Assembly of the Missouri Legislature, H.B. 424, *An Act Relating to Education for Inmates*, January 15, 1998; S.B. 336, *An Act . . . Relating to Offender Education*, February 3, 1997; H.B. 1372, *An Act Relating to Education for Inmates*, January 15, 1998.

10. Several responded affirmatively, with the president of the University of Missouri System writing, "I have spoken with our lobbyist in Jefferson City and indicated our support for these [424 and 336] bills. We will do what we can to encourage passage so as to provide educational opportunities for prison inmates" (personal communication, March 25, 1997).

11. Missouri DOC mail policy dictates that all inmate correspondence must be deposited unsealed for inspection before posting, except for legal mail and correspondence to elected governmental officials. Thus my 50 two-ounce envelopes to the Missouri legislature were deposited sealed, rendering them noninspectable before posting. Shortly thereafter, an interview in *The Christian Science Monitor* (Marks, 1997) noted, "From his prison cell, Jon Marc Taylor sits at the heart of a national debate over prisoners' access to higher education. . . . In taking on the fight, Taylor enters a renewed national debate over how society should spend its limited education resources. . . . [He] has offered a legislative proposal that would require Missouri to replace Pell grants with profits from its prison phone system."

12. Strip search procedure requires the subject to remove all clothing, placing it in a pile before him. He then raises his arms over his head, exposing his armpits

and fronts and backs of his hands, spreading the fingers, and lifts his scrotum. The subject then turns his back to the officer, runs his fingers through his hair, lifts his feet to expose their soles, and bends at the waist and spreads the buttocks to expose the anus. After being performed the first time, the routine becomes rote, requiring no more instruction than the order to commence.

13. Grievance procedures in the Missouri DOC provide a set number of days between the time of an incident and when the prisoner must file a grievance. If late by one day, the petition is permanently dismissed. On the other hand, administrative response times, while specifically stated, are not enforced, nor do they carry any penalty for not being met. A full grievance cycle in Missouri, combining the maximum possible filing days and response periods, consumes seven months by policy. If a final response is received within a year, a convict is on the fast track for their denial.

14. Richard E. McFadin, known as the "Matlock of Missouri." In a telling observation, the first time McFadin visited the prison, two guards immediately recognized him, asking, "Is he your lawyer? He is very good." It is my assumption the administration was made aware of this development as well.

15. Courtesy of the Comprehensive Antiterrorism Act of 1995, which, among many other things, eliminated the previously waivable court filing fees for prisoner pro se filings. As a result, prisoner court filings have been significantly reduced.

16. To the best of my knowledge, I am the only prisoner criminally charged from the Crossroads Correctional Center that has not received additional time. This has more to do with the quantity of resources available to the state and the paucity of those available to the prisoner defendant than with the quality or worthiness of the case itself. Since I was able to effectively participate in my own defense and employ competent private counsel, the prosecution of my case was a much more balanced affair. The legislature provides counties containing prisons with tens of thousands of dollars for the prosecution of inmates. The local prosecutors then have the incentive to bring as many cases as the counties' relatively light rural dockets permit, allowing them to accumulate easy convictions for reelection publicity. It should also be noted that the legislature has not provided adequate funding for public defenders.

17. For discussion of gulag, see Solzhenitsyn 1973, 1975, 1978; Richards, 1990. I wrote most of this chapter in 2003, while in the hole at Crossroads Correctional Center, Missouri Department of Corrections. The victim of assault by another prisoner, I was under "protective custody investigation."

| 2 |

The Realities of Special Housing Units in the Federal Bureau of Prisons

Seth Ferranti

The summer of 1991, I was 19 years old and living in the affluent suburbs of northern Virginia. The feds busted me for conspiracy to distribute LSD. They made a big deal of it, like I was the John Gotti of the suburbs or something. But it wasn't really like that. Not that it matters. I copped to a plea and took off. The feds weren't getting any prison time out of me.

But I was wrong. They placed me on the U.S. Marshals Service "15 Most Wanted" list and hunted me down like I was a violent criminal. I was captured in St. Louis by a special fugitive task force in the fall of 1993. The feds extradited me back to Virginia and sentenced me to 25 years with no parole, a mandatory minimum sentence for a first-time nonviolent offender. This is American justice, right?

Wrong. I have been incarcerated for 20 years now, with a few more to go inside and then the remainder to be served in the community. My release date from prison is November 2015. When I entered prison, I was 21; when I get out, I will be nearly 45 years old. I will have done 25 years for a minor drug offense, suffering the harsh realities of the Federal Bureau of Prisons (BOP), which is a corrupt bureaucracy running overcrowded prisons.

Since 1993, when I first came into the BOP, conditions have gotten steadily worse. Now, as I revise this essay in 2013, the prisons are overcrowded with nonviolent drug offenders. There aren't many, if any, killers in this joint. And with no parole, there is no relief in sight. The prisoners are doing time with no incentive to behave. What is the BOP's answer to this problem? More prisoners being locked down 24 hours a day in special housing units, sometimes called segregated housing units in state prisons.

Before 2002, I had never encountered "the hole." But since my writing about the corrupt system run by the feds was published, I have been spending a lot of time in the hole. So I thought I would inform you all about the realities of the special housing unit (SHU) in the federal prison system.

What Is the SHU?

I am a federal prisoner writing this chapter while locked down in the hole. The SHU is a prison within a prison. Commonly referred to by prisoners as "the hole," "the box," or "the bucket," it is a separate unit on the compound of a prison where prisoners are placed for a variety of reasons, mostly disciplinary. The cells in the SHU are usually 7 by 12 feet and each have a stainless steel toilet-sink apparatus, a small metal desk, a tiny metal bunk bed, and a small metal shelf. All items in the cell are bolted to the walls or floors. The cell door is made of steel with a 24-by-3-inch slit window built in. A lockable steel trap opening in the door allows the correctional officers contact with the prisoners inside. The SHU is designed to keep a prisoner locked in a cell 24 hours a day without opening the door. Imagine being locked in your bathroom with a slit in the door through which your keepers slide you your food.

In the federal system, they call it lockdown. The correctional officers and administrators use the threat of being locked up in the hole to control and maintain order in the prison. Federal prison policy is to provide a safe and orderly environment for all inmates. If a prisoner's behavior violates or disrupts their orderly environment, that prisoner will be going to the hole.

You can be sent to the hole at the whim of any staff member. If the staff members do not like you, watch out. You might be spending years in the hole for some reason or another. Whatever they say goes. They are the masters, and they let you know brutally when you step out of line. Even 30 days in the SHU can be disheartening.

At most federal prison institutions, the hole is the most dreaded place to be on the compound. You get little recreation, are allowed minimal showers, and are confined to roughly 84 square feet of space. It's like being in a cage. It makes you feel like an animal or beast. Your whole life is dependent on the guards, who bring you your food and mail, take you to the recreation cage for an hour a day Monday to Friday, take you to the shower three times a week, and bring you clean clothes after a shower. And to make it even worse, you're even locked into the showers.

Whenever you move from your cell, you are handcuffed with your hands behind your back. The handcuffs are placed on you through the steel trapdoor that the food goes through. You cannot move about in the SHU without being handcuffed. If you are moving to recreation or the shower, the correctional officer comes to the door and shouts, “Rec time” or “Shower time cuff up.” He then opens the steel trapdoor. You must place your hands behind your back into the slot in the cell door. The guard then reaches into the slot and cuffs you and then your cellie, if you have one, before unlocking the real door. The correctional officer, who keeps a hand on your arm or handcuffs, escorts you to the recreation area or shower cage. When you arrive at either destination, the guard locks you in before removing the handcuffs through the bars or fence.

At no time while you reside in the SHU are you free to move unshackled or unwatched. You are locked down at all times like a violent criminal or the second coming of Hannibal Lecter, like a wild vicious beast that will lash out at any time. As a result of this misguided thinking, you are controlled, suppressed, and completely dependent on your keepers.

The Official Line

The official line is spelled out in the Code of Federal Regulations (CFR 541.10) and the Federal Bureau of Prisons Inmate Discipline and Special Housing Units Program Statement (BOP PS 5270–07): “Each institution having the need for facilities to house inmates separate from the general population will establish a special housing unit consisting of two categories of cells: administrative detention and disciplinary segregation.” According to the BOP, it maintains the SHUs for the following reason: “So that inmates may live in a safe and orderly environment, it is necessary for institution authorities to impose discipline on those inmates whose behavior is not in compliance with Bureau of Prisons rules.” The official line further states, “Staff shall take disciplinary action at such times and to the degree necessary to regulate an inmate’s behavior within bureau rules and institution guidelines and to promote a safe and orderly institution environment.”

The BOP uses disciplinary segregation as “a form of separation from the general population in which inmates who commit serious violations of Bureau rules are confined by the Discipline Hearing Officer (DHO), for specified periods of time, in a cell removed from the general population.” It defines administrative detention as “a form of separation from the general population used when the continued presence of the inmate within the general population would pose a serious threat to life, property, self, staff or other inmates, or to the security or orderly running of the institution.”

Why Are Prisoners Sent to the SHU?

Prisoners end up in the hole for a variety of reasons. Special reasons—that is why it is called the special housing unit. You might be locked up in the bucket because of incident reports, or "shots," or due to a pending special investigative supervisors (SIS) investigation. Maybe you are waiting to be classified and need a formal captain's review before you hit the compound, or maybe your life is at stake and you check into protective custody (PC). Explanations of the many reasons follow.

Shots

As of 2014 there were over 119 federal prisons. All federal prisons issue an *Inmate Information Handbook* to new inmates. These documents are typically less than 50 pages and may be updated at any time, with new policies and rules. Prisoners may collect copies issued with different dates of publication at the various prisons where they have done time, with diverse formats and details dictated by the whims of individual wardens. Disciplinary policies include some variation of the following statement: "It is the policy of the Bureau of Prisons to provide a safe and orderly environment for all inmates. Violations of Bureau rules and regulations are dealt with by the Unit Discipline Committee (UDC), and for more serious violations, the Discipline Hearing Officer (DHO)" So when you break the rules, they write you up. The official name for these write-ups is incident reports, but they are commonly referred to by inmates and staff as "shots." The severity of the shot determines whether you go to the hole or not. The *Inmate Information Handbook* lists the levels of severity of the various shots.

There are four categories: greatest, high, moderate, and low moderate. The 100 series and 200 series shots are the most severe. Usually, if you receive one of them, you go right to the hole to await a DHO hearing. These shots carry the highest sanctions and sometimes can lead to street charges, which means new federal indictments. Prosecutions can lead to being sentenced in federal court to many more years in prisons. The 300 and 400 series shots are less severe and often don't necessitate hole time unless there are repeated violations. Many prisoners refer to 300 and 400 series shots as "petty" shots. They might also refer to these shots as "charges" or "tickets."

The 100 series shots are in the greatest category. These are for prohibited acts including killing; assaulting any person, including sexual assault or armed assault; attempting an escape; setting a fire (to facilitate a riot or escape or if found to pose a threat to life); possessing, manufacturing, or introducing a gun, firearm, weapon, sharpened instrument, knife, dangerous chemical, explosive, or any ammunition; rioting or encouraging another to riot; taking hostages; possessing, manufacturing, or introducing a hazardous tool; refusing to provide a urine sample; introducing or using narcotics or drug paraphernalia; using the telephone to further criminal activity; interfering with a staff member; or having conduct that disrupts the security or orderly running of the institution (this conduct must be of the greatest severity nature).

The 200 series shots are in the high category. Prohibited acts in this category include escaping from camps or walkways, fighting, threatening others, extorting others (blackmail), engaging in sexual acts, making sexual propositions or threats, wearing a disguise or mask, possessing a lock pick or damaging a lock, adulterating any food or drink, possessing staff clothing, participating in a group demonstration, participating in a work stoppage, introduction of alcohol, bribing others, destroying government property, stealing, practicing martial arts, boxing, wrestling, being in unauthorized areas with a person of the opposite sex, possessing or using intoxicants, refusing a Breathalyzer test, using a telephone for abuses other than criminal activity, or interfering with or behaving in a way that disrupts staff members.

The 300 series shots are in the moderate category. Prohibited acts include indecent exposure, misuse of medication, possession of money, loaning property, contraband, refusing to work, disobeying a direct order, being out of bounds, insolence, lying, counterfeiting, participating in a group meeting, poor sanitation, using unauthorized equipment, interfering with the count, failing to stand count, gambling, conducting a gambling pool, possession of gambling paraphernalia, giving anything of value to another inmate, destroying government property, being untidy, possessing nonhazardous tools, smoking where prohibited, using a telephone for abuses other than criminal, or conduct that disrupts a staff member.

The 400 series shots are in the low moderate category. This category includes possessing another inmate's property, possessing too much clothing, malingering, feigning illness, using abusive or obscene language, tattooing, unauthorized use of mail, unauthorized conduct with visitors, conducting a business, and unauthorized physical contact.

These are all of the prohibited acts listed in the *Inmate Information Handbook*, which every prisoner receives upon arrival at the institution. Much of the stuff is overlooked, though, depending on the correctional officer. But if you get a guard mad at you, watch out. He or she will write you up for anything and everything. A guard who's mad may even make stuff up and write you multiple shots for the same thing, stacking charges, so to speak. It depends on the joint, but these days, most of the federal prisons are extremely petty.

It used to be that the cops didn't care what you did as long as you stayed away from the fence, didn't kill anybody, and didn't mess up the count, but nowadays, they go all out for anything and everything. Any reason to put you in the hole or take away your privileges is fair game to the cops. Unlike years ago, when 300 and 400 series shots were deemed minor, prisoners now are losing good time and doing hole time for petty shots.

The sanctions or punishments for being found guilty of a prohibited act by the UDC or DHO can include hole time, loss of good time credits, disciplinary transfer, or monetary restitution. They usually include loss of privileges, such as family visits, phone use, recreation, commissary, or job, and can involve a housing change, restriction to quarters, removal from a program, or extra duty like mopping floors or cleaning bathrooms. A minor shot might result in just a warning and reprimand or an inmate's personal property being impounded.

Usually for a 100 or 200 series shot, you do hole time and lose good time credits. For 300 and 400 series shots, you usually lose commissary, phone, or visiting privileges, or you may have to do extra duty. How the sanctions are enforced depends on the institution you are in. UDCs or DHOs can do what they want with the use of the sanctions, but most prison administrators have little or no creativity and stick to the same routine punishment.

Some DHOs are vicious, even brutal. I've heard of men getting 200 series phone shots and losing their phone privileges for one or two years. I've seen dudes who get their third dirty urine lose their visits, phone, and commissary privileges for five years. It depends on the joint and the DHO. The problem is that the DHOs aren't consistent. One might be lenient at one prison, while another at a different prison will be a hardass. So you never know. These feds like to play games. Basically, though, if you get lots of shots, you are going to the hole. And once you start getting shots, the cops will keep writing you up so that you are in and out of the hole on a seemingly never-ending random and rotating basis.

Special Investigative Supervisors (SIS) Investigations

Another way you can find yourself in the hole is to be placed under special investigative supervisors (SIS) investigation. This occurs whenever the SIS lieutenants decide that something you did or are doing or are supposedly doing merits investigation. Most people put under investigation are usually written a shot in the end.

Much of the time, the investigations are bullshit, too. For instance, a dude may drop a "kite" (a note given by an inmate to staff) about you saying that you did this or are planning that. You may be completely innocent, but the SIS still puts you under investigation because this dude ratted you out for who knows what or perhaps to get himself out of doing some hole time. At any rate, you might be in the hole under investigation for 30, 60, or 90 days for nothing. It is the price you pay for being in prison. The SIS lieutenants don't need an honest reason to lock you up. They can put you in the hole because they don't like you, and you have no way to get out of the hole until they decide their investigation is up. I've seen SIS investigations keep people locked up in segregation for years like this. They have no proof of anything, just suspicion or hints or the word of a rat. For example, if a lieutenant or captain suspects a person is a gang member, selling dope, or planning to kill another inmate, they will begin an SIS investigation and, pending a decision, keep the man in segregation. Some "mainline" penitentiaries like United States Penitentiary (USP) Atlanta or Leavenworth keep hundreds of men in the SHU.

Being under investigation sucks, because you don't know when or if you will get out of the hole. You just have to wait it out. SIS uses this tactic to get prisoners to tell or rat on other prisoners. They let prisoners rot in the hole until they get the information they are after. It doesn't matter if you don't know what the SIS lieutenants are talking about. If they think you know something and are not telling them, you will sit in the hole forever. Maybe they just don't like the way you look. For example, you may have too many muscles or gang tattoos. You never know with these guys. A lot of them are FBI "wannabes" that couldn't make the cut. They are infuriated when they encounter a "solid prisoner" or "stand-up" convict who won't give them the information they are seeking in their investigation. So they make those prisoners pay the price. Across the nation in federal prisons, those solid prisoners are rotting in SHUs or control units at USP Marion or Administrative Maximum Facility (ADX) Florence because of the corrupt nature of SIS lieutenants who maintain that at whatever compound they are employed, they may hold their own private inquisitions.

Classification Problems

Some prisoners go to the SHU right off the bus in the BOP because of classification problems, which arise when they arrive at their destination without the proper paperwork. At the medium- and maximum-security prisons, this is the common practice. If the prison officials have no record of you, such as if they can't locate your central inmate file on their computer system, they will not let you on the compound in the "general population," so you go straight to the hole.

Other types of classification problems can occur when you are either transferring down in security level or going up in level as a result of a disciplinary, administrative, or closer supervision transfer. In this case, upon arrival at the new institution, you will be thrown into the hole to await the captain's review. The captain who oversees security and custody checks you out and gives you the guidelines you have to follow to stay on his compound. This usually consists of him telling you, "If you screw up on my compound, I'm locking you up forever!" Prison officials often use scare tactics, thinking they can intimidate prisoners.

Sometimes a new convict might be transferred into an institution with a prison file, or "jacket," filled with violent or subversive actions. The warden or captain will then refuse to release him into the "general population," claiming the prisoner is a threat to the security and orderly running of the institution. Dudes labeled like this are stuck in the hole until the "region" (the BOP has six administrative regions across the country) approves a transfer to a different institution—a penitentiary or supermax. You will also be thrown in the hole if you have a "separate" with anyone on the compound. "Separate" is prisoner slang for keeping specific prisoners apart, for reasons such as gang affiliation, a previous fight, investigation, or because one inmate testified in court against the other. In general, the BOP tries to keep prisoners separate that might attack one another.

The Revolving Door

By writing prisoners numerous shots and keeping them in trouble, the prison officials create a revolving door at the SHU. The UDC and DHO will give D/S time for serious shots (100 and 200 series) and put D/S time on the shelf for moderate shots (300 and 400 series). By doing this, they keep the hole full of prisoners and have a bunch more who will go to the hole with their next shots. So it is a revolving-door system that is constructed to keep you in trouble and in the hole. Because it doesn't matter if the new shot is minor; the accumulation will get you more hole time. It keeps stacking up.

Prisoner Status in the SHU

When a prisoner is put into the SHU, he will be assigned to a status of administrative detention (A/D), disciplinary segregation (D/S), or protective custody (PC). The DHO will inform the prisoner of his status in a written memo. Usually, he will get a shot and be left waiting to see UDC or the DHO, or he will be under some type of investigation.

Administrative Detention (A/D) or Disciplinary Segregation (D/S)

Administrative detention separates an inmate from the general population. This may be in the SHU, a separate cellhouse, or a dormitory, depending on the security level of the prison. To the extent practical, inmates in A/D shall be provided with the same general privileges as inmates in general population. This means they might even be allowed family visits, phone calls, mail, and commissary privileges. They may also retain more personal property, including uniforms and toiletries, as well as bed sheets and towels. An inmate may be placed in A/D when the inmate is in holdover status awaiting transfer, is a new commitment pending classification, is pending investigation or a hearing for a violation of bureau regulations, is pending investigation or trial for a criminal act, is pending transfer, for protection, or is finishing confinement in disciplinary segregation (D/S).

In comparison, disciplinary segregation refers to time to be served after being found guilty of a shot, as a sanction for violation of bureau rules and regulations. Inmates in D/S are usually in SHU and will be denied many privileges listed above. Personal property will usually be impounded. An inmate placed in D/S is given only an old blanket, a thin mattress, a pillow, toilet tissue, and eating utensils (as necessary). Inmates may possess legal and religious material while in D/S, and staff may provide a reasonable amount of nonlegal reading material.

In the BOP, A/D is used to lock up tens of thousands of prisoners every day that are in "holdover" status. Holdover refers to inmates that are being transported by car, bus, or plane from one prison to another. Some prisoners spend years being shipped from prison to prison, and at each prison, they are kept separate from the general population for a few days or weeks. In contrast, D/S inmates are confined to the hole for designated time periods of days, weeks, or months, which may add up to years, after being convicted of either one major shot (100 or 200) or multiple minor shots (300 or 400).

Protective Custody (PC)

The most looked-down-upon reason you might go to the SHU is if you are a protection case who checked into the hole for protective custody (PC). Instead of being a man and dealing with your problems, you ran to the lieutenant's office and probably snitched on somebody in the hope of avoiding a confrontation with another convict over a drug or gambling debt. The PC unit may also include prisoners who are gay or have HIV or AIDS; those who are mentally ill, retarded, or suffering from a mental breakdown; or those unable or unwilling to defend themselves from predatory prisoners. In some prisons, men on suicide watch are also designated PC and placed in the hole. Some BOP medium- and maximum-security prisons may have hundreds of men in PC. Prisoners in PC may do many months or years in the hole.

The BOP is home to many politicians, judges, police officers, and witnesses in high-profile federal cases that are PC. In fact, the BOP has entire minimum- and medium-security facilities filled with PC prisoners that would not survive if placed in maximum-security penitentiaries. Federal prisoners have little respect for PC prisoners, as they are understood to be weak or at odds with the convict culture.

Different Types of Cells

In the SHU, a variety of different cells are employed. A prisoner's status of A/D, D/S, or PC and his "jacket" determines which type he will be placed in. Two-man cells are the most common, but recently the BOP has been employing three-man cells with triple bunk beds. This type of cell has about 60 square feet of usable area, which amounts to 20 square feet per person when filled with three prisoners. Imagine living in your bathroom with two other people for 24 hours a day. It isn't pleasant. The two-man cells are better, although still crowded.

Someone who is a snitch or is in PC usually gets his own cell or an isolation cell. Inmate orderlies are given nicer single cells with showers. The doors are usually left unsecured, as the orderlies work in the SHU cleaning the floors, showers, and recreation cages; washing the clothes; and helping out with meal distribution. As the SHU cellblocks are loud, with prisoners screaming and banging doors, not many prisoners want the orderly job. So the "hacks" (guards) might order a PC prisoner to work as the orderly in the hole. I have also seen two gay prisoners share a cell and do the same job.

The SHU has a few special types of cells as well. One is a "dry cell" with no running water. This cell is used for someone who has flooded his cell repeatedly by clogging the toilet or is suspected of smuggling in drugs through balloons. A prisoner suspected of smuggling drugs must remain in this cell until he shits out the evidence. Stories have been told of prisoners in these cells eating their own excrement in an attempt to swallow the balloons of drugs again before detection.

Another is a "rubber cell," where the guards will put a prisoner if he is a continual disruption. It has rubber-padded walls and no lights, water, or mattress. This is a severe punishment room where shit slingers, urine throwers, suicide attempters, or violent crazies are put. In this cell, the prisoner might be placed in four-point restraints or handcuffed to the bed. It is supposed to be used only for extreme measures, but during my incarceration in the BOP, I have heard many stories of staff abusing prisoners confined in these cells.

The BOP also employs temporary strip cells where they process you in and out of the hole. Here they strip you down, take your property and clothing, and issue hole attire—orange jumpsuits, or what we call "carrot suits." The strip search routine includes searching your mouth, under your tongue, behind your ears and running fingers through your hair, under your arms, under your nut sack, showing the bottom of your feet, wiggling your toes, bending over and spreading 'em (which has to be every correctional officer's favorite part of the job). They are getting paid to look at naked men. What a career choice for the heterosexual man!

Whatever cell you are assigned to in special housing sucks; believe me, there is nothing special about it! And depending on the joint you're in, the sanitation level can vary from bad to detestable. The older prisons' holes are usually more akin to dungeons, but even the newer, more modern holes are dirty in comparison with the typical general population cellblock. That's why prisoners call the hole "the jail within the jail." Think about it—no movement, no freedom, minimal recreation, minimal human contact, no privileges (commissary, TV, radio, visits, phone, programs, church), restricted mail, chow hall food, always handcuffed, and limited reading material. The hole means you're in a perpetual state of boredom that seems designed to alienate you and make you crazy.

Who Is in the Hole?

The spectrum of prisoners found in the hole is as colorful as any rainbow. The only thing is that this rainbow is painted red, white, and blue with the Department of Justice seal of approval on it. You might think that if you avoid getting shots and the drama of prison intrigues, you can stay out of the hole, but that isn't necessarily true. In these politically charged times since September 11, prison is the last place you want to be if you are considered a little radical or your political views are somewhat off-center or un-American.

Terrorists, Arabs, and Non-Christians

Ever since 9/11 and the writing of the first antiterrorism bill by U.S. Attorney General John Ashcroft, the FBOP has resorted to congressionally approved Gestapo-like actions. If you are unfortunate enough to be in federal prison and also happen to be a suspected terrorist, Arab, or non-Christian, you are hit. It is lockdown city, baby! With resolutions passed in the antiterrorism bill, federal prisoners classified as terrorist, Arab, or non-Christian have absolutely no rights at all and can be held incommunicado for up to one year. That is correct. No due process, no shots, no investigation, no visits, no phone, no mail, no lawyer—no nothing. All because you just happen to be a Muslim extremist or a radical. All is justified and legal for the BOP thanks to the anti-terrorism bill and U.S. Attorney General John Ashcroft.

After 9/11, prisoners from Arab countries just started disappearing off of federal compounds across the nation. I have seen them since I have been in the hole numerous times. They treat these guys like public enemy number one. And don't get me wrong, I am American. Maybe the restrictions are necessary, but what I don't like is when the prison administrators apply their new Gestapo-like powers to incarcerated American citizens.

Politicals, Writers, and Hard Cases

It used to be when the SIS held you in the SHU under investigation, after three months they had to get approval from administrators at the region. This was supposed to provide some administrative oversight of what happens at individual prisons. Now it has become common practice to hold some prisoners indefinitely in the hole for years. The region won't transfer them to other prisons, and the warden, captain, or SIS won't let them on the yard. Prisoners in this category include political activists, known as "politicals," writers, and hard cases.

"Politicals" are prisoners with differing views on government. They might be right-wing Christian militia members, anarchists, communists, revolutionaries, or radicals. They might be Americans or nationals from different countries like Cuba, Puerto Rico, or the aforementioned Arab countries. They could include Black Panthers, militia extremists like Timothy McVeigh (the U.S. soldier who bombed the Federal Building in Oklahoma City in 1995 and was executed at the Terre Haute Federal Correctional Complex in 2001), Neo-Nazis, Native Americans, Marxists, or leftists of any faction. The BOP looks down on these prisoners and will lock them up for any perceived indiscretion.

"Writers" include any literate prisoners trying to report on conditions within the prison. The BOP administrators don't want the public to know what is going on in the prisons and attempt to keep writers in the hole, where they won't have access to copy machines or typewriters. The administrators are especially hard on prisoners that write letters to members of Congress or submit stories or editorials to newspapers. Their correspondence is closely monitored and restricted, and all federal prisoners are limited to five books in their cells.

"Hard cases" are convicts who won't snitch or cooperate with the "man." Some hard cases are men or women who think it is dishonorable to inform on others in criminal investigations. For example, this includes defendants that refused to cooperate in federal drug cases, pled not guilty, retained their right to remain silent, demanded due process, or fought their cases through jury trials and appellate court. Upon conviction, they usually receive longer sentences and are designated to higher-security prisons. Information about fighting their cases and refusing to testify against others is included in their presentence investigation (PSI) report contained in their jacket. SIS lieutenants hate these types and will attempt to keep them locked up in the hole forever. They know that if these dudes are released on the compound, their stature and respect among the prisoners will grow because of their open defiance of the system.

Prisoners with Lawsuits Pending, Custody Problems, DC Guys, and Riot Ringleaders

Another type of prisoner usually confined to the hole under some type of pretense is anyone who has filed lawsuits against the prison, the BOP, or individual staff members. Prison administrators will keep these men locked up for much the same reason as writers. It is extremely hard to file legal work, keep up with court dates, and coordinate lawsuits when you are in the hole under 24-hour lockdown. You have no access to a typewriter, copier, or phone, and your access to legal materials is very limited and controlled.

The BOP locks up prisoners in the hole as a means of obstructing justice. Prisoners are unable to file timely motions, miss court-ordered deadlines, and have their writs, suits, and motions dismissed in due course. "Jailhouse lawyers" are prisoners that do legal work for other convicts. When they are especially talented and get their cases into appellate court, they will be sent to the hole or transferred to another prison.

"Custody problems" are men that find themselves locked in the hole long-term under the auspices of SIS investigation. These are prisoners who have political influence, a lot of money, or outside connections such as mobsters or gangbangers; high-profile or celebrity prisoners; and prison gang members. Sometimes, for example, the prison administrators might lock up all the Latin Kings on the compound if they hear that something is about to go down. Much of the administrators' justice is preventive in nature. If they have even an inkling that hell might break loose, they lock down all the suspects.

When I first went to prison in the early 1990s, I heard a lot about the "DC guys" or "DCers" from Washington being in the hole. Because the District of Columbia is ruled under federal jurisdiction, all local crimes there are federal. So people from DC convicted of either misdemeanors or felonies both are sentenced to do time in the BOP. In general, DC prisoners tend to be common street criminals, somewhat less sophisticated than most federal prisoners. Rumors would float around such as "They got 30 DC guys in the hole ready to hit the compound." DCers are sentenced under different guidelines than regular federal prisoners and are still eligible for parole. Supposedly, they were the meanest, roughest, toughest, and worst prisoners on earth. OK, at least that was the word going around. The DC prisons were allegedly corrupt, and all of the DC prisons like Lorton were being closed down, meaning that the federal prisons had to absorb the DC prisoners. Well, it is 2013 now, the DC prisoners are fully integrated into the federal system, and I have not really noticed any difference.

Another type of prisoner confined to the hole under the guise of investigation is the supposed or purported riot ringleaders or organizers of a food strike or work stoppage. At times in prisons, as tensions erupt and the prisoners get sick of the overcrowding, bad food, and overall hostility and abuse of their keepers, they organize a food strike or work stoppage. Sometimes a full-scale riot may occur. When this does happen, the administrators go to their snitches to locate the leaders. Then it is payback time. Whoever is found guilty or is held to be guilty is punished with extreme hole time or even diesel therapy.

Prisoners in Diesel Therapy

"Diesel therapy" is when any of the above-mentioned types of prisoners are put in transit and kept in transit for a significant amount of time, sometimes even years. They are transported from institution to institution, hole to hole, kept in perpetual motion. They do not know where they are going and have no designated destination. The prisoners call this "diesel therapy," and although it is not an officially sanctioned method of punishment, it happens—frequently. On any given day, there are over 20,000 federal prisoners being transported from prison to prison. Many men ride the buses for years and do time in numerous prisons.

Other Types of Prisoners in the Hole

Other types of prisoners found in the hole include those held in protective custody because they are testifying in court cases. These prisoners may be shipped out to county jails or federal prisons in cities called metropolitan correctional centers (MCCs), which look like bank buildings and are usually located near federal courthouses. Federal courtrooms also may be located in the MCC.

Suicidal prisoners may be housed in the hole. The BOP does not like to admit that they have many prisoners committing suicide by diving off of cellblock tiers, hanging themselves, poisoning themselves with cleaning chemicals, or walking through prohibited areas so that the guards will shoot them, known as "death by gun tower." A prisoner simply walks out on the yard and approaches the wall or fence too closely, where he is cut down by machine gun fire from the gun towers. A prisoner that attempts suicide without success will be housed in the PC unit.

Prisoners with AIDS who are either dying or in an advanced state of the illness are often put in the hole. Nowadays, most of these prisoners are shipped out promptly to federal medical center (FMC) prisons to deal with their particular problems. Locations such as the U.S. Medical Center for Federal Prisoners in Springfield and FMC Lexington now have hundreds of prisoners dying of AIDS, many of them in the hole.

Why and How the BOP Uses the SHU

The BOP uses the SHU to control and punish prisoners. The federal prison staff constantly threatens prisoners with going to the hole. Officers say, "Do this, comply with that, obey this order, put up with our bullshit, or go to the hole." A favorite question the correctional officers always ask the prisoners is "Are you disobeying a direct order? Because I gave you a direct order." They act like we're in the military.

Whatever the situation, BOP staff members use the threat of going to the hole to get the upper hand. Many of them are power trippers. As a prisoner, you cannot talk common sense to them, and don't even try to argue. If you do, you will get locked up in a minute. It doesn't matter if you are right or wrong. The prison administrators feel that "it will all wash out in the end." But in the meantime, you might be in the hole for 30 days.

The hole is a tactical weapon employed by all BOP staff members, from SIS to kitchen supervisors, to get whatever it is they want out of the prisoners, be it information, work, compliance to their personal whims, or whatever. Writing you a shot or locking you up in the hole is a weapon, and the staffs in prisons across the nation brandish it unconscionably.

Refusing to Do a Work Assignment

A prisoner who is assigned to the kitchen might be paid less than $20 a week to work 84 hours a week (12 hours a day, seven days a week), so most of the prisoners don't do anything. They just sit around at work and then slip away to their housing units during mealtimes, if they can get away with it. When it is cleanup time after meals, they try to make themselves scarce, but there will always be one power-tripping hack running the kitchen detail trying to get every prisoner to work.

There might be an overflow of pots and pans in the dish room, and the kitchen guard will tell a prisoner from the dining room to go back and help. If that prisoner refuses because it's not his job or says, "I ain't washing no dishes," the kitchen hack will call the lieutenant and have the prisoner locked up in the hole for refusing to obey a direct order. You'd better bet the next prisoner he gives an order to will jump to it and go help to avoid going to the hole.

Going Out of Bounds

Sometimes prisoners go to other units to see their fellow prisoners. Most compounds have "controlled movement," which is only 10 minutes long, so a prisoner may just duck into another housing unit and go to his buddy's cell to kick it. But don't let the guard find out you are not from his unit, because if he does, he will lock you up.

Any time a prisoner is not in his supposed assigned area, he is out of bounds. The BOP administrators use the threat of the hole to keep prisoners where they want them to be even on a totally enclosed and fenced compound. It's a joke. You are locked up in the prison, and you are out of bounds. Go directly to the hole.

Refusing to Rat

The custody staff and SIS lieutenants will also use the threat of the hole to get information out of prisoners. They'll say things like "Tell me who did it, or I'll lock you up in the hole forever." They will give you a chance to be a rat and snitch, but if you don't cooperate with them, you will be in the hole locked down for as long as they want under some pretense or another.

It's a vicious system that spawns snitches, rats, and informers. The custody and SIS staff will divide and conquer by threatening to lock up one prisoner if he doesn't tell on another. They are maintaining control through intimidation, treachery, and deceit. And these are supposed to be the good guys? We all know that the snitch system results in more prison violence.

Gambling and Using Dope

The lieutenants use their network of snitches to police inmate recreation. They keep tabs on the gamblers and dopers, and they bust them every now and then by raiding their lockers, having random shakedowns, or using piss tests. If they get something on you, watch out. You will be going to the hole unless you offer them something such as the head bookie, someone who is bringing drugs into the institution, or a prisoner who is making big sports bets. If you give them the 411, they will go easy on you, throw out the shot, and let you back on the compound. But it is a double-edged sword, because once a prisoner is branded a snitch, he might get checked back into the hole for protective custody, or worse, somebody might stab him. The SIS lieutenants have numerous people on each compound, though, who are always in trouble and are always working for the man to avoid future problems and trips to the hole. It is eerily similar to the tactics the feds employ on the street. If you snitch, you walk. If not, you get big time.

Life in the SHU

The SHU is 24-hour lockdown with maybe three showers a week and maybe one hour of recreation a day. Life isn't pretty in the hole, but when you are there, you make do. Imagine being trapped in a 12–by-7-foot cell. The floor is white tile, dirty and dingy. White paint flecks hang off the ceiling, ripping off in pieces from disrepair. The 12-foot-high ceiling is your only view as you lie in the metal triple bunk bed staring at the off-white concrete brick walls. There is a 2-by-4-foot window with two hollow steel bars in front of it to look out of, but the world is obscured by a thin piece of plastic that lets the light in but doesn't allow you to see out.

The steel door with its 24-by-3-inch window is painted blue and has etches in it from different prisoners who occupied the cell. The stainless steel toilet-sink apparatus is almost mirrorlike in its appearance as it sits like some machine ready to let your wastes and trash escape into the plumbing while you are still trapped. Everything is bolted down as though the BOP is afraid the prisoners will steal something. There won't be any rearranging of the furniture in this room. The air is stale and the cell muggy, as the air-conditioning and ventilation system barely work to move and cool the air.

You have a skinny plastic mattress, a pillow if you're lucky, maybe two sheets, a wool military blanket, and your orange jumpsuit, which most prisoners wrap and tie at the waist in the summer heat. In the winter, you freeze. Your property consists of one pair of socks, one pair of underpants, one undershirt, maybe one towel, and a washcloth, which you can exchange on shower day.

Once a week, you are allowed to clean your cell. Most of the cells are so dirty and unkempt, however, that it isn't worth the trouble. You can also change your sheets once a week. Every 21 days, the guards move you to a different cell. They call this cell rotation. I guess they figure you might be digging a hole in the concrete block wall with your plastic spoon!

Most of the time, you are just trying to fight off the boredom that is driving you crazy. You stare at the ceiling, the walls, and the graffiti that covers everything. You read Spanish and English gang signs, along with cryptic messages warning about who is a rat, or who sucks dick, or what cops are assholes. You can spend a couple of days just reading the graffiti in your cell.

If you get mail, it is the highlight of your day. This is a brief relief from the monotonous boredom that rules your world in the hole. You learn to look forward to the little things in the SHU, such as a shower, recreation, mail, commissary, or any chance to get out of the cell. Unless you are going to UDC, captain's review, SIS interrogation, or DHO, however, you most likely aren't leaving the cell. When you do go, it is with handcuffs on behind your back, because you are a special prisoner when you are in the special housing unit. Even if you have no violence on your record, it doesn't matter. You are still treated like a deranged killer, an animal, or a rabid beast.

The inmate orderly might bring you some books—nothing you want to read, but you read them anyway. You crave a diversion, maybe a newspaper or magazine, whatever. You sleep a lot, try to write letters if you can get a stamp, and have no privacy with your cellie or even two cellies right there all of the time. If you have some cards, you play gin or spades until you hate the game.

During the regular working week, the prison administrators come by, looking in the tiny window and asking if you are OK. "Of course, I'm not fucking OK," you want to say, but you don't because it will only cause you more trouble. Your unit manager, counselor, Federal Prison Industries (UNICOR) boss, or case manager might roll through, asking if they can get anything for you, but it is all for appearances because they can't do jack shit for you. You hear dudes asking them all the time, "Can you get me out?" The answer is always "No, you have to see UDC. You have to see DHO. You are under investigation."

With all the prison staff looking in at you, you feel like an animal in a zoo. You know it's hot in the room when the metal toilet starts to sweat. You stink. Your cellie stinks. You need to take a shower, but it's Friday night and you won't get one until Monday. Eat, shit, read, sleep, and fart. That's the routine.

Prisoners coming into the hole that have never been in the SHU before start crying and whining. Banging on the door, they ask when they're getting out. Lie down, son. Take it like a man. The orderlies can bring you paper, envelopes, and pencils to write a letter, but anything else is contraband. Don't get caught with a pen. That's a shot. The pencils are broken in half into minipencils, because the hacks are afraid you might stab someone with your hands handcuffed behind your back on the way to a shower.

Effects of the SHU on Prisoners

The effects of the SHU are many and varied, depending on the individual. First, you are treated like a wild animal, a rabid dog. This tends to affect the psyche. Being locked in a cell for 24 hours a day and handcuffed every time you leave the cell is not healthy for the mind. Some dudes in the SHU lose it and go off the deep end, digging themselves in deeper and deeper holes by displaying animalistic behavior and getting more shots and more hole time. What do the feds expect? When treated like animals, some people will act like animals.

A few prisoners get so stressed out by being in the hole that they commit suicide. You hear about it all the time. They hang themselves with their sheets. The noise, minimal human contact, frustration, and sheer hopelessness of being locked in a room for 24 hours a day drives them to take their own lives.

Other prisoners become violent and antisocial. A prolonged stay in the hole can cause prisoners to become paranoid, deranged, claustrophobic, and psychotic. A thin plastic film covers the small window only letting sunlight in but denying the prisoners the ability to see. The inability to see outside for extended periods of time can cause sensory deprivation.

Long-term confinement in the SHU takes both a mental and physical toll on prisoners. The lack of fresh air, poor ventilation, and mugginess contribute to sickness and respiratory problems in the summer. The chilled air and freezing conditions in winter can lead to exhaustion, illness, even death for older or disabled prisoners unable to do calisthenics to stay warm. The lack of showers and generally poor sanitation lead to poor hygiene and overall filth. Prolonged lying in bed is bad for your back, shins, and legs. After spending months in the hole, prisoners always complain of shin splints and backaches. The absence of serious physical recreation and lack of movement can cause your muscles to atrophy.

Sleep is also a problem. You can only sleep so much. After the first couple of weeks of sleeping all day, a man may not be able to sleep. A lot of prisoners in the hole have trouble sleeping after being there for a while, and any little noise will wake them up. They will lie there in the dark wondering what kind of hell they are in.

Gaining weight is also a problem. Prisoners look forward to the meals and will eat to kill the constant boredom. By doing this, they are taking in maximum calories while burning few because of the lack of movement and minimal recreation. This can cause a prisoner to get fat and can affect his overall health.

There are many bad effects on prisoners from being in the SHU. To do a long stint in the hole, you are going to have to be strong in mind and body. You have to stay focused, have a workout routine, and keep yourself occupied to fight the boredom. If not, you might become despondent and unmotivated or suicidal. Some men can do segregation, while others get crazy. The hole can bring out the worst in some prisoners.

Cell Gangstas

A "cell gangsta" is someone who acts real tough behind a locked door in the SHU. You can't imagine how tough prisoners become when they are locked in the SHU. Dudes talk mad shit in the hole and sell "crazy wolf tickets." They cuss out counselors, hacks, prison administrators, and other prisoners. Whomever. When they know you can't get to them, the monster comes out. Hollering down the hall, calling dudes out, disrespecting cats left and right.

And dudes buy into that shit. "All right, muthafucka, you betta shut you mouth. I'm gonna kill you ass nigga." It's crazy, the shit you hear in the hole. Dudes are real disrespectful. When they get back on the yard, they never talk shit like that, but in the hole, locked in a cell with no face-to-face contact, you might not even know who is cussing you out.

Feeding the Warden

About the worst thing about being in the hole is when you have to take a shit. Prisoners call this "feeding the warden." It sucks because you are in a little tiny cell with one or maybe two other people, and you have to do it right in front of them. There is no privacy whatsoever. Talk about unpleasant, dehumanizing, and demoralizing.

The smell, the sounds, the sight of a dude straining on the pot, it sucks. Dudes will be like, "Sorry guys, I gotta feed the warden." When your cellie says this, you try to retreat under your sheet and bury your head in your pillow. You usually yell out, "Flush, man, flush. Keep the water running," while your bunkie is feeding the warden to lighten the atmosphere in a situation that is uncomfortable for both of you.

Going Hard

When some prisoners get locked in the SHU, they "go hard." This means that they are going to cause a ruckus. The prisoners do this by various means. They flood the tiers and incite other prisoners to flood the tier. They do this by clogging their toilet with a T-shirt or sheet, and then they flush the toilet continually. When you have seven or eight prisoners on a tier doing this, it creates a flood sometimes with water up to 2 or 3 feet high. It is crazy. It disrupts the normal operations of the SHU officers and is a nuisance for them and the other prisoners in general. The hallway, tier, and cells are flooded, and watch out if it is a tier on the second floor. Then there might be a waterfall action. Usually the inmate orderlies are left to clean up the mess and sop up the water with mops. The guards aren't doing any janitorial duties. It's not in their job description.

Another way prisoner "go hard" is by slinging shit and piss out the trapdoors at meal times. They target the cops, trying to splatter them with feces or urine. The guards aren't too fond of this, for obvious reasons, and sometimes they bring in the Special Operations Response Team, aka SORT team, a group of cops in Teenage Mutant Ninja Turtle outfits, to subdue the culprit in a cell removal. They wear helmets and pads and carry shields.

A "cell removal" is when a prisoner is physically and often violently removed from a cell. This also might occur if a prisoner refuses to cuff up or is belligerent to the guards. I have heard of dudes stripping down to nothing and rubbing baby oil all over themselves to combat the SORT team when they attempt a cell removal. Sometimes it will take five or more Ninja Turtle hacks to subdue and remove a determined, prepared, and violent prisoner from his cell. Makes you think, why don't they just leave the prisoner in the cell? But the feds aren't having that. If you are a shit slinger or refuse to cuff up, you are probably going in the rubber room and being four-pointed to the bed.

"Breakfast in Bed"

A lot of prisoners view trips to the hole as a vacation. They'll say, "I'm going to lay it down." They say that the room service, breakfast in bed, and no work is a vacation. Sometimes it can be a permanent one, depending on how long they stay. For someone who can adapt, doing hole time is easy. It is just a real slow lifestyle.

The food in the hole is served in trays through the steel trap in the door. The hacks come by at mealtime three times a day and open up the slot and shove the food through. You get a cold tray, a hot tray, maybe a piece of fruit, and a drink. The cold tray usually consists of cereal in the morning and lettuce, bread, and a dessert at the other meals. The hot tray will usually have whatever the main line is serving and will include some rice, beans, or vegetables. The food is usually cold or semiwarm and is not the highest quality, as it has been sitting for a couple of hours after being prepared by prisoners in the kitchen, put on a segregation cart, and pushed over to the SHU.

Some dudes who are going hard will throw the food trays out of the steel trap in the door, trying to hit the cops or just to make a mess. Some prisoners take it one step further and refuse meals, declaring a hunger strike to protest their presence in the hole or to force the prison administrators to look into their situation.

"Checking In"

Some prisoners use the SHU like a hotel, checking in and out. When a prisoner checks into the hole, it means he goes to the lieutenant and asks to be put into the hole. This might be because the prisoner needs protection (PC), has a drug problem and wants to detox, or owes a lot of money for gambling or drug debts and doesn't have the ability to pay at the moment (he stays in the hole until he can get the money), or may be just for the simple reason that the prisoner wants to lay it down and take a break.

Whatever the reason, convicts look down on "checking in." It is seen as an escape route chosen by prisoners who can't handle their business. Some dudes have reputations as "check-in artists." They are always hitting different compounds as a result of frequent transfers, running up drug or gambling debts, checking in, snitching, and then getting transferred to other prisons.

The Noise

Let me tell you, life in the SHU is not a picnic. Despite the claims of vacation or breakfast in bed, it is hard to lay it down in the SHU unless you can make yourself immune to the noise. The noise is outrageous. Dudes are banging on the doors, kicking it, and calling for the guards. Prisoners are hollering back and forth, yelling down the halls, through the vents, just trying to make some noise.

Prisoners sing and scream at the top of their lungs just to hear their own voices, I guess. You can't see anybody, so that makes everyone crave human contact, so they holler, yell, and scream. The pounding is unbelievable. Sometimes a whole tier will start pounding on their doors and playing the drums on their metal desks or toilets. The din that reverberates can drive you crazy. In the hole, you don't get a moment's peace; it's like being in an insane asylum.

Hustling Cigarettes

On the compound, the hustle is drugs. In the hole, it is cigarettes. There are many ways prisoners smuggle cigarettes into the hole. Dudes are dying to get their smokes and have invented numerous ways to smuggle cigarettes into the hole. Prisoners do pretty much all of the work there is to do in a prison. Cops supervise or monitor them, but they can't catch everything. Men that work in the kitchen or laundry will stash cigarettes in the food or laundry cart going to the SHU. The orderlies in the SHU have access to these carts and, through a prearranged deal, will be notified when the cigarettes are coming. They then grab them and give them to the person they are sent in for. Everybody gets a cut out of the deal. The cops are pretty hip to this hustle; perhaps they are in on the deal.

In the hole, if you have a pack of smokes and some matches, you're a rich man. Prisoners sell cigarettes at the rate of three for a book of stamps. At $7.40 for a book of stamps, that is almost $45 a pack. Talk about inflation! I've seen guys run hustles that involved getting locked up in the hole on purpose just to cash in. These dudes might be in some serious debt on the pound, so they stash cigarettes, sometimes keistering them, on their person and smuggle them into the hole to sell for stamps. They then come out of the hole loaded with books of stamps to pay off their debts.

Another way prisoners smuggle cigarettes to their buddies is through the institutional mail system. After count every day, the cops will have mail call in the units. Much of the time, they will call the name of someone that is in the SHU. The prisoner's buddy will grab the letter or envelope, put in the tobacco and matches, and tape it back up, then return it to the cop, saying, "Oh, yeah, he's in the hole." If the cop doesn't notice the cigarettes, the letter will be rerouted to the hole.

A trickier method is to make up a bulky envelope with three or four packs and matches in it, address it to a lawyer with your buddy's name as the return address but without stamps on it, and put it in the legal mailbox. All legal mail is closed, so when the mailroom gets it, the letter is rerouted to the prisoner in the hole. Voilà! Cigarettes and instant riches for that prisoner.

Most SHUs have an outside recreation yard with cages that the prisoners are put into for recreation. Many times you can see this SHU rec yard from the regular rec yard or the pound. Often prisoners on the compound will throw packs of cigarettes over the fence to the SHU rec yards. Then the prisoners can retrieve them. If they can't, the orderlies usually can. But sometimes there are asshole cops who go out on the SHU rec yard and make sure there are no packs of cigarettes around the cages before they take dudes out to rec.

The most trusted and time-honored way to get cigarettes into the hole is the "toiletries move." When you know you are going to the hole, you can prepare tobacco and matches by wrapping them in plastic and submerging them in your shampoo, conditioner, or lotion. You can also break open your soap bars and stash tobacco in them, resealing them so the cops can't tell. About the only property they will give you in the hole is your toiletries, so a lot of dudes use this move.

In 2004, the BOP banned smoking cigarettes in all federal prisons. Today getting caught with a cigarette means a shot and you go to the hole. All this means is that some hacks are getting rich supplying convicts with smokes. Every day they bring in a few packs that they sell to prisoner merchants for $20 each. The prisoner then sells individual cigarettes for $2 to $5 each. On some days, it seems everybody in the prison has smokes, even the convicts in the hole.

Your Tax Dollars at Work

With the prison population growing at a phenomenal rate, there will only be more and more prisoners locked down in the hole. Prison overcrowding forces the BOP to struggle with maintaining order. They have resorted to the tactics discussed in this chapter. Today, in most medium- and maximum-security federal prisons, hundreds of prisoners are locked in the hole every day. Cruel and unusual punishment comes to mind, but who will listen?

Perhaps the taxpayer will begin to listen, because right now the BOP is just warehousing men and women. With the main theme in prison being punishment, where can this lead? There is no attempt to rehabilitate anymore. Vocational and education programs are limited, and what is offered to prisoners is a joke. Prisoners are losing decades of their lives to prison. The BOP staff doesn't care about the prisoners' rehabilitation. In fact, they seem to want to keep all prisoners in prison for as long as possible. Perhaps they are worried about their job security.

If the sentences were shorter and prisoners had some incentive to be good inmates, such as parole, maybe the BOP wouldn't need so many segregation cells. What is the point of all the security and lockdown procedures in SHUs nationwide when most of the prisoners that occupy them are nonviolent? They even lock down minimum-security campers in the hole. It is really ridiculous. Minimum-security prisoners reside in a prison camp without a fence, but if they get a shot, they go to the hole, where they're under 24-hour lockdown. Does that make sense?

The point is that if prisoners were serving shorter sentences, the prison would not have to resort to using corrupt practices like the hole to control prisoners. If the sentences were shorter, there would be less need for the gun towers, razor wire, SHU cells, and all the expense to the taxpayers. If prisoners had a chance at getting out earlier for exemplary behavior, were given some educational opportunities, and received sentences that actually fit the crimes they committed, then they might have a reason to behave the way the cops want them to.

But now, I just don't know. It only seems to be getting worse in here. I keep thinking to myself, "When will it explode?" It's got to sometime. The pressure is building.

| 3 |

Going to the Hole in California: Cauldron of Solitude

Eugene Dey

August 2, 2006, the sirens blare. Running feet stampede the hall. My pulse racing, I search for a spot out of harm's way. Contingents of correctional officers converge, wielding batons and pepper spray. "Get on your stomachs!" they scream. "Don't move a muscle!" The officers bind our hands behind our backs using plastic flex ties that are much stronger than the zip ties they resemble. The officers' panic only adds to the pandemonium.

My mouth is dry. I've been breathing open-mouthed, out of control. Once the rush of adrenaline subsides, my pulse will return to normal and my mouth will moisten again. A few feet away, a prisoner is pressing a shirt against his throat. It's been cut open. He stanches the wound while waiting for the ambulance to arrive. After he's whisked away, prisoners begin to complain. "My hands are turning blue, this is fucking bullshit!"

To take my mind off the pain in my hands—the tingle rapidly turns to a sting, then to pinpricks of fire—I listen to the officers' talk. I watch them as they watch us. Some take photos and write notes. Others stand around and look bored. A fan of the reality competition *Rock Star Supernova*, I wonder who will be voted off tonight. Lying on my stomach with my arms tied behind my back, I try to look cool. It doesn't work. The smell of disinfectant and moldy mop is a humbling experience.

Prisoners secured in their cells come to their windows and stare. They are unimpressed by the chaos. This is how we do it—just another day. Most are happy they aren't cuffed up. I'm happy for them. Running out of distractions, I fix my gaze on the solid steel door of what looks like the lid to my concrete casket. Lockdown looming large, my concrete coffin beckons.

The California Model: Lockdown

Lockdown has become the norm in the prisons of my native Golden State. When an incident occurs, prisoners are "slammed" in their cells. If the incident is racial, we are sorted out by gang affiliation and race. While the guards determine what tactics to employ in controlling the prisoners, all prison activities come to an abrupt halt, with no movement whatsoever. Those involved in or suspected of institutional transgressions are carried off to administrative segregation (Ad Seg). Sequestered 24 hours a day, convicts on lockdown are allowed to live and not much else. The human mind can only take so much. California's suicide rate for prisoners is the highest in the nation.

It's all bad; California's prisons are racially segregated and prone to chronic violence. Simple solutions to the unending conflicts don't exist. We're forced to live next to and on top of our friends and enemies. Reluctantly, we tolerate one another. It's a nightmare. On July 31, 2006, there was a huge race riot at the California Correctional Center in Susanville. Just a few days later, a number of white prisoners had their throats cut. We call it "cleanup." Prisoners suspected of betrayal or cowardice—not to mention sex offenders and snitches—are violently removed from the population. Like nefarious alchemists, convicts turn grown men into "victims."

Automatically, I knew it when I saw it—one man failed to stand and fight when the fight began. I couldn't care less if someone fought valiantly at the riot, but most do not share my indifference. Not participating during a riot is a serious betrayal, and this particular person ran. To say we are harsh critics of those who don't toe the party line would be an extreme understatement. The following night, two more "vics" had their throats cut. We heard the Skinheads did it. In the vernacular of the underground, "Susanville is rocking and rolling."

If rehabilitation were truly the goal, then placing the institution on lockdown would be counterproductive. When more than two-thirds of the prisoners in the California Department of Corrections and Rehabilitation (CDCR) have substance abuse issues, a system of treatment and training would be a more logical approach. But under the California model, lockdown is the main staple on penology's pungent diet—treat 'em bad enough for long enough and they'll correct their behavior. What a sad joke.

Lockdowns are the norm. The practice of trapping two grown men in a concrete cage produces an amalgam of mind-numbing isolation and disagreeable conditions of cohabitation. For those with preexisting conditions, seclusion exacerbates mental disorders. Deviance is reinforced as the prisoner is pressured into a state of desperation. Subtle are the strains isolation places on the psyche.

While some institutions allow visiting during lockdowns, Susanville takes a harder line. Family photos become the only solace. My cellie, a young man from Los Angeles, stares at pictures of his wife for hours to counteract the pressures of being locked up with me 24 hours a day. Maybe he's just lonely as hell. I'm not qualified to make a diagnosis, but I don't need a doctorate in psychology to recognize the damage he's enduring because of severed family ties.

Each extended session of solitude takes something away from me I'll never get back. As I try to maintain a grasp on sanity, no matter how tenuous, I manage to keep writing and exercising in order to keep myself busy. Testing the patience and sanity of my cellie, I rarely stop moving. I made a permanent departure from the ranks of the sane long ago, so why bother to pretend. I just do the best I can. Institutions generally return to normal routine, but not always. Even when the lockdown is lifted, we know that peace is always temporary. Our escape from the confines of two-man asylums never lasts long.

Hard Times

On August 2, 2006, I spent three hours as a piece of "physical evidence" at the crime scene of the stabbing. It ended with being escorted back to my cell. I had mixed feelings. Relieved this torturous session of being treated like physical evidence was about to come to an end, I resisted the temptation to yearn for the familiar comforts of my concrete coffin. Escorted like a dead man walking past a number of cuffed-up suspects, I knew some of them to be innocent. Rarely do the guards get it right. But they had their own problems and I had mine. In times like these, it's every man for himself—doing time isn't a team sport.

The process starts in the first few days of a lockdown. Enveloped by the warm embrace of the cell, I begin to fight my own personal demons. It's a struggle. Through a regimen of litigious, literary, and physical exercises, I try to expand the claustrophobic parameters of the coffin. Only time will tell if I'm successful.

On lockdown, hard times can hit someone like a ton of bricks. Everyone has a method. Some men sleep all the time, others read. Most, however, watch endless hours of television. When we're finally let out of our cells, it's like being released from one form of hell into Hades. A few weeks into this lockdown, I was given a breath of not-so-fresh air. Starting with a strip search in the doorways of our cells, we're then escorted in boxer shorts and shower sandals back into the dayroom. Seated at tables, separated by race, we're held like hostages in the middle of a standoff.

Once again, I was cuffed up in the dayroom, the scene of the previous crime. Though no longer in the middle of an emergency, "search teams" of correctional officers ripped through our belongings like Nazis through Warsaw. They confiscated a multitude of books, clothes, and small appliances. There is a policy about excess property. It seems more about the constant pressure of correctional managers who use policy to draw the walls of an already restricted environment even closer. As I awaited the completion of this stripping—materially, physically, and emotionally, I caught it staring at me, the solid steel door of my cell, much like the lid of a coffin in shape and form, locked into the open position. This was going to be a bad trip.

The Chill Effect

While group punishment rolls on, investigations of individuals continue behind the scenes. Periodically, suspects are taken away, excised from the whole. In order to catch their prey off guard, raids are usually executed around sunrise. Dulled senses diminish the likelihood of resistance.

For me, my turn came a few months after the cell search, on the morning of Friday the 13th in October 2006. "Dey. Get dressed," an officer ordered as the electric door to my cell was opened. An early riser, I put down a book I was reading. I stared at two officers who filled the narrow doorway and took my time putting on my clothes. They tried to look mean. Most guards are regular folks and many are decent. The nature of their job, however, turns them into the enemy. I've seen this movie a million times as they become faceless ghouls. Already knowing the cause, I inquired about my destination. "Where am I going?" I asked, as if unconcerned. "R&R," replied a third. Receiving and Release is where we pick up care packages from home.

Three against one hardly seemed like a fair fight. Having worn many hats throughout my crazy life, a hustler's cap being one of them, I recognized a game of dirty pool a mile away. Picking up packages at R&R had been taken away long ago. Dangling a coveted box of morsels in front of the stupid prisoner added insult to injury. I don't care if they lie. It's us against them, and they lie just as much as we do. The enemy isn't privy to the truth. With distinct lines of demarcation that I won't cross, my convict honor and integrity are at stake, not to mention my life. As they say, snitches get stitches.

Going to R&R to pick up a package sounded so stupid I felt like refusing. I would make my stand. Like a soldier, I would go out on my shield. But I was in no position to initiate a debate; I just did what I was told. I knew the deal. A list had been assembled, and we were in trouble again.

My third handcuffed sojourn into the dayroom in as many months, and this would be my last. Under heavy escort, I was now the suspect. I saw many staring from the cells. Some just looked. Others just looked scared. Trying to look tough, I mainly looked busted. Paraded around like a punk, I made my penological "perp walk."

The chill effect is age-old. By intimidating the masses and terrorizing them from speaking out, those in positions of power effectively scare them. The chill effect is a control mechanism. I don't blame someone for being afraid. Oppression defeats the spirit. For me, it's a matter of principle. I'm too stubborn—or stupid—to allow fear to take control of my emotions. "Eugene," screamed a friend. "Is it good or bad?" "It doesn't look good, bro!" I yelled, to the irritation of my escorts. Oppressors prefer their captives quiet. Given the circumstances, I couldn't care less. "Take it easy, Eugene!" he replied. "Give 'em hell, brother!" hollered another. My heart growing heavier by the second, I held my head up high and smiled. They whisked me away, and out of the corner of my eye, I caught it staring at me. It's a wicked miscreant, my concrete coffin. Good riddance.

The Quagmire

The officers of the CDCR are a lawless lot. A lack of competence, compounded by corruption, caused the federal judiciary to take control of various functions of the mammoth agency. After numerous class-action lawsuits ranging from unconstitutional delivery of mental and health-care services to malfeasance and contempt of court, the Supreme Court validated a population cap placed on the agency by a three-judge panel.

Stacking prisoners high and tight like oily cords of human firewood forces us to compete like savages for scarce resources. Negative resources are tattooed on our minds. Riots, stabbings, and fights—not to mention the "homies" carted off to the hole, the infirmary, or the morgue—are all too familiar sights. While most taken to the hole are guilty of something, many have not done what is charged—or have done nothing at all. After the August stabbings, without an iota of evidence, a friend of mine had been charged with orchestrating one of the assaults. Every document had been falsified in a sad example of police work.

While the right to seek redress against the government is absolute, the courts give wide deference to the actions and decisions of correctional officials. The stifling of prisoners' civil liberties hit an apex during the tough-on-crime 1990s, until serious officer misconduct at the notorious Pelican Bay State Prison blew up in their faces. Officers attempted to conceal numerous instances of guard-on-prisoner assaults, and the media discovered a cover-up going all the way to Edward Alameida, the director of what was then the CDCR. Under threat of a federal contempt charge, he resigned in 2003, citing personal reasons. Despite the ensuing scrutiny, including federal oversight and unending negative media, a higher standard for correctional officer conduct has not materialized.

Fighting the Good Fight

Prison administrators can always be counted on to viciously reciprocate. It's the nature of the game. Following the August 2006 stabbings, after confiscating from the prison population mass quantities of personal property under the catchall label of contraband, the officers made sure white prisoners would bear the brunt of the administration's nefarious quid pro quo. This time us, next time prisoners of color. Waves of punitive methodologies are unleashed just to let us know who's in charge.

It's difficult to pinpoint exactly what I did during this lockdown to become a target of corrupt officials. While in prison, I've covered many facets of "prisondom" for numerous publications (e.g., Dey, 2005a, 2005b, 2005c, 2006a). These legal actions don't coalesce with the malicious goals of prison officials. A complete ban on the press implemented in the tough-on-crime 1990s gave corrections a much-desired cloak of secrecy. Penitentiaries are closed societies by their very definition. Keeping investigative journalists out of prisons gives the agents of government absolute power.

Incarcerated activists like me are an anomaly. Corrupt government officials have little respect for free speech. Whether they are covering up malfeasance or choosing not to weather some well-deserved criticism in the press, the CDCR will never voluntarily end their embargo on free speech. Retaliation is assured.

The Constitution is the ultimate loser. My activism took shape in late 2006. On behalf of those on lockdown, I filed an administrative appeal in early October. Severed family ties caused by the total denial of all visitors for months based on race, not individual culpability, motivated me to file the administrative class action. Exercising my rights on multiple levels, I also covered the story for a publication for which I served as an "inside" reporter (Dey, 2006b).

With corrections mired in crisis, one must take chances. The CDCR medical services were placed in federal receivership when found to be in violation of the Eighth Amendment of the US Constitution (see *Plata v. Schwarzenegger* and *Coleman v. Schwarzenegger*). Perhaps if enough prisoners spoke out about how the overcrowding contributed to racial violence, the entire California prison system would face a similar fate. The CDCR was operating prisons way beyond legal capacity. The federal judiciary hovered over the prison system like an angry parent. The time to act was now. Prisoners have few constitutional protections for their use of literary or litigious expression. Still, I thought I needed to make a stand. Generally motivated by a sense of social responsibility, not gang or race-based intolerance, I placed cause over self.

Falsified Evidence

Such were the factual circumstances under which the guards took me to the hole. Having already worn me down from months of lockdown, my captors then took me to an even worse place. On the morning of October 13, 2006, I found myself seated and handcuffed waiting to be dragged away; with no abundance of racial tattoos or gang affiliation, I was horribly miscast for this production of *The Usual Suspects.*

As if being treated like a recently captured enemy combatant weren't bad enough, each of us had been served identical documents alleging our instrumental roles "in promoting racial unrest" as members or affiliates of the Skinheads. I'm not a gangbanger. Not one to accept a total fabrication of charges without a court battle, I took such charges very seriously. Instinctive reflexes on how to fight false charges fired in the back of my mind. But the first order of business involved survival.

I recalled memories of the six months I spent in 1999 as a prisoner in the secure housing unit (SHU) in Corcoran State Prison. Corcoran SHU is infamous. Throughout the late 1980s and early 1990s, Corcoran applied a morbid doctrine of pitting rival gang members against each other on the concrete exercise yards. Roughly 50 men were shot point-blank by guards. Seven were killed. Convicts were forced to fight their rivals or be shot by the guards. Nothing has changed.

When I arrived at Corcoran, I was mad at the world for an unjust life sentence for drugs and determined to fight back. From the platform of the chair's position of the inmate council, I took on one of the most notorious prison administrations in the nation. Corcoran's administration made short work of me. After a riot between the whites and the Crips, I was sent to the hole. So when the Susanville faction of the correctional oppressors came to get me, I felt as if I had come full circle.

They did me a favor. In Corcoran, I learned how to really do time. I entered a notorious hellhole an undisciplined and angry quasi-activist. In such settings, with absolutely nothing to lose, the guards have no choice but to show respect for the convicts. We give it like we get it, and the calming effect of mutual respect is almost therapeutic. I emerged a better man, an accomplished convict activist who desired to become a jailhouse lawyer—and to start writing again. I would now rather die than submit. By the hard times that seem to be in abundance, I'm empowered.

The Vortex

That Friday morning in October, an explosion of barbed wire, chain-link fence, and one-man holding cages overwhelmed my senses as I entered the abyss. My heart rate elevated. The reality that a torture chamber resembling a housing unit would serve as my new home slapped me hard in the face. As my mind raced, I tried not to lose my cool. I had to fight back the instinct to cry out like a wolf caught in a steel trap. Preparing for the rigors of confinement in supermax is an exercise of extreme difficulty. I struggled to maintain control at all costs.

Ritualistic greetings and salutations peppered the air as I entered the abyss. Those who had gone MIA days, weeks, and months earlier welcomed us into the vortex. "Eugene!" I heard someone scream over all the noise. "That's fucked up!" The convicts knew that the administration arbitrarily deemed us insurgents. My inclusion seemed like a capricious stretch of the evidence that everyone knew didn't exist. "I never expected to see you in here, Dey," said the guard performing my inaugural strip search. Such disingenuous small talk did little to diminish the indignation of unjustified subjugation and the feeling of being flushed down the toilet. "Neither did I," I lied. I shrugged off his comment with a grin. My demeanor was calm, as if it were just another day at the office. "Dey, you're going to cell 24/7." It was a bad dream that kept getting worse. I tried not to make eye contact—my cauldron awaited.

Afterward

If life imitates art, then my body of work chronicles my existence as an activist. One of my hometown newspapers ran a part of this piece that I drafted while on lockdown (Dey, 2007b). Since the charges were so poorly crafted, I determined to flesh out the entire episode as an example of correctional corruption. My effort (Dey, 2008c) won third place in the PEN American Center's annual writing contest for prisoners. With the perpetual assistance from Jessie, my PEN writing mentor, I further developed two PEN pieces, "Cauldron" and "A Requiem for Freddy" (Dey, 2007a, 2007c), which both won honorable mentions in 2007. Since the events of "Cauldron," I feel I've progressed as an advocate for social justice.

After going to Ad Seg in 2006, for the next couple of years my litigation took on a sense of purpose. In the hole I met J. P. Cuellar, and for him and the cause, I edited and revised his poorly written prisoner appeals, earning my first "Order to Show Cause" (Cuellar, 2007). When released from another trip to the hole in 2007, I managed to have my case joined to Cuellar's (Dey, 2008a, 2008b, 2008d).

With the appointment of counsel, evidentiary hearings, and the attorney general deposing the prison staff, the pressure was on the correctional administrators that covered up the staff violence against prisoners. I broadened the scope of my case to cover how complaints of misconduct against guards are systematically covered up. As my petition worked its way through the state courts, I found myself in a streak of litigious success. I had attorneys appointed in the state and federal courts for over half a dozen guys, covering an assortment of claims. In 2009, I secured the release of a lifer.

My all-out reactions to the actions of dirty cops made me a hero in the eyes of my people. The experience made me a better person. Advocacy is serious business. I may be mad, but I treat it like a game. By not taking it personally, I kept my sanity. After I finally transferred from Susanville back to Soledad (both medium-security state prisons), I still couldn't stop my advocacy efforts and wrote my article "Grey Goose" (Dey, 2010a). But a reporter at my other hometown newspaper used my case as part of a larger piece about correctional corruption (Piller, 2010), and being part of a newspaper story that led to statewide changes in the appeals process allowed me to achieve closure.

Preferring to write literature rather than litigate court cases, I restarted my literary activism in Soledad. I prefer to write social commentary about prison life, rather than motions to court. The prison administrators at Soledad, a lower-security institution than Corcoran, did not respond in a brutal or felonious fashion to my public advocacy in the press. When I determined to illuminate the injustice of forcing racial integration on prisoners, a minor act of retaliation by the prison staff didn't warrant a response. I kept my cool while continuing to submit my written work to newspapers and academic journals. Only battles with merit and substance move me.[1]

Because jailhouse journalists are frequent targets for punishment and sanctions,[2] our underappreciated work deserves a place in the literature.[3] Prison writers understand that they are taking risks when expressing their views in published works or lawsuits. Prison officials will go to great lengths to defeat the resistance of prisoners in higher-custody institutions. However, convicts should not be locked in solitary confinement or violently attacked by guards for submitting articles to newspapers or bringing their concerns to a court of law. Having experienced many months of solitary confinement in Corcoran SHU and then again at the California Correctional Center at Susanville, making it out of the war zone and then to the medium-security prison at Soledad felt like a miracle.

Times are changing, and I'm adjusting my focus. In my last year at Susanville and my first year and a half at Soledad, I've been working with a team of "qualified offenders" to develop and deliver evidence-based programs. With the assistance of a well-connected nonprofit organization, through a group we call Inside Solutions, I'm holstering some of my "acidic views" (Dey, 2009, p. 122) as I chase transcendence in the form of unleashing systemic restoration to the community.

Notes

1. See, e.g., Dey, 2010b, 2011b.

2. Prisoners that publish editorials or articles in newspapers or magazines often suffer harsh reprisals. See, e.g., Hucklebury, 1999; McMaster, 1999b; Dey, 2009.

3. Prisoners have few outlets for their social commentary on prisons. See, e.g., Gaucher, 1999; Piché, 2008.

| 4 |

The Boy Scout in Solitary at USP Lompoc

Brian Edward Malnes

I was raised a Boy Scout to become a soldier. Then I became a bank robber, and now I do time in a U.S. penitentiary. I must be clear at the beginning. I am insane, made this way by continued existence inside a box—solitary confinement in United States Penitentiary (USP) Lompoc, California. Here, the lights never go out. Continued brightness bleeds everything together into a single fluorescent tube, searching behind steel mesh. Closing my eyes is like lighting a road flare. Nothing is hidden, especially the man I was, melting in the corner.

Before now, I existed outside of not only this box, but also the prison that contains it. I was a middle-class kid, an Eagle Scout. I got a swimming scholarship to Pacific Lutheran University, but then dropped out and decided I wanted to serve my country as my father did. In the 1980s, I joined the U.S. Army and found myself on the demilitarized zone in South Korea with little more than a clue where I was. I learned that North Korea keeps a grudge.

When I came home, I wanted to see the truth I'd learned on every face, but no one but the dope man seemed to listen. Heroin solved so many things for me. However, even a $100 a gram habit costs a tidy sum of $36,500 per annum. So I decided to step up my game, and in 1991, at age 24, I robbed my first bank. I robbed three banks total along with Michelle, my fiancée, age 25, but I only got prosecuted for the last one and was sentenced to 36 months in this maximum-security penitentiary. I didn't use a gun, just a "mysterious bulge" a teller took for a gun. I took my case all the way to trial, and so as punishment, I was sent to Lompoc to do my sentence. Damn bad speculative venture. Bank robbery is just a bad bust waiting to happen. At the time, the FBI suspect demographic for bank robbers like me was 20- to 30-year-old white male heroin addict. Damn, the FBI is good at what it does.

Michelle is free because I took the fall. I am happy for her but scared every day she'll leave me. I never hurt anyone. Now I am sitting in this bad box doing more than just time. I'm doing everything I've ever done, over and over. Because I will never tell on another man, I am here, writing on the walls. A convict "shanked" this other guy right in front of me, stabbing him with a homemade knife, and I simply saw nothing.

Please understand that I am sorry. Sorry for the infractions of prison rules that have brought me here to wallow in my sin. I was a witness to violence, as I have been every day of my sentence. But in this bloody case, I was seen seeing. A "hack" (prison slang for federal guard) pointed me out and said I knew something, and because I told the lieutenant nothing when asked what I knew, I was remanded to this very box to consider my crime.

I hope I do not break, but fear I already have. Conversations I've had over the last couple of weeks are strung together. Any sense of the straight line of my life has broken into an ever-changing amount of rivulets flowing away from me. Always away, as if my own past is escaping, afraid of what must be ahead.

Time and Space in the Box

Time becomes very particular in a brightly lit box. I am aware of every second, the beating of my heart. I read somewhere that every animal has approximately 1 billion heartbeats, and the fast heart rate of tiny creatures like hummingbirds makes them die much quicker than large ones like hippos. Somewhere in between the two are humans. As for how many heartbeats I am up to, I cannot say, but I am very guarded.

I have devoted several cinder blocks—like all the walls, a pleasant beige—to my ongoing calculations regarding how long I have to live. To begin with, there are 86,400 seconds in every single day. That means there are 31,536,000 seconds in a year, which is a massive number. Figuring this out took several days, because focus is becoming a major problem for me. Carrying the math a bit further, I have determined the average person should have roughly 30 years of heartbeats.

I am 25, so I have five years left of God-given heartbeats. Something must be done. I want to outlive my sentence, so I need to lower my heart rate. Nothing is more important than adding years to my life. I desperately want to feel freedom again. So I have begun meditating, yogi style.

Each morning, which is only determinable by when the food slot in the door opens, I strip naked and sit cross-legged on a towel in the middle of the cell. Here I begin counting heartbeats and seconds. I focus my mind and will on slowing down time, giving myself much-needed grace. I believe that I have gotten down to about 70,000 heartbeats a day, maybe five years of net gain. I am proud of the discipline I have mastered. Soon, I should be gaining years. Possibly someone deals in time and can buy some of mine. I can only hope I will be released very soon, younger than when they put me in this box.

The box itself is a measurable reality, 7 by 9 feet, making the cell 63 square feet (I've checked this several times). I realize that sounds massive. But I will tell you that I occupy approximately 1 square foot of space when I stand up. So there are 63 possible spaces I can stand in this cell. But that, of course, is amendable by objects that also consume space in this cell.

The concrete slab where I sleep is 7 by 3 feet, which equals 21 square feet, leaving 42 square feet. I also calculate that 1 square foot is used for the combination toilet-sink so cleverly placed in a corner of the cell. The combo sink is stainless steel and provides flushing of sewage as well as cold water for drinking, washing, and spiritual cleansing. This easy math establishes a free range of movement of approximately 40 square feet. Considering my constant movement pacing back and forth across the box, I calculate there are 3,000,000 possible upright movements per day.

This box does not provide much space for my movement. Believe me, having systematically explored every possibility in this cell, I decided that a human being needs more space than what has been provided, maybe even much more. Of course, I am not an expert in the design of cells. This work is left to the Federal Bureau of Prisons (BOP), my careful caretakers who maintain the delicate balance of sanity in this box of mine.

Ghosts in the Box

I realize this is not really my cell, as I share it with many ghosts. I am simply one convict in an endless line of occupants. I wonder how many men have sat on this concrete and stared at the paint peeling on the vent that always brings in bad air. How many men have calculated their own movements, right here?

USP Lompoc was constructed in 1946, the last of three "big house" federal penitentiaries built on the West Coast (the other two are USP McNeil Island and USP Alcatraz). That means that as of 1992, this "joint" has been here for 46 years. A hack informed me that guys usually do about two months on average in the hole. That makes an average of six men per year, which times 46 equals 276. But for this thought, I'm going to round it to 300.

I am thinking 300 in memory of King Leonidas and his Spartans. Greek warriors were forged on deprivation, solitude, and hatred, making them savage. They stood their ground at the Battle of Thermopylae and were slaughtered by the Persians. At least they are remembered as brave soldiers, the murderers they were. It is I who now wish for that same bloody death, alone in this cell.

Alone, like 300 other men before me. I shudder at the magnitude of that. Because I know what punishment has been handed to me. I am living it right now, a pressure that mounts by the moment, shaving off more of my mind. An inexact bloodletting performed by those whose job it is to watch over human misery, to count people in their boxes, day after day.

In the past 46 years, how many different guards have strolled by that slot in the door, making certain of the lives they count every day at 4 P.M.? Right now, there are three shifts of six that rotate on a schedule, which I estimate must come near to 100 different hacks a year. Taking into account an attrition of plus or minus 10 per year, this totals about 560 guards since this prison first opened. For this thought, I'm going to be kind and estimate that in the life of the door slot I'm looking at, 550 different people have walked past on behalf of the BOP.

I figure 550 guards watching 300 prisoners just in this one cell. That is a lot of hacks counting a lot of prisoners, right where I am sitting. I figure that at least 850 people have shared in this punishment and intimacy that are exchanged, with this daily witnessing of naked men wasting away inside this very box. I cannot know the prisoners that have slept here, although I know them like my very flesh. We, like all those who have been sentenced here, are one. I know what the hacks think, or at least what they want to believe. They think the prisoner's mind is simply "tabula rasa," a blank slate like the beige walls that entomb me. But the horror is, the mind never stops beating.

So those starched-uniformed BOP guards walk the spaces between cell doors, ignoring us, thinking we have faded into the abyss. Patrolling the tier outside my door, they are the outsiders. To treat people like animals, you must make them animals and feed them like animals. Wash them three times a week, give them minimum space in their pens, and most important, collectively shut out the noise coming from inside the doors. Turn that noise into the rutting yelps of a caged beast. Then, being a hack can be a walk in the zoo.

They know not what they do. Like many before me, I prostrate myself, my lips so close to the slot I can smell spilt Kool-Aid, thirst killing me because they shut off the water, another clever trick to make me a better man, and it is now at least 100 degrees Fahrenheit. Like an animal yipping for mealtime, I've begged that set of blue pants for water. Just some water, sir, please. How many men in this cell have gotten nothing in return but the fading click of highly polished boots? I do not remember a time when I ever denied another human being water. God help me if I have. I guess I simply do not have the fortitude for corrections.

Food in the Hole: Brown Bag

Let me show you something written on the outside of this brown bag: 08547–023. That means it is mine. My food. I am so very hungry, and it takes everything I have to carefully open the brown bag and take account of what is inside. The contents of the brown bag are the same every day: four pieces of white bread, two cheese slices, two meat slices (there are three different meat styles: red, gray, and brown), one fruit (typically apples or oranges; however, occasionally they have slipped in an overly ripe black banana), and three to eight carrot and celery sticks. I am told that these sticks are supposed to curb the desire for nicotine, but they do not. Further, I think it is cruel and unusual to provide celery, a food that uses more calories to eat it than are contained within. No one in the hole is trying to lose weight. I also receive one pint-size carton of warm milk. My personal policy is to never look at the expiration date. It is better to close one's eyes and nose and drink than to think about the oyster like consistency of the product. Finally, my favorite, the pièce de résistance—on some days I get two cookies. Too bad, they are often too hard to eat until soaked in water for a bit, but then they are quite delicious.

Without change, that is the brown bag. I am being punished for acting like a dog. So the brown bags replace the normal meal trays—everything the "general population" eats at Food Service. I still get the Styrofoam cup of Kool-Aid (since I've been here, they have only served red and orange). Occasionally the brown bag must accommodate not only a meal, but sometimes a day of meals—one brown bag to last 86,400 seconds. In no way is this common except in cases of behavior modification.

Here is an example of a crime that garnered me the one-brown-bag-a-day punishment favored at USP Lompoc in 1992. It began with the casual observation that every time the door slot opens, I instantly feel hungry. In the course of 86,400 seconds, the slot typically opens six times: three times for meals at 5 A.M., 1 P.M., and 5 P.M.; one time for the BOP 4 P.M. stand-up count; and one time each in the morning and evening for medications (these are the wild cards and can happen seemingly anytime).

The morning medication administration is often accompanied with a mental and medical evaluation or a visit by the deputy warden when "kites" (inmate requests of staff) are answered and general complaints are heard through a 2-inch metal door. I typically do not even acknowledge these medical and administrative interruptions, except when I feel like I'm dying, or bleeding, which has happened more times than is reasonable. Instead, I often choose to make a statement when the morning observations occur.

On occasion, I grunt and bark at the nurse's intrusion, choosing to speak in tongues as he or she offers the standard dosage of Prozac. I am unimpressed with the results, having saved three days' dosages and taken them all at once. No noticeable difference was experienced. Food for thought: Prozac is not for getting high. However, the first week on the drug is a high-wire act of euphoria and inescapable laughter. I remember the first time I was dosed in Lompoc. I was astonished by the uncontrollable laughter I was hit with as I cried in the shower, understanding that I was no more than a slave. Most everyone in the hole here gets the green and white capsule. In a way, it acts as Judge Dredd, the judge, jury, and executioner, all in one pill.

Anyway, one day I got the idea to lather up some toothpaste and rub it on my lips. I was sure I looked like a salivating dog, like Pavlov's dog that craves food when a bell is rung. Well, to me the bell was the opening of the food slot in the door. To be funny, political, human, whatever, I decided to be Pavlov's dog when the door opened for the morning medication dispersal. On my hands and knees, my mouth foaming, I viciously barked at the overweight face peering in the door slot. It took one heartbeat to realize I was looking at the deputy warden (DW). This fact gave the dog act a serious downside. To his credit, the DW said not a word, just shut the slot. The voices of the DW and his retinue of hacks stopped at the next cell door, and I listened to the one-sided exchange. I believe the guy in the next cell over, named Red, had gone at the neck of some other guy with a handmade awl. Now he was relaxing and letting off steam. The DW wanted to know if he was ready to explain what had happened. In answer, I heard Red mumble something negative and then the slamming of the door slot. I assume Red threw fecal matter or a Styrofoam cup of urine.

I kept kneeling naked on the ground in front of the food slot, eagerly listening while licking the foam from my lips. I was quite relieved that the DW had another focus besides me. What was more important was the drama. I was listening to the world that was not in this box. I don't get a lot of action down here at the end of the tier, with only one neighbor, as the segregation tier ended at my cell. So I was grateful to Red, who was now going to be punished for his transgressions.

Soon he would learn what I did about the extraction team and the cold metal table in the lieutenant's office. He would know what it was to lie naked on the table, strapped and simply left. Under the blinding light, he would have to shit and piss on himself and be fed baby food hand-to-mouth by a guard. Red would stop being. The man left from this treatment lacks any recognizable humanity, a disheveled bag of flesh whimpering to simply be heard. "It's for his own good" is a phrase I heard a female guard say to another guard administering my issue of food jelly as I lay there naked in front of them, very possibly with a hard on. I am certainly glad someone was looking out for what is good for me.

But after the DW left, there was no more drama. I sat for quite a while, waiting at the food slot for any action, but none came. However, the next morning at chow, I was greeted not with a tray, but with a brown bag with my number on it. The hack who delivered the good news offered this advice: "Make it last." Make it last? So I did what I've done with all my food since coming to prison: I ate it all save for the fruit and cookies. Prisoners know that keeping a little aside is always a good plan. It was, for sure, because when I was awakened by the opening of the slot for lunch, instead I got, "I hope you made it last." I immediately asked what he meant several times, louder each time. What I got in response was the slow closing of the food slot as I started yelling and pounding on the door. When the pounding started to really hurt my hands, I kicked the door and sat down on the bed. A few days later, hunger and I had finally become one.

I am alone, knowing that every moment must be filled with my mind. Focus is needed to make it through today. On my food slot door frame opening, I write a timetable. The following schedule is helpful in planning the one-brown-bag-a-day diet:

4:30 A.M. Food slot opens and brown bag is born out of the steel door.

4:31 A.M. I take a full accounting of contents, then eat one bread, one cheese, some fruit, one carrot (the beta-carotene does a great job of protecting the skin from the ever-buzzing fluorescent lights), drink milk, meditate, and hold back vomit. I save the two cookies for later. Then I go back to sleep.

6:30 A.M. The guard raps door with something, checking for movement. Still hungry, I eat one bread, one meat, celery already turning, rotting. Go back to sleep.

Noon The guard raps door with something, checking for movement. Still hungry, I eat one bread, one cheese, and one cookie.

4:00 P.M. Stand-up count. Hunger is now very active. I have difficulty with balance. I am lightheaded from lack of food. I eat the rest of vegetables and one last cookie. Now, wrapped in the napkin under my pillow, I have one bread, one meat, and condiment packets. My mouth is wet with food, but several breaths later, hunger has returned. Wait.

9:00 P.M. The guard raps door with something, checking for movement. I am so happy because I get to eat one meat. The moment is short but fulfilling. I now know the next seven hours will be a test, and there is no doubt tomorrow will bring the very same test. Mind must become other than hunger. Hunger must now be something different, apart from the growling and biting of a stomach gone rogue. Starvation becomes an intimate thing, a lover wrapping her arms around you. The bones of a person begin to speak. Hunger and I return. Wait.

Midnight The guard raps door with something, checking for movement. Only four and a half hours left. During this well-lit time, hunger is a race. I might have a taste of toothpaste, the mint a reminder as saliva fills the mouth, then wait for sleep.

This, of course, is only one way the brown bag can be consumed over 86,400 clicking seconds.

The reason I was on "dietary restriction" for five days was bad luck, really. Red had pissed off the DW, so they put that loser Red on brown-bag dietary restriction. I was put on because the DW said, "That clown could stand to lose some weight too." He didn't appreciate my dog routine. So it was that my new buddy Red put me through hell. He's still over there right now, figuring out some new shit to throw at them. I'm not really mad at Red. I simply hate him. If this gets over, I won't look for him on the yard. I will just be so happy to feel the breeze on my face, breathe fresh air, stand in line for chow, and be back home in "general population."

A Scout Is Brave

Right now I am scared, and why wouldn't I be? I am alone in this box under a blinding light, exposed, separated from everyone else in the world. I must certainly be insane. I know what it is to be a ghost, a person judged to be something less. I am just a number. But I am also a Boy Scout. One of the mottos is "A Scout is brave." So when I can remember, I am brave.

In this box, I am allowed up to three books, hygiene items, linen, legal papers, and little else. One of the books I have here with me is *The Official Boy Scout Handbook*, the 1979 version. My girlfriend, Michelle, sent it in the mail. It is the one I grew up with, not the very one, but the same cover and everything. On the cover is a pastoral Norman Rockwell painting of a Boy Scout troop by a lake. A fire is burning as a young man samples the soup. All other eyes are focused across the water. A new troop has come to share the space. The two primary people in the picture are the scout master and an eager young Scout pointing to the new arrivals. It is a picturesque scene that I would stare at for hours, imagining the heat of the sun on my face.

Then one morning, I was looking at the cover picture and the eager young Scout started to talk with me. He told me it was all right. I didn't want to blink. I knew it wasn't happening, but I couldn't deny myself the company of another Scout. So it was that Baden came into my life. Now he is a constant fixture in this cell. Constant because I said it was true. Actually, I wrote it on the wall right here: Baden is the better part of myself.

Coming Apart

Every inch of space on the beige walls has been written on with my tiny golf pencil, one of the few items available on the commissary list in the hole. The guards won't sharpen them, so I have a supply of 2-inch-long sticks that are variously used as a calculator, Lincoln Logs, even hygiene devices. I have written down all the song lyrics I know. You can see that I'm a huge Butthole Surfers fan. I must have listened to "Rembrandt Pussyhorse" and "Psychic . . . Powerless . . . Another Man's Sac" a thousand times right here in my head. My favorite Surfers song is definitely "John E. Smoke." As the great and glorious Gibby Haynes proclaims, "and they said no, you are the flame itself and you shall burn pure in the South American sky where the blood dogs worship the stairway." Amen.

"And I love to travel, so I've mentioned traveling to him. And finances are no problem. But he says that he did all the traveling that he wanted to do while he was in the service." That isn't me, it's Butthole Surfers again, in "22 Going on 23" from *Locust Abortion Technician*. It's a strong idea, knowing you've been everywhere you will be, satisfied with what has been. Sadly, I am never still. Patience has become ingrained, tattooed on the inside of my gums. I want freedom and someone who will listen to me when I talk. As it is, I'm the only one listening.

You can see that my musical tastes are varied. Here's Jimi singing, "After all jacks are in their boxes, and the clowns have all gone to bed." Here is my rap section and this great line: "Just who had the power? The whites? The blacks? Or just the gun tower!" Thanks Ice-T. But Mr. Steve Albini said it nicely, as you can see by the underline: "I'm tough as dirt, I'm mean as blood. Where, where I blow out comes spiders, where I step a weed dies. No smokes with diapers for Pete, King of All Detectives. Fall down on your knees, fall down and worship King Dick."

The reason the writing gets smaller in spots is due to some nervous disorder associated with my insanity. I seem to think better in small print. Large print like over here, "Groovy," a great line from *Evil Dead*, indicates wide-open emotion and flushing understanding suited to the one-word line. Freedom is seriously in double jeopardy, hosted by Alex Trebek. Note how the smaller, tighter words give exactitude of meaning. Clarity is always found in small places. Cells and boxes serve nicely as those small places where clarity is found.

This cell is a depository of whom I am, tirelessly written, recorded, counted, examined, and constantly edited. Reality can be washed off the walls, taking a part of who I am with it. Is there some heartbeat thing for being erased? Like a person can only be washed off a wall 10 times in life, or would it be nine lives like a cat? Either way, it is a limited number, a number you do not want to surpass.

Being remembered is very important. Under the towel I use as a pillow are the most valuable items in my possession: my letters from Michelle. Look at how worn they have become. My reading them has lessened them as well. I hope I don't read them away. But they say my name, Brian or Honey Bear, not 08547–023. In a real way, these artifacts keep me from being a ghost, a man who has been forgotten by everyone save possibly the victims, people who righteously owe him hate. Instead, I have Michelle and her lifeline that passes over miles and through these concrete walls to rest here and be read, over and over again.

I have kissed the fading lipstick marks and think fondly of her always. But we know that isn't true. Because thinking of one person always truly would be insane, and I pride myself on not being that insane. Certainly I am holding more marbles than that peckerwood Red sitting over there. I'm laughing because he doesn't know he's wasting heartbeats right now, on the other side of the wall, that bastard Red.

My Boy Scout Oath

I try to keep the Boy Scout oath "To keep myself physically strong, mentally awake, and morally straight." I realize this sounds like an impossibility, especially given the insanity thing I have going on in this cell. However, I am always doing push-ups and sit-ups. I run in place for hours, shadow box, do taekwondo, anything I can to pass the time. I realize that these activities are detrimental to my heartbeat count, but I qualify the fact that some heartbeats work to erase what I call dead heartbeats.

They're dead heartbeats because they were not used in hard work. I will die if I am not engaged in hard work. I work to battle insanity, keep myself fit, and work on my morality. In short, all hard work is an effort to make me a better Scout. I want to be a better Scout because I see how successful Baden has become.

The clearing in Rockwell's painting shows the happiness enjoyed by the troop. Baden told me everyone is happy. I believe him because a Scout is trustworthy, and I want to be trustworthy. I am a pillar of honesty and integrity. If you put $10,000 on the floor right here, I guarantee I wouldn't steal it. However, if you put a Big Mac down, I would take it.

Right now I am doing a deck of cards. The shuffled deck is placed facedown on the concrete. Its placement has never changed, positioned so as to leave me room to do push-ups. I turn over the first card. It is a seven of hearts, so I do seven push-ups. Next card is the ace of spades; all aces are 15. All face cards are 10 push-ups. That makes 396 push-ups a deck. Today I will most likely do 100 decks, which are 39,600 push-ups. In truth, I am totally "yoked," in the best shape of my life probably. It truly sucks to pass good heartbeats in this box. I'm looking to sell if you are looking to buy a few extra heartbeats.

I have two decks of cards, a luxury in the hole, so I have knocked out the two decks of cards. That is, I flip a card and it is the eight of diamonds. Now I will do eight decks of cards. Following the two-decks-of-cards rule, that is 3,168 push-ups. In total, it comes out to 156,816, which I did in just over 172,800 standard heartbeats (SHBs). I find this fascinating, given the relative closeness in the number of SHBs over two days and the number of push-ups I do blasting out the two decks of cards. I gotta say, my guns are busting out of my skin right now, not to mention the pectoral muscles, which have become like iron.

So that is a bit of my fitness thing. My addiction to counting and using the numbers keeps me mentally sharp. I am brought to peace by the smooth logic of figuring numbers. Finding the patterns like concrete blocks stacked forever around you is order. Chaos is unbelievable in this cell. This box is routine, like my inmate number on the brown bag, a cycle that continues, a merry-go-round with this box at its exact center. I watch what I can of that which spins by, but almost everything is a colorless blur of grays and white and beige. If I look too long, I get dizzy; that is why my eyes are so tightly shut, praying for darkness.

The Wizard of Id

One cartoon I love to read in the newspaper is the Wizard of Id. It isn't exactly funny, but I just love the hanging prisoner living his days in the gaol (another word for jail). Obviously, his crime was heinous—I imagine him a bread thief—so he hangs from his wrists. Horrible stuff, right? It is, but what is interesting is that the prisoner is a character, a viable human being, albeit he is a cartoon. He is given a voice, seen openly by another human being, not through a narrow slit in the door. No, the hanging prisoner is a person in a bad situation. I am a blur seen during count, kept in a box that ensures I have no voice. The hanging prisoner is pitied. I am invisible, a ghost save for Michelle.

Tonight, like every night, I read. Mostly I read the Bible, the *Boy Scout Handbook*, and an Army survival guide. It helps me to remember what it is to be human, what it is to care. I have carefully read, and learned, what a good person does. You are the first good person I've met in a long time, please don't forget me. A Scout is brave, please don't leave . . .

| 5 |

Long-Term Solitary Segregation in the United States and Canada

Gregory J. McMaster

This is my personal observation on isolation and deprivation in long-term solitary segregation. Your tour guide is 56 years old and 35 years into two concurrent life sentences. I have spent half my life in prison. My uninterrupted incarceration began in the late 1970s. At times it feels like I was sentenced to death but the government conveniently forgot to execute me.

My history includes segregation punishment units in different states, provinces, and countries. I have served more than seven years in segregation cells, mostly during my younger days. I used to tell people that ZZ Top was my favorite rock band and it had a song that said it all: "I'm Bad, I'm Nationwide." Now that I am older and wiser, I sing a different tune and leave the chest pounding to the youngsters.

I have been there, seen it, and done it. Over my episodic journeys and battles, I have accumulated significant excess baggage and a footlocker full of regrets. Some scars never heal. I wouldn't wish the road I traveled down on anyone. My soul carries an everlasting burden. I am opening up some old wounds hoping to share some useful information. This is my feeble attempt to educate the keepers and the kept, the lawmakers and the voters. I especially write for all the students out there who may stumble across this story in who knows how many years to come. Solitary confinement is eternal; it never goes away.

Take a journey with me, a walk on the dark side. Traverse the dungeons that blacken men's hearts and wreak havoc on their souls. Solitary segregation cellblocks have different names depending on the state or province, country, or specific joint (prison). They may be called control units, segregation, special housing units, special handling, disassociation, "the digger," or "the back end." Call it what you will, fancy correctional titles or back-home regional slang, the bottom line is that you are going to "the hole."

Going to the Hole

Imagine you are a convict doing time in a maximum-security penitentiary. It makes no difference what institutional infraction you allegedly violated. It does not matter if you are innocent or everything is a simple misunderstanding. A floor officer has made the call, and the "Goon Squad" cometh. You are handcuffed behind your back, and a gorilla firmly clamps on to each arm. Investigative questions are not asked, explanations are not given, and your convict associates stare bewildered as you are crudely shuffled off to the hole. Incarcerated life as you know it just changed dramatically. This is your first peek at the belly of the beast.

As you walk through the door of the segregation punishment unit, your senses are assaulted. There is an odor that you recognize at once. It is the stench of human misery and despair. You instinctively know that shattered minds and unwashed bodies dwell here. A chill runs down your spine. Your eyes detect no movement. This is a wasteland, bleak and empty. No bodies hustling about and no card games in progress. No tables on the main "flag" or "range" (the Canadian and U.S. words for the cellblock floor, respectively). The wide-open space is cold and unnerving. Your ears have not popped, nor have you lost your hearing. It takes a few seconds to comprehend that every single sound is different. There are no televisions blaring or radios competing for your attention. Gone are the loud, boisterous conversations. Taunting challenges and slamming dominoes cease to exist. The constant loud buzz and din that took you so long to adjust to in the penitentiary has suddenly disappeared. What you hear instead is every footstep of the escorting goon squad members, the pounding of their boots on the cement floor, the rustling of their pants as they strain to drag you down the hall, the breath on their lips as they breathe in your face, and the beating of your own heart. You have entered the netherworld, a dungeon within a prison.

The Shakedown Cell

You are taken to a shakedown cell and strip searched. The goon squad and segregation guards surround you at close proximity. "Show me your hands, arms over your head," a guard barks. "Run your fingers through your hair, then pull your ears forward. Open your mouth and move your tongue. Let's have a look under those lips. Lift your sac." Then he orders, "Turn around, show me the bottom of your feet and wiggle your toes. Bend over and spread 'em." All of this is done while the guards joke about how fat you are, what a small cock you have, and how pink your asshole is. Dehumanization and degradation are the name of the game. Your blood boils. You want to lash out, but you are completely naked and it is eight against one. You stockpile this rage with all the rest and silently swear, "Someday, pig, someday . . ."

Personal clothes are bagged and tagged, and you put on the segregation-issued clothing. Your skin crawls at the indignity of wearing communal underwear and socks. You remember the stories about lice, crabs, and scabies. The jumpsuit is torn, tattered, and two sizes too large. Nobody looks good in head-to-foot fire engine red. You fight the gag reflex as you slip on the worn-out cheap plastic deck shoes. The insides are blackened with black crud and blue-green fungus. Your toes begin to itch immediately. The guards write down some brief medical information on a form. They are required to make notes about a convict's cuts, bruises, and broken bones, but don't expect them to look real close or care about what they might see. In some joints, you might get one paper-thin sheet and a small, lumpy pillow; in others, a worn-out military-style wool blanket or plastic mattress, if you are lucky. In many segregation cellblocks, the convicts get nothing to comfort them on the cold cement floor or sleeping platform. You are given a sheet of segregation rules and regulations and told, "Keep your mouth shut and your nose clean, and you might make it out of here."

Walking to Your Cell

Handcuffed and leg-ironed, you are led out of the shakedown cell and shuffled down the main flag. Suddenly, you are the center of attention. Convict faces are crammed against the cell bars, checking out the newcomer. Rows and rows of cells stretch down a long corridor. There are too many to count. The enormity of the punishment unit hits you. The cellblock is four tiers high, each 32 cells long. The prison has bigger blocks, but you never imagined all of these men were in the hole. You are reminded of a scientific research laboratory with animals in cages stacked to the ceiling. The similarity ends when you realize mankind is the subject of this experiment.

You walk past the rubber room, with its toilet hole in the floor and padded steel door, which the guards have left opened to air it out. Next are the two elongated open-faced observation cells. High-powered external security lights illuminate them 24 hours a day. The two cells are completely barren except for what remotely resemble human beings curled up in the fetal position, legs and arms drawn tight to the body, trying to stay warm as they lie on cement block beds. The men are totally naked except for the disposable fireproof paper gowns that drape their bodies. These are the infamous "baby doll" outfits that inmates are issued to prevent suicide. These paper gowns are used to humiliate and punish the prisoners. They offer no protection from the cold. An ominous reinforced solid steel door is next. This is "the quiet box." You hear a soft whimpering emanating from within.

Too much is happening too fast; your brain cannot process this nightmare. With your mouth hanging open and eyes unable to blink, you stumble along. You tell yourself that none of this is real, that it cannot be true. These are the scenes of horror stories and demented fiction. A screaming prisoner snaps you back to reality: "What the fuck are you staring at, Punk!" There is a steel-meshed cage attached to the last six cells on the main flag. The cage forms a narrow walkway in front of the cells. The bars of the individual cells are covered with the same steel wire mesh. The overhanging walkway of the second tier above your head creates dark shadows inside. Peering through the offset steel mesh on the cell bars into the dimly lit cage, you can barely make out the human figures within. This is the assaultive cage, containing individual cells reserved for men accused of assaulting staff or other inmates. You didn't realize you'd been staring and mumble some feeble apology. The guards chuckle and prod you along.

Finally, you reach the stairs. You can handle this. You understand stairs. Then you notice that the handcuffs restrict you from grabbing on to the wrought iron railings, and the leg irons are dragging and clanging on each metal step. You're just relieved to be slowly climbing three stories of metal stairs and away from the macabre insanity of the main flag. All too soon you are rounding the corner on the third tier, passing through the grilled doorway, and walking past cells again.

This tier is caged in with the same wire mesh as downstairs. Each cell contains one man with a set of eyes that burn right through you. Half naked and surly, these are the monsters of the midway, complete with tattoos, muscles, scars, and assorted personality disorders. Black, white, and brown, they all look dangerous. These are the living legends that all prisoners hear about in the penitentiary, but only a few get to meet. You are marched forward to the middle of the tier. The guards halt at cell 316 and order you inside. They slam the cell shut and remove your handcuffs and leg irons through the cell bars. Quickly, you inventory your new 9-by-6-foot surroundings. The cell has a steel toilet and sink, a metal bunk hanging from the wall, and a woefully thin, piss-stained mattress. Somewhere in the recesses of your confused mind, it registers that your body is actually wider than the bed. The pitiful bedding you carried up with you from the shakedown cell completes the picture. This is your new "home sweet home."

When the guards' departing footsteps are no longer heard, you are bombarded with questions by numerous prisoners in adjoining cells: "Who are you?" "What are you back here for?" "Who are you with?" "Know anybody here?" "Did you bring any dope?" "Did Crazy Bob make parole?" You ask yourself, who the hell is Crazy Bob, and what am I doing here? That covers the first-timer's 30-minute introductory experience, leaving you dazed and confused. Now it's time take a look at the utter depravity of long-term segregation and the inevitable problem of sensory deprivation. Put on your helmet—this ride is about to get bumpy.

Life and Death in the Hole

Banishment to isolation is like falling off the end of the earth. I became an inanimate object to be treated like garbage rotting at the dump. I received no medical care. My mail was usually withheld, sometimes destroyed or thrown away, never to be seen again. Meals become bean cake and cheese slice sandwiches. It's as if the Constitution, the Geneva Conventions, and human decency all ceased to exist simultaneously. When I was doing time in solitary confinement, it didn't matter what country I was in. I found doing segregation time in the United States about the same as in Canada.

Time

Wanting to know and even needing to know what time it is has been ingrained in the human psyche for thousands of years. That's why watches are contraband and there are no wall clocks in segregation punishment units. It is one of the most obvious tools of deliberate sensory deprivation. The resourceful mind of a disciplined prisoner soon learns to roughly tell time by the meals he is served, daily body counts, the distant prison industry work whistle, and lights-out at night. On the other hand, knowing what day it is can be a bit more difficult. Men in solitary confinement are constantly asking each other, "What day is it today?" Once an answer is given, a second question is routinely asked: "Are you sure?"

Time in solitary seems to drags on forever. From wake-up call in the morning to lights-out at night, you'd swear a week went by. Every week passes as slowly as a month, and each month seems as if it were a year. Time stands still. With the massive sensory deprivation and an almost total lack of external stimuli, time takes on a realm of nothingness. Every day is excruciatingly repetitive, as if the same thing always has been, always will be. Yesterday was the same as today, and we have already done tomorrow. Segregation means an endless parade of Xeroxed days and carbon copy nights. Seasons flicker by the window. But, of course, that's only if you are fortunate enough at some point to be chained up and actually escorted somewhere past a window so that you can even notice the seasons.

Another month come and gone means another page turned on my mental calendar. I learned to estimate the day and date from receiving letters. During my years in segregation confinement, any time I was moved to a new cell, the first thing I did was clean the space from top to bottom to the best of my limited ability. The second thing I did was to crudely draw or scratch a calendar on the wall. In segregation cellblocks, convicts are not allowed paper calendars, as they are considered contraband.

Contrary to popular belief, convicts don't mark X's on their calendars to count down how much time they have left. We mark calendars so we don't get lost—lost in our minds, lost in time. We are the original time travelers. Without our little X's on the calendar, Tuesday becomes Thursday and early June is actually late July. Already lost to the world, we can't allow ourselves to get lost in time too.

Reading

In segregation, you are not allowed access to the prison library. Forget what you saw in the movies where the old grizzled convict, like Brooks in *The Shawshank Redemption*, pushes the wooden library cart past your segregation cell, handing out books and taking requests for popular magazines. That's pure Hollywood bullshit and not on the sensory deprivation agenda. The prison system can't break a man down if it's letting his mind escape through literature. The only books available to me in segregation were the Bible and the ever-popular Chaplain Ray's prison ministries testimonial books. There were no newspapers, magazines, and novels, just religion to read.

Family Visits

Prisoners in segregation look forward to visits, as it may give them an opportunity to get out of their cells. For most people in prison, it is difficult to maintain meaningful relationships with family and friends. When I spent years in segregation, it became nearly impossible. I was flat out denied visits while in the hole. When I was allowed visits, they were severely limited to a few hours a week, by appointment only, and always with no contact. This means they took place in a booth, partitioned by security glass, over a phone that was bugged. Canceled and missed visits became despondently predictable. Many times, my family would travel great distances to the prison to visit, just to be turned away because I was in the hole.

On a scheduled visiting day, I would anxiously stand at the bars of my segregation cell, groomed to the best of my limited ability, waiting. My heart would gradually sink as the reserved visiting hour passed. I had no way of knowing if my family even showed up. It would be a full week before another appointment could be made. My former excitement and anticipation were now crushing depression. I needed to see my family. Desperate for contact with anyone who said they loved and cared about me, I now just needed to be left alone with my misery and despair.

If you are a person of interest, the mailroom staff reads and photocopies all your letters, both incoming and outgoing. The major difference when you are in the hole is that the segregation guards receive perverse pleasure from reading your mail too, possibly to see if their demented actions are having the desired effect. Phone calls are strictly monitored by the guards, if allowed at all. They listen in and record them. The calls are very short in duration, unless you are dumb enough to say something the guards think they can use against you.

All private or confidential contact with the outside world is severed. Your communications become superficial and suppressed as a result of the prison system's pandemic paranoia. This has dire consequences for all of your personal relationships, particularly affecting spouses and children. Having never been in your shoes, they cannot grasp the concept of being smothered through perpetual audio, visual, and psychologically intrusive surveillance techniques.

Unfortunately, if you are fortunate enough to have dedicated family members, they start serving their own kind of time. The closer the bond, the harder their time. I wish it weren't so, but my observations conclude that the average family can sustain only 12 to 18 months of long-term segregation before permanent damage is done. Bridges are burned, and dramatic changes take place in the psyche and personality of the prisoner subjected to many months or years in segregation. Unquestionably, segregation causes psychological damage, and the longer the stay in segregation, the greater the harm. The convict becomes more alienated from his family. Eventually, his family may abandon him.

During my segregation years, my older sister let me know she wasn't pleased with our sporadic phone conversations and letter exchanges. When discussing our disintegrated family, she flatly stated that I only remembered the bad times. It took me a few years of being out of segregation to realize just how accurate her assessment was. The sterile environment of a segregation punishment unit offers no sights, sounds, or smells that would remind anyone of any pleasurable experiences. Segregation units simply aren't designed that way. There is nothing that would encourage favorable recollections. All around me was pain and suffering, which triggered my memories of pain and suffering. Concrete and steel and constant oppression are not catalysts for generating positive memories.

Survival

Purely as a survival technique, I couldn't afford to dwell on the missed visits or lack of privacy with mail or phone calls for too long. I had to focus on staying alive. A minimum of 23 hours per day is spent locked in your cell. My one-hour exercise period consisted of walking the length of the caged-in tier. It is crowded with men stretching their legs and working out the kinks. Pointless arguments are settled, and the "cock of the walk" is king. There is a pecking order, even when there is nothing left to peck.

One cell on the tier, which was converted into a communal shower room, bustles with activity, men wrapped in towels moving in and out, as everyone has to scheme. An inmate orderly is usually assigned to clean the showers. The cleaner gets an extra two hours a day out of his cell to do the necessary cleaning, so the least he can do is do a decent job for health reasons. Apparently, as he does not live on my tier and use my shower, he does not care. I decide to make him care, making a note to bring to his attention that, as usual, the shower is filthy again. Mold and fungus add an interesting color.

Outside Recreation

Outside exercise is offered only twice a week. I take the available hour outside or forfeit the day. The guards play a dirty little trick and go from cell to cell at 7:30 A.M., waking everyone up and telling the prisoners to be dressed and ready to go outside at 8 A.M. The choice is to get dressed and go outside or wait for food. The guards know the convicts are always hungry. They know most of the men are going to roll back over in their beds and wait for the breakfast trays to be passed into the cells. Especially on a cold winter day, this is preferable to being handcuffed and shuffled outside to stand in the freezing cold for an hour. From the guards' perspective, they fulfilled their statutory obligation of offering outside exercise.

I always took the opportunity to go outside, no matter how hungry I was, how bad the weather was, or how early in the morning it was. This was my only opportunity for fresh air. I would circle inside the large cage, using the extra room for much-needed stretching. Modern correctional systems have brought back the dog kennels, dividing the exercise cages into individual runs. I know dog kennels all too well. The early morning sun has barely risen above the penitentiary walls, and there is no direct sunlight. The surrounding buildings cast shadows over the exercise cage, buttressed up against the wall of the segregation unit. The lack of vitamin D, which would normally come from direct sunlight, becomes evident in everyone you see in prison. All the convicts have a light or pale complexion. I have been known to climb the cage and suspend myself from the ceiling, craving the warm sensation, trying to catch the life-giving properties on my face. It may have been for only a few minutes, but desperate men truly know no shame.

Staying Busy

You read, write, and exercise, and masturbation becomes a favorite pastime. There is not much else to do locked in an empty cell all day. You ask yourself if you are turning into a pervert, and you hate for that too. The steel toilet becomes a Stairmaster for leg exercises and Roman chair for sit-ups. I honed my writing skills and wrote extensive poetry about, you guessed it, hate. My first pro se prisoners' rights civil lawsuits were drafted in the hole. Creativity surfaces in surprising forms. With only a pencil, artists turn cell walls into elaborate murals. Craftsmen resort to soap carvings with contraband paper clips. Spiders are kept for pets, traded, and fought. Once I had a dead bug collection, with 22 different kinds hanging from my cell bars with dental floss. This was my executioner's row for insects. I must have been really fucked up that month.

The segregation punishment unit houses many illiterates, and I often wondered how they maintained. Unable to read or write, their miniature world was half the size of mine. They became fantastic storytellers and the keepers of our oral history. Yes, some of us were back there that long, and there was the need to pass on our oral history to the younger prisoners. I spent many nights gratefully lost in their renditions.

Segregation Food

Meals can be a test of your character and resolve. Years go by without once tasting whole milk or real butter. The weekly food menu is fixed and never varies. The processed pap is tasteless and sparse, undercooked, and always cold. Mystery meat becomes a test of bravery, while nourishing meals are restricted to memories and fantasies. You know it is food poisoning when all the men on the tier get sick at the same time. If you can get past the smell, you swallow it or slowly starve to death.

Your so-called "brothers" in the kitchen have forgotten all about you. Out of sight, out of mind. Prison food was never anything to write home about, but a trip to the chow hall is like a four-star restaurant compared with this. You close your eyes and eat the slop. It is the only sustenance you are going to get. Once in a while, untouched food trays are thrown from all the cells in protest. You are rewarded with bean cake and cheese sandwiches for a week. The show of unity does little to reduce your hunger pains, but it serves to bolster your pride.

Sensory Deprivation Agenda

My first five months on the fourth tier I spent all by myself, never once seeing another convict, or getting out of the solitary cell. I received no exercise on the tier or outside. I was not allowed to take a shower, receive mail or visits, or make a phone call. The guards strictly enforced the silent treatment in their attempt to break my spirit and shatter my will. It was just as well, as I had nothing to say to them anyway. I was lost in mind, hate, and time.

Most isolation cells don't have mirrors or any type of reflective surfaces. It's all part of the sensory deprivation agenda. Not seeing trees, animals, or automobiles is one thing, but never seeing yourself is a whole different experiment. The man in solitary confinement quickly discovers he can see himself reflected in his toilet water. Just as a child peers into a still pond, a desperate prisoner can look into the toilet bowl and identify with himself again.

The old, 19th- and 20th-century maximum-security penitentiaries were composed of cellblocks of cages. New high-security supermax prisons use boxes constructed of concrete floors and steel walls, usually with bars and security glass as a front door. Different prisons, old or new, use many types of isolation or segregation cells, each one a miniexperiment in inmate torture. These might be cells with padded walls, no lights, or lights on all the time, or strip cells where you live naked, freezing, sleeping on the cold concrete floor, with a hole in the center called a French toilet. Typically, the keepers experiment with various regimens of architecture, bad food, lack of adequate clothing, and excessive heat or cold to punish convicts that refuse to conform to the rules and procedure in segregation cell blocks. I have chosen to discuss two examples: the quiet box and the dark box.

The Quiet Box

I used to suffer from a moderate form of claustrophobia, which I was unaware of prior to going to prison. I learned to manage most caged and confined situations by confronting the rage and anxiety swelling within me. I made it deeply personal by directly challenging my youthful sense of pride and manhood. I refused to let my tormentors know that they were getting to me, that there was a chink in my armor. The quiet box, on the other hand, was a totally different matter. It tore at me something terrible, and I fought like a demon not to be thrown into it. Once the guards realized my internal weakness, they instigated and manipulated situations that on paper justified returning me to the quiet box. The guards laughed at my torment and celebrated my suffering. The warden needed a psychologist's approval to keep anyone in the quiet box for more than a week at a time. The shrinks always showed compassion by ordering my release, usually to the assaultive cage.

It took me a while to figure out the quiet box, and we had to go a few rounds before I finally won. Sitting there one day, I realized it was all in my head; the quiet box was just another cell. Sure, the steel toilet-sink and bed were all heavily reinforced, but it was still just another cell. The only real structural difference was the 4-foot-long indestructible light fixtures that were on 24/7 and the floor-to-ceiling solid steel plates welded on to the cells bars.

My miniature world stopped at those steel plates, whereas before I had always had some line of vision past my physical confinement. Normally, I could see down the tier, out into the cellblock, a line of vision 50 yards to my left or right. There were steel bars and wire mesh cages to contend with, but it was still a line of vision. There was a whole world just on the other side of my cage with activity that I could see. This included watching meals being served, guards arguing amongst themselves, and cons passing items from cell to cell. In the quiet box, that was all gone, and everything stopped at those fucking steel plates. The damn things weren't even painted, just bare, rusted cold steel.

I realized it wasn't the cell or the steel plates. I had lost my peripheral vision. It was that simple, that basic. It didn't help that I only had one blanket, no sheets, pillow, exercise, or shoes, and maybe one shower per week. Sure I was uncomfortable, because the mattress would be removed at 6 A.M. and not returned until 10 P.M., and I was experiencing sleep deprivation from the glaring light. Still, it wasn't any of those things, as I was quite familiar with being uncomfortable and had experienced far worse deprivations.

I tired of the guards' daily games and my own weakness and finally took the quiet box head-on. It was the box or me, and I was damned if I was going to lose. I orchestrated an incident that resulted in my return to the quiet box. I then refused to come out when the first week was up. The psychologists were puzzled and the guards laughed, thinking they had fractured my mind. When the second week was over, I refused to come out again. I also rejected the shrinks' request for an interview and ceased all interaction and communications with the guards. When they suited up in full riot gear and cracked open the solid steel door to take me for my weekly shower, I just ignored them till they became frustrated and slammed the door shut. They filmed everything and probably showed it at the Rookie Corrections Officer Academy, with other tidbits of my sordid history. I would love to have a copy for my home movies.

I had created my own little world within my head inside that metal and concrete box, a place where my tormentors simply didn't exist. In short order, the guards figured out my use of reverse psychology tactics and brashly assumed I couldn't last much longer, so they'd simply wait me out. When I refused to come out at the end of the third week, the prison administration actually got upset with me. It seems I was interfering with their ability to torment other souls by occupying their punishment box.

After four weeks, the warden ordered my removal—by force if necessary—from the quiet box. Although I had a scruffy beard and greasy disheveled hair, and I smelled something awful, you couldn't miss the Cheshire cat grin and arrogant strut as I stepped out into the corridor. I showered and shaved and was then escorted back to a regular segregation cell. Later that day, the prison psychologist stopped by my bars for a chat. He said, "They might not understand, but I certainly do. Well done. Very well done." The psychologist walked away down the tier, glancing over his shoulder and shaking his head with admiration. I was never put in the quiet box again, although I continued to suffer at the hands of my segregation keepers for the next couple of years.

Dark Boxes

Some isolation cells are dark boxes. This type of cell has a small foyer added to the front, which allows the guard to step in, feed you through the cell bars, and then step out, closing the solid door behind. This was a lights-out strategy. The only light is in the foyer, and it is always off unless the guard is present. My longest stretch in one of these isolation cells was two months. It was at a different prison in a different state, a different penal experiment. I had already dealt with the quiet box and slain my personal demons. I lay there in the darkness, tucked away in a concrete cocoon.

At times I found lying there in the dark very cathartic. I had long deep sleeps, unimaginable dreams, and journeys of self-awareness. I used this time to conduct intensive self-evaluations. I restructured my thinking while lying there in the pitch dark, set new goals and guidelines, formulated my morality, and for the first time ever enacted self-imposed restraints.

The Guards

Generally speaking, segregation guards exhibit major attitude problems. Many of them appear to enjoy abusing prisoners and request work assignments in segregation cellblocks. Sometimes they ask to work in segregation after they have had problems with inmates in the general population cellblocks, where they must relate to hundreds of inmates. So they request or accept duty in the hole, where they have more control and the inmates are all locked down in cells or behind doors. Many of these guards appear to find it entertaining to torment inmates. I once asked a particularly nauseous sergeant what was behind his bullshit head games. "The instant you walk through that door, you become an asshole," he said. "You wouldn't be here unless you were an asshole. Everybody back here is an asshole, and they will be treated like assholes until they walk back through that door."

I suggested that he hurry home and strip search his children, as I was sure they missed him. He failed to see the humor and became quite upset. Unbeknownst to me at the time, I had struck a very raw nerve. Approximately one year later, the same sergeant was arrested and given administrative leave from the Department of Corrections for allegedly molesting his own 12-year-old daughter. Several other neighborhood children also came forth with allegations of sexual assault. Without access to a television and newspapers, I was unable to track the sergeant's progress through the criminal courts. As usual, the Department of Corrections clamped a lid on the story as quickly as possible, and guards experienced disciplinary sanctions for discussing the matter with prisoners. But apparently the allegations were false or the charges were dropped, as he returned to work at the prison.

Long-term segregation prisoners see themselves as prisoners of war. No other analogy comes close. Behavior modification is the scheduled agenda. Everything becomes a test to break your spirit and bend your will. The longer you resist, the harder the enemy tries. If you cannot be broken, prison administrators and the hands that do their dirty work take it personally. It is their dungeon, they are in control, and you cannot be seen to have beaten them at anything. Your keepers interpret convict determination and unity as a virulent disease that must not spread. Instead of setting an example for other prisoners to follow, you are made the example. Prisoncrats clearly understand rule number one of ultimate power: use it or lose it.

Behavior Modification: Hate and Insanity

For most prisoners, as the months in solitary confinement pile up, they begin to lose touch with reality. All they know is the hole. Guards become your mortal enemies, and the warden is the dictator of the evil empire. Ironically, you have become totally dependent on the very guards you despise and distrust. Food, clothes, shaving supplies, and mail are all delivered to your bars. Everything you have, everything you do, is facilitated through these bastards. You cannot wipe your ass unless a guard brings you a roll of toilet paper. They get indignant and withhold the toilet paper when you do not say please and thank you. You feel neutered and emasculated for having to ask for such basic human needs. Neither side comprehends the other's ill will, and the tension stays thick.

After a year or two in solitary confinement, your world collapses around you. No sunlight, total lack of stimuli, and the constant oppressive atmosphere lead to spiraling depression. The stress leads to fear, as any time of day or night you can be assaulted by gangs of guards. Meanwhile, your delusions grow as your memory fades. Sensory deprivation is a malignant cancer that slowly eats away at you. I crashed and burned for months at a time. I virtually lived off of hate.

Death becomes your neighbor in the hole. As the months and years pass, the body count mounts from suicide, murder, drug overdoses, and heart failure. Attention-seeking suicidal gestures become common occurrences. Men hang themselves just as the guard walks onto the tier. I have seen lightbulbs eaten and handfuls of Drano swallowed. Spraying blood from cut wrists becomes routine. Self- mutilation turns into an art form. One man wrapped his entire body in toilet paper and torched himself. The nylon jumpsuit melted into his flesh, and the pungent odor of burning flesh lingered for days. Amazingly, he didn't die; he just looks like he did, our very own Freddy Krueger.

During an emergency situation, a rookie guard got locked onto my tier. Within minutes, he started trembling, crying, and ripping his hair out. Like a pack of vultures tearing into carrion, prisoners tormented and cheered him on. Later that night, the rookie died of a brain aneurysm. A blood vessel in his head exploded from the stress. Not a single prisoner knew his name, but most rejoiced in his death. Hate was all encompassing.

Some of that hate is justifiable. If one accepts the reality that physical and psychological abuse takes place in prison, common sense dictates that the segregation punishment unit is the hotbed of this activity. Beatings, being chained to the bars, four-point restraints, forced injections of psychotropic drugs, chemical irritant abuse (mace, tear gas, pepper gas), and being denied needed medical attention are all on the menu.

You hate for what has been done to you. You hate for what you have seen done to others. Totally forgotten is the crime that brought you to prison and the infraction that landed you in the hole. Insanity rules the day. The very people charged with your rehabilitation are themselves committing acts of brutality on a daily basis. Nothing makes sense, and hate becomes your only constant. Hate is pure, focused, and reliable; it will never let you down or leave you alone. Hate stimulates your stagnating thought process with twisted fantasies of retaliation and retribution. As long as you hate, you have something to live for.

Screaming nut cases keep you awake all night. They belong in psychiatric hospitals, but the government ordered the closing of many federal psychiatric institutions, and state governments followed suit by shutting down many more. The end result is that mental health patients are sent to prison for beatings, neglect, and abuse, instead of psychiatric hospitals for therapy and proper medications. Unfit or unable to cope with the daily realities of a prison's general population, the mentally unstable serve their entire sentence in the hole. You learn to appreciate it when sadistic guards apply "physical therapy" to silence crazies. You never want it too quiet, though, for the moans and muffled sobs of "normal" men will drive a stake into your icy heart. Your mind works the night shift, and you sleep sporadically throughout the day.

Riots, Revolts, and Hunger Strikes

Most convicts know that riots, revolts, and hunger strikes are common in segregation units in many prisons. Whether you call him "the mayor" or "the boss of the floods," when a charismatic leader gives the word, most of the segregation unit rocks. Plugged and overflowing toilets create massive amounts of water, which rolls off the upper tiers and thunders to the floor below. Niagara Falls never looked or sounded better. Toilets and sinks are ripped from the walls, and broken water pipes spew like open fire hydrants. Fires are lit and everything is burned, including mattresses, blankets, old letters from Mom, everything. You're losing it all anyway, so you might as well burn it. Burning sailboats made from milk cartons cruise by your cell on the outgoing tide. Stainless steel toilets become battering rams, and you wear yourself out chipping away at your steel and concrete cage. It feels good to be alive again, to unite and make a stand against the Beast.

Eventually, the goon squad shows up in full riot gear, and these guards go from cell to cell dealing out their personal brand of retaliation. Even though you hadn't done anything to them as individuals or destroyed a single thing they personally own, they sure act like you did. You pray they start at the other end of the tier so they are less energetic when it is your turn. There's not much you can do to defend yourself from the assault of a 10-man emergency response team as they storm into your cell with body armor, helmets, shields and clubs. The guards rotate and 10 fresh ones take over. You take your lumps and hunker down for the beating.

For the first week of the riot, the entire tier becomes a floating toilet, and shit and piss are everywhere. Without a sink or toilet, you have no choice, as you can't leave it in your cell. Remnants from the flood and piles of ashes mix with the human excrement. The acrid ammonia tortures your smoke-scorched lungs. The guards serve bag lunches three times a day. Now they spit in your food and in your face. My friend is naked and hog-tied with chains in a padded cell. He had tied his cell door shut, greased the flooded cell floor, had a "shank" (homemade knife), and defended himself as they gathered to enter his cell. First he was gassed into respiratory arrest, and now he is getting the full treatment. War is hell.

A maximum-security penitentiary is a small world where men know each other. Over many years, they develop friendships and do not passively accept their friends being assaulted by convicts or guards. In general, the public never learns about prisoner insurrections, unless buildings burn, prison staff members are taken hostage, or people are killed. I recall another riot that happened in a general population cellblock, in response to a popular prisoner being assaulted by guards in the segregation unit. I listened helplessly while a close friend was severely beaten by guards in the cell directly below mine. My buddy suffered a fractured skull, a broken nose, four broken ribs, and a punctured and collapsed lung. They put the boots to the wrong man this time, as he was a much-loved radical leader. Three hours later, the general population cellblock rioted in response. Numerous guards were sent to area hospitals, some with particularly gruesome (and highly unnatural) internal injuries. The outrage of the prisoners became evident through the depravity of their retaliation against the guards.

I had a front-row seat when the rioters were brought into the segregation punishment unit one by one, all 90 of them. Every man was naked and cuffed behind the back. Hanging from each man's mouth was a brown paper bag with his last name boldly printed on it with a black marking pen. The rioters were forced to walk their already bruised bodies through the gauntlet. Twenty guards, 10 on each side, armed with ax handles and nightsticks, rained down blows on legs, abdomens, and backs. In order to deny abuse, they deliberately avoided facial bruising. If a prisoner dropped his paper bag, he was made to walk the gauntlet a second time. The perceived leaders of the riot were set aside for special beatings in the shakedown cell, with lead-lined Zap gloves that make a distinctive thud.

One man's riot is another man's sudden release from segregation. Other than the 15 special-handling cases, incorrigibles, and psychotics, the segregation population turned over in a matter of hours. Those of us left behind suffered right along with the rioters. No distinction was made between those who did riot and those who did not. Within a couple of days, I acquired yet another assault on staff charge. My segregated existence made sense again; there was a cause and effect I could relate to and personalize. I was being dogged for a reason.

Once every year or so, you skip the destruction and do the hunger strike. On my best effort, I lost 47 pounds in 52 days and thought I was going to die. Unlike Bobby Sands, the Irish Republican Army political prisoner, martyr, and legend who died during a hunger strike in Her Majesty's Prison Maze in Northern Ireland in 1981, I did not have what it takes. I lost weight but not my life. Sands died at age 27 after a 66-day hunger strike for better prison conditions. In total, 10 IRA prisoners died during the same hunger strike. Still, my co–hunger striker and chief of the Native American convicts organized 400 free citizens to march on our behalf. We did the perfunctory media interviews and actually won a few concessions. Oddly enough, I had a toilet for this excursion but had no use for it: nothing in, nothing out.

Reflecting on Maturity and Change

Christmas in the hole is a trip down misery lane. The prison's general population has tournaments, movies, religious services, and illicit parties with contraband food, alcohol, and drugs to offer as necessary distractions. Segregation offers the darkest blues and deepest depressions, with haunting memories from Christmas past. I recall family, friends, and children's glowing faces, and happiness, love, giving, and sharing. It hurts deeply; tears silently roll down my face. I sit on the cell floor, my back to the cold concrete wall, drowning in guilt and self-pity.

As a young man, I was responsible for the deaths of several other young men. I found myself thinking of their families and their Christmas without them. I realized that I had done much more than commit murder. I had ripped the hearts and souls out of several families: theirs and mine. Apparently, I had to bottom out completely—prison, the hole, Christmas Day—in order to understand the magnitude of my actions. Sometimes it takes sinking to the bottom before you can start climbing to the top.

Setting aside psychological defects, most of us experience the maturation process as the years tick by. Our thoughts and feelings change, sometimes completely. Men who had never slept in the government's dungeons puzzled me. I assumed that segregation was a rite of passage, that you could not be a stand-up convict unless you had howled with the hounds from hell. Now that I am older and wiser, I realize it was my thinking process that was faulty, not the men that had somehow managed to honorably avoid the insanity. There is nothing but despair, systemic abuse, and hatred going on back there. Nobody needs or deserves that in their life. Incarcerated life is hard enough without dragging physical and psychological torture into the mix.

At the time I served those four straight years in the hole, prison psychiatrists had little experience or interest in the effects of long-term segregation. Since the Marion experiment, we have had maximum-security special housing units or segregated housing units (SHUs) springing up all over the United States and Canada, and correctional watchdogs and the courts are finally taking notice. Now, here in Canada, the shrinks ask me how I managed to survive and why my eggs are not scrambled. Unbeknownst to me, I have become an unofficial case study. I saw no point in asking if I passed the audition.

I entered prison at the age of 21 a violent, volatile youth who believed himself to be indestructible and eternal. Such is the folly of young men, particularly those of the criminal mindset. Having grown, matured, and survived the insanity of prison, I now find myself at the high end of middle age. After two knee surgeries and a reconstructed shoulder, and with chronic back problems and arthritic joints, I am all too aware of my mortality. Each day, fresh faces enter the prison system. Many are young men full of energy, hate, and confusion, just as I once was. Somewhere along the way, I crossed over from being a player to becoming a wise old hound dog with energetic and unstable puppies nipping at my heels.

This observation brings us to the most important aspect of time: change. Since the age of 30, I have openly credited prison with having kept me alive long enough that I could evolve into a sane and rational human being. This is quite a contrast from the 21-year-old runaway train that desperately needed incarceration for the safety of society and protection from himself. The journey from chaos to reality was long, arduous, and constantly interrupted by the actualities of prison. Personally, I believe that I was ready to reenter society 20 years ago. Let's face it: If a man hasn't changed his way of thinking after 10 straight years of incarceration, he may never understand the self-evaluation process and work that needs to be done.

There truly are prisoners who have changed—the ones on whom time and life's natural maturation process have had the desired effect. Ironically, one of the biggest obstacles on the road to rehabilitation is the average citizen's concept of time. Although 35 years have passed in my case, many still insist on treating me as if it were 1978 and I am 21 years old. Rehabilitation and the developing of a moral compass and social conscience are never easy. The tasks become increasingly difficult when society seems to demand that an individual not change. It is quite clear that many in society need many of us in prison to remain their evil monsters and arch villains. I am proud to say that untold thousands of prisoners across the country can no longer fill those roles. Although many would have us remain the same, we absolutely refuse. Time moves on, and with time comes change. Hundreds of thousands of us are no longer drug addicts, drunks, uneducated, self-destructive, thieves, users, and abusers. We were given time, and we used that time to cleanse ourselves of the personal demons that led us astray.

One of the hardest realizations for me to come to grips with was that all the time I spent in segregation and solitary confinement had at least one extremely positive effect on me: It provided me with the opportunity to conduct an intense self-evaluation. Why did I think the way I did? What led me to prison? How did I end up in the quiet box again? Why were people afraid of me? Why was I always in physical confrontations? What could I do to change myself and how others interacted with me? In short, how could I make myself a better person?

Please don't misunderstand the point I am trying to make. I am not suggesting or recommending that anyone be subjected to what I went through. I witnessed too many men die needless deaths. Untold numbers of human beings suffered mental collapses. Long-term segregation and isolation are insanely inhumane. In my case, it just so happens that I was deep within the hole when I found myself. I would be remiss if I did not acknowledge such. We'll never know if I could have or would have found myself had I not spent all those years in segregation. Would the maturation process have taken place at about the same age without segregation? I wasn't afforded the opportunity to find out. A well-meaning psychologist fondly refers to me as an "eternal optimist." Working off of that sentiment, I would like to believe that the changes in my life could have happened naturally, without all the pain and violence of long-term segregation.

PART II

The Effects of Solitary Confinement

Turning and turning in the widening gyre
The falcon cannot hear the falconer;
Things fall apart; the centre cannot hold;
Mere anarchy is loosed upon the world,
The blood-dimmed tide is loosed, and everywhere
The ceremony of innocence is drowned;
The best lack all conviction, while the worst
Are full of passionate intensity.

—William Butler Yeats, "The Second Coming"

| 6 |

Theorizing "Marionization" and the Supermax Prison Movement

Kevin I. Minor and Marisa M. Baumgardner

When living or working in prison, people become acutely aware that prospects exist in these environments for danger and extreme disruption. The reality is that a relatively small group of incarcerated individuals either pose serious threats to the physical safety of others or present a high possibility of attempting to escape or inciting major disturbances. Most people, other prisoners included, likely would agree that at times such individuals need to be temporarily segregated from the general population until whatever threats are posed subside. However, these recognitions do not necessarily justify what has become a national movement over the past three decades to devote entire institutions or large units of wider facilities to protracted, ultrasecure, high-tech solitary confinement that is largely wedged off from outside scrutiny.[1] This chapter draws on recent theoretical work in the sociology of punishment to examine forces behind, and effects of, this movement.

In the introduction to this volume, Stephen Richards discusses "Marionization" as "the spreading of design features and operational procedures from USP Marion" to prison redesign and new construction following 1983. He conceptualizes USP Marion as a blueprint for the nationwide proliferation of both ultrasecure control units embedded in more traditional prisons and stand-alone supermax institutions. Other scholars have also documented this trend.[2] As a penological movement, Marionization is rivaled in scope and pace only by analogous movements that preceded it, such as in the earlier penitentiary, reformatory, and correctional institution eras.[3]

Questions of why the supermax movement took place, why it has not been more staunchly opposed, and what its effects have been ought to be of central interest in the bourgeoning theoretical work on punishment and society, chronicled recently by Simon and Sparks (2013). But this has not been so. There are works that discuss the supermax movement peripheral to larger theoretical analyses of mass imprisonment,[4] and there are also exceptions. One exception is Pizarro, Stenius, and Pratt's (2006) examination of shifting, myth-infused ideologies that spurred the supermax movement. These authors emphasized the relevance of imageries of government toughness on crime and bureaucratic efficiency that comported with a broader punitive shift in penology away from welfarism and rehabilitation toward retribution and control.[5] These imageries operated together with what Pizarro et al. called a "commercialization of crime control" (p. 11).[6] Other exceptions include Mears, Mancini, Beaver, and Gertz's (2009) public opinion explanation of supermax prisons and Welch's (2009) application of Foucault's (1975/1979) work on power relations to Guantanamo Bay.

All around, however, there has been a dearth of attention to the supermax prison movement per se drawing on theoretical analyses of the wider punitive turn in U.S. society. Consequently, the supermax has often been theorized rather narrowly as a largely self-evident outgrowth of "get tough on crime" politics and public sentiment or, more narrowly still, as a classification tool within corrections to enforce order and safety in prison systems. While useful, such approaches are no substitute for coming to better terms with the supermax movement and its effects in relation to broader structural and cultural trends. Theoretical literature on punishment and society can be thought of as a tool for making better sense of the supermax movement as a sociological phenomenon in and of itself. So the aim in this chapter is to help bridge this gap in theoretical application in the hope of promoting a deeper and more complete understanding of the social significance of Marionization as a movement.

The Supermax Movement

Antecedents

Supermax confinement did not materialize from scratch. Two of the most direct antecedents, solitary confinement and administrative segregation, have lengthy histories as penal strategies. In fact, the practice of solitary confinement far precedes the rise of prisons (e.g., its use in monasteries), and it was for many decades a mainstay of Pennsylvania penology at Eastern State Penitentiary as a means of encouraging penance and reformation.[7] By contrast, although solitary confinement is integral to contemporary supermax facilities, these facilities have few if any rehabilitative pretenses. The express function is incapacitation and control of dangerous prisoners.

Administrative segregation consists of transferring a prisoner from the institution's general population into segregation based on the desire of prison officials to prevent future misbehavior through incapacitation.[8] Although the line between the two can become blurred, administrative segregation is technically distinct from disciplinary segregation. Whereas the latter is imposed for a definite period of time (e.g., one month) in response to specific rule infractions so as to promote retribution and deterrence objectives, the former is imposed for an indefinite period of time to achieve incapacitation.

The supermax movement constitutes a new take on traditional solitary confinement and administrative segregation and is distinguishable from them in at least three ways: the designation of entire institutions to perform segregation functions; much longer durations of segregationist confinement (i.e., an entire sentence, or a substantial portion of one, versus an indefinite but shorter portion of a sentence); and tighter control and more restrictions (e.g., no human contact rules, showers installed in cells, and ubiquitous automated surveillance of prisoners). In supermax facilities, then, administrative segregation becomes the rule rather than the exception. Supermax confinement can be thought of as the revving up and systematic institutionalization of solitary confinement and administrative segregation—the quintessence of Marionization.

Proliferation

In addition to traditional administrative segregation housing units in various prisons, 30 years ago the United States had one stand-alone supermax prison operating in Marion, Illinois, a federal penitentiary opened in 1963 and retrofitted into a supermax facility two decades later in reaction to violence against staff. United States Penitentiary (USP) Alcatraz, which closed the same year USP Marion opened, is sometimes described as the nation's original supermax institution and was Marion's main predecessor.[9] Pizarro and Narag (2008) estimated that by the end of the 20th century, approximately 60 supermax facilities (stand-alones and embedded units) were operating in the United States. This is remarkable growth, given that supermax facilities are two to three times more expensive to build and operate than lower-security institutions.[10] Similar to the chronology of prison boot camps,[11] the supermax growth pattern is indicative of a certain "keeping up with the Joneses" or "everyone wants one" atmosphere.[12]

Baumgardner (2011) conducted an extensive search of correctional agency websites and American Correctional Association materials in an effort to describe the number and location of supermax facilities in the United States. She found that as of 2011, 37 states had at least one supermax prison or housing unit. Eleven of these states had at least one freestanding supermax facility. Furthermore, 17 states had at least two supermax prisons or units, and six of the 17 had three or more. Texas had the largest number of facilities, followed by North Carolina. Across all 37 jurisdictions, Baumgardner found a total of 87 supermax facilities or housing units. This estimate is conservative because it excludes facilities in jurisdictions such as Missouri (Petosi), Pennsylvania (Greene County), and Indiana (Wabash Valley), which are known to exist but could not be verified applying the study's methodology. Indeed, Mears et al. (2009) reported the presence of supermax institutions in 44 states.

Based on such findings, one would be hard-pressed to argue that the previous history of institutional corrections in the United States has witnessed a construction and retrofitting movement of faster pace or wider spectrum. Of course, the morphing of traditional solitary confinement and administrative segregation practices into the supermax movement is partly explicable by innovations in construction and computer technology that transpired since the penitentiary and reformatory eras. But this explanation sidesteps the fact that Marionization was not inevitable. The supermax movement arose out of conscious policy choices and deliberate planning by state agents, which launched technology into motion.

Nor can the supermax movement's scope and speed be accounted for exclusively as a reaction to institutional violence and the need to corral a growing population of the "worst of the worst" prisoners.[13] This explanation also presupposes inevitability that never existed. Many of the nation's prisons were plagued with rashes of violence during the 1970s and early 1980s, as illustrated by serious riots at penitentiaries in Attica Correctional Facility in New York (43 killed in 1971), the Oklahoma State Penitentiary at McAlester (three killed in 1973), and the Penitentiary of New Mexico at Santa Fe (33 killed in 1980), as well as by scores of less publicized incidents. But despite declines in prison homicide rates since 1980, contemporary prisons, like their pre-supermax-era counterparts, can hardly be characterized as nonviolent places.[14]

Even more fundamentally, there is not a clear consensus among penologists on which prisoners constitute the "worst of the worst"[15] and thus no agreed-upon criteria about precisely who should be placed in supermax environments. Likewise, the goals of supermax confinement are not as clear-cut as incapacitationist logic ostensibly suggests.[16] Threats of such confinement are used to dissuade prisoners at less secure institutions from serious rule infractions (especially assaults on staff), thus helping promote smoother and less scrutinized bureaucratic operations at these institutions. When prisoners disregard such threats, supermax placement decisions can be driven as much by retributive motives as by a desire for incapacitation.

All this underscores the point that the supermax movement was a choice pursued by state agents over alternative decisions. There were clearly other ways to counter high rates of prison violence that, from a policy perspective, made at least as much sense as the supermax option and likely more. At a minimum, these alternatives included slowing the incarceration boom and curtailing prison crowding, taking steps to deal more constructively with racial tensions inside prisons, and devoting budgetary resources to improving unconstitutional conditions of confinement found in many institutions.[17] But in terms of responding to prison violence and disorder, for many jurisdictions these choices represented the path not (or less) taken. Given the existence of sensible, viable, and less costly alternatives, the paucity of organized opposition to the supermax movement is all the more remarkable. It is this state of affairs with which theory must reckon.

Theoretical Conceptualization

Application of theory from the sociology of punishment literature can provide a fuller and deeper understanding of how supermax prisons have blended in to become a stable and more or less unquestioned aspect of the penological and cultural landscape in the United States. At first glance, this may appear inconsequential in that persons housed in supermax confinement constitute a small percentage of the prison population (Pizarro et al., 2006). However, an inconsequentialist argument overlooks the substantial cultural symbolism and ideological impacts of such facilities, and these features are exactly what help make supermax institutions important in the larger scheme. As Lynch (2013) stated, "the supermax is the ultimate physical embodiment of the changes inherent to mass incarceration" (p. 250). Without focusing on ideology, there is really no way to get at how Marionization became an accepted, normal, and indeed expected format of social control, almost a mode of default for extreme deviance, at the same time that it costs considerably more money than traditional modes of incarceration and exists in a state of tension with humanistic tenets fundamental to liberal democracy.

Hence, one way of framing the larger theoretical question is to inquire why, following the opening of Eastern State Penitentiary in 1829 and the subsequent abandonment of protracted solitary confinement, the United States opted for a return to systematic use of the practice, with rationales and technologies of total control and containment substituted for reformation. In deliberately simplistic terms, what changed in the approximately 150 years leading up to 1983?

Late Modernity and Its Discontents

A number of theorists have identified shifts in U.S. social structure and culture during the second half of the 20th century that profoundly shaped both the nature of social control and public sentiments regarding the targets thereof.[18] For instance, Garland (2001) contended that social and cultural changes accompanying the transition to the postindustrial late modern era,[19] combined with a socially conservative polity that glorified free market solutions to social problems, resulted in a "culture of control" in both the United States and Great Britain. Owing to the near constant economic uncertainty surrounding deindustrialization and globalization, diminished informal social control in local communities, and public discontent with government, late modern life came to be experienced as volatile and unpredictable. Therefore, the culture of control is characterized by, among other things, angst-driven obsession over risk and security.

Around the mid-1970s, out of the medley just described began to emerge a conception of criminals, especially the more serious and incorrigible ones, as given "facts of life" that have to be managed and contained as part of a zero-sum contest of wills played out against "decent" members of society. Garland (2001) posited that these offenders came to be construed as "dangerous others," individuals presumed to be fundamentally distinct in character from the rest of "us" without need to contemplate the role of environmental context (see also Haney, 2006). This concept is akin to the stereotype of the "bogeyman"[20] or the notion of "symbolic threat."[21] In stark contrast with the welfarist and rehabilitative orientation of the late 1950s and 1960s, then, tolerance for deviation atrophied amid a reversion to "back to basic" social control.

In a conceptualization similar to, but more economic than, the one just described, De Giorgi (2006) analyzed changes in punishment as part of the transition of western economies from industrial to postindustrial form. Relatively stable labor markets of the post-Depression era gave way to markets featuring highly uncertain employment prospects. People faced swelling inequality and growing concentrations of economic disadvantage. Along with the unemployment and underemployment characteristic of the decline of industrialism were various radical social movements of the 1960s and 1970s and a fiscal crisis of government on the heels of the Great Society era. These factors, De Giorgi posited, culminated in a conservative backlash with more rigid conceptions of morality and the kind of diminished tolerance for deviance described by Garland (2001). The focus of government shifted from assisting and placating the underclass to achieving protection from it through overt control and oppression.[22]

Expanding on seminal work by Piven and Cloward (1971), Wacquant (2009, 2010b) described this same transition as one from welfarist to penal state. Starting in the 1960s in the United States, postindustrialism and a concomitant upsetting of the institutionalized racial hierarchy gave rise to a culture of social insecurity. This cultural atmosphere, in turn, shifted the government modality of regulating the poor away from the liberal welfarism of the post–New Deal era toward coercive Clinton-era workfare and mass incarceration, or what Wacquant (2010a) called "hyperincarceration." Wacquant saw the transition to penal statehood as an attempt to help shore up the ideological legitimacy of government, which was threatened through the abandonment of welfarism. He thus concluded that "the root cause of the punitive turn is *not late modernity but neoliberalism*" (Wacquant, 2010b, p. 209; emphasis in original), which he described as a "close articulation" of government deregulation of economic markets, devolution of the welfare to workfare state, penal expansion, and increased cultural emphasis on individual responsibility and scaled-back government (p. 213).

For our purposes, it is instructive to note that the deregulative tendencies of the neoliberal turn stretched beyond the economy to include attenuated judicial regulation of prison administration. Of particular relevance to Marionization, the federal appellate judiciary migrated away from the hands-on activist posture of the prisoners' rights era toward a due deference philosophy characteristic of post-1970s correctional law.[23] The move to scale back concern with prisoners' rights and grant deference to prison official expertise was ushered in with the bellicose rhetoric of the U.S. Supreme Court in *Bell v. Wolfish* (1979) and *Rhodes v. Chapman* (1981) and, earlier and more fundamentally still, by inconspicuous passage of the Prison Litigation Reform Act in 1995–1996.

This act seriously curtailed prisoner access to the courts and placed important restrictions on the remedies courts can impose.[24] But the most germane linkage of the due deference doctrine to supermax penology can be found in requirements by the court that a piecemeal (versus totality) approach be taken to evaluating Eighth Amendment confinement condition claims and that prisoners must demonstrate "deliberate indifference" on the part of prison officials in order to prevail (*Wilson v. Seiter*, 1991). While the court did recognize transfer to supermax housing as departing sufficiently from the "normal" aspects of a sentence to warrant minimalist due process (*Wilkinson v. Austin*, 2005), there are usually few judicial checks and balances over executive decisions about who can be transferred to supermax and what confinement conditions will be. This breakdown of judicial constraint and diminished inhibition and callousness toward the possibility for the supermax to contribute to penal harm[25] go a long way in helping account for the full-speed-ahead nature of Marionization after 1983.

Simon's (2009) analysis sheds added light on why the changes discussed above took the directions they did and culminated in what Wacquant (2010a) described as "revanchist American penology." Simon saw this brand of penology as a component of a larger strategy of governance. The legitimacy of the welfare state eroded in the wake of the 1960s as riots, protests, assassinations, and antigovernment movements undermined citizen confidence in government. In response, political agents sought out new imageries and representations of government to regain and bolster legitimacy. Representations of protection and security resonated with a cultural ethos of fear, vulnerability, and victim-proneness that government agents themselves had helped construct. Simon demonstrated that greater government power and control permeated social institutions besides law (e.g., schools and workplaces), and state agents gradually came to be construed as acting legitimately any time they claimed to be pursuing protection and security for the populace. In this manner, extended government control fed upon itself to beget more of the same, so that state actions that might previously have been defined as civilly suspect were instead defined as acceptable and even necessary to achieve protectionist objectives.

It turns out that these wider trends have a great deal to do with the supermax prison movement. As part of these trends, the wayward but redeemable citizen of penal welfarism became the immutable "other" targeted as an enemy by the penal state. This helps account for the oft-invoked metaphors of war—the war on crime and the war on drugs—to characterize the polity's response to criminals, metaphors that in turn lend ideological legitimacy to extremist penal measures that stubbornly defy civic accountability.[26] Such measures act as symbols to assure a fidgety, insecure public that something is being done about deviance and disorder regardless of the tolls on people or public coffers. So while the supermax movement is a microcosm of wider shifts in social control, it is also a potent cultural symbol in its own right for state-sponsored security.

As a precursor to the supermax movement, prison unrest was in no short supply during the 1960s through the mid-1980s.[27] Well-publicized prison protests and episodes of violence no doubt fueled citizen insecurities and discontent with government. It is not hard to see how prison unrest helped undermine confidence in government. The imagery prompted was one of the government losing control of an institution where, after all, citizens should expect to see control most marked and public safety epitomized. The prisoners' rights movement of the era added insult to injury in the minds of many people, helping galvanize movements on behalf of victims. Here we find important raw material for the construction of zero-sum ideology pitting competing imageries of good against evil.[28]

These factors led to the prison itself being defined as a ripe target for governance through crime. Culprits of prison unrest were sought out to blame and shame for pervasive cultural insecurities, fears, and anger. The symbolism of the dangerous other provided a ready outlet. People demanded that something be done, that those responsible for violence and disorder be contained. Supermaximum confinement symbolized a type of ultimate remedy. It is in one sense irrelevant whether the dangerous other is a predatory serial killer, a ravaging drug dealer or sex fiend, a foreign or home-grown terrorist, or a recalcitrant prisoner deemed in need of supermax classification. The underlying "us" versus "them" differentiation is constant across such categories in legitimating total incapacitation. But in another sense, the more despicable and depraved the symbolic representation of the other, the more potential for robust ideological assurance of governmental control and public protection, and, quite conveniently, the less the need for worry over human rights. Some high-profile offenders and obstinate prisoners were easily construed to fit this very mold, the "worst of the worst" who necessitate and deserve "prison within prison."

The supermax prison sits at the far end on Foucault's (1975/1979) "carceral continuum" of government control, second only to capital punishment. Supermax penology has a strong affinity with the retributive, deterrent, and incapacitative mantras of the penal state. Promising security and governing through crime control foster public expectations for achieving these goals, and the supermax is meant to deliver. In emulating Eastern State Penitentiary, prisons modeled after Marion represent back-to-basics penology at its finest—a logical and necessary extension of the traditional penitentiary, minus any pretense of reformation and attendant humanistic concerns.

It is in a conception of the supermax as increasingly necessary to combat danger and evil, as relieving angst and promoting a cultural sense of safety and security, that we begin to achieve a richer understanding of the movement's social significance. In turn, this better positions us to appreciate the staying power and self-sustaining legacies of the supermax. What remains, then, is to examine just how this representation process transpires and with what potential consequences for cultural sentiments and penal practices.

Voyeuristic Mysticism, Reaffirming Otherness, and Constructing Governing Authority

For the supermax to help palliate the insecurities and fears of late modernity that penal welfarist ideology was ill equipped to allay, the symbolism of complete segregatory control had to capture mass attention and be internalized by people in a way consonant with cultural sentiments about civility. Thus understanding the ascent of the supermax as more than a mere artifact of the punitive turn in penology, and also appreciating its role as an icon for tight-fisted control of dangerous people (i.e., as an ideological medium of governance), requires analysis of what Wacquant (2010b) called the "theatricalization of penality" or "the crystallization of law-and-order pornography" (p. 206). This trend, once it took hold in culture and linked up with the due deference posturing of the judiciary that was already well in place, rendered the supermax movement only loosely leashed to the usual restraints imposed by fiscal realities and concern over legalistic fundamental fairness.

Brown's (2009) work on mystiques surrounding the culture of control is useful in understanding this process. It is safe to say that few citizens ever directly access an operational ultrasecure prison unit, such as by visiting or touring. Rather, most are able and content to remain comfortably removed. Conceptions get developed through highly select and indirect encounters with symbols in popular culture that invite shared intrigue, something Brown calls "voyeuristic sensationalism" (p. 4). People are drawn toward media-filtered representations of these prisons. There may be a sense of awe over symbols depicting the physical structure and internal workings, and even fascination and fast acquiescence when media reporting efforts are curtailed by security considerations that necessitate deference to prison official expertise.

Media representations of supermax penology thus oscillate between first stimulating and then soothing the curiosity accompanying distanced spectatorship. The experience from these encounters is analogous to individual and collective sensations experienced when driving by a serious car accident being attended to by emergency responders. But a major difference in the case of the supermax is that the dangerous other is readily available as an outlet for a poignant mixture of blame, shame, anger, and fear, in contrast to attributions of amorphous fate or circumstances in the case of accidents. The outcome is a collective sense of reassurance. In holding the Ramzi Yousefs, the Ted Kaczynskis, and the Jerry Sanduskys, these places keep "us" safe. While the solidarity-evoking impacts of supermax penology theorized by Durkheim (1893/1964) are not hard to spot here, it is instructive to remember Garland's (1990) point that the deeper impact is the fortification of relations of governing authority.

As these cultural sentiments and images are interpreted and manipulated by media agents and governing officials, particular versions of penal practice are able to trump reservations and simultaneously blur and overshadow alternative visions. More specifically, a penality of exclusion and tightly contained suffering comes to be conceived as natural and deserved, given the choices offenders have made—inevitable prices that have to be paid to exact justice and secure safety. Brown (2009) saw the distancing of citizens from penal practice as crucial in providing absolution from personal responsibility for penal harms and excesses. As Rhodes (2009) pointed out, the designation of supermax prisoners "as a distinct and dangerous class" (p. 203) produces social and moral indifference to their plight.

Over time and repeated exposures, these cultural images and ideologies take on a commonsense flavoring. The need for the supermax grows ever more self-evident, with its embeddedness feeding its embeddedness. Marionization thus assumes objectivist and essentialist qualities widely seen as requiring no special justifications and few civil restraints; critical appraisals are easily dismissed as ramblings of the naïve and bleeding heart. We can think of this process, in short, as cultural hegemonization of the supermax, an integral part of a self-legitimating and self-perpetuating "correctional Leviathan" (Useem & Piehl, 2008). This helps account for the continual expansion of expensive segregatory penology over the last 30 years despite scant evidence of achieving stated goals and solid evidence of deleterious effects on prisoners.[29]

Crucial to the hegemony of the supermax movement is an ideology of a prerogative of correctional expertise, created largely by judicial and correctional administrative elites and propagated by the media. The supermax is represented as a complex, professionally managed, rationalistic institution where complete, but humane, control is achieved through specialized penal architecture, bureaucratized routinization of life and movement, as well as strategic use of the latest automated technologies.[30] Supermax staff members are cast as experts in high-stakes, big-league penology, trained professionals who ought to be granted deference to carry out work only they understand how to perform. This portrayal prompts a certain "backing off" of public scrutiny and a cushioning of any uneasiness people may have about civil injustices and penal harm. In essence, then, the prerogative of expertise helps shield the supermax from scrutiny and provides ideological fuel for highly discretionary handling of the dangerous other therein. Officials are thereby enabled to blend stated incapacitationist objectives with deterrence and retributive motives.[31]

Slippery Slopes and Moving Edges

It is, then, through analysis not only of supermax penology as a product of late modern neoliberal society, but also of its reciprocal effects on culture that we can better appreciate the sociological significance of the Marionization movement. Gaining appreciation of the sociological significance of any phenomenon almost always obligates consideration of cautionary implications, and Marionization is certainly no exception. Drawing on Bourdieu (1977), we might say that theoretical scrutiny of supermax calls forth heterodoxy in thinking through implications.

One way of coming around to these implications is to consider the popularized, commonsense knowledge people use to interpret select aspects of the culture of control they encounter, both directly and symbolically. The framework of knowledge can be seen as having three characteristics. The first of these is that the framework is embedded against and charged by sensibilities like insecurity, fear, and anger. The second is that the knowledge is necessarily fragmented and partial; this is due to the distancing of supermax penology from everyday experience and deference to the prerogative of correctional expertise. These two features function to inhibit and relieve citizens from systematic critical appraisal of complexities and contradictions underlying supermax confinement, such as the tension between the need for prison order and safety on the one hand and the need to preserve humane confinement conditions on the other. Hence, that we would build and operate ultrasecure segregation units for criminals of the most intractable and despicable kind seems to defy question or reason for debate; the need appears self-evident. Simple seems better—and easier and more comforting too.

If one thinks of this affect-laden, partial, hegemonic knowledge as serving as an accelerator toward supermax confinement and analogous control initiatives of the penal state, the third characteristic of the framework can usefully be seen as a brake—or at least a flashing caution light. As such, the third characteristic exists in dialectical tension with the first two (i.e., angst and partiality). To identify this characteristic, it is useful to draw on the work of Smith (2008). Based on historical analyses of the rise and fall of various technologies of punishment, such as the guillotine, Smith analogized crime and deviance to a form of cultural pollution, threatening the cultural purity and sanctity of person and property. Punishment is, above all, about containing pollution, decontaminating that which is culturally offensive. But the main point here is that if punishment gives off more cultural pollution than it controls, offending more moral sensibilities than it upholds, there is a threat that its legitimacy will be questioned by large numbers of people. This point is easily seen by considering contemporary controversies over the handling of military detainees.[32] To sustain legitimacy, then, it is necessary that punishment conform to the parameters of cultural sensibility and thus be construed as fair, humane, and sanitary. As Smith observed, "The range and extent of disciplinary possibilities have been as severely constrained by the sacred status of the sovereign human being as they have been energized by the quest for the docile body" (p. 175).

The supermax prison thus hovers on a dicey tipping point vis-à-vis the cultural hegemony of the penal state. While it helps further and sustain hegemony through varied imageries and representations, given the extremity of its very nature, it simultaneously possesses strong potential to undermine hegemony by serving as a reservoir of exposable and potentially scandalous inhumanity. In short, the supermax impends to offend the very moral sensibility that it purportedly upholds.

The cultural danger in all this is that, concerns with legitimacy notwithstanding, common-sense-bound, self-legitimating, and self-perpetuating control movements are not prone to reach a particular level and go static. Instead, after establishing fixity in culture, they are prone to push on toward greater extremes. And it is in testing and pushing the bounds of sentiments in this manner that the supermax movement can have the effect of gradually moving those bounds, thus creating relatively lasting impressions on the cultural landscape that make ever more extreme forms of punishment seem normal, acceptable, and necessary. This line of reasoning is integral to appreciating how the transmuting of exclusionary policies and practices into systematic genocide gave rise to the National Socialist German state.[33]

What should arouse deep concern is that cultural sentiments become especially vulnerable to this slippery slope, these edge-moving effects of penal practices, when large sectors of the population disengage from civic and democratic participation in favor of apathy and directionlessness. People thereby not only become susceptible to moral crusades emphasizing exclusion and punitiveness, but also default toward acceptance of escalating governmental authoritarianism.[34] This kind of de-democratization creates a fecund climate for the pushing of cultural sentiments to the edge and, by implication, a moving of the edge in the direction of ever greater punitiveness and callousness toward penal harm. Cultural sentiments that should be exerting civilizing and restraining effects on penal policy and practice, epitomized by such concepts as "evolving standards of decency," effectively become neutralized and give ground to decivilizing tendencies (Pratt, 2013).

Considered in these terms, the supermax movement takes on an entirely new importance. It becomes a unit for theoretical analysis in its own right as an agent shaping culture. Marionization is a pungent reminder that the practice of being inattentive and uncritically accepting of what is done in the realm of penal policy and practice, of acquiescing to the prerogative of government expertise and, as Pratt (2013) put it, "looking the other way" and "not asking awkward questions," can do more than control and dominate the incorrigible. It can also shape what we are willing to accept and thereby become as a culture.

Notes

1. For more discussion, see Rhodes, 2009.

2. For a discussion of trends in construction of supermax prisons, see King, 1999; Mears & Reisig, 2006; Sundt, Castellano, & Briggs, 2008.

3. For a discussion of earlier trends in prison construction, see Hirsch, 1992; Irwin, 1980; Rothman, 1971, 1980; Rotman, 1995.

4. E.g., Bosworth, 2010; Lynch, 2013; Simon, 2009, 2013; Useem & Piehl, 2008.

5. See also Cullen & Jonson, 2012.

6. See also Selman & Leighton, 2010.

7. See Shalev, 2009a.

8. See Minor, Wallace, & Parson, 2008; Pizarro, Stenius, & Pratt, 2006.

9. See King, 1999; Ward & Werlich, 2003.

10. See Mears & Bales, 2009; Ross, 2007.

11. See Bergin, 2013.

12. See Massing, 2001.

13. See National Institute of Corrections, 1997.

14. See Byrne & Hummer, 2008; Commission on Safety and Abuse in America's Prisons, 2006; Irwin, 1980, 2005.

15. For detailed discussion, see Ahn-Redding, 2007; Butler, Griffin, & Johnson, 2013.

16. See Lippke, 2004; Mears, 2008.

17. For an excellent discussion of more humane ways to manage prisons, see Haney, 2006.

18. See De Giorgi, 2006; Garland, 2001; Simon, 2009; Tonry, 2011; Wacquant, 2009; Western, 2006.

19. Also see Giddens, 1991.

20. Irwin (1985b) discussed the felon as the "bogeyman."

21. See Mears, Mancini, Beaver, & Gertz, 2009.

22. See Western, 2006; Wilson, 1987.

23. See Feeley & Rubin, 1999; Minor, Wells, & Soderstrom, 2003.

24. See Human Rights Watch, 2009.

25. See Clear, 1994.

26. See Bosworth, 2010; Tonry, 2011.

27. See Irwin, 1980, 2005; Jacobs, 1983.

28. See Gottschalk, 2006.

29. See Briggs, Sundt, & Castellano, 2003; Haney, 2003; Mears & Reisig, 2006; O'Keefe, 2008; Sundt, Castellano, & Briggs, 2008.

30. See Rhodes, 2009.

31. See Lippke, 2004.

32. See Welch, 2009.

33. See Friedlander, 1995.

34. See Barker, 2009; West, 2004.

| 7 |

Female Prisoners and Solitary Confinement

Dennis J. Stevens

The scholarly literature informs us about many female prisoner issues, such as sexual assault and misconduct against them, prison sentencing, medical neglect, discrimination, and contraband initiatives.[1] Organizations such as Amnesty International, the Pennsylvania Prison Society, and the John Howard League pride themselves on emphasizing various female prisoner concerns, and rightfully so. However, a gap in the literature exists about female prisoners and solitary confinement, or what is commonly called segregation (Seg) or "the hole." It is hoped that this chapter will enhance an understanding of the impact of Seg practices on female prisoners and detainees, those who have not been tried but are in custody. The term "female" is used throughout this chapter rather than "women" because many confined females are not yet women, but juveniles, and juvenile prisoners experience harsh Seg initiatives.[2] Female prisoners tend to be viewed as "fallen women" regardless of the crime for which they were convicted.[3]

Solitary Confinement, or Segregation (Seg)

Solitary confinement, or segregation (Seg), is a specific area or group of cells within a local jail or prison where prisoners and detainees are held in isolation from the general confined population (Bosworth, 2005). Specifically, Seg is the placement of a local, state, or federal prisoner or detainee into a space isolated from other prisoners, usually as a form of discipline, protection, or prevention (Hill & Hill, n.d.).[4] Prisoners are "written up" for various disciplinary reasons, such as fighting, wandering into restrictive areas (known as "going out of bounds"), or unruly or disorderly behavior.[5] Sometimes custody officers may be compelled to confine a prisoner in the "hole" because of the number of write-ups, the seriousness of the offense, or the restricted area breached. Other times, Seg can be a sanction related to protecting a prisoner from other prisoners, such as in the case of a celebrity, a cop, or a child killer, or it may be a method of preventing a prisoner from attacking others prisoners, correctional personnel, or correctional volunteers or damaging correctional property. Although prisoners can request Seg for personal reasons, which may or may not be approved, it is often used as tool for protection or prevention without the consent of the prisoner. Most female detention facilities have Seg wings, a "prison within a prison," often an isolated structure away from other prison activities, or a few single cells used for the purpose of isolating prisoners for disciplinary, protection, or prevention solutions.

The Number of Females in Prison and in Seg

Nationally, females make up approximately 5% to 10% of the correctional population. According to the Bureau of Justice Statistics (2010, 2011a, 2011b), of an estimated 2.1 million prisoners incarcerated in state, local, and federal detention facilities, 198,600 prisoners are females ranging in age from 16 to 73. In individual states, the California Department of Corrections and Rehabilitation (2011) reported that of an estimated 158,000 prisoners, 9,000 were female. The New York Department of Correctional Services (2011) stated that of 56,000 prisoners, almost 2,300 were females. The Illinois Department of Corrections (2011) estimated that of 48,000 adult prisoners, 3,000 were female. Additionally, some 60 female prisoners are on death row across the country (Sourcebook of Criminal Justice Statistics, 2009), and an estimated 20,000 females are confined awaiting trial, of which a large number are immigrant detainees.[6]

Solitary Watch reported that more than 240 female prisoners experience Seg annually (Rodriguez, 2011). Yet my experience as a prison adviser, program facilitator, and teacher in several female prisons suggests that the number of female prisoners in Seg is probably 10 times greater than that, with perhaps 2,400 or more females experiencing Seg annually. Many Seg prisoners are "in the hole" more than once in a 12-month period, and others are locked down for years at a time.

Female prisoner statistics may be sketchy because many correctional units do not keep records of the number of prisoners that are in Seg for only short terms, such as a couple of hours or days. Also, they may not count prisoners in protective custody. Moreover, female immigrants detained in temporary and private "jails," including Native Americans in tribal custody facilities, female juveniles at detention centers, and female detainees held for trial, may not be counted accurately in general prison population counts. However, those prisoners can be placed in Seg for disciplinary, protection, or prevention rationales without consequence to custody personnel, opening the door for mistreatment and abuse.

The fact is that the mental and sexual abuse of females in Seg and in general prison populations is probably underreported. Frankly, correctional authorities appear to have few concerns about females in Seg cells, let alone about a few thousand immigrant, Native American, and juvenile prisoners. For example, the National Prison Rape Elimination Commission (2009) noted that rates of sexual abuse appear to be much higher for confined youth than they are for adult prisoners. According to the Bureau of Justice Statistics (2010), the rate of sexual abuse in adult facilities, based only on substantiated allegations captured in facility records, was 2.91 per 1,000 incarcerated prisoners in 2006, whereas the parallel rate in juvenile facilities was more than five times greater, at 16.8 per 1,000. The actual extent of sexual abuse in residential facilities and Seg units remains a mystery.

Effects of Seg on Females in Supermax Prisons

A difference exists between separating prisoners through correctional classification practices, which results in segregating prisoners, and Seg as used throughout this chapter.[7] As a correctional response to what many perceived as unmanageable prisons, prison systems radically turned to lockdown and administrative segregation (Ad Seg), locking down entire prison populations, such as mental health and sex offender units, as a way to manage prisoner behavior and to provide programs, services, and supervision styles.[8] Sections of prisons and new structures were built dedicated to Ad Seg, and thus the supermaximum security prison emerged.[9]

Studies of supermax facilities largely have been about male prisoners, but we can take some guidance from those studies. For instance, Riveland (1999), the former director of the Washington State Department of Corrections, stated in a report for the National Institute of Corrections that "insofar as possible, mentally ill inmates should be excluded from extended control facilities [as] much of the regime common to extended control facilities may be unnecessary, and even counter-productive, for this population" (p. 12). Five years later, Collins (2004) declared that mental health conditions in supermax prisons were a major litigation-related issue. On the one hand, correctional managers are cognizant of their constitutional legal and moral responsibilities toward prisoners when attempting to provide care with custody. Trying to find a balance between human rights and the security requirements of custodial supervision is a difficult endeavor. Yet an alternative and productive method of supervising prisoners has to be found. Most of the evidence that follows emphasizes both deterioration of mental health and sexual assault as the primary outcomes for female prisoners in Seg. Nevertheless, some prisoner accounts of Seg have claimed some advantages.

Advantages of Seg

There can be some advantages of isolation for female prisoners, but they are rarely documented. For example, a female prisoner at the Federal Detention Center at SeaTac, Washington, said that she had heard that short times of 3 to 10 days in Seg would provide locked-down prisoners "time to refocus, to think, to re-evaluate what they were doing. My own experiences in isolation, first for 3 days and later for 30 days, were the beginning of a spiritual quest that I've been on for many years now." She also observed that "many of the guards made a point of talking through the doors to the women in [solitary confinement], using their unique humor, being human, showing compassion" (Casella & Ridgeway, 2011b).

Disadvantages of Seg

Regardless of the length of time a female prisoner spends in Seg, she faces particular hardships because of both her specific needs and her extreme lack of privacy. Prison personnel maintain a presence over prisoners almost every minute of their time while isolated, regardless of the issues that brought a prisoner to Seg, meaning that strangers observe the most intimate functions of female Seg prisoners. I can argue with a great deal of confidence that for most female prisoners, this could develop into an extreme form of oppression and, in some respects, trauma. The distress of female Seg prisoners is made all the more acute because of the number in prison with long histories of abuse at the hands of violent men in particular.[10]

One Seg prisoner described isolation this way: "The doors on the bathrooms lock on the outside instead of in. There is just no way out . . . they go inside a pit, like an empty swimming pool, to exercise, so that you don't know where you are. . . . Part of the plan here is sensory deprivation" (Correctional Forum, 2007). From another perspective, Seg is literally torture.[11] Just imagine being locked in a backed-up public toilet for a few days with strangers who randomly come and go. The mental health of Seg prisoners can easily deteriorate as a result of the oppression and trauma experienced during and after isolation.

Mental Health of Female Seg Prisoners

The mental health problems of female Seg prisoners are complex because their experiences are often linked to histories of abuse, which may manifest in high levels of drug addiction, and they are compounded by the effects of imprisonment.[12] How to help female prisoners with their needs, which may include mental illness, dyslexia, illiteracy, and disabilities, remains a matter of debate among experts and personnel who provide treatment, services, and supervision to female prisoners. For example, a 19-year-old female prisoner hanged herself as correctional personnel watched (CBC News, 2010). Many female prisoners placed in Seg are abruptly taken off antianxiety and other medications. Understandably, these prisoners would have a harder time than others, especially those prisoners who are forced to go "cold turkey" without drugs, legal or otherwise.[13]

More specifically, Quigley (2010) reported on a federal court case in which the following conclusions were presented as medical testimony:

> After 60 days in solitary people's mental state begins to break down. That means a person will start to experience panic, anxiety, confusion, headaches, heart palpitations, sleep problems, withdrawal, anger, depression, despair and over-sensitivity. Over time this can lead to severe psychiatric trauma and harms like psychosis, distortion of reality, hallucinations, mass anxiety and acute confusion. Essentially, the mind disintegrates.

In another case, a woman prisoner in Seg wrote in the blog *Stopmax Voices* (2008):

> I knew I couldn't just sit here and pass time, and I would emerge from this abyss unchanged. I had to do something, something different from my first stay (where I broke)—I had hung myself and was cut down by my "torturers"—revived and sent to an outside hospital for observation (lack of oxygen and throat damage). I'm lucky I didn't break my neck. . . . I couldn't live like this—so deprived of everything because I'm a "needy" person and [this prison] is not a place for the needy. . . . There were a lot of different factors at play that pushed me to decide to kill myself before they killed me. Nevertheless, here I am again, back in prison—chewed up and swallowed by the beast that didn't get its fill of me the last two times and here I am . . . [with] a history that marks an inability to live in open population without disrupting the orderly running of the facility—yeah! (smile) and being a threat to the security of the institution. I have been indigent since August and owe $28.00 to medical. . . . So I can't get anything [medication] to make myself semi-comfortable or (get) the proper food to eat for my Hep. C. I can't get any more batteries, nor can I even buy (wear) sneakers or shorts

> or t-shirts on cool days. . . . I would be floored if I could eat tuna & drink V-8, listen to the radio, have my own writing paper, a stock of hygienes and whatever is close to a "necessity!" I would love to be able to order stuff once a week, like 66 of the women here (only 4 of us are "poor").

The evidence that mental health suffers in solitary confinement has accumulated in both court cases and the academic literature. Reviewing dozens of academic studies published over the last four decades that looked at the mental health of prisoners in nonvoluntary solitary confinement, Haney and Lynch (1997) did not find one study without negative psychiatric outcomes.

This testimony implies that prison regimes can exacerbate mental distress, especially through Seg isolation practices of female prisoners and detainees. Additionally, once in Seg, female prisoners lose their participation momentum in prison programs, such as the social programs that have been established to help incarcerated mothers attend to parenting skills and other family concerns.[14] Unfortunately, they're not permitted to attend any prison programs, including parenting classes or 12-step programs in Narcotics or Alcohol Anonymous, until released from Seg. Most often, they must wait until a similar program starts up to reapply.

Given all of the effects on mental health, perhaps Seg initiatives should be eliminated from the practices of correctional systems. But evidence about sexual assault suggests that the word "perhaps" might be replaced with the word "absolutely."

Sexual Assault

Evidence suggests that female prisoners held in Seg are frequently sexually assaulted by correctional personnel.[15] Both male and female custodial personnel engage aggressively in the sexual assault of female prisoners. Rape in the context of female prisoners in Seg is relevant because of the nature of rape by correctional personnel and ultimately the prison as an institution. Regarding the crime of rape in women's prisons, MacKinnon (1989) explained that if heterosexuality means males over females, gender matters independently. Heterosexuality is a fusion of the two, with gender a social outcome, such that the acted upon is feminized, is the "girl" regardless of sex; the actor correspondingly is masculinized and made strong. This occurs whenever females are victimized, regardless of the gender of the perpetrator. As MacKinnon put it, "Whenever powerlessness and ascribed inferiority are sexually exploited or enjoyed—based on age, race, physical stature or appearance or ability, or socially reviled or stigmatized status—the system is at work" (p. 179).[16]

Rape is more than just a crime of violence and sex. It is a crime of hierarchies. The rapist uses power over the victim, MacKinnon emphasized. Gendered systems of power exist in the correctional system. Rape in prison is a crime asserting power over the powerless. However, the literature does not always support that perspective.[17] Research on rape, which does not seem to have been influenced by feminist politics, shows that lust plays a central role in the motive or trigger of many chronic rapists. Most often, it appears that this is what motivates correctional officers more often than does power. Put another way, although the research of Wilson, Goodwin, and Beck (2002) sounds indecisive, they argue that up to 50 percent of men report some likelihood of raping if they know they can get away with it. The indecisive part is linked to their sample, because in my experience, 100 percent of sexual predators will rape, and as correctional officers they already know they will most likely get away with it.[18]

The thinking goes something like this: If a female prisoner is put like a piece of meat in a cage, handcuffed, made helpless, and given no way to communicate with anybody—and if she did, nobody would believe her—then rape might be the most obvious conclusion. On the other hand, a high percentage of males might care less about sex than expected, and being responsible, respectful, and honorable are qualities that help them decide that rape is not an option for them.[19] Nonetheless, of those correctional personnel, both male and female, who do engage in sexual assault of prisoners, the majority may have been criminal in their intentions to rape prior to obtaining employment in the correctional industry. That is, criminals often seek initiatives and occupations that allow them the opportunity to exploit others at the levels they seek. One conclusion of Wilson, Goodwin, and Beck (2002) is that the self-reported likelihood of raping among criminals, and that would include some correctional officers, relates to an individual's moral reasoning or development and general attitude toward rape. Who applies for those jobs in prisons, anyway?

Because of a lack of regulation and poor hiring, training, and monitoring practices, and because females tend to be devalued in American society, sexual assault of female prisoners, especially those in Seg, occurs often. The victims may be females with no previous sexual experience. This may happen even to young girls or nuns. It is not uncommon to see females as young as 14 imprisoned in adult facilities. The federal prison system incarcerates nuns convicted of crimes associated with social or political protests, such as maintaining information pickets about social causes in front of federal courthouses or trespassing on nuclear missile bases. Letters written by Susan Crane in 2011 (Casella & Ridgeway, 2011b) contained the following description:

> While at the Federal Detention Center (FDC) SeaTac [prison in the state of Washington], S[iste]r. Anne [Montgomery] and I were in cell 11 in one of the women's units. Cells 2–10 are filled with women wearing orange, held

> in solitary (Special Handling Unit as it is officially named). These sisters [nuns] eat all their meals alone in their cells. They get out of their cell for a 15-minute shower three times a week (M, W & F). They are offered no exercise or outside time. They [are] not allowed to communicate with other prisoners, and we were not allowed to motion or talk to them. There is no yelling between cells. They can't participate in group prayer, or any group activity. No one offers them Eucharist. . . .
>
> Some of the women in solitary are pre-trial, some have been sentenced. They are probably here for some sort of write-up for an infraction of a prison rule: some have had a hearing with a BOP [Bureau of Prisons] officer and have been found guilty, and so continue to sit in the solitary cells. The write-ups might be, for example, for fighting, making a three-way call, or the result of mental illness.

Solitary Watch was among the many cosponsors of a public panel discussion on "Isolation Units within U.S. Prisons," organized and hosted by the Center for Constitutional Rights in San Francisco (Id, 2011). One issue was on what the Federal Bureau of Prisons called communication management units (Center for Constitutional Rights, 2011), also known as lockdown for female prisoners or what this chapter calls Seg.

Other than the large number of Muslim female prisoners in CMUs, other examples include Michelle Ortiz, who was serving one year at the Ohio Reformatory for Women (ORW), a state prison in Marysville, when she was molested by a male guard (Id, 2011; Torry, 2010). Ortiz reported the first sexual assault to prison official Paula Jordan, whereupon Jordan informed Ortiz that the male guard was transferred to another prison. However, the male guard turned up in Ortiz's cell, much to her surprise, and raped her again and again. Rebecca Bright, another prison official, launched an investigation and ordered Ortiz placed in Seg. She was handcuffed and helpless. Bright reportedly argued that Ortiz was talking about the incident with other inmates. Eventually, a jury awarded Ortiz $625,000 in damages. An entry in the Ohio Prison Watch blog dated May 1, 2010, discussed an April 26, 2010, Associated Press report that Jordan and Bright appealed the verdict, and the U.S. 6th Circuit Court of Appeals ruled 2 to 1 that the prison officials had qualified immunity, so they did not have to pay damages. The third judge, however, issued an outraged dissent.

Another example is the Black Panther activist Assata Shakur, a New Jersey prisoner who explained in her 2006 autobiography that when she was one month pregnant, she was taken to Roosevelt Hospital and shackled to a bed for 10 days. She was then moved to Middlesex County Jail for Men and kept in solitary confinement for four months. On being extradited to New York, she was imprisoned at Rikers Island, where "the treatment" continued. A day later, she went into labor and gave birth. When Shakur was returned to Rikers Island, she was shackled, beaten, and put into solitary confinement for a month.

Just Detention International (JDI, 2009) reported that sexual abuse of prisoners by guards at the Ohio Reformatory for Women (ORW) was an ongoing crime. Ohio female prisoners described a range of incidents, including violent encounters, threats and pressure to submit to sexual advances, trading of sex for goods and favors, and relationships that were seemingly consensual. JDI concluded that a "climate of abuse" existed at this detention facility. It was implied that a similar climate of abuse existed at most female facilities across the country, as long as administrators see sex between their staff and prisoners as consensual. Yet for females under near total control by prison staff, the concept of "consenting" to sex is virtually meaningless (and Ohio law reflects this thought, consistent with most state laws).

The problems arising from this power imbalance are compounded by the past history of sexual abuse that many female prisoners have endured. In many prisons prisoners who complain of sexual abuse are transferred to Seg, losing their privileges, which include family visitations, purchasing personal products from prison stores, participating in prison programs, and interacting with other prisoners and prison volunteers. This policy is usually explained as being necessary to protect the prisoner while officials investigated the incident, but this doesn't explain why inmates should be stripped of basic privileges and locked in isolation for 23 hours a day.

Consistent with the above accounts, Talvi (2007) described sex between prison personnel and prisoners. In one case, an officer named K. P. Price had sex with a female prisoner. When the prisoner discovered that she was pregnant, an abortion was provided. I read that to mean an abortion was performed without Price's consent. Four years later, Price pled guilty to a misdemeanor concerning the same prisoner, and he was placed on probation. At the same facility, another officer, Michael Sneed, was charged with having sex with a female prisoner in solitary confinement. He also received probation.

Talvi also discussed the case of Bobbi Bolton, a nonviolent offender incarcerated at Federal Correctional Institution, Tallahassee, who had been first sexually harassed and then raped twice by guard Jeffrey Linton in her own cell. When she produced evidence of her attack by saving his semen on her clothing and filed a complaint, she was punished with four months in solitary confinement. Linton was charged with a misdemeanor and ended up with two years' probation.

Lesbian or Transgender Prisoners in Seg

Although solitary confinement refers to the placement of a local, state, or federal prisoner into a space isolated from other prisoners, usually as a form of discipline or protection or to prevent the prisoner from causing trouble, it can be argued that a lesbian or transgender female prisoner is always at risk of being isolated. For instance, reports from Fluvanna Correctional Center for Women in Virginia reveal that females who "appear to be lesbian" have been segregated and put in a "butch wing" (Canzi, 2010). A no-touching policy has been instituted. Female prisoners walk single file everywhere. Access to religious services has been curtailed. Canzi also reported that a number of female prisoners were discriminated against because they looked "butch." When butch-appearing prisoners take showers, they are led, shackled and naked, down the hall, with a dog leash attached to their shackles, by a male guard.

Across the United States, correctional personnel refer to transgender prisoners as "it" and worse. Transgender and lesbian prisoners are placed in solitary confinement for long periods because of their status rather than their behavior, purportedly "for their own protection." Abusive and discriminatory treatment against transgenders and transvestites is not unique to American corrections, but appears to be a global phenomenon (Hanif, 2008). Hanif explains the findings through culture. That is, prison culture, rather than being divorced from larger society, is in effect able to articulate and elaborate on the processes of social exclusion faced by transgenders.

Yet in my experience, each American prison is unique unto itself, even when facilities operate under the same authority. For instance, although Attica and Elmira Correctional Facilities are both operated by the New York Department of Correctional Services and house similar security-level prisoners, the cultural differences among prisoners and staff are more than striking (Stevens, 2000). A prison's culture is developed by its specific managerial regime, physical structure, and unique history, among other variables, which also include the staff and prisoners. Prisoners and correctional personnel transferring from one similar security-level prison to another typically remark that they have "to learn the ropes" or perish. However, most often, little is heard from female Seg prisoners.

Following is an excerpt from a story in *Wicked Women: A Journey of Super Predators* (Stevens, 2011) about a pretty, petite, 24-year-old transgender prisoner called Margo Clinton (not her real name). Because she had been born a male, the state sent her to a male prison instead of a female prison. After her conviction and incarceration, rumors had spread about her gender, and she was kept in "protective custody," but really in Seg.

> Once released, Margo brought suit against the state prison system, alleging that she had been handcuffed to her bunk and repeatedly raped and sodomized by three correctional officers for two days. Her suit stated that rumors spread about her [before the attack], based on her civil suit linked to obtain her transgender drugs, and she became fair game for anybody wanting to victimize her. When the guards learned that Margo had been born a male, they "wanted to see for" themselves. Upon discovering she had a vagina, they raped her, and two of the officers anally assaulted her "to be sure." When Margo was asked what "to be sure" meant, she said that she had no explanation other than, "Well, they're men and who knows what men think."
>
> The lawsuit was dropped for lack of evidence, other than Margo's medical report describing her bruised and battered body, and the lacerations on her thighs, vagina, breasts, and anus. There was no sperm found on or in her body. Margo explained that the guards used condoms and latex gloves. Correctional staff reported that Margo had harmed herself, and that she was always a "suicide and psycho case."
>
> The movie *Boys Don't Cry* [about a young transgender man] made such an impact on Margo and [her twin sister] Madelyn, they sought more information about it. They also sought out heroin, got high for a week or maybe longer, had sex, and were eventually arrested at the beach house [family vacation home]. A neighbor had called the police, reporting loud, continuous music, flames seen in different rooms of the eighteen-room house, and crashes coming from all over the beach home.
>
> During the trial, the magistrate decided that Margo had not only violated the terms of her good-time release, but this second drug conviction [the judge decided at the request of the prosecutor] was actually her third conviction. [Margo and her lawyers objected to the judge's decision, but it was made clear that she was an "evil and deviant person" because of her transgender state.] Therefore, she was a habitual criminal. In the jurisdiction where Margo was convicted, the sentencing guidelines mandate a life sentence for a habitual criminal.
>
> Also, the judge reviewed Margo's PSI [pre-sentence investigation official records], earlier civil suits based on gender segregation, and the accusations against male correctional officers. The decision of the court was to ship Margo [out of state] to a jurisdiction that recognized transgender rights. (pp. 159–160)

In part, this decision further isolated Margo from family members and her friends. Margo related how she was transported from the county jail to the airport for a flight to another state, where she would be locked up for life.

> "Without so much as a blink of an eye, the judge said, life without parole for you, young lady. I almost passed out. I couldn't believe it! Here I was,

a twenty-five-year-old woman who decided to go back to college to better myself, and the only way I would leave prison is in a pine box. My hands were already in restraints and I was dressed in a brown jump suit from the county jail. My hair was godawful and dirty and my sneakers didn't fit right, but I was pulled from the court into a vehicle, chained and locked, driven to the airport, onto the tarmac, and up metal stairs into a small, official-looking aircraft." (p. 161)

The treatment Margo experienced while under the care and custody of a correctional system is consistent with other accounts offered by female prisoners in group meetings. The point is that female prisoners are more likely to be raped once incarcerated than when they are walking the streets in a free society. Most often those rapes happen while female prisoners, especially lesbians and transgenders, are in placed in solitary confinement, as Margo had experienced.

The Prison Rape Elimination Act of 2003

Females fear sexual assault and rape in prison.[20] Mann and Cronan (2002) referred to rape and sexual abuse as "one of America's oldest, darkest, and yet most open, secrets." Sexual assault anywhere is devastating, both physically and emotionally (Stannow, 2010). When such abuse happens in prison, especially among Seg prisoners or prisoners isolated from the general prison population, victims face tremendous challenges, such as suffering in silence, and they may be forced to endure contact with their attackers. Prisoners have no access to rape crisis counselors, functional grievance systems, or anyone else to help guide them through their victimization. Isolated and vulnerable, female prisoners, once targeted, are attacked more often than expected.

The Prison Rape Elimination Act of 2003 was passed unanimously by the U.S. Congress to reduce rape in prison, and most assuredly, some policymakers wanted to reduce or monitor arbitrary practices such as Seg. The act established a system of grants and reforms that cost over $60 million a year. Its centerpiece is an annual survey by the U.S. Department of Justice (2006), which has been one of the most sweeping studies ever made of sexual assault in prisons. In prisons across the country, especially among female Seg prisoners, many face similar horrors every day.[21]

Final Thoughts

Curbing Seg practices will reduce many of the problems explored in this chapter, including custodial rape.[22] As I have argued, most custodial rape is a product of the isolation of prisoners coupled with the out-of-control, lustful motivators of custodial personnel.[23] Thus prisons need to reduce the use of segregation cells for females because of the issues that have arisen from a lack of regulation and poor hiring, training, and monitoring practices.

Sometimes I wonder if there are indeed criminals in prison or just broken souls. Empirical evidence shows that once an individual is incarcerated, regardless of his or her guilt or degree of innocence, the individual decisions of that prisoner have forever changed.[24] Once a defendant, particularly a female, is sentenced to prison, in the words of one female prisoner whom I counseled at Massachusetts Correctional Institution–Framingham, "If a girl is not a whore or junkie when she arrives here, she will be when she's released . . . especially if she's thrown in Seg."

Many female prisoners never recover from their experiences in prison. For the record, only one-third of the females serving state prison sentences are incarcerated for violent offenses, and nearly one-third of female convictions are linked to drug charges (Bureau of Justice Statistics, 2011b). Do females who serve prison time change? Do they conform to the rules once released? Recidivism rates suggest that they change for the worse.

Society has attempted to control criminals and criminal behavior throughout recorded history. We've tried dismemberment, crucifixion, entombment, impalement, and relocation. We fried them, butchered them, burned them, drugged them, lobotomized them, electrocuted them, and hanged them. Now we incarcerate and bury them in segregation cells, and still . . . criminal behavior is pervasive.

Notes

1. See Buchanan, 2007.
2. See Papen, 2011.
3. See Davis, De-Groot, & Shaylor, 1998.
4. See Stevens, 2006.
5. See Fraser, Mosley, Thornion, Belknap, & Rogers, 1984.
6. See National Prison Rape Elimination Commission, 2009.
7. See Stevens, 2005.
8. See Kupers et al., 2009; Stevens, 2006.
9. See Riveland, 1999; Scharff-Smith, 2006.
10. See Buchanan, 2007; Stevens, 1999; Wolff, Jing, & Siegel, 2009.
11. See Gawande, 2010; Seamons, 2011.
12. See Ford, 2009.
13. See National Institute of Corrections, 2011.
14. See Cecil, McHale, Strozier, & Pietsch, 2008.
15. See Buchanan, 2007; Gaes & Goldberg, 2005; Talvi, 2007; Amnesty International, 2011.
16. Also see Landis, 2005.

17. See Stevens, 2000; Thornhill & Palmer, 2000.
18. See Stevens, 2011.
19. See Stevens, 2000, 2010, 2011.
20. See Wolff & Shi, 2011.
21. See Mann & Cronan, 2002; Stannow, 2010.
22. See Thompson, 2009.
23. See Antonaccio & Tittle, 2008; Stevens, 2000; Thornhill & Palmer, 2000.
24. See Stevens, 1994, 1997, 1998a, 2010.

| 8 |

The Scene of the Crime: Children in Solitary Confinement

Christopher Bickel

I heard Danny's screams before I met him. I was playing dominoes when all hell broke loose in the adjacent unit. A Code 2 blasted over the radio, and guards were rushing to the scene, congregating outside the unit where Danny was housed all by himself, isolated from the rest of the youth in juvenile detention. "Fuck you, I'm not going back into that fuckin' cell," Danny yelled as he backed against the wall, facing a number of guards preparing to take him down. The guards must have looked like giants to him. They towered over him, just 13 years old and barely five feet tall.

Then I heard a loud thump as his body was slammed to the thinly carpeted floor. I peeked into the hall to see five large guards pile on top of him. One grabbed his right wrist, another his left, two more were on his legs, and one beefy guard pressed his knee into the back of his neck. "Get the fuck off me, I can't breathe!" he yelled at the guards, who were methodically twisting his body in unnatural ways to handcuff him behind his back. "Fuck you!" Danny shouted, gasping for air, as blood dripped from his mouth.

"Stop resisting," the guards shouted at the young man, who was screaming in pain more than resisting. They lifted his body in the air and forced him into his cell, a place where he would eventually spend months in isolation. Outside in the hall, guards excitedly patted each other on the back for a job well done.[1]

Solitary Confinement of Youth

The use of solitary confinement and the accompanying violence are common in juvenile facilities throughout the United States. The Office of Juvenile Justice and Delinquency Prevention found that 24% of the youth in juvenile facilities had experienced solitary confinement. Barry Krisberg (2003), director of the National Council on Crime and Delinquency, reported that "on any given day, between 10–12 percent of wards were housed in units in which they were confined to their rooms for 23 hours a day, with one hour permitted outside their rooms under close supervision" (p. 51). At the juvenile detention center where I conducted research, it was not unusual to see at least two of the 10 children in each unit placed on cell restriction, some of whom were denied running water, basic hygiene products, and writing materials.

Internationally, many countries disapprove of the use of solitary confinement for juveniles. During the 20th century, much of Europe eliminated or severely curtailed the practice in its juvenile facilities. In 1989, the United Nations ratified the Convention on the Rights of a Child, which states that "no child shall be subjected to torture or other cruel, inhuman or degrading treatment as punishment." Later in 1991, the United Nations ratified the Rules for the Protection of Juveniles Deprived of Their Liberty, which explicitly states that "all disciplinary measures constituting cruel, inhuman or degrading treatment shall be strictly prohibited, including corporal punishment, placement in a dark cell, closed or solitary confinement, or any other punishment that may compromise the physical or mental health of the juvenile concerned" (United Nations, 1990). Only the United States and Somalia have refused to sign the Convention on the Rights of the Child.[2]

Accompanying the international condemnation of solitary confinement is a growing body of academic literature that documents the physical and psychological dangers of solitary confinement, including lethargy, hypersensitivity to sounds, a sense of hopelessness, rage, self-mutilation, and ideations of suicide.[3] While existing research studies document the consequences of solitary confinement for adults, few focus on the effects on juveniles. Most research on juvenile facilities relies heavily on surveys or interviews with the functionaries of juvenile justice, leaving researchers more susceptible to institutional rhetoric that veils solitary confinement in a euphemistic cloth: "dorm confinement," "reflection rooms," or "special intervention units." Ethnographic accounts of day-to-day life in juvenile facilities are few.[4] It is within this gap in the literature that I situate my research at a county juvenile detention center in the United States with approximately 180 to 200 juveniles aged 12 to 17. "Rosy Meadows" is a fictional name for the institution I studied, as a representation of what additional studies might find across the United States.

In this chapter, I argue that the practice of holding children in solitary confinement is a fundamental component in the process of criminalizing youth and preparing them for the adult criminal justice system, rather than successful reentry to society. Most detention guards and officials maintain that cell confinement is an important "teaching tool" that encourages detained and incarcerated youth to follow the rules. In contrast, I contend that it accomplishes the opposite by degrading the relationship children have with their keepers, exposing them to increased institutional violence, and reinforcing their belief in the sham of rehabilitation. Rather than teach valuable lessons, or even secure behavioral conformity, solitary confinement increases resistance from youth as they bang on their cell doors, shout profanities at their keepers, and flood their cells. This response to solitary confinement conveniently becomes the institutional justification for further punishment and degradation. Thus this cycle of punishment and resistance traps young men, who were often accused of minor property crimes, into a cycle of criminalization that paves a path toward adult jails and prisons.

To make this argument, I draw on my two years of experience conducting research at a juvenile detention center. I began my fieldwork at Rosy Meadows in October 1998. I spent 20 hours a week for nearly two years inside the detention center. I ate the bland food, played cards, and attended church services with the youth. I also spoke with 25 guards, asking them questions as they went about their work. This more informal way of speaking with guards proved highly effective, as guards were far more comfortable talking to me during their daily routine. I also formally interviewed eight additional detention guards and a detention supervisor in the summer of 2002.

I obtained most of my interviews through "convenience sampling," in which I simply sat outside the detention center and asked guards if I could interview them. Three interviews I obtained through "snowball sampling" with the assistance of guards who helped set up the interviews. All formal interviews were recorded.[5] After I completed my ethnographic research in July 2002, I remained in contact with several youth over the years and am still in contact with a few today, who are now adults. With their permission, this study also relies to a great extent on my correspondence with the young men as they have come of age in the adult prison system.

In the following sections, I draw heavily from the experiences of young men in juvenile detention centers and youth prisons as they experience solitary confinement. In the first section, I describe the rules and regulations that govern life in detention centers and youth prisons, paying attention to how one young man, Mario, understood the rules he was expected to follow. As juvenile facilities increasingly resemble adult prisons, the restrictive rules guarantee that many youth will spend considerable time inside cinder-block cages, alone and isolated from the rest of the youth. In the second section, I tell the stories of three young men—Andre, Phil, and Danny—as they confronted a juvenile justice system that employs solitary confinement to secure conformity.

Mice in a Maze: "We're Treated Like Animals in Here!"

Rosy Meadows, similarly to juvenile facilities across the United States, has a strict body of rules that children are expected to follow. These rules govern everything from how to walk down the hallway—hands to the sides, quiet, head forward—to how they wear their institutional garb, with shirt tucked in, pants pulled up, and identification band on the right wrist. In all, hundreds of rules govern a young person's behavior inside these detention institutions. These rules are the backbone of what detention officials call in in-house handbooks the "behavior management program," an incentive-and-punishment system viewed as a "teaching tool" intended "to change behavior."

The behavior management program, also known as the "level system," establishes an artificial hierarchy within the detained population, marking those with and those without certain privileges. Ideally, if detained children follow the rules and obey the instructions of their guards, they are rewarded with extra time out of their cells and more access to the telephone. If, however, they break institutional rules or defy the guard's orders, they may be punished with cell confinement, which in theory should last anywhere from eight hours to three days, but in reality may last for months. If the blue-uniformed children, for example, have a pencil in the cell or possess more than five books, they may be locked in their cells for 16 hours. If they yell to another youth in an adjacent cell, they may be locked for 24 hours. If they tuck their pants into their socks or are found with sagging county blues (pants), they may be locked in for two days. If they flood their cells, they may be locked in for a minimum of three days, with additional punishment depending on how they behave while confined to their cells. On several occasions, I have observed children placed in solitary confinement for a period of three months for 23 hours a day.

Solitary confinement is used even more heavily in state youth prisons. It is not unusual for children to be locked in their cells for weeks and even months at a time. For example, Danny, from the opening story, explained that he spent nearly 80% of his time in solitary confinement at Rosy Meadows. While Danny said he was released from solitary confinement for a few days here and there, I never once saw him in the general population.

Grounded in simple operant conditioning, the underlying assumption of the level system is that if compliance is rewarded and noncompliance punished, the youth, like mice in a "Skinner box," will eventually learn to adhere to institutional rules and, by extension, those of society (Skinner, 1953). The level system is the primary tool of social control inside the secured walls at Rosy Meadows. The administration believed that if detained juveniles could be trained to follow rules inside the detention facility, these newly instilled disciplinary values would help them when they are eventually released to return home.

Shalev (2009b) documented the rise of behaviorist approaches to rehabilitation in the Federal Bureau of Prisons. In 1973, the Federal Bureau of Prisons introduced the Control and Rehabilitation Effort (CARE) program at United States Penitentiary (USP) Marion penitentiary and the Special Treatment and Rehabilitation Training (START) program at the United States Medical Center for Federal Prisoners in Springfield, Missouri. Federal prison administrators and psychologists conceived of the CARE and START programs as tools to rehabilitate "problem prisoners" through the use of solitary confinement as a punishment for institutionally unacceptable behavior. As the incarcerated fell in line with institutional rules, they would graduate to the next level and enjoy more time outside of their cells. However, Shalev (2008) wrote, "rather than rehabilitating prisoners . . . programs like START and CARE aimed to make prisoners more docile and more susceptible to rehabilitation programs through solitary confinement" (p. 19). According to Shalev, the therapeutic justification of solitary confinement, widely considered ineffective in the rehabilitation of incarcerated people, was replaced by the logic of risk management and the need for institutional safety and security.

In juvenile facilities, however, the therapeutic justification of cell confinement is still alive and well. Through behavior management programs, the cell becomes the primary and sometimes the only "teaching tool" for the rehabilitation of detained and incarcerated youth. As Peter, a juvenile detention guard at Rosy Meadows, explained:

> The level system is an essential element of what we do. Without the threat of room confinement, it'd be difficult to motivate the kids to improve their behavior. It provides incentive and gives motivation. If we didn't have it, we'd be hard-pressed to motivate the kids to behave well. And it's really the first step to teaching them to be more responsible when they get released.

While Peter justifies the threat of cell confinement on more therapeutic grounds, the level system and the threat of cell confinement make it easier to control and manage the youth in blue uniforms. In his study of a Rhode Island training facility, Reich (2010) reported that guards often "conflate rehabilitative assumptions with managerial prerogatives" (p. 128). Reich's point is not lost on the youth confined at Rosy Meadows, who often question the strict rules and regulations that govern their behavior.

Detention guards often lament that the "detainees" simply don't know how to follow the rules. In my conversations with the young men at Rosy Meadows, however, it's not that they don't know how to follow the rules, but rather that they make a distinction between rules that are designed for their benefit—their safety and rehabilitation—and those that serve only to control them. The youth make two fundamental arguments against the institutional rules: first, the rules are unnecessarily restrictive, and second, the rules are not designed for their rehabilitation and pose a threat to their identity as children worthy of human dignity and respect. The following section details the experience of Mario as he confronted detention rules. His story is representative of what many youth go through at Rosy Meadows.

Mario's Story: "The Rules Are Crazy"

Mario was a fierce card player. He was one of the best, and he never missed an opportunity to challenge me in a game of 13. If he won, I would smuggle in a candy bar, but if I won, he had to write a one- to two-page essay. He won most of the time, but he did a fair amount of writing as well. The 16-year-old Mario, who identified as Latino, had arrived at detention a month earlier, charged with joyriding in a stolen vehicle and possession of a small amount of crack cocaine. He stood about 5 feet, 7 inches tall and had curly hair braided into cornrows. Mario was an artist and spent a lot of time drawing low-rider cars, action heroes, and biblical images of Jesus. His talents came in handy, as they helped pass the time in his cell, where he spent most of the day. He was a self-identified "soldier," a word the youth use to describe someone who isn't afraid to stand up to the guards and break the rules when they feel they have been unjustly treated. But all battles carry a steep price: days and even weeks locked in a cinder-block cell for 23 hours a day.

I met up with Mario one evening to play our regularly scheduled card game. Throwing a card on the table, Mario explained his view on detention rules, a topic especially salient because he had just finished spending most of the day in his cell for having a golf pencil he used to draw low-rider cars and write letters to his mother and father. Institutional rules forbid the use of pens or markers and limit the use of pencils to the living units outside the cells. A pencil found inside a young man's cell is considered contraband and is an offense punishable with up to a day of cell confinement. "The rules in here, man, they're crazy!" he said, shaking his head. "I don't understand why they have most of them. It's like they try to control every little thing we do. We can't do nothing on our own."

Mario grabbed a card from the table, and then asked a series of questions:

> I mean, what is this, you can't have a pencil in your room? What's that all about? What are we supposed to do in our cell? And, why is it that you can only have five books and magazines in your cell? Man, they'll give you hours for shit like that. I've seen it happen. I mean, if we have extra books in our cell, that's a good thing, isn't it? And then, why do they only allow us to have two shirts and two pairs of pants? They will give you hours for that too. It's like they enjoy giving hours [in solitary lockup], so they make everything against the rules.

Mario's voice was laced with frustration as he continued:

> They're constantly nagging at me for every little thing. They tell us when to eat, sleep, shit. They tell us when to do everything. They think they can treat us like shit just 'cause they've got the power, just 'cause they can. We're treated like animals in here. They're always giving us hours [of cell confinement], and it's not for no big shit, either. It's always for some petty shit.

Mario is not alone. Many youth vehemently disagree with many of the rules that govern their behavior inside detention walls. They argue that the rules are unnecessarily restrictive, designed not for their safety or well-being, but rather to control them. To many, this flies in the face of the officially stated goals of the institution to provide rehabilitation and educational programs. Detention officials, however, argue that the rules are designed to teach good behavior and are necessary to provide safety when dealing with "dangerous" populations. Uniforms are used to prevent escapes, and uncomfortable flip-flops limit the youth's ability to run. Items like toothbrushes, hairbrushes, combs, and pencils must be kept locked away because the youth might chisel them into weapons. All of this, detention officials argue, is necessary for the "safety and security" of the youth and staff.

The rules are the material manifestation of ideological assumptions about the perceived pathological character of detained children. This particular way of framing youth—as pathological, troubled, and dysfunctional—shapes every aspect of juvenile facilities. The very architecture of the detention center suggests that the youth are dangerous: the thick steel doors, countless locks on every door and drawer, listening devices built into each cell, and the many security cameras. Although the overwhelming majority of youth are detained for nonviolent offenses, the architecture of Rosy Meadows resembles that of an adult prison.

In addition to the institutional rules and the architecture, guards are trained to accept these commonly held stereotypes in their daily interactions. During their mandatory training, guards are given a handbook replete with warnings about the dangers of detained and incarcerated youth. The handbook suggests that guards beware of criminals with a sociopathic personality who may attempt to manipulate and take advantage of them. Guards are then instructed never to turn their backs to the youth, never to share personal stories, and to maintain their social distance, almost as if the youth are suffering from an infectious disease that threatens to contaminate all who come too close.

Given these stereotypical assumptions, when guards enforce the rules, they are not simply maintaining order, but rather they are communicating a powerful message to the youth that they are a different category of human beings who are disreputable, pathological, and untrustworthy. Speaking to the communicative power of rules in mental asylums and total institutions, Erving Goffman (1961) wrote:

> Once lodged on a given ward, the patient is firmly instructed that the restrictions and deprivations he encounters are not due to such blind forces as tradition or economy—and hence dissociable from self—but are intentional parts of his treatment, part of his need at the time and therefore an expression of the state that his self has fallen. (p. 149)

It is not surprising, then, that the confined children experience the rules not as teaching tools but as an attack on their identity. Mario, for example, took issue with the assumption that he could not be trusted with a pencil. After all, he was not just a detainee but also an artist who loved to draw, and he was a son who loved and missed his family. A rule forbidding a pencil in his cell, he argued, was unnecessary because he wouldn't use it to "tag" his walls. At the same time, Mario's statement that "we're treated like animals in here" highlights that he was keenly aware of how the staff viewed him.

For Mario, to accept the legitimacy of the rules was to accept the image that guards had of him. Given this, Mario had become somewhat of an expert at evading the rules. He spent much of his day figuring out how to get around detention regulations. To circumvent the rules limiting pencils in his cell, Mario broke off the lead tips wrapped them with cardboard and rubber bands, so he could smuggle them into his cell at night and draw and write letters to his parents. This is an example of what Goffman called "secondary adjustments," practices that allow the confined to obtain restricted items without being detected by staff. When Mario sneaked a pencil into his room undetected, when he lifted a permanent marker from underneath his teacher's nose, he felt alive, as if he had won a small victory against an impossible opponent. Mario took great pride in these moments. As Goffman (1961) explained, "Secondary adjustments provide the inmate with important evidence that he is still his own man, with some control of his environment; sometimes a secondary adjustment becomes almost a kind of lodgment for the self, a churinga in which the soul is felt to reside" (p. 55).

Although Mario took great pride in evading the rules, he was sometimes detected and paid the price. Since Mario's placement in detention, he spent most of his time locked inside his cell, doing what many of the youth call "hard time." Guards confined him for eight hours for possessing a pencil, 72 hours for possessing a permanent marker, eight hours for instigating, 24 hours for threatening to fight, eight hours for refusing staff orders, eight hours for chewing gum, 24 hours for refusing to go to his cell, and another 72 hours for waving to his friend, a gesture mistaken by guards as a gang sign. Mario served all of this time on top of the 14 hours each day that all prisoners have to spend in their cells regardless of how well they follow the rules.

Known by guards as a "troublemaker," Mario found that he spent a lot of time staring at the white walls of his cell. With each day confined, he became noticeably more frustrated and angry. He developed what he called an "I don't give a fuck" attitude. I visited him one day after he had spent 72 hours in his cell. His demeanor was sullen and detached. As we played cards, I asked, "What's it like to be locked in a cell?" Mario responded:

> It's hard to describe, man, you don't really never know what it feels like unless you've been locked up. It's crazy, man. I get tired of being in my cell all day. Imagine this, man. Imagine having to stay in your bathroom all day. Take out the tub and put a metal bed in it with a thin-ass ghetto mattress. Imagine having to stay in there all day and having to depend on somebody you hate to let you out. That's what it's like. I hate being locked up. It's doing things to me, man, it's fucking me up, I can tell.

"How so?" I asked. Mario continued:

> It makes me real angry, man, being locked up in that cell. The only thing I keep saying to myself is, at least I don't have to do years, you know. I know this dude in here. He got out, and then two weeks later he was back in, facing three years. Three years! Do you know what that's gonna do to him? He's fucked! So I just keep thinking, it could be worse, but even with the time I've done, I can tell it's fucking with me. Sometimes I just want to run down the hall as fast as I can. I haven't run, I mean really run, in so long. Sometimes I think about jumping on that basketball court and breaking up outta this place. I know I can do it, but they'll end up catching me. I don't have no place to hide, so, you know, I'll just do my time. Fuck it.

Mario would end up doing more time in the future than he imagined. Although Mario's probation officer initially said he would be a good candidate for release on house arrest, the list of disciplinary infractions hurt his chances of an early release. Although his probation officer didn't have the direct authority to release Mario, his recommendation carried weight with the judge.

Mario's record of disciplinary actions weighed heavily on his probation officer's decision to recommend detention while Mario awaited his trial. Mario was later sentenced to nearly two years at a state youth prison.

Looking at Mario's list of disciplinary sanctions, they all seem quite petty: possession of a marker, allegedly throwing a gang sign, instigating, and chewing gum. As juvenile institutions come to resemble adult prisons, detention guards view these minor infractions not only as a threat to "safety and security," but also as evidence of the pathological, disreputable character of the children in blue uniforms. Mario's distaste for the rules did not simply revolve around his desire to wave to his friends or even to possess a marker, but rather reflected his desire to have rules that acknowledged his worth as a human being. He refused to accept that he was an animal to be corralled from place to place, under degrading and inhumane conditions. His frustration with the rules was only amplified by the guards' frequent use of solitary confinement.

The Caging of Childhood: "The Scene of a Crime"

In the 1970s, investigative journalist Kenneth Wooden toured juvenile facilities across the United States and documented his findings in the classic book *Weeping in the Playtime of Others*. Wooden wrote about children in Texas who were trapped in cells while guards threw tear gas canisters inside and others in Alabama who were locked in rat-infested cells. Wooden (1976/2000) explained, "I personally feel, after visiting staff and talking with students, that solitary confinement has only one purpose and that purpose is control" (p. 130). Around the same time, Jerome Miller was appointed as director of the Department of Youth Services in Massachusetts. He began touring reform schools throughout the state. At one boys' industrial school, Miller made an unannounced visit to one of the cottages, where the boys called their housing unit the "tombs." Miller (1991) later wrote, "The coffin-like rooms were aptly named. I asked to look inside one. The master unlocked the steel mesh door, and there, on the floor, nude in the darkness of his own tomb, sat a 16-year-old." These early tours of reform schools, Miller reflected, "touched something that would make the reform schools my personal ghosts" (p. 65).

Nearly 30 years later, the ghosts of solitary confinement continue to haunt the juvenile justice system. At Rosy Meadows, I routinely witnessed children held under lockdown for days, weeks, and even months at a time. It was difficult to see so many young people trapped behind their steel doors, some barely tall enough to see outside their narrow windows. On an average day, guards confine the young men at Rosy Meadows to their cells for 12 to 14 hours. However, a sizable number of young men spend far more time in their cells, isolated and separated from the other youth, who are forbidden to speak or interact with those placed under lockdown. Few staff and administrators at Rosy Meadows call the practice of holding children in 7-by-8-foot cells solitary confinement; instead, they prefer euphemisms such as "special intervention program," "restrictive status," "quiet time," or "dorm confinement." The terms are simply a feat of verbal gymnastics that glosses over the rising trend in juvenile justice to rely heavily on cell confinement to manage and control low-income children.[6] Wooden (1976/2000) observed the same trend decades before: "Institutions who claim they no longer have solitary confinement have simply adjusted their terminology, deceived or lied outright" (p. 134). The youth use different names: "the hole," "solitary," and even "hell."

In the following sections, I tell the stories of three young men—Andre, Phil, and Danny—as they tried to make sense of their time enduring days, weeks, and even months in solitary confinement. For the young men at Rosy Meadows, the use of solitary confinement damages their physical and psychological well-being, poisons their relationship with detention guards, and ultimately reinforces their desire to resist an institution that they see as designed more for their control than their rehabilitation.

Andre's Story: "Nobody Belongs in a Cell, Not Even My Worst Enemy"

Andre was a 17-year-old with a voracious appetite for books. I often spoke with him at night through the cracks of his cell door, where we talked about everything from life on the streets to the latest books he had just finished reading. Andre was profoundly mature for his age, and I often had more interesting discussions with him than I did with the students during graduate seminars at a nearby university. One evening, he explained to me why so many young people, especially youth of color, are behind bars:

> There are the people on top, there are the people in the middle, and then there's us at the bottom. Society tries to make people believe that it's us who is causing the problem, 'cause as long as the people in the middle fear us, and think that we're the criminals, they won't look at the stuff the people on top are doing. It's like they set up this fear, but it's not real; they think it's real, but we're not the ones they need to fear. Society has everybody fooled.

Andre confided that he dreamed of attending college and eventually becoming a counselor to incarcerated youth:

> I want to be a counselor when I get out of here. I see a lot of white, Latino, and black kids in here who don't have family. You know, kids who never felt the love a family can bring. They don't have money or nothing. And if they have parents, they're struggling to get by. I know what it's like 'cause I've lived it. I've been to hell and back. I've seen it all. Most of the guards in here don't

> know nothing about that. You know, they came from middle-class homes. They don't really understand. But I understand—I've been through it. That's why I want to be a counselor. I could explain things to kids in a language they would understand.

Andre had spent most of his teenage years in and out of juvenile facilities. When I met him, he was facing a charge of possession of crack cocaine with intent to sell. Undercover police had caught him downtown in an area undergoing gentrification, an attempt by the city to bring middle-class whites back to the area to dine and shop. Over a game of dominoes one night, Andre told me the story of his arrest by the police:

> They caught me with 6 grams and $320. I was at hard at work that night. I was out there all night, and they got me. . . . I wouldn't have done none of that, but my cheese was low from when I was locked up, and my kids were living with me at the time, so I had to do something. I had to do something to put clothes on their backs and food in their stomach. I'm not gonna let them starve, and none of the places I applied to were hiring, so I did what I had to do.

Andre's time in juvenile facilities had taught him many lessons, and he was deeply reflective of how his experiences had affected him, particularly the time spent alone in his cell. He regarded the cell as one of the most damaging punishments a human being, let alone a child, could experience. He spoke of the boredom, the lack of human contact, the lights that never completely turned off, the smells of piss and disinfectant, and the anger it all produced. The cell, he told me as I stood next to his door, is one of the main reasons why there is so much conflict between the guards and the youth. Andre continued:

> I don't know why they think we're just going to accept that we belong in there. Nobody belongs in a cell, man, not even my worst enemy. They used to put me in my cell a lot. That didn't do nothing, though; it just made me more angry, you know? I don't even know why they think that's gonna do anything. If a kid is angry, why are you gonna put him in a little cell with nothing to do, nothing to write with, nothing to read, nothing for you to do anything positive, nothing to help you grow? It's like they try to keep knowledge from you. There's a lot of staff in here who do that. They don't want to deal with us, so they put us in cages where they don't have to see us.

I asked him why he thought they used cells as punishment. Andre explained:

> Well, a lot of guards don't respect us, and they think we're not human, like we don't respond to the same things other people do. You know, treat me like a human being and you don't need a cell, but they don't see us like that. A lot of guards come to work here thinking they know all about us. But they don't

> know shit! You know, they judge us and think that all we are is criminals. They don't never take the time to listen to us and hear where we coming from. That's why they don't understand why we do what we do. They see a kid explode and don't have no idea why he did it. If they had been listening, they would have known.

Like Mario, Andre saw his treatment by guards as an attack on his identity as a human being. The rules, the architecture of confinement, and the cell were powerful reminders that the guards saw him as a danger and as a threat that must be controlled. Andre's belief that the use of solitary confinement is purely about control echoes the thoughts of Kenneth Wooden decades earlier. Wooden (1976/2000) wrote that solitary confinement "is the staff's trump card; it is a substitute for comprehensive and dedicated treatment and rehabilitation" (p. 130). Andre explained that it's not only a substitute, but also a poison that impedes any attempt at meaningful rehabilitation within juvenile facilities. A growing body of research suggests that solitary confinement has several detrimental physical and psychological effects.[7] As Krisberg (2003) explained in his review of the California Youth Authority:

> It is hard to imagine that 23-hour confinement over several months has any therapeutic value. Most psychologists and mental health professionals would argue that this severe isolation is antithetical to sound treatment practices. Since the invention of solitary confinement by the Philadelphia Quakers in the 18th century, we have learned that this approach produces hostility and illness, not health. (p. 58)

Whereas most guards and detention officials believe that solitary confinement teaches powerful lessons about the importance of following the rules, Andre argued that it only creates more anger and inevitably leads to more conflict between youth and their keepers. As the guards rely increasingly on cell confinement to manage their units, their relationship with the youth deteriorates, as does the respect the youth afford them.

Over the years, Andre had developed a profound distaste for detention officials. It was an issue of respect. Given the pathological view that many guards hold of detained youth, they treat the youth as criminals, as members of a disreputable category, deserving of punishment. Andre commented:

> The thing I don't like is when the staff disrespects us, and then expects us to respect them. I don't like it when it's one-way. How can they expect us to respect them when they don't respect us? That's the shit that will make you go mad. Man, there are a lot of staff who are just here for the money, and they don't even talk to us or nothing. They just give orders like we [are] animals or something. But when a staff don't respect us, we gonna cause trouble.

Andre believed that guards should be trained counselors who should talk with the youth about their lives, offer advice, and help nurture their growth. The reality of detention, however, is a far cry from his more rehabilitative vision. Faced with an increasingly punitive institution, Andre had learned how to limit his time in a cell. He avoided interacting with guards, and when he did, he never let them know what he was thinking. Guards were not to be trusted, he felt, especially with one's emotions. Andre explained:

> You know, when I first came in here, I was angry all the time. I spent a lot of time in my cell because I let them get to me. All that stuff they were saying to me, yelling at me, it's like they were trying to get me to act out. It's like they knew if they pushed me just a little bit further, they knew I'd do something so that they could put me back in the cell. I used to fall into that trap, you know. Until I figured it out. Now I just laugh at them, and I can tell that it makes them even angrier. So they try to push me more and more, and I can see what they're doing, so I don't play their game. I know they got the key, and as long as they got that, they have the power. I can't do nothing, so I don't even play their game. That's why I play around a lot. They don't know what I'm thinking that way. I don't let them know how angry I am. I just joke around a lot and smile. You see, 'cause if they know what you are thinking, they can control that. If they see you are angry, they can push you a little bit and set you off, and put you right back in your cell where they want you. . . . It's like they get a kick out of seeing you get in trouble. They don't understand that what they do affects our lives forever. For them, it's just a job. For us, it's our life.

For his part, Andre tried to remain invisible and avoid interacting with the guards as much as possible. From the perspective of the guards, his coping strategy was viewed as a managerial success story. "He finally learned his lesson," a guard with a bulging belly told me as we walked down the long corridor. "He's not causing trouble anymore, like when he first came in here."

Andre no longer spent as much time in his cell as he had earlier. However, it's difficult to imagine how any meaningful growth, let alone rehabilitation, can happen when young men avoid the very people who are supposed to help them grow and stay free from juvenile facilities. When I asked Andre if he ever tried to talk to the guards about his life, he replied, "Man, I don't even try to talk to them about that stuff anymore, because they can't even see me."

Far from being a success story, Andre believed that his time in detention, particularly his time in solitary, had done him irreparable harm, preparing him more for a future in an adult penitentiary. "This place, man, doesn't prepare you for the outside," he said. "There's nothing in here to help you grow. And you know, the things we have to do to survive in here are the things that will get us arrested on the outside." "How so?" I asked. Andre replied:

> Well, when you do time, you have to become another person, and toughen up and be ready for anything. And the longer you're locked up, the more you forget who you were on the outside. I've spent way too much time in my cell and, man, when you're in there alone, the demons come out, you know, the anger, and shit, you forget who you are. I should be learning to live life on the outside, things like how to get into community college and pay my bills, but I'm only learning the things that will keep me here. . . . I know how to survive detention, but what good does that do me out there?

Andre's dreams of becoming a counselor to incarcerated youth had to be put on the back burner when he received more prison time. One evening in the gym, a young man walked up to Andre and challenged him to a fight. Not wanting to lose his reputation as a leader, Andre answered with a fist to his opponent's jaw. The young man had to be taken to the hospital. He later pressed charges, at the urging of several guards, and before Andre could finish his 15- to 36-week sentence, he was sentenced to two more years at the state youth prison. He never even made it out the door. His fears had proved prophetic.

Phil's Story: "They Fucked Me Up!"

Phil was 15 years old and skinny, and whenever I was at Rosy Meadows, he was always confined to his cell. He got a day in his cell for mouthing off at a guard, another day for having a pencil in his cell, then three days for alleged gang activity. I spoke to him for weeks through his cell door before I was actually able to talk to him without a steel door between us. Phil had arrived in detention after attempting to take his stepmother's car for a joyride to another state. She reported it stolen, and the police caught him soon after. His trip ended in detention, and he faced charges for stealing a motor vehicle. Accused of a relatively minor offense, Phil was an excellent candidate for diversion programs like probation or house arrest, but his time in detention changed all of that, as the days of isolation in his cell set the stage for several disciplinary actions that weighed heavily on his adjudication.

One evening, while confined to his cell for yet another rule infraction, a known snitch told Jennifer, the guard on duty, to check Phil's room for matches. Jennifer enlisted the help of another guard, Jonathan, who went to search Phil's cell, but Phil slammed the door shut. Jonathan left the unit and returned with three exceptionally large men. Phil then capitulated, and the guards removed him from his cell, took him into a small bathroom, strip searched him, and checked his clothes for contraband. Phil was humiliated by the experience, as he had never been strip searched by grown men before, but still he maintained his cool. While he was in the bathroom, two other guards searched his cell.

Cell searches are a daily reality for detained children like Phil. Guards remove the youth from their cells, inspect their living spaces, and check for rule violations. For the youth, there is no sacred ground on which the keepers can't walk, and this, in and of itself, is a thorn in their side. Given the vast amount of time spent inside a small, drab cell, many youth take to decorating their walls with pictures of family members, significant others, low-rider cars, or their favorite television stars to make their cells a bit more habitable and less sterile. These decorations help children maintain their identity and individuality in the face of an institutional drive toward behavioral conformity. The rules of detention, however, prohibit placing anything on cell walls, leading to a sterile uniformity of detention cells.

After Phil was strip searched, he returned to his cell to find it a disheveled mess. Many of his pictures had been torn from the wall, and he couldn't find several of his girlfriend's letters, which he read every night to remind him of his life outside the walls. Phil began to yell at the guards, breathing heavily and shouting cuss words—"Fuck you, what'd you do with my letters?"—as he searched through his folder. In detention, this is one of the most valued possessions because it contains letters, pictures, and court documents.

Phil approached Jennifer, the guard in charge, but before he reached her, two well-built detention guards lifted him into the air and slammed his skinny, 120-pound body to the ground. The guards later claimed that they feared he was going to attack Jennifer, which Phil adamantly denied. His body made a loud thump as it hit the ground. The sound attracted all of the youth in the unit to their windows, where they watched Phil being jumped by the guards. As he moaned in pain, several youth yelled out to the guards from inside their cells. "He's down, leave him alone," Fernando shouted as he looked out the window of his cell. "You gonna break something." "He's not resisting, let him go," yelled another young man. "Get out from the window or you're goin' to get taxed," a guard called back, reiterating the detention policy that punishes young men for standing in their windows during altercations between guards and detainees. This policy eliminates potential witnesses.

All four guards piled on top of Phil. One guard grabbed his left leg, another grabbed his right leg, while a third pulled Phil's arms behind his back so he could be handcuffed. The fourth guard placed his knee on the back of Phil's neck. Phil screamed in pain. His face rubbed against the thin carpet until it was raw. Once Phil was handcuffed, the guards forced him into his cell. Two hours later, after complaining of extreme pain in his wrist, Phil was taken to the emergency room, where his wrist was fitted with a cast.

I visited Phil the next day at the health clinic, where he was placed on suicide watch. He was in a slightly larger cell in his underwear, with nothing but a mat on the ground and a sheet to keep him warm. He was shivering.

He came to the door and I could see his face through the window. He had several bruises over his body, rug burns on his arms and face, a black eye, and a badly swollen lip. "How are you doing, man?" I asked. "They fucked me up," Phil said through the cracks of his door. He sounded depressed and his face was sullen. His watery eyes looked down at the cement floor as he tried desperately to hold back a flood of tears. "I don't understand how they can get away with that," he said, wiping the tears from his eyes. "One of them even hit me in the jaw with a closed fist."

In the end, the guards didn't find what they were looking for. They found only a safety pin and a pencil, but no matches. Phil had to serve 24 hours in his cell for the contraband. He wasn't punished, however, for the physical altercation with the guards, which usually carries a penalty of 72 hours. The guards had violated procedure when they handcuffed Phil without a supervisor present. The guard named Jonathan and a detention supervisor later apologized to Phil, but no guards were officially reprimanded.

A week after Phil was slammed, he looked unusually happy, even though he was confined to his cell for 16 hours for wearing his identification bracelet on the wrong wrist. I walked up to his cell and asked how he was doing. "It looks like I might be getting out on electronic monitoring until a bed in a treatment center opens up. I'll be able to get out of this hellhole," he said with a rare smile. Phil's optimism, however, was short-lived. A few days later, his probation officer informed him that he had been deemed too dangerous for electronic monitoring. His behavior in detention, coupled with his mother's fears that he would run away, weighed heavily on the probation officer's recommendation to the court to keep him in detention.

I saw Phil shortly after he found out that he wouldn't be leaving detention any time soon. He was crying by the pay phone. "I can't believe the court went back on its word," he said. "How can they do that? I can't take another day, man, I'm telling you, Chris. I'm going to get out of here one way or another." After the guards had "slammed" Phil, he spent most of his time confined to a cell. The guards now considered Phil a troublemaker. His name was mentioned repeatedly during their daily debriefings, and as a result, they had been instructed to tighten their control over him, which meant more cell time. They taxed him with several petty violations that ordinarily would have passed beneath the eyes of detention staff. He received 8 hours for possession of a pencil, 8 hours for taking a book out of the library, 16 hours for failing to appropriately wear his identification bracelet, 24 hours for tagging his desk at school, 24 hours for tagging the walls of his cell, and another 8 hours for writing the names of his friends on his cast.

With so much time in his cell, Phil believed the walls were closing in on him. He was reaching a boiling point. As time passed, Phil's sense of hopelessness seemed all-encompassing. His demeanor changed noticeably. I talked with him one evening about the treatment he had received in detention. Phil told me:

> You know, I just want to go home and get away from this place, man. I'm sick of it. I'm sick of all of it. I hate everybody here. They treat you like shit, and we're just supposed to take it. And the minute I try to say something about it, they say I'm a troublemaker, and then they tax me even more. [Phil begins to pace inside his cell.] I'm tired of this cell, man. I'm going crazy in here. Man, I'm bored. I can't stand it in here. I've already slept as much as I can, and I can't read no more. So I just sit here doing nothing but think, and that's making me even angrier, man, angry at this entire place. Fuck this.

Like Andre, Phil spoke of a boiling anger that turned into rage. Anger and rage are common effects of solitary confinement in adult institutions. In his review of the literature on solitary confinement in maximum-security prisons, Craig Haney (2003) reported that the overwhelming majority of supermax captives experience an intolerable sense of frustration, anger, and rage. This, then, results in further hostility toward guards, a hostility that is used to justify even further confinement and isolation. While most of the academic literature focuses on the experiences of adults in long-term solitary confinement, my ethnographic research suggests that these symptoms appear much sooner for confined children, especially when confronted by hostile guards who lack the training to counsel youth and de-escalate conflict. Guards then rely on violence to force young men into their cells and secure behavioral conformity.

Phil promised that once released from his cell, he would never return to it again. "I'll die before they put me in here again," he said. The next day, nearly two weeks after guards first slammed him to the ground, Phil held to his promise and refused to go to his cell. This time, Tyree, a guard known among the youth for being particularly brutal, slammed Phil to the ground. Four additional guards joined Tyree and forced Phil into his cell, handcuffed and screaming in pain. In the end, Phil received another black eye, a large rug burn on his chin, bruises on his arms, a bloody lip and nose, and a mild concussion from hitting his head against the wall. During the altercation, Phil reinjured his wrist. Later, Tyree passed by Phil's cell and asked, "How's your wrist, punk?" "Fuck you," Phil shouted back from his cell, where he remained for the next three days.

These displays of force figure prominently in children's stories about detention guards, reinforcing feelings of frustration, anger, and powerlessness. The physical assaults from guards are particularly traumatizing, because the youth cannot fight back, lest they face additional charges for custodial assault. When Phil was slammed, he didn't fight back, he threw no punches, but he did resist their attempts to handcuff him. He squirmed and wriggled his hands from their grasp. This "resistance" led to the guards' use of even more force.

I made sure to visit Phil every day that I was in the detention center. Our conversations, however, were usually blocked by a heavy steel door, so we spoke through the cracks. Phil had endured a lot of loneliness inside his cell, and it had taken its toll on his spirit. He spoke of feeling hopeless. "There's just nothing to look forward to in here," he told me. "You know, if I had something to look forward to, it wouldn't be that bad. Nothing is looking up. Every time I think it can't get any worse, something else comes up. I'm losing hope, man." I noticed a few cuts on his hands and arms. "How'd that happen?" I asked. "I did it," he admitted.

Phil, like several other youth in detention, had begun cutting his skin. He explained that he had started cutting his arms during the past week, after the guards slammed him. "I like the rush from the pain," he said. "In here, I just feel numb, like I'm empty, but at the same time, I'm so angry. When I cut myself, I feel something; I feel alive." Phil found comfort in self-mutilation, and it was a habit he picked up in detention. Although some youth come to detention with a tendency to self-mutilate, others develop the habit inside detention walls. Phil told me that he had never cut himself on the outside, but inside his cell, cutting provided a release from all of the anger and frustration he held deep inside. Phil was certainly not alone. Psychologists have consistently found self-mutilation to be a common response to prolonged exposure to solitary confinement.[8]

He wrote a particularly poignant essay about self-mutilation, his thoughts of suicide, and life in detention. He slid the essay underneath his door one evening, saying, "This is for you. I thought you might be able to use it for your research." The essay read:

> *Death, is it the way out? I wonder as I cut myself and watch the blood as it puddles on the cell floor. When I tell people that they look at me like I were a fool, but they can't know the amount of pain, remorse, anger, and fear that I hide deep inside. I go on a pass to see my mom, and she cries. I know why, it's because of me. I don't understand how she can love something that's not hers, something she picked up at a place, like a store for kids with lost souls. Maybe in those first minutes of life when my parents decided to disown me, evil decided to own me. But, what if this is all a blessing from god? What if he chose us before we were born to live this life to test society?*
>
> *We aren't criminals, we don't need your bars. Yes, you can lock us up, but you can't stop our minds. I sit and listen to the kids locked up with me and they are some of the smartest and most dedicated people I know. Maybe it's because we are a different race, not bound by color or our society. I can learn more from a "criminal" who has*

> *been through what I have been through better than any school or rehabilitation center can teach me.*
>
> *My mom looks at me as a criminal that gang bangs. You know why there are gangs? It's because we all understand each other. The court looks at me as a felon, but the things I did were mistakes you make growing up in a world they can't see. My world, not made by choices, but a world that I was born into. Treatment that means nothing. You want to know what works? Love, love is the only thing that will "fix" us.*

Phil's essay captures the sentiment of most of the youth I talked to in detention, who have spent considerable time in their cells, isolated from their peers. It highlights his changing conception of himself, an ambivalent conception molded out of months of confinement. Phil knew he was seen as a criminal, and in moments of deep reflection, he wondered if the guards were right—if he truly were evil. The brutality from guards, the days of loneliness in his cell, and the aggressive way guards spoke to him all had degraded his conception of self. He cut his arms and even contemplated suicide.

Suicide, unfortunately, is relatively common in juvenile institutions. The National Center on Institutions and Alternatives (Hayes, 2004) identified 110 cases of suicide in juvenile facilities between 1995 and 1999. It found that children with a history of cell confinement accounted for 62% of all suicides, and nearly 50% of the suicides occurred while children were penalized with cell confinement. Phil had spent more time in his cell than he thought he can handle. It was in these moments, as he stared blankly through the narrow window of his cell, that he looked down at his feet and wondered if this was what his future held. He was scared, but there was nobody to talk to about it. He wondered if death might be "the way out."

It was clear to me, and many other outside observers, that the use of solitary confinement caused an incredible amount of harm to Phil and other youth like him. The cuts on his arms, his ideations of suicide, his growing frustration and anger were all warning signs ignored by the staff at Rosy Meadows. Detention officials instead viewed these symptoms as proof of his pathological character, rather than recognizing them as having been caused by the dehumanizing situation that has become the hallmark of juvenile justice. As a result, guards tightened the bolts of his confinement and confined him to even longer periods of isolation. Reflecting on the lessons learned from the Stanford prison experiment, a psychological study on life inside prison, Haney and Zimbardo (1998) reported:

> Widespread prison management problems . . . are best understood in systematic terms, as at least in large part the products of worsening overall institutional conditions. Viewing them instead as caused exclusively by

> "problem prisoners" who require nothing more than isolated and segregated confinement ignores the role of compelling situational forces that help to account for their behavior. (p. 716)

In the cases of Phil and many other youth locked up in juvenile facilities, these punitive institutional conditions have become normalized and spawn resistance from the young men. This in turn requires even more force, creating a cycle of violence that threatens to spin out of control, leaving the lives of children in detention and youth prisons in ruins. The capacity of juvenile institutions to inflict harm on detained and incarcerated young people has increased with the rise of the "get tough on crime" movement. A growing number of young people are held in institutions that resemble adult prisons. Many juvenile facilities have added maximum-security units to control and manage "problem youth."

Accompanying this shift in juvenile policy is a poisoning of the interactions between guards and youth. Guards are no longer trained to counsel the children under their charge; instead, they learn the proper use of physical force techniques, how to engage five-point restraints, and how to recognize the "sociopathic" personality. The binary of social worker and law enforcer that characterized juvenile justice work in the past has shifted toward the extreme of law enforcement. In my years of researching at Rosy Meadows, not a single guard believed the institution did anything positive for the youth. Some guards lamented that it was only about "safety and security." Given these shifts in juvenile justice policy, most youth no longer trust detention officials to protect their safety, let alone provide for their rehabilitation.

As many of the youth lash out at their ill-equipped state-issued guardians, their behavior is viewed as further evidence of their pathology, rather than a symptom of a pathological institution. For example, Phil's response to weeks of solitary confinement was used against him in juvenile court. The judge didn't see how Phil was treated in detention or how he was slammed to the ground by guards twice his size. The judge saw only his list of disciplinary infractions, his institutional file, so Phil was eventually sent off to a youth prison for a year, where he spent even more time in a cinder-block cage for children. It's hard to believe the state couldn't find a better solution to deal with a young man whose initial crime was taking his stepmother's car for a joyride.

Danny's Story: "I Am an Average Man at the Scene of a Crime"

I can still hear Danny's screams, even though he was slammed to the ground more than a decade ago. It was hard watching a 13-year-old yelling in pain as five grown men twisted his body into unnatural positions. I wanted to protect him, but I felt powerless. While Danny was in detention, I made a commitment to visit him four days a week. I sometimes ate the gut-wrenching bland dinner with him and played cards, or if a cool guard was on duty, we played basketball in the courtyard for 15 minutes—his only exercise. I brought him books to read and made the same agreement that I made with other youth: read a book, write a report, and I'll bring another.

I was in graduate school at the time, and Danny damn near broke my bank account. I started out buying new books, but after he had read so many, I scoured the used bookstores. I began by smuggling in street novels by Donald Goines, a favorite of the young men in detention. As he developed, I pushed his reading farther and brought books like *Makes Me Wanna Holler* by Nathan McCall and *The Autobiography of Malcolm X* as told to Alex Haley. We talked a lot about the books he read, and it was clear that he was serious about his education. He had a thirst for knowledge, but it was being stifled by the detention center, which kept him from attending school with the other youth.

In all of his interactions with adults in juvenile detention, I was one of the few who took the time to listen to him, and I learned more than my 25-year-old mind could possibly have imagined. Danny was just 13 when he was brought to detention. He was charged with taking a motor vehicle, possession of crack cocaine, and eluding arrest. His father had taught him how to break into vehicles when he was 9 years old. While in detention, he was placed on what is euphemistically called a "special intervention program," where he was kept in solitary confinement for months at a time in a unit all by himself and completely isolated from the other youth. He spent 23 hours a day in his cell, with one hour out to eat, exercise, shower, and sometimes talk with me. When his case was reviewed every three days, detention supervisors always decided to extend his time in solitary. They considered him incorrigible, a lost cause who was better off kept in a cell. The entire time I volunteered in detention, he was never released from solitary confinement.

While in his cell, he would sometimes lash out at his keepers, shout profanities, bang his feet against the steel door, and flood his cell. I was never quite sure what the guards expected. Did they think that at age 13, Danny would sit quietly in his cell with the discipline of a Buddhist monk? As Danny lashed out at the guards, they responded with even more force. They turned off his water, removed his mattress, and cleared his cell of books, letters, and personal items. Some days he would go 24 hours without the ability to flush his toilet. I observed guards make fun of him, laugh at him, and say things about his mother, just to get a rise out of him. He didn't back down and would fight back, at least as much as his 13-year-old body would allow. This only led to more time in his cell, and with every day, I saw him descend into a sense of hopelessness, confusion, and anger. Danny was convinced the guards were trying to "break him" and tear away his spirit. He felt alone.

After my visits with him, I drove home, grabbed a bottle of wine, and cried, something I hadn't done in years. Growing up, I'd considered myself hardened. By that time, I had already lost three friends to suicide and murder, and even more to the adult prison system. I had seen a lot and rarely cried when I lost a friend, but there was something about Danny's story that shook me to the core. I worried that Danny would take his life, because deep down, I knew that if faced with the same treatment, I probably would. One evening, about a week before his trial, I decided to write a letter to the judge about what I had seen during my visits with him, hoping that it might lead to a lesser sentence and finally get him the treatment he deserved. I penned the following letter:

> *Your Honor,*
>
> *My name is Christopher Bickel and I have been a volunteer and mentor to detained and incarcerated youth for two years. Today, my fingers type with a profound urgency because I am terribly alarmed by how Danny Rockford has been and continues to be treated by the functionaries of juvenile justice. He has spent the last three months in solitary confinement-like conditions, living 23 hours a day in a 6 × 8 cell. This is the context in which Danny's behavior inside the detention center must be understood. That thick, official file from which you must base your decision is disturbingly one-sided. It tells of his actions, his behaviors, but it doesn't tell you about the other side, about how he has been treated inside the secured walls and how that affects his behavior, or more importantly, his view of the world.*
>
> *I have spent the last four months mentoring, teaching, listening and learning from Danny. In that time, I have witnessed first hand Danny's struggle to deal with the feelings evoked by his confinement, neglect and abuse. He is strong, much stronger than any 14 year-old should ever have to be, but I worry that he will falter under the weight of it all if he sent to a state institution.*
>
> *Danny is an exceptionally bright young man with a lot of potential. At first, I was surprised and even overwhelmed by his desire to learn. I made a deal with Danny. I promised that I would bring in a new book of his choice as long he wrote a four-page report, expressing his feelings about the book. At the time, to be honest, I had no idea how many books he would eventually read. Everyday I came in, three times a week, he had finished reading and reporting on the previous book I gave him.*
>
> *Your honor, I have worked with a lot of incarcerated teenagers and I sincerely believe that Danny is on the cusp of change. He is now thinking critically about his life, about his past and his future.*

Drug and alcohol treatment, I hope will be a part of that future. It certainly will help him grow to his potential rather than stifle him as the state institutions have so clearly done. Danny is ready to change, and I hope the court has the courage to change with him by offering the help he needs. Please, your Honor, allow Danny the treatment he needs. His life, his hopes, his dreams depend on it. Thank you for your time.

Respectfully, Christopher Bickel

I submitted the letter on a Thursday and was kicked out of the detention center the following Monday, despite the years I had dedicated to working there with detained youth. Although there were no rules stating that I couldn't write a letter to the judge, the director of the detention center decided that I was a liability and asked the volunteer coordinator to relieve me of my duties. I later persuaded the director to allow me to say good-bye to the youth I had worked with over the years. I was given permission to say good-bye, but I had to be escorted by two guards.

My letter, of course, didn't work. The judge later sentenced Danny to three and a half years, during which he was housed at several different facilities throughout the state. Luckily, I was also Danny's mentor through a program offered by the state juvenile rehabilitation system. I was able to visit him occasionally at a maximum-security facility for young men. At the youth prisons, Danny was again placed in solitary confinement, in what is called the "intensive management unit." He spent 23 hours a day in his cell, and during the one hour a day out of his solitary confinement cell, he was placed in a larger room with bright white walls, a pull-up bar, and a surveillance camera—nothing else. Every time he wrote a letter to me, he was in solitary confinement. I asked Danny, "How long have you been in solitary confinement?" He told me,

The short answer is 90% of the time. Any time I was let out, I would be back within two to three weeks without fail. The long answer is, in juvenile detention, I spent 70 to 80% of the time in solitary, and the majority of that was spent in a pod all by myself with nobody to interact with, nobody to talk to. As for the youth prisons, I spent 90% of the time in solitary. I would go two to three months on essential "strip cell," with no books, writing paper, etc. The swine would take all my bedding, mattress, paper, books, any property in my room at 6 A.M. and only return it at 10 P.M. And it all would happen again the next morning. Bear in mind that I am only allowed one T-shirt, socks, underwear, and a pair of shorts in a bare

> *concrete- and steel-filled cell that is freezing all day. This forced me to do anything and everything to get out of my cell (threaten suicide, cover the window with toilet paper so the guards would come in and ultimately attack me!) or at least to keep warm by way of kicking my door, yelling at the guards, and breaking my sprinkler system.*

The yelling, kicking, and attempts to resist his keepers only led to more time in solitary. He wore an oversize orange suit, and any time he was moved from his cell, he was forced into five-point restraints. He wore shackles on his ankles and handcuffs on his wrists, and both were connected to a chain around his waist. During one visit, I requested that the chains be removed. The large, muscular guard refused, stating that the 5-foot, 4-inch 15-year-old was a security threat. I became angry but tried not to show it. "Don't trip, Chris," Danny said. "I'm used to it. And, man, I don't want them to cancel our visit."

He received few visits in detention. His father was in prison, and his mother couldn't afford the long trips to visit him. As time wore on, Danny picked up a number of charges for custodial assault and was eventually given a juvenile life sentence by the court. Danny described one example of a custodial assault in a letter:

> *I was jumped by guards at Shady Acres [a youth prison]. I don't really know what started it all, but I do remember them coming into my cell to take me down. They were kneeing me in the side of my head when I was laying on the ground, which caused part of my ear to be ripped from my scalp and blood was all over the place. On top of that, they did something to my wrist, which caused everything from my elbow to my hand to swell up. I thought it was broke, because I couldn't move it. Finally after two or three days, they took me to an outside hospital for x-rays. It wasn't broke but I had a really bad sprain. . . . I was charged with custodial assault, because they said that during the "use of force" I elbowed one of the guards when I yanked my hand from their grasp.*

When guards deploy violence to control youth in solitary confinement, they gather a group of four or five large men to secure compliance. The use of physical force is a frequent occurrence in juvenile facilities across the United States. In his review of the California Youth Authority, Krisberg (2003) found that in one institution with a population of 872 youth, the guards had used physical force 109 times, pepper spray 535 times, and mechanical restraints 236 times.

Although Danny was housed in a different state, he said that physical force was a regular occurrence for him and other youth in solitary. Danny told me in another letter:

> *Force was used on me around once a week, and it was almost always unjustified. I was given more criminal charges for defending myself against their assaults, and they made me out to be the perpetrator. How are four to five grown men a victim to a 15–16 year old, 5'7", 160-pound kid, when they had the choice to come in the cell. Not to mention, I was the one that had to be treated by medical for injuries, and/or taken to the hospital.*

Some might be tempted to doubt the truth of Danny's recollections. Perhaps I would, too, had I not witnessed similar circumstances at Rosy Meadows and other juvenile institutions. I watched guards use physical force on youth on several occasions, and it was difficult to watch. Quite often guards would unnecessarily knee young men in their ribs and bend their wrists back, and on occasion they would take shots at their faces with closed fists. Anita, a guard who was appalled by the use of violence in detention, shared this story with me:

> There was one time when a staff beat up a kid. You know he was taunting the kid. The kids know when the staff don't like them. The guy actually followed the kid into the cell and started hitting him in the chest and face with his fist. Three staff saw it and the guy was written up. He was under investigation for a while, but he was never fired. He was back on the floor. I mean, everybody knew about it to the point where everybody was talking about it out in the open. But nothing happened. Nothing changed. The management wouldn't do anything. Those that blew the whistle were punished for speaking out. They weren't promoted when they should have been, and they never will be.

There is a well-documented culture of violence among guards in juvenile facilities. Part of the problem lies with the training they receive at the academy. Guards are told to be prepared at all times, to watch their backs, and to use physical force in ways that are acceptable only inside detention walls. Guards learn how to use chemical sprays, self-defense tactics, five-point restraints, and takedown techniques, all of which are framed as normal and legitimate operating procedures when dealing with "potentially violent" detainees. "Safety and security" is the mantra, and all forms of violence are justified under its banner.

Aside from the training, there is a hypermasculine culture among guards that is reproduced and maintained through interactions that place a high value on the ability to use physical force and violence. Guards gain acceptance from their coworkers by exhibiting their toughness, a peacocklike display that proves they can handle their jobs and enforce the rules. When new guards, particularly women, arrive at the detention center, they must prove to their male coworkers that they can handle the job. For example at Rosy Meadows, Alana, a recent college graduate, experienced weeks of harassment from her male coworkers before they accepted her into their ranks. She heard rumors that they thought she was too soft. Alana consulted with other women on the job. One said they had done the same thing to her until she wrestled a kid to the ground. They left her alone shortly after the takedown. After Alana, too, responded to a fight and had to physically take down the youth, a few guards stopped by her unit later in the day to pat her on the back and say, "Nice job." In this way, the bodies of children become mere props on the stage where guards act out their toughness and prove their worthiness as detention officers.

The problem of violence in juvenile facilities is amplified because most guards receive little if any training on how to de-escalate conflict. So when young men like Danny flood their cells or break their sprinkler system, the guards respond in the only way they know how: with force. The time spent in solitary confinement, coupled with the violence required to enforce it, takes a terrible toll on the youth who must endure it. Danny reflected on the time he had spent in juvenile facilities when I asked him what it had been like to spend so much time in solitary:

> *I would constantly feel weak and fatigued, sleeping sometimes for over half of the day. It would sometimes be a struggle just to do 10 pushups, because I never had any physical exercise. The psychological effects, however, were far more intense. I often cut on myself to relieve the stress and anxiety. I was constantly having thoughts of suicide, and sometimes I would hear voices. I would feel aggravated for little to no reason. The simple sounds of doors opening and closing, toilets flushing, and vents blowing would irritate me.*

Danny's experience with solitary confinement was remarkably similar to that of adults in supermax prisons across the United States. In their review of the literature on solitary confinement, Arrigo and Bullock (2008) found that fatigue, lethargy, self-mutilation, hypersensitivity to noises, and ideations of suicide were common responses to long-term isolation. Shalev (2008) reviewed the contemporary research on the effects of solitary confinement and found the common physical side effects to be heart palpitations, lethargy, hypersensitivity to noises and smells, and insomnia. The list of psychological effects includes a sense of hopelessness, hostility and anger, poor concentration and memory, social withdrawal, self-mutilation, and suicide. Haney (1993) studied men held in solitary confinement at Pelican Bay State Prison in California, who were confined to their cells for 23 hours a day with limited social interaction and sensory stimulation. He found that 91% of the men suffered from anxiety, 77% endured chronic depression, and 70% feared they were on the edge of a mental breakdown.

Danny, however, was only 13 years old when he began to experience these same symptoms. In 1999, he sent me a statement from a psychiatrist that was submitted to the court during one of his cases:

> *I am firmly convinced that Mr. Rockford suffers from an extreme version of Complex Posttraumatic Stress Disorder. This disorder started in early childhood and has been both chronic and severe. But, the consequences of the years spent inside a cinderblock cage are far more than physical, or even psychological; they have also dramatically shaped how he sees the world, the prison, and the guards who maintain it. A world that allows a 13 year old to be kept in a cage for years is a world he will resist until the day he dies.*

Danny wrote in a letter to me:

> *My years in solitary confinement have taught me great lessons about the level of inhumanity of people. Solitary reinforced my hatred and discontent for the guards, and really it reinforced my desire to fight back. I honestly believe the institutional purpose of solitary confinement is nothing more than their way of "breaking" us in order to capture and control our thoughts and actions. This experience has provided me with a great insight into hell here on earth.*

It is now more than a decade since I first met Danny, and he has not seen freedom since that day I heard his screams at Rosy Meadows. His three-and-a-half-year sentence turned into an 11-year sentence, and he doesn't expect to be released until 2020. When he turned 18, he was immediately sent to adult prison, where he hoped he would finally be able to see his father. At prison, he picked up additional custodial assault charges and was again placed in solitary confinement. When I have told his story to my students at the university where I teach, they have been horrified at the injustice of such an inhumane juvenile justice system.

One of my university students, however, asked a question that was probably on the minds of others: "Why does he continue to resist the guards when they keep giving him more time?" I understand the question. As a friend and mentor to Danny, I desperately want to see him free, to be able to hug him and tell him that life is better outside prison walls, to show him that people are better than what he has seen so far in his life. Yet I also understand his resistance. From a young age, the state took one of his most valuable possessions: his childhood. All he has left is his sense of humanity, which he clings on to with all of his energy. When I relayed my student's question in a letter to Danny, he replied by mail:

> *In fighting back against a system and situational forces, one does not disillusion themself [sic] to believe that they are going to win the actual war and bring the system to its knees in surrender. Rather one fights in hopes of winning battles, requiring the system to change its tactics. I believe the civil rights movement to be an example of such resistance. The masses that were resisting and demanding change did not actually believe that they would trigger an immediate change within the system, rather they realized that with continued pressure throughout time, eventually the system would change. Somebody has got to do it, and, as a person who has endured more than most, I feel obligated to resist and sacrifice myself for the greater cause. I would like you to stress to your students that my actions are not an attempt to satisfy "Maslow's Hierarchy of Needs" or some twisted sense of self-actualization, or to be some type of martyr; but rather, I am an average man at the scene of a crime, doing what needs to be done to seek the furtherance of justice.*

Solitary Confinement and the Theft of Childhood

In this chapter, I have documented what Danny called "the scene of a crime," as witnessed and experienced by the young men at Rosy Meadows. Following the "Marionization" of adult prisons, an equally dramatic shift has occurred in juvenile justice policy toward more incarceration and punishment and less rehabilitation (Immarigeon, 1992; Richards, 2008). Since the 1980s, federal and state legislators have passed several punitive laws designed to target youth, particularly youth of color. At the federal level, the Violent and Repeat Juvenile Offender Act of 1997 encouraged the prosecution of more juveniles as adults, steepened the penalties for gang-related offenses, and increased the use of mandatory minimums for juvenile offenders. At the state level, an increasing number have passed laws to lower the age at which juveniles can be tried as adults. Some states allowed children as young as 14 to be tried in adult criminal courts, while others have no minimum age at all.

The push toward incarcerating more juveniles in secure facilities, where children will endure the pains of solitary confinement, has produced troubling results. If success is measured by how many children are arrested after their release, then most states are failing miserably. For example, according to the Center for Juvenile and Criminal Justice (2007), nearly 91% of those released from the California Youth Authority (now called the Division of Juvenile Justice) were arrested within three years. Krisberg (2005) reported that in Pennsylvania, nearly 55% of released juveniles were rearrested within 18 months, and in Utah 79% were rearrested within a year.

The stories of Mario, Andre, Phil, and Danny provide insight into this tragic failure of juvenile justice policy over the past 30 years. Juvenile justice officials and criminologists have grossly underestimated the physical and psychological damages that cell confinement causes youth trapped inside cinder-block cages. Most officials justify the use of solitary confinement as a tool for rehabilitation or for the management of "dangerous" youth. The young men in this essay, however, suggest it is an instrument for the cruel, inhumane, and degrading treatment of children, who are ultimately robbed of their childhood.

Solitary confinement poisons the young men's relationship with their state-issued guardians, perpetuates and even requires institutional violence to secure compliance, and reinforces their desire to resist the guard's attempts to control them. As the young men lash out at their keepers, bang their fists against steel doors, and flood their cells with toilet water, the guards see their behavior as further evidence of their pathological character and push for even more punitive measure to control the youth under their supervision. These acts of resistance, however, are symptoms of a pathological institution that is designed more to control and manage low-income children than to provide for their rehabilitation.

The use of solitary confinement is a human rights tragedy and a violation of international law, particularly the United Nations Rules for the Protection of Juveniles Deprived of Their Liberty (United Nations, 1990). The consequences of confining thousands of children to prison cages are heartbreaking, not only for those condemned to captivity, but also for the detention guards, who must ultimately come to terms with the fact that their jobs do little to help the children they deal with on a daily basis.

The story of Rosy Meadows juvenile detention center, like the stories of most penal facilities for juveniles, is not simply about an ineffective institution that fails to rehabilitate children. It is a far more catastrophic story about how the functionaries of juvenile justice cast children as "criminals" and, in the process, rob them of their childhood.

Mario, Andre, Phil, and Danny were never accused of violent offenses on the street. Their charges were only property and drug related. But Rosy Meadows treated them like violent criminals and ultimately ushered them into the adult prison system.

Mario eventually served adult time in prison. Andre is still incarcerated. Phil spent time in adult jail, although he is now out. And Danny still does time in a prison, never having experienced freedom since the age of 13. As documented in this chapter, the use of solitary confinement in juvenile institutions serves to further criminalize youth, preparing them for adult prisons. The experience of confinement leaves scars and wounds for those young men who, in many ways, were simply victims at "the scene of a crime."

Notes

1. All names have been changed to protect the youth I interviewed, some of whom may still be incarcerated. I have changed the name of the detention center as well.
2. See Amnesty International, 1998.
3. See Arrigo and Bullock, 2008; Haney, 2003.
4. See Inderbitzen, 2007.
5. For a more detailed discussion of my methodology, see Bickel, 2010.
6. See Shelden, 2008.
7. See Arrigo and Bullock, 2008; Haney, 2003.
8. See Grassian and Friedman, 1986; Haney, 2003; Shalev, 2009b.

19

Colorado Supermax Study: What the Critics Say and the Future Holds

Russ Immarigeon

The accelerating growth of American prison populations has been given widespread public attention in recent decades, but somewhat less known is the steep increase in the use of high-security prison operations, including the use of administrative segregation, punitive isolation, and "supermax" confinement. Several years ago, the widely touted Commission on Safety and Abuse in America's Prisons (2006) reported a 40% increase in the use of solitary confinement between 1995 and 2000 (during this same period, the American prison population experienced a 28% increase).

However, the current fiscal crisis in the United States, as well as state-by-state shifts in correctional policy and practice, may be changing the extent to which prison managers use solitary confinement, and perhaps the ways they do so. Johnson (2010) reported that in some states, for example Illinois, Mississippi, and Texas, "state prison officials are reducing the number of offenders in solitary confinement—once among the fastest-growing conditions of detention—as budget pressures, legal challenges, and concerns about the punishment's effectiveness mount."

Interestingly, in this context, the Colorado Department of Corrections released a research report in October 2010 that has stirred an already simmering pot of prison reform activity into a stranger—and clearly unresolved—brew of concerns about academic research, psychological intervention, and media coverage. The report, mildly titled *One Year Longitudinal Study of the*

Psychological Effects of Administrative Segregation (O'Keefe, Klebe, Stucker, Sturm, & Leggett, 2010), described an intensely focused research project on the impact of administrative segregation, another term for solitary confinement, on mentally ill and non–mentally ill prisoners at the Colorado State Penitentiary (CSP), a supermax prison in Colorado Springs. Despite the widespread belief that solitary confinement is damaging, the report suggested that administrative segregation has little comparative psychological damage on either mentally ill or non–mentally ill prisoners subjected to solitary confinement in Colorado.

In this chapter, I provide some historical and other background to this study and the response it has received so far. I describe the primary contents of the report and summarize the responses of various academic researchers, mental health practitioners, and prison reform activists who have provided commentary on the study. The chapter concludes with some observations of what the future holds for the use of solitary confinement.

Background

In August 2010, the National Geographic Society presented a documentary about the use of solitary confinement at the CSP. One of the Colorado study's principal investigators, Kelli Klebe, remarked in a symposium at an academic conference that "this was initially proposed to us as a documentary about the study." However, "it has very little information about the study, but it was filmed at CSP and the warden gave an interview as well as did CSP inmates" (Klebe 2010).

The National Geographic Society's website for this documentary included a variety of background pieces, one of them from Dr. Stuart Grassian, a Boston-area medical researcher who conducted interviews of high-security prisoners in Massachusetts in the mid-1980s. Grassian has been widely cited in newspaper and other media coverage of solitary confinement, and he was an invited consultant on the Colorado study. Grassian (2006) wrote:

> This literature as well as my own observations, have demonstrated that, deprived of a sufficient level of environmental and social stimulation, individuals will soon become incapable of maintaining an adequate state of alertness and attention to the environment. Indeed, even a few days of solitary confinement will predictably shift the electroencephalogram (EEG) pattern towards an abnormal pattern characteristic of stupor and delirium. (pp. 330–331)

How endemic is the practice of solitary confinement in American prison history? The historian David J. Rothman (1971) told us that early American prisons were of two types. In "congregate" prisons,

> prisoners were to sleep alone in a cell at night and labor together in a workshop during the day for the course of their fixed sentences in the penitentiary. They were forbidden to converse with fellow inmates or even exchange glances while on the job, at meals, or in their cells.

"Separate" prisons, however,

> isolated each prisoner for the entire period of his confinement. According to its blueprint, convicts were to eat, work, and sleep in individual cells, seeing and talking with only a handful of responsible guards and selected visitors. They were to leave the institution as ignorant of the identity of other convicts as on the day they entered. (p. 82)

"To both the advocates of the congregate and the separate systems," Rothman added, "the promise of institutionalization depended upon the isolation of the prisoner and the establishment of a disciplined routine" (p. 82).

Approximately two centuries after these congregate and separate prison systems were established in the United States, it is tempting to suggest that Rothman used the term "isolation" differently than we might when considering the contemporary practices of solitary confinement in state and federal institutions. While Rothman described the general isolation of all early American prisoners from their communities, today we think of isolation as a practice applied to those confined persons within prisons who violate rules, harm themselves or others, or threaten disruptive behavior.

Still, there are distinct differences in the uses of isolation as a disciplinary tool in the evolution of prison design, management, and operations. Rothman (1971) continued:

> Convinced that deviancy was primarily the result of the corruptions pervading the community, and that organizations like the family and the church were not counterbalancing them, they [advocates of the congregate and separate systems] believed that a setting which removed the offender from all temptations and substituted a steady and regular regimen would reform him. Since the convict was not inherently depraved, but the victim of an upbringing that had failed to provide protection against the vices loose in society, a well-ordered institution could successfully reeducate and rehabilitate him. The penitentiary, free of corruptions and dedicated to the proper training of the inmate, would inculcate the discipline that negligent parents, evil companions, taverns, houses of prostitution, theaters, and gambling halls had destroyed. Just as the criminal's environment had led him into crime, the institutional environment would lead him out of it. (pp. 82–83)

Unfortunately, American prisons no longer hold or nurture the visionary values they once aspired to achieve. Instead, they have increasingly become "holding tanks," with record numbers of prisoners being held for short or long terms and frequently for life terms.

Contemporary prisons are organized around classification systems that place prisoners at different security levels, each generally defined by one or another characteristic or purpose. Classification systems,[1] particularly those involving discretionary decision making, seem ill fitting, especially for some. Maximum-security custody, for example, was classically designed for the "worst" prisoners, those most dangerous to themselves, other prisoners or staff members, or the larger society outside prison walls. But new forms of confinement were eventually designed to hold "the worst of the worst" (Ward, 2009, p. 4; Mears, Mancini, Beaver, & Gertz, 2009), separate institutions (e.g., supermax prisons) or specific units (e.g., intensive management units) where prison officials could house those convicts deemed unsuitable even for maximum-security confinement.

United States Penitentiary (USP) Alcatraz, opened in 1934, was a notorious prison where the federal government locked up a large number of infamous gangsters and bank robbers. While Alcatraz was not a supermax prison, as the convicts took their meals in the dining hall, worked in shops, and went outside to the yard, it did discipline convicts by removing them from their normal cells to do short or long periods in "the hole." The use of solitary confinement at Alcatraz was widely believed to have caused psychological disorders in the prisoners. However, the criminologist David Ward, who has reviewed the case files of former Alcatraz prisoners and conducted interviews with many of them, reported in 2009 that confinement in this prison did not generally cause "the onset of psychosis" (p. 453). Ward found mental health problems identified in only 41 of 508 case files, and only three of the 54 former prisoners he interviewed reported to him that their own mental health had been affected by their time at Alcatraz.

If prisoners in fact survive "the psychological challenges" of long-term confinement in solitary, how does this occur? Ward answered this question as follows:

> The inmates themselves had a clear idea of who was "crazy" and who was not; they made an important distinction between genuine mental illness and feelings of depression, frustration, anger, and hopelessness that almost every man experienced at one time or another. The majority of Alcatraz inmates—those not in the "crazy" category—were simply better equipped to stand up to the challenging conditions; after all they were old hands at doing time, including considerable time in tough state prisons [and federal penitentiaries]. They

> understood that spending some years behind bars was an inherent risk of the life of a bank robber or ransom kidnapper, and they brought to Alcatraz ways of adapting to, and coping with, harsh prison conditions. (p. 453)

Were the mid-20th-century bank robbers, kidnappers, and other men at Alcatraz better at adapting to and surviving their harrowing conditions of confinement than contemporary prisoners? Or was Ward's analysis just deeply flawed?

Perhaps this is why solitary confinement remains controversial. Many people, even those working in the field of corrections, have reservations about its use and consequences, because it is not the way they would want to be treated. "I would go crazy myself under those conditions," they might say. Or they may notice the effects that solitary confinement has on prisoners, and this raises certain concerns or at least some skepticism.

Accepting Ward's conclusion for the moment raises another question that resonates and merits inquiry. Assuming, as Ward suggested, that doing time at Alcatraz did not cause significant, long-lasting mental health effects for most of its inmates or preclude their successful adjustment in other prisons and later in the free world, is it possible that a penal environment designed specifically for severe punishment actually promotes the possibility of reform or rehabilitation in prisoners, even when the government does not expect or plan for that outcome? Well informed about "the worst of the worst," Ward still held out for reformation and rehabilitation.

The conflict between despair and hope, or between complete control and salvation, probably fired the sparks set off by the Colorado study and similar reports. The results have pushed us in different directions. What do we really know about mental or physical deterioration as a consequence of supermaximum-security solitary confinement? What do we know about individual survival as a consequence of supermaximum-security solitary confinement? And what do we know about the consequences of supermaximum-security solitary confinement that lies between these opposing outcomes?

The Colorado Study

Maureen O'Keefe of the Colorado Department of Corrections and psychologist Kelli Klebe and colleagues from the University of Colorado–Colorado Springs published the results of their research in *One Year Longitudinal Study of the Psychological Effects of Administrative Segregation* (O'Keefe et al., 2010). They reported being surprised by their findings, which suggested that administrative segregation was far less harmful than they had expected. Their study found that segregated prisoners experienced elevated measures of psychological and cognitive change, much like nonsegregated prisoners in the study's control group. The condition of mentally ill prisoners was more aggravated by their experiences of isolation than that of non–mentally ill prisoners, but this was true whether they were in segregation or general population. Moreover, prisoners seemed to improve as they initially entered administrative segregation.

The Colorado study involved 237 male prisoners (so any implications may not apply to women prisoners) who were held in administrative segregation (AS) or general population (GP). Each of these general groups was subsequently divided into mentally ill and non–mentally ill groups. Paper-and-pencil tests were administered to both groups at three-month intervals for approximately one year. Of the mentally ill prisoners, 56% had a serious and pervasive disorder.

A dozen psychological constructs were measured, including anxiety, cognitive impairment, depression or hopelessness, hostility or anger control, hypersensitivity, psychosis, somatization, withdrawal or alienation, malingering, self-harm, trauma, and personality disorder. The 12 self-report instruments used in the study were intended to demonstrate data reliability and validity, identify multiple data sources, conduct multiple assessments of each construct, and enable ease of use in a prison setting. Additional information was also culled from official records and clinical staff assessments.

Like other studies on solitary confinement, the Colorado study found that segregated prisoners had higher psychological and cognitive measures than "normative adults," but these elevated test scores were also found in nonsegregated prisoners. Non–mentally ill general population prisoners were the only test takers who seemed similar to normative adults. All test groups improved over time, with the bulk of this improvement occurring between the first and second test periods. Afterward, all seemed to settle down. Interestingly, withdrawal was the only measure that worsened over time, and this occurred only for the non–mentally ill groups.

All groups, except for the general population non–mentally ill group, showed signs of what Grassian (2006) had described as "severe psychiatric harm" (p. 333) in his numerous studies, which was also present throughout the Colorado study but more seriously for mentally ill prisoners. This harm included hyperresponsivity to external stimuli; perceptual distortions, illusions, hallucinations, and panic attacks; difficulties with thinking, concentration, and memory; intrusive obsessional thoughts; overt paranoia; problems with impulse control; and delirium (pp. 335–336.). Moreover, the Colorado researchers found few predictors of who would or would not be damaged by solitary confinement.

Much dialogue over the past few decades on the use of solitary confinement has revolved around the notion that solitary confinement is harmful, although the extent and nature of this harm has not always been clear. Still, stories of harm from prisoners who have experienced solitary confinement are compelling and worthy of review. Moreover, American and European studies have chronicled the deterioration and survival of severely isolated prisoners. Therefore, criticisms of the Colorado study quickly emerged: Was it methodologically sound? Was it conducted properly? What do its findings actually mean, not just for the treatment of prisoners, but also for the extent and nature of solitary confinement in penal institutions?

Almost immediately, controversy over the Colorado report erupted in public.[2] However, criticism of the study's design, implementation, and results was an internal, as well as external, aspect of the study from its beginning. As the report noted, critics of solitary confinement were invited not only to consult during the development of the project, but also to sit on the project's advisory board, which they did. In an update on the National Institute of Corrections website (Shalev & Lloyd, 2011), O'Keefe and Klebe, the principal investigators of the study, reported that advisory board members, including those who have been critics of solitary confinement, "ripped the study design apart and put it back together again in the best possible way." Before and after the report was released in October 2010, the principal investigators traveled to various venues to present their findings. At the annual American Psychological Association meetings in San Diego, O'Keefe was on a panel with Grassian, who had shared his perspectives with the principal investigators earlier in the study and perhaps was now the most outspoken critic of the study.

As of January 2012, the major sources of critical commentary published on the Colorado study were *Solitary Watch*, a website written and edited by journalists James Ridgeway and Jean Casella that focuses on solitary confinement; the May–June 2011 issue of *Correctional Mental Health Report*, which Fred Cohen edited for the Civic Research Institute and includes articles from the Colorado researchers and two advisory board members, as well as several critical overviews; and *Corrections & Mental Health*, which I edited for the National Institute of Corrections and contains the Colorado report's executive summary, six responses from American and European researchers and practitioners, and a response to the responders from the study's researchers. The report has also received coverage in Colorado, where prison reform advocates and state officials are involved in legal and legislative initiatives addressing conditions of confinement at the CSP, the supermax site of the study.

Overall, the Colorado study received praise from its detractors as well as its supporters on some matters. Notably, the Colorado corrections researchers have persistently examined administrative segregation over time.[3] However, the period of confinement in solitary was just one year. Observers seem to agree that the current study was an exceptional empirical undertaking. Some have noted that the researchers were especially careful in the organization and writing of their final research report, which undoubtedly stemmed at least in part from their own surprise at their findings.

However, criticism of the Colorado study remains, including the following:

- Some findings were not surprising, such as improvements experienced by AS and GP populations between the first and second testing periods, a time when both groups were returning from stressful disciplinary processing.
- Particular prisoners were removed from the AS group, including those with learning disabilities.
- AS prisoners had greater experience in solitary confinement than their GP counterparts.
- Prisoners were decontextualized from their solitary confinement.
- Prisoners respond differently to solitary confinement depending on their attitudes toward it.
- Prisoners received incentives to advance from one stage of solitary confinement to another, and these incentives were not integrated into assessments of prisoner perspectives of their confinement. (Also, these incentives may distinguish, and therefore separate, solitary confinement in Colorado from that in other states.)
- Prisoners often concealed not only symptoms of disturbance, but also overall perspectives on their confinement to researchers and to themselves, often as a means of masking the appearance of weakness.

Beyond these and other divergent perspectives, one observation by Shalev and Lloyd, (2011) may be particularly prescient:

> Solitary confinement is not a natural state for us as social creatures who require human contact and human touch to maintain our very sense of "self." It is difficult to see how prison systems, which officially aim to rehabilitate offenders and assist their reintegration into society, propose to provide prisoners with the social skills and tools necessary for living alongside others by withholding social contact. In many super-maxes prisoners spend many years and in some cases even decades in conditions of extreme solitary confinement. It is possible that some of the deeper and longer lasting deficits that result from solitary confinement only reveal themselves once the prisoner is exposed again to the real world. Certainly interviews with former prisoners who have spent long stretches of time in solitary confinement suggest that the pains of isolation remained with them long after their release and that those who did not manifest serious mental illness were nonetheless deeply scarred by the experience. In this context, the finding that withdrawal/alienation increased over time in the segregated group is worrying in terms of potential impact on rehabilitation and resettlement. (p. 5)

In short, as other researchers have suggested, the study does not actually—or accurately—depict the deterioration of individual prisoners held in solitary confinement. Instead, this is a matter left for a further study, unless the results of past research, including that done in Europe, are given renewed attention.

The Future of Solitary Confinement

The Colorado study and the responses that have come forth suggest contrasting prospects for the future of solitary confinement. On the one hand, it is not likely to disappear from the penal landscape. On the other hand, the extent and nature of its future use are unclear, subject to the endurance or volatility of a variety of correctional, economic, legal, political, or programmatic spheres of influence. Currently, we do not know much about how correctional administrators, managers, superintendents, or wardens will respond to the Colorado research. No members of these groups, as far as I know, have commented, at least in print, on the Colorado report. But in time, they probably will. The report will likely become a topic of discussion at prison manager meetings or in mainstream corrections-oriented publications such as *Corrections Today* or *American Jails*. And at some point, too, the study's findings may become a centerpiece of policy- and practice-oriented deliberations on the use of solitary confinement.

Or it's possible that the study will have little influence. The Colorado report referred to Canadian research (Zinger, Wichmann, & Andrews, 2001) investigating the short-term impact of administrative segregation and finding roughly similar results. Little evidence is available that this study affected Canadian solitary confinement practices one way or another. In their article, Zinger and colleagues stated that the study results should not be used to justify the practice of administrative segregation. In a conversation during my preparation of this chapter, Zinger, now executive director and general counsel for the Office of the Correctional Investigator in Canada, observed that while administrative segregation has long been overused, its general use has not increased over the past decade or so. He said that the lack of research on the fundamental questions about the psychological impact of administrative segregation is shameful. In Canada, he added, alternatives to administrative segregation, such as transitional units, intermediate care units, and structured living environments, have not been given adequate attention or implementation.

Although for different reasons, consensus among the Colorado study's researchers and critics does not seem to suggest that its findings are immediately applicable to solitary confinement practices in other jurisdictions, and they may not be clearly applicable even within Colorado. The study was done in part to collect data that could be used in court to defend the Colorado

Department of Corrections from a series of pending lawsuits. In 2011, Tom Clements became the new executive director of the Colorado Department of Corrections. Clements was critical of the use of long-term segregation of prisoners in solitary confinement. He made a number of changes in supermax custody, including reducing by half the number of prisoners confined in administrative segregation. This included transferring hundreds of mentally ill prisoners to residential treatment housing units. He was especially concerned about prisoners that had suffered months or years in solitary confinement being released directly to the streets upon completion of their prison sentences (Greene, 2013).

Tragically, and perhaps with some irony, Director Clements was assassinated by a newly released convict who had been in solitary confinement. On March 19, 2013, the gunman dressed as a pizza delivery person rang Tom Clements's doorbell and shot him dead. Apparently, the convict released from a Colorado supermax just two months prior had no idea the man he killed was working to dramatically reform the prison policies that had caused his own mental deterioration. As Erica Goode reported in the *New York Times* (2014),

> Tom Clements, Colorado's previous executive director of corrections, was convinced that many inmates in segregation cells—Colorado made extensive use of solitary confinement—did not need to be there. He was particularly worried about the state's habit of releasing some prisoners from long-term isolation directly onto the streets, with no transition. Mr. Clements's killer, Evan S. Ebel, who died in a shootout later with the police, was one such prisoner. (p. A16)

In 2013, Rick Raemisch, the former head of the Wisconsin Department of Corrections, was hired to manage Colorado's prisons. Seven months after he was hired, Raemisch decided to spend 20 hours inside a solitary confinement cell, just to see what it was really like. In his own *New York Times* opinion piece, Raemisch (2014) wrote,

> I would spend a total of 20 hours in that cell. Which, compared with the typical stay, is practically a blink. On average, inmates who are sent to solitary in Colorado spend an average of 23 months there. Some spend 20 years . . .
>
> My predecessor, Tom Clements, who was as courageous a reformer as they come, felt the same way. Mr. Clements had already gone a long way to reining in the overuse of solitary confinement in Colorado. In little more than two years, he and his staff cut it by more than half: from 1,505 inmates (among the highest rates in the country) to 726. As of January, the number was down to 593. (We have also gotten the number of severely mentally ill inmates in Ad Seg down to the single digits.)

> But Mr. Clements had barely begun his work when he was assassinated last March. In a tragic irony, he was murdered in his home by a gang member who had been recently released directly from Ad Seg. This former inmate murdered a pizza delivery person, allegedly for the purpose of wearing his uniform to lure Mr. Clements to open his front door. A few days later, the man was killed in a shootout with the Texas police after he had shot an officer during a traffic stop. Whatever solitary confinement did to that former inmate and murderer, it was not for the better.
>
> When I finally left my cell at 3 P.M., I felt even more urgency for reform. If we can't eliminate solitary confinement, at least we can strive to greatly reduce its use. Knowing that 97 percent of inmates are ultimately returned to their communities, doing anything less would be both counterproductive and inhumane. (p. A 25)

In short, there is no indication yet about what, if anything, Colorado prison officials are going to do in response to the Colorado Prison Study research findings. It may be the report gathers dust on a shelf, and that may ultimately be all the attention it deserves. Although prison reform activists, legislators, and journalists in Colorado have been carefully monitoring and reviewing solitary confinement practices in the state, the long-term policy changes are equally uncertain. However, despite what the report says, and how by design it obscures the harm done by solitary confinement to prisoners, it does appear that the unfortunate death of Tom Clements and the hiring of Rick Raemisch have resulted in significant reductions in the use and abuse of solitary confinement in Colorado.

The Colorado Prison Study, and subsequent events discussed above, will at least attract attention in some other jurisdictions. Still, other prison systems may totally ignore what Colorado does or be inclined to fashion their own responses, and this raises some cautionary red flags. In particular, I am reminded of Robert Martinson's 1974 report on correctional rehabilitation, which has become a major case study in the misuse of correctional research.

After reviewing a massive collection of research evaluations of diverse correctional intervention programs and practices, Martinson concluded that nothing works. His report was misinterpreted by the media, politicians, and correctional administrators. Then the research was used to support new policies that reduced vocational and educational program expenditures in some prison systems. This is not what Martinson had intended. He became so distraught that his academic work had been misappropriated by political forces determined to terminate prison rehabilitation that he committed suicide by jumping out a window. Like the Colorado Prison Study, which reported that not much separates those in solitary confinement and those in the general population, Martinson also had reported that not much was different as a result of correctional intervention.

One lesson of the Martinson meta study was that the grand scale of the research may have masked important findings buried under the weight of a large database. A second lesson was that even the original reports had not been adequately reviewed by policy makers or practitioners, which resulted in serious misunderstanding, misinterpretation, and misapplication, and this may have contributed to the termination of prison programs that did work. Few policy makers ever bothered to read Martinson's original report, which eventually was published as a book (Lipton, Martinson, & Wilks, 1975), earlier magazine article (Martinson 1972), or subsequent journal article (Martinson 1979) commenting on his research findings. Instead, the idea that nothing works to rehabilitate convicts became an official excuse for cutting funding for educational and vocational programs that operated inside the prisons.

Finally, the Colorado report by O'Keefe et al. (2010) concluded:

> Questions about the efficacy of AS will be asked until more is known about whether the use of AS in prison systems improves conditions for the rest of the system, whether and how they improve inmate behavior within and beyond the prison walls, whether they are cost-effective, whether they increase risks to public safety, and whether there are settings or individuals that are prone to psychological deterioration. (p. 11)

Thus this study did not claim to tell us much about whether AS changes prisoner behavior for the better. Moreover, it claimed no insight into the effectiveness of AS to produce a safer prison system through significant reductions in prisoner movement with access to other prisoners, prison services, or even so-called prison amenities. Or as Rhodes and Lovell (2011), critics of the Colorado study, have suggested:

> The "adaptation to isolation" tested by the Colorado study is not the solution to super-max confinement; rather, it is a problem not only for the individual, but also ultimately for those around him. We should ask instead whether requiring individuals to adapt to extreme conditions, and then approaching them as the non-relational beings that those conditions suggest, does more than potentially justify solitary confinement as the study's authors rightly fear. Perhaps it also reinforces the underlying assumptions that make solitary confinement appear as the logical solution to problems within prison systems. (p. 7)

Learning from the State of Maine

For better or for worse, the correctional system does sometimes change from within. In the summer of 2010, for example, a legislative committee on public safety asked the Maine Department of Corrections to work with the state's human service and substance abuse agency to review due process procedures and policies for special management prisoners. In Maine, high-security or supermax custody was available for both juveniles and adults, and much concern was being expressed about careless use of these highly restrictive and harsh options. In January 2011, the newly elected governor Paul LePage (R) named Joseph Ponte as the state's new corrections director. Some in Maine were skeptical of the governor's choice, but skepticism soon turned to approval. In March, the corrections–human service group issued a 22-page report (Sherrets & LeBel, 2011) that recommended a range of changes in the way correctional facilities use their highest level of custody. Commissioner Ponte responded to the report, or at least issues related to the report, by replacing high-level central office administration personnel and security staff members. Within a short time, the number of supermax prisoners was reduced significantly.

The corrections–human service group took its mission seriously, logging in more than 100 hours of groundwork. The group's work was based on several premises: research and science should guide its work; special management units (SMUs) should not be used as punishment per se; some individuals are dangerous, to general population prisoners and others, and require severely restrictive confinement; and mentally ill prisoners should be addressed separately. The product of the group's work is not so much a program for what should be done, but rather an offering of "ideas to shape directions, culture, and planning" (Sherrets & LeBel, 2011, p. 3). In particular, the group's recommendations are designed to address due process and behavioral change for prisoners in special management units.

Prisoners are sent to the SMU for adverse behavior in the community as well as behavior within correctional institutions. Sherrets and LeBel noted that "'high-risk' inmates are included in the SMU population. These include individuals who make up the most dangerous population in the State of Maine and who have a history of repeated violent and antisocial behavior." The authors cautioned that "careful consideration needs to be used when applying the [report's] recommendations with this population. Because high-risk classification is partially based upon behavior prior to coming into the institution some of the recommendations will have a limited impact on the numbers of individuals being placed there" (p. 4). This last comment is notable because almost immediately after Maine started implementing these recommendations, the SMU population began to plummet.

Overall, the report made 48 recommendations concerning general overview issues, the use of high-risk and administrative segregation units, data monitoring, and the mental health unit. Recommendations for overview issues included developing alternatives to administrative segregation and disciplinary units; hiring mental health specialists to improve confinement for both general and SMU populations; meetings by SMU staff to review operations and ideas; routinely collecting statistical data; and reviewing SMU prisoners on a regular basis. Disciplinary and administrative segregation unit recommendations included developing additional sanctions for prisoner misbehavior in confinement; tracking prisoner time in SMU confinement; reconsidering an inmate advocate position that had been previously eliminated; and reviewing written legal materials for prisoners and revising them where necessary. Sherrets and LeBel (2011) noted:

> From what we could discern, the required checks by mental health and medical staff were completed on a timely basis. There was however clearly no consistent definition or data kept on what was assessed. There was also little evidence in any of the units that there was sufficient time for the mental health staff to do any true consistent therapy. Subjectively, it appeared and was reported to us that many of the individuals in the SMU's (outside of the Mental Health Unit) had a history of mental illness. The SMUs are also used to house a variety of inmates beyond the narrow definition of the original purpose. (p. 9)

The report also recommended improving staff selection; improving the air quality and sensory stimulation components of the SMU; providing more training for staff; developing more appropriate supervision protocols; improving staff-prisoner ratios; devising a consistent behavioral checklist; making security staff part of intervention plans; and implementing increased out-of-cell time. Additionally, a clearer mission statement was necessary.

Data collection concerns focused on developing a comprehensive data collection process, with collected data being relevant to the mission and achievable goals. Mental health unit (MHU) recommendations were also made for milieu therapy, access to medications, access to relevant therapy, and interventions related to personality disorders and criminogenic risk factors. The report stated that the MHU should be separated from other SMUs and used only for prisoners with major mental illness or crisis stabilization, given increased education, training, support services, and enhanced milieu treatment space.

Significantly, in a short period of time, Commissioner Ponte cut in half the number of prisoners sent to SMUs in Maine. This suggests that when directors of Departments of Corrections do their homework and consult the scientific and mental health literature on the potential harm of solitary confinement, they may decide to raise professional standards, seeking to do less harm to both dangerous and vulnerable prisoners. It is hoped that officials and administrators in Colorado and other states read the Maine report before deciding to construct more supermax units.

Notes

1. See Richards & Ross, 2003b.
2. See Grassian, 2010a; Greene, 2010; Prendergast, 2010.
3. See O'Keefe, 2005, 2008.

| 10 |

Revisiting the Mental Health Effects of Solitary Confinement on Prisoners in Supermax Units: A Psychological Jurisprudence Perspective

Bruce A. Arrigo and Heather Y. Bersot

Solitary confinement, a correctional strategy used to physically isolate inmates, has been employed in penal facilities since their inception.[1] Although incarcerates are placed in isolation for both administrative and disciplinary reasons, the objective in all cases is to increase control over those deemed incapable of being housed among the general prison population.[2] The American public, ever fearful of criminals, demands legislative responses that seemingly ensure that these offending individuals will be punished severely.[3] As harsh crime control policies have grown in popularity, the use of solitary confinement of convicts has become widespread.[4] Consequently, increased limitations placed on the personal freedoms of prisoners raise serious civil rights issues.[5]

This chapter critically reviews the mental health consequences of short- and long-term isolation on incarcerates. Although the extant literature has devoted some attention to this concern,[6] limited research "has directly examined the effect of supermax confinement on inmates' psychological and physical health" (Pizarro & Stenius, 2004, p. 255). Some investigators[7] have asserted that "the very nature of isolation precludes investigators from gaining meaningful access to those whom they seek to study" (Arrigo, Bersot, & Sellers, 2011, p. 68). Although incomplete, the growing body of literature largely supports early findings suggesting that solitary confinement, particularly for protracted periods of time, is detrimental to prisoners' overall well-being.[8]

The origin of this disturbing correctional practice is rooted in the history of the penitentiary in general and the case law pertaining to solitary confinement in particular. Thus drawing attention to this history is useful in that it identifies the public and political sentiment that has fueled the growth of secure housing units (SHUs) and supermax facilities in the United States and the increasing deployment of segregated housing as a customary tool for punishing and managing the nation's burgeoning prison population.[9] Moreover, reviewing the relevant case law helps situate the plight and suffering of those subjected to the practice of solitary confinement in an important and timely evaluative context.[10]

Accordingly, following a summary presentation of these historical and legal matters, we present the pertinent empirical (and related) literature documenting the psychological effects of such isolation. Where useful and appropriate, we consider these effects in relation to both long- and short-term segregation. We also look at the impact of correctional isolation on persons with preexisting mental illness and review studies examining race, gender, and class dynamics. Finally, mindful of the research to date, we make several recommendations for correctional policy reform as guided by principles and practices emanating from psychological jurisprudence.

Solitary Confinement in U.S. Prisons: Historical and Legal Considerations

During the early 1800s, two prison systems developed in the United States: the Pennsylvania system and the Auburn system. The Auburn system, developed in New York, was characterized by silent but congregate labor. Thus prisoners in this system were exposed to some degree of physical and mental stimulation. In contrast, the Pennsylvania system was characterized by rigid isolation of prisoners both from society and from each other.[11] This system was based on the premise that compulsory seclusion would give prisoners time to reflect on their crimes and become penitent, hence the term "penitentiary."[12] The extreme isolation that was characteristic of the early prisons operating under the Pennsylvania system ultimately resulted in serious physical and psychological consequences for convicts.[13] Because of the detrimental mental health effects of penal solitude, the system was eventually discontinued.[14] In 1890, the U.S. Supreme Court commented on the adverse effects of solitary confinement in prisons:

> A considerable number of prisoners fell, after even a short confinement, into a semi-fatuous condition, from which it was next to impossible to arouse them, and others became violently insane; others still, committed suicide;

while those who stood the ordeal better were not generally reformed, and in most cases did not recover sufficient mental activity to be of any subsequent service to the community. (*In re Medley*, 134 U.S. 160, 1890)

The adverse psychological effects of solitary confinement were also documented in German prisons, which were modeled after early U.S. institutions. Numerous articles appeared in German medical journals chronicling cases of psychosis attributed to conditions of imprisonment.[15] Indeed, among the accounts published delineating the harmful effects of solitary confinement is an 1854 report prepared by the chief physician of Halle Prison. He noted that prisoners suffered from what he termed "Prison Psychosis," which appeared to have "a very injurious effect on the body and mind and seem[ed] to predispose [incarcerates] to hallucinations (Nitsche & Williams as cited in Shalev, 2008, p. 10). A later report, published in 1863, described a number of symptoms exhibited by isolated prisoners, including "vivid hallucinations, delusions, apprehension and psychomotor excitation" (Shalev, 2008, p. 10).

Despite the lessons learned during the 1800s about the devastating psychological impact of solitary confinement, rigid isolation of prisoners has once again become a commonly employed strategy for managing incarcerates deemed dangerous or disruptive to the correctional order.[16] The development of supermaximum security units, also referred to as "control units," can be traced to the opening of the United States Penitentiary (USP) Marion in Illinois in 1963.[17] Called "one of the most significant U.S. prisons built in the past century" (Richards, 2008, p. 6), USP Marion was constructed to serve as a replacement to the federal prison at Alcatraz, which was decommissioned the same year.

Unlike maximum- or medium-security facilities, USP Marion was designed exclusively as a disciplinary supermax prison capable of isolating for years incarcerates who pose the most significant challenges to correctional administrators (e.g., those who are high escape risks, are gang members, or exhibit assaultive behavior toward staff).[18] Indeed, offenders confined at USP Marion are subjected to such extreme solitude that they "sleep, eat, exercise, live, and die in their cells alone" (Richards, 2008, p. 8).

Over time, USP Marion increased its use of solitary confinement to coerce prisoners to participate in therapy and to control dissident convicts, such as those who led a work stoppage to protest the beating of a minority prisoner by a guard in 1972.[19] As the use of correctional isolation at USP Marion grew, so did the duration of internment. After two prison guards were murdered by inmates in 1983, the entire prisoner population at USP Marion was restricted to their cells, with many inmates living for years in isolation.[20]

The Administrative Maximum Facility (ADX) Florence, in Colorado, has since replaced USP Marion as the primary supermax facility in the federal system.[21] Unlike its predecessor, ADX Florence truly represents a "prison of the future," in which a plethora of the most advanced surveillance technologies are employed to ensure that nearly every aspect of an inmate's life is observed and managed. In addition to the ubiquitous monitoring, one prisoner, Ray Luc Levasseur, described how he and other incarcerates at ADX Florence were frequently subjected to invasive control strategies, including "four-point spread-eagle restraints, forced feedings, cell extractions, mind-control medications, and chemical weapons" (Richards, 2008, p. 16).

Nevertheless, USP Marion has served as the leading model for state secure housing units throughout the country.[22] According to the National Institute of Corrections, as of 1996, 34 state jurisdictions operated or had plans to operate one or more supermax facilities (Pizarro & Stenius, 2004). During this time, more than 55 control units operated nationwide, providing housing to nearly 20,000 prisoners (Mears & Reisig, 2006; National Institute of Corrections, 1997). More recently, based on a 2004 Urban Institute survey of self-identified supermax wardens, 44 states reported the presence of at least one facility, and they collectively house approximately 25,000 prisoners (Mears, 2005; Shalev, 2008).

The structure and routine within solitary confinement facilities and units can vary somewhat, depending on the jurisdiction and the type of segregation (i.e., administrative or disciplinary). Typically, isolated prisoners are housed in steel door reinforced cells that measure approximately 6 by 8 feet in size. Incarcerates are confined in this manner for 22 to 23 hours per day. As long as inmates follow prison rules, they are permitted one hour of exercise time in a secured area each day.[23] Those serving time in isolation frequently refer to the exercise pen as "the dog run," as its size is often similar to that of their solitary cells and is typically enclosed by concrete walls or wire fencing (Haney, 2003, p. 126). Nevertheless, inmates are rarely released from their holding cells. When they are, they are restrained by a variety of mechanical apparatuses, such as handcuffs, waist chains, and leg chains. Indeed, "in addition to imposed seclusion, mechanical, physical, chemical, and technological restraints are utilized to ensure minimal psychological stimulation and to control nearly every aspect of an inmate's existence" (Arrigo et al., 2011, p. 61).[24]

In general, prisoners placed in segregation are not permitted any contact visits, and they are often required to talk with visitors via closed-circuit television. Furthermore, they do not benefit from any congregate activity, such as exercise, dining, or religious services. Access to personal belongings, including reading materials, is strictly limited. These convicts typically have no opportunity to work or participate in educational or therapeutic programming. Prisoners in control units are given insufficient room to exercise and often have no access to recreational or athletic equipment. Most isolation units lack windows, so there is little to no opportunity for exposure to natural sunlight. The cells are often illuminated by artificial light 24 hours a day, with prisoners having no means of controlling the brightness or dimness in their cells. Under these conditions, convicts may have difficulty determining whether it is day or night. Prisoners are assigned to control units for indefinite periods of time, which typically last for months or years. Overall, SHU convicts are extremely isolated and are offered very limited mental stimulation.[25]

While the quality of and access to medical and psychiatric care vary according to jurisdiction, prisoners in both administrative and disciplinary solitary confinement often receive less than adequate attention. This is particularly troubling given the likelihood of inmates being placed in such conditions who have preexisting mental health conditions.[26] In the case of *Madrid v. Gomez* (1995), the U.S. District Court for the Northern District of California was presented with a challenge to the conditions of confinement at the Pelican Bay State Prison secure housing unit. The court found that Pelican Bay staff exhibited deliberate indifference to the health care needs of prisoners in the SHU. The medical services at the SHU were chronically understaffed, and medical personnel were provided inadequate training and supervision. Convicts were offered no routine physical examinations or other medical or psychiatric screening. They often faced significant delays in accessing health care or experienced outright denial of health care services.

Mental health services in particular were found to be markedly deficient at the Pelican Bay SHU. The court in *Madrid* determined that a significant number of prisoners at the correctional facility, both in the SHU and in the general population, suffered from serious psychological problems. As with other forms of health service, psychiatric care staffing at Pelican Bay was found to be grossly inadequate. Pelican Bay offered no screening of incarcerates entering the SHU for mental illness. Convicts who were psychiatrically disordered or otherwise exhibited emotional problems were not screened out of the SHU. Because of inadequate screening for and monitoring of mental health conditions, many psychiatrically ill prisoners did not receive treatment until they became flagrantly psychotic or suicidal. Furthermore, the SHU offered a very limited range of intervention options for mentally disordered prisoners. There were no provisions for psychiatric inpatient treatment or intensive outpatient services for this population in the SHU. The *Madrid* court therefore determined that the Pelican Bay SHU was in a state of "mental health care crisis" and concluded that "conditions in the SHU [we]re sufficiently severe that they [could] lead to serious psychiatric consequences for some prisoners" (*Madrid v. Gomez*, 1995, pp. 1216–1217).

The inadequate system of psychiatric care as documented in *Madrid* is not limited to the SHU at Pelican Bay State Prison. Similar conditions at

Wisconsin's Supermax Correctional Institution (now the Wisconsin Secure Program Facility) at Boscobel were reported by the U.S. District Court for the Western District of Wisconsin in the case of *Jones'El v. Berge* (2001). This case revealed a strikingly deficient ratio of mental health staff to incarcerates in the facility. Terry Kupers, a noted psychiatrist and expert witness, described what he assessed as inadequate methods for screening incoming prisoners for mental illness. Despite efforts to screen psychiatrically disordered convicts out of the supermax, many prisoners were found to be suffering from serious mental illness. The court also noted that ongoing monitoring of the prisoners' mental health was woefully inadequate.

The conditions of confinement in supermax prisons and SHUs are typically characterized by hostility and violence.[27] Incarcerates are shackled and restrained occasionally while within their holding units and always when they are removed from their cells. They are accompanied to showers or exercise under heavy guard. Correctional officers frequently employ violent "cell extractions" in response to minor infractions committed by convicts, such as failure to return a food tray. During cell extractions, prisoners are subdued with batons, shields, tasers, and rubber bullets. The use of force in secure housing units is often excessive. This was reported by the U.S. District Court for the Northern District of California in *Madrid v. Gomez* (1995). In the *Madrid* case, the court found that SHU staff engaged in assaults on prisoners, used fetal restraints for purposes of "hog-tying" convicts, caged incarcerates outdoors in inclement weather, relied on unnecessary and violent cell extractions, and employed the unnecessary and reckless use of lethal force.

The characterization of SHU convicts as being "the worst of the worst" contributes to an "us against them" mindset among correctional staff. This orientation serves only to heighten the potential for abuse of prisoners.[28] However, the primary purpose of secure housing units is to exercise complete control and dominion over convicts. Typically, prisoners are assigned to the SHU because they are thought to be too violent and dangerous to be managed in the general population.[29] The public's impression is that secure housing units are reserved for the vilest and most despicable offenders found within the U.S. penal system. Thus the severe confinement conditions are justified and deemed necessary in order to maintain the security of the prison, the safety of the correctional staff, and the welfare of other prisoners.[30]

However, in reality, most convicts in secure housing units are not incorrigibly violent.[31] Prisoners are often placed in the SHU because they accumulated a number of nonviolent disciplinary infractions, were identified as gang members, or were involved in a single fight. Secure housing units are also used to suppress activity defined as dissident. Examples of this dissidence include protesting prison conditions, assisting other convicts with habeas corpus appeals, or initiating litigation against correctional administration. Typically, the conditions of confinement in the SHU are excessively severe relative to the prison's legitimate security and management objectives.[32]

The Mental Health Effects of Short- and Long-Term Solitary Confinement

At this time, the empirical evidence on the harmful consequences of placing inmates in isolation for brief time-limited periods of 60 days or less is rather scarce.[33] The research exploring the effects of short-term administrative segregation has largely been conducted under carefully controlled conditions. As such, these conditions do not typify the experience of most prisoners subjected to secure isolation.[34]

Among the findings on short-term administrative segregation, Bonta and Gendreau (1995) noted that "solitary confinement may not be cruel and unusual punishment under the humane and time-limited conditions investigated in experimental studies or in correctional jurisdictions that have well-defined and effectively administered ethical guidelines for its use" (p. 86). Indeed, in actual practice, the environmental circumstances of solitary confinement do not resemble the safe and sanitized conditions that are typical of research studies.[35] Moreover, as Roberts and Jackson (1991) asserted, the effects of short-term incarceration may not be revealed in experimental research because of the limitations of the instruments used to measure psychological consequences.[36]

Similarly, Zinger, Wichmann, & Andrews (2001) did not find evidence of psychological deterioration among Canadian prisoners who spent 60 days in administrative segregation. However, they commented that their findings were not applicable to the United States, where offenders remained in segregation for longer periods of time and under harsher conditions of confinement than their Canadian counterparts. Zinger and colleagues also noted that the nature and quality of prisoner-staff interaction affected how well convicts coped with their temporary administrative segregation. As described above, correctional staff typically harbored very negative views of prisoners in solitary confinement. Abusive or capricious behavior by staff, documented in SHUs in the United States, can also lead to increased psychological stress.[37]

Roberts and Gebotys (2001) pointed out that although Zinger and his research team found no *detectable* psychological deterioration among prisoners who spent 60 days in administrative segregation, even short-term solitary confinement may have subtle effects on psychological functioning that are not so easily discernible. Furthermore, Jackson (2001) asserted that punitive, short-term isolation might have a long-lasting impact on offenders. Specifically, Jackson explained that qualitative analyses of prisoners exposed to solitary confinement revealed that incarcerates were at risk for developing post-traumatic stress disorder.

Suedfeld, Ramirez, Deaton, and Baker-Brown (1982) also studied convicts in solitary confinement and concluded that "there was no evidence to support the hypothesis that SC [solitary confinement] [was] universally or uniformly aversive or damaging to prisoners" (p. 330). However, the investigators did acknowledge that adverse psychological effects were more often observed with longer durations of administrative segregation. Moreover, they conceded that certain conditions of internment, such as maltreatment by staff or lack of access to sensory stimuli, were likely to produce negative psychological consequences. These are the very conditions that are typical of long-term solitary confinement in U.S. prisons today.[38] Finally, they noted that certain personality types demonstrated less tolerance for the stress of secure isolation. It is important to note that psychotic or suicidal prisoners were excluded from the study conducted by Suedfeld and associates. This is important because in the United States, mentally disordered prisoners are frequently placed in solitary confinement.[39]

The damaging psychological consequences of long-term solitary confinement have been well documented.[40] The adverse effects of solitary confinement appear to be related primarily to the duration and conditions of internment.[41] While it has not been conclusively established that short periods of segregated housing produce negative outcomes for the emotional well-being of incarcerates, long-term solitary confinement does, especially in relation to the psychological adjustment of prisoners.[42]

Incarcerates segregated for extended periods of time suffer from what Toch (1992) termed "isolation panic." Indeed, he observed that prisoners in solitary confinement experienced the following:

> a feeling of abandonment . . . dead-end desperation . . . helplessness, tension. It is a physical reaction, a demand for release or a need to escape at all costs. . . . [Segregated individuals] feel caged rather than confined, abandoned rather than alone, suffocated rather than isolated. They react to solitary confinement with surges of panic or rage. They lose control, break down, and regress. (p. 49)

Haney (1993, 2006) also described the psychological consequences of and adaptations to long-term solitary confinement particularly well. Haney served as an expert witness for the plaintiff convicts in *Madrid v. Gomez* (1995), the class-action suit challenging the conditions of confinement in the SHU at Pelican Bay State Prison in California. The SHU at Pelican Bay is a particularly notorious example of the extreme social isolation found in supermaximum custody units. Prisoners at the SHU are almost completely isolated from human contact and receive virtually no opportunity for mental stimulation or activity.

Haney (2006) pointed out that the rigid conditions of solitary confinement offer individuals no opportunity to engage in social reality testing. Human beings rely on social contact with others to test and validate their perceptions of the environment. Ultimately, a complete lack of social contact makes it difficult to distinguish what is real from what is not or what is external from what is internal. As Haney (1993) explained, "social connectedness and social support are the prerequisites to long-term social adjustment" (p. 7).

In the absence of social context, Haney (1993) noted that people become "highly malleable, unnaturally sensitive, and vulnerable to the influence of those who control the environment around them" (p. 5). Paradoxically, long-term social isolation often leads to social withdrawal. Individuals move from craving social contact to fearing it. Prisoners housed under conditions of confinement such as those found at the SHU grow to rely on the prison structure to limit and control their behavior. A consequence of this is that convicts are no longer able to manage their conduct when returned to the general prison population or when released to the community. Alternatively, incarcerates may become unable to initiate behavior on their own due to severe apathy and lethargy. Convicts may resort to acting out behavior as a means of testing their environment, or they may retreat into fantasy. Haney (2003) indicated that prisoners in the SHU experience intolerable feelings of frustration, anger, and rage. Acting out based on these feelings is often used to justify placing offenders in isolation; however, Haney (1993) noted that "rage is a reaction against, not a justification for, their oppressive confinement" (p. 5).[43]

Haney (2006) also cautioned that prisoners in long-term solitary confinement are at increased risk for developing symptoms of mental illness. Social isolation is correlated with clinical depression and long-term impulse control disorder. Prisoners with preexisting mental illness are at particular risk for developing psychiatric symptoms in solitary confinement. Psychosis, suicidal behavior, and self-mutilation are commonly seen among prisoners in long-term solitary confinement. Additionally, offenders with mental illness are already at increased risk for being placed in solitary confinement because they have difficulty adjusting to prison and are often unable to manage their behavior in the correctional population.[44] Behavior that stems from mental illness is often used as a justification to place convicts with mental illness in the SHU. To compound the problem, psychiatric resources are scarce in the overcrowded prison system, and adequate psychiatric evaluation and treatment typically are not available in control units such as the SHU.

The adverse mental health consequences of long-term solitary confinement have also been documented by Grassian (1983, 2006). He conducted psychiatric evaluations of 14 prisoners who were plaintiffs in a class-action lawsuit challenging the conditions of their solitary confinement at the Massachusetts Correctional Institution at Walpole. These offenders were housed in 1.8-by-2.7-meter cells with solid steel doors that were kept closed, shutting off any contact prisoners may have had with staff or other prisoners. Each cell was illuminated by a single 60-watt bulb and had no natural light. Prisoners were allowed no personal belongings, including reading materials, except for a Bible. The convicts were housed under these conditions on average for two months.

Grassian (1983) identified a psychopathological condition known as "SHU syndrome" among these prisoners.[45] The syndrome is characterized by perceptual changes; affective disturbance; difficulties with thinking, concentration, and memory; disturbance of thought content; and problems with impulse control. Grassian found that these incarcerates were hypersensitive to external stimuli and frequently experienced distortions of perception, hallucinations, or feelings of derealization. Most suffered extreme generalized anxiety and symptoms of panic disorder. Many were confused, and some suffered amnesia regarding some of the events that had occurred during their confinement. Further, prisoners reported frightening and disturbing violent fantasies of revenge against their captors. A number of inmates suffered paranoia and believed they were being persecuted. Several prisoners reported problems with impulse control, characterized by violent or destructive behavior or acts of self-mutilation. Notably, most of these offenders had no previous history of psychiatric problems. In all cases, their symptoms subsided after they were released from segregated housing. Grassian (1983) noted that the effects of solitary confinement varied according to the degree of social isolation and sensory deprivation that was imposed, concluding, "The use of solitary confinement carries major psychiatric risks" (p. 1454).[46]

Grassian and Friedman (1986) discussed some of the factors that influence how an individual responds to segregated housing. They noted that individuals exhibit different responses to this form of containment, with some demonstrating greater ability to tolerate it than others. The investigators identified the complexity of sensory deprivation, the duration of the confinement, and the prisoner's perception of the internment's purpose as important variables influencing the effects of solitary confinement. They also noted that the individual prisoner's personality organization affected his ability to tolerate solitary confinement and the development of psychiatric symptoms.

With regard to the complexity of the sensory deprivation associated with solitary confinement, Grassian and Friedman indicated that the quality and intensity of the available stimuli were important. For example, the amount and quality of light, the size of the room, the ability to perceive sounds in the surrounding environment, and the color and appearance of the environment were all essential components to the convicts' experiences of solitary confinement.

The duration of the isolation was also significant in predicting adverse psychological consequences. For example, Grassian and Friedman noted that the length of solitary confinement operating at the Massachusetts Correctional Institution at Walpole was too long to protect against serious psychological harm. Prisoners at Walpole were isolated continuously behind solid steel doors for up to 15 days at a time.

Grassian and Friedman also reported that the individual's expectation and perception of the containment's purpose was important. Solitary confinement that was perceived as punitive produced greater potential for adverse psychological effects. For example, the convicts evaluated by the investigators at Walpole perceived their isolation as a deliberately punitive attempt to drive them crazy. Other researchers have also indicated that the prisoner's perception regarding the purpose of solitary confinement and the manner in which the offender is treated while in segregation influence whether the convict will suffer adverse psychological consequences.[47]

Finally, Grassian and Friedman noted that the individual's personality organization affected how the person responded to solitary confinement. As the investigators explained, the personality types generally found in prisons were particularly vulnerable to the adverse psychological effects of solitary confinement. Overall, they concluded that greater degrees of sensory deprivation and longer periods of internment were most likely to produce the psychopathological SHU syndrome described by Grassian (1983) in his previous work.[48]

In 2010, the results of a longitudinal study conducted by O'Keefe, Klebe, Stucker, Sturm, and Leggett on the mental health effects of long-term administrative segregation on incarcerates at the Colorado State Penitentiary were published. Prisoners in both administrative segregation and the general population were examined over a one-year period. Inmates who participated in the study were divided into two groups: those with mental illness and those without mental illness. A comparison group composed of incarcerates with severe mental health problems housed at a psychiatric care prison was also included in the investigation. The findings, which were based on self-report data, suggested that the mental health of administrative segregation inmates with preexisting conditions did not decline at a rate that was more rapid or more severe than the mental health of those without psychiatric disorders. According to the empirical evidence, the researchers noted that there was an "initial improvement in psychological well-being across all study groups" (p. 8).

Although O'Keefe and colleagues acknowledged that their investigation suffered from several limitations and the results could not be generalized to prisoners held in other facilities and under different segregation conditions, their study's findings have drawn considerable criticism from a number of solitary confinement experts and human rights activists. One of the chief concerns raised regarding the empirical investigation was the fact that the researchers relied exclusively on self-report data.[49] Shalev and Lloyd (2011) argued that given the "damaged nature of the population under study and the essential unreliability of their self-report data," the potential for measurement error was significantly high (p. 4). Grassian (2010) commented that "these minute dissections reveal *nothing*, because the data they dissect does not in any meaningful manner reflect the psychiatric pathology they are supposed to be studying." Further, Shalev and Lloyd (2011) opined:

> Beyond any methodological criticisms of the Colorado study, there remains one key, much wider problem. Solitary confinement is not a natural state for us as social creatures who require human contact and human touch to maintain our very sense of "self." It is difficult to see how prison systems which officially aim to rehabilitate offenders and assist their reintegration into society propose to provide prisoners with the social skills and tools necessary for living alongside others by withholding social contact. . . . [It] would be tragic indeed if departments of corrections decided to invest in further supermax facilities on the basis of a flawed study. (p. 5)

It is imperative to note that the extant body of research on solitary confinement comprises studies that differ in context, location, and perhaps most important, methodology. Nevertheless, researchers generally contend that empirical evidence suggesting that isolation does not have psychologically damaging effects on prisoners is not representative of the conditions of correctional solitude in the United States. Furthermore, nearly all investigators acknowledge that long-term segregation, mistreatment by correctional staff, and preexisting psychological vulnerability contribute to negative mental health consequences for convicts. Contrary to the widely accepted findings on protracted isolation are the results of the recent Colorado study conducted by O'Keefe and colleagues (2010). The empirical evidence presented, however, has and will likely continue to be a source of intense debate among solitary confinement experts and human rights activists.

Vulnerability of Prisoners with Preexisting Mental Illness

It has been amply demonstrated that the conditions of solitary confinement can produce psychopathology even in healthy prisoners. Convicts with preexisting mental illness are especially vulnerable to suffering damaging consequences from such routine confinement. Indeed, mentally disordered offenders are at greater risk for being placed in secure housing units. According to Haney (2009), approximately one-third (29%) of supermax or SHU prisoners are suffering from a "serious mental disorder" (p. 14). He further estimated that at least two-thirds of these inmates experience a "variety of symptoms of psychological and emotional trauma, as well as some of the psychopathological effects of isolation" (p. 15). Lovell (2008) estimated that nearly half (45%) of supermax incarcerates endure a number of "psychosocial impairments" (p. 990). Given the scarce psychiatric resources in correctional facilities, many prisoners suffer from debilitating and undiagnosed psychiatric disorders for which they receive no treatment. These prisoners are unfortunately the most likely to be placed in isolation and the least equipped to modify their behavior to conform to correctional rules.[50]

Behavior stemming from psychiatric illness is often used as justification to place prisoners in solitary confinement.[51] For example, prisoners with mental disorders are more likely to refuse to leave their cells, destroy property, set fires, smear urine and feces on walls or themselves, or engage in suicide attempts and self-mutilation than their non–mentally ill counterparts. When inmates engage in such activities, including those that involve self-harm (e.g., cutting, hanging, or swallowing sharp objects), they often receive rule infractions. Because incarcerates are in state custody, these behaviors are deemed "destruction of state property—to wit, the prisoner's body" (Fellner, 2006, p. 397). Interestingly, of the inmates who succeed in committing suicide, "approximately half occur among the 6% to 8% of the prison population that is consigned to segregation at any given time" (Kupers, 2008, p. 1009).

Psychiatrically disordered offenders may be at a greater risk for both violence toward and victimization by other prisoners.[52] Indeed, McCorkle (1995) found that male prisoners suffering from mental illness were more likely to be confined in a maximum-security facility or SHU than female prisoners similarly suffering from mental illness. Both males and females with prior or present psychiatric disorders had significantly more rule infractions than their non–mentally ill counterparts.

The extreme isolation and harsh conditions of confinement in secure housing units typically exacerbate the symptoms of mental illness.[53] This position was described by psychiatrist Terry Kupers while testifying as an expert witness for the plaintiff prisoners in a suit challenging the conditions of confinement at Wisconsin's Supermax Correctional Institution. Kupers indicated that isolation and inactivity in the unit aggravated and worsened a person's psychiatric disorder by depriving the prisoner of any opportunity for reality testing (*Jones'El v. Berge*, 2001). The *Jones'El* case focused specifically on the effects of supermaximum security confinement on convicts with mental illness. The court acknowledged that "confinement in a supermaximum security prison . . . is known to cause severe psychiatric morbidity, disability, suffering, and mortality" (p. 1101). Thus the court held that placing a seriously mentally disordered prisoner in such a facility violated the cruel and unusual punishment clause of the Eighth Amendment.

Race, Gender, and Class Dynamics

In general, incarcerated persons in the United States are disproportionately poor minority males. Similarly, prisoners in long-term solitary confinement largely represent economically disadvantaged racial and ethnic minorities. For example, Haney and Lynch (1997) reported that 90% of a random sample of convicts in punitive isolation at a California prison was composed of nonwhite individuals, with 70% of the members of the sample being Latinos. Haney and Lynch remarked that this overrepresentation of minority prisoners, particularly Latinos, might be a result of the prison's policy of placing alleged gang members in solitary or supermax confinement.

Several studies have documented the differential treatment of black versus white offenders in terms of disciplinary action for prison rule violations. For example, Ramirez (1983) found that black convicts received a disproportionate number of conduct reports compared with their white counterparts in a medium-security federal correctional institution. Additionally, Ramirez indicated that a disproportionate number of black prisoners received multiple conduct reports. Ramirez explained that there were more opportunities for extralegal factors such as race to influence treatment in the criminal justice system at stages where officials were afforded greater discretion. Because of the relative seclusion of prisons from the public view, prison officials had significant discretion.

Similarly, Poole and Regoli (1980) found that although black and white offenders were equally likely to commit prison rule infractions, black convicts were more likely to be written up for rule violations. Furthermore, prisoners who received prior disciplinary write-ups were also more likely to obtain them for infractions in the future. Poole and Regoli noted that this process served to reinforce correctional officers' stereotypical conception of black prisoners as aggressive and more prone to rule-breaking. Therefore, "to guards, given their stereotypic conceptions, a pattern of greater control of black inmates having a history of disciplinary infractions represents sound custodial practice" (p. 944). As correctional officers increase their attempts to control black prisoners, convicts respond with increasing hostility. In this way, correctional officers may inadvertently cause the very behavior they are attempting to control.

This differential treatment of white versus non-white convicts is mirrored in the treatment of prisoners in secure housing units.[54] Given that non-white prisoners are more likely to be perceived as dangerous and disruptive in prison, they are more likely to be placed in solitary confinement for disciplinary infractions. While working in the SHU, prison staffers afforded greater discretion in the management of prisoners than when not working in segregated housing. This is because of the heightened isolation found within these units and the fact that they are generally not accessible to public scrutiny.

Gender issues are also relevant in the discussion of solitary confinement and their effects for prisoners.[55] Indeed, the placement of women in punitive isolation presents special concerns. Although incarcerated persons in the United States are disproportionately male (over 90% of the U.S. prison population is male), the rate of incarceration for women has increased dramatically over the last 20 years.[56]

Shaylor (1998) described the conditions at the SHU at Valley State Prison for Women in Chowchilla, California. SHU conditions in women's prisons are very similar to those in male facilities; however, Shaylor noted that women face unique challenges. For example, women convicts in the SHU are particularly vulnerable to sexual harassment and abuse by male correctional staff. Male guards are able to view women prisoners in the shower and on the toilet, and male correctional officers (COs) are often present when women prisoners are strip searched. Additionally, cell extractions are typically performed by male guards, making the experience particularly traumatic for women. Violent cell extractions by male COs may trigger post-traumatic stress reactions in women subjected to prior trauma, such as rape. Shaylor also argued that women are more likely than men to be sent to the SHU for minor infractions. For example, women may be placed in punitive isolation for attempted suicide. Shaylor concluded that harsh treatment of female prisoners is used to control women who fail to conform to societal standards of femininity. As she noted,

> A central function of prisons in general is to punish women who fail to subscribe to a model of femininity that historically has been (re)produced in discourse as white, pure, passive, heterosexual, and located in motherhood. When women operate outside of this model, even slightly, they are disciplined harshly for doing so. (p. 394)

Minority women are more likely than white women to be perceived as aggressive or otherwise nonfeminine. Thus they may be subjected to harsher treatment in prison and in solitary confinement. Similarly to male convicts in solitary confinement, Shaylor found that minority women were overrepresented in secure housing units compared with nonminority female offenders. Likewise, McCorkle (1995) found that black women prisoners suffering from mental illness reported being cited for rule infractions at a rate that was significantly greater than what was reported by white women prisoners with mental illness.

Some commentators have suggested that American penal institutions merely serve to "warehouse the poor" (Herivel and Wright, 2003, p. 6).[57] With this in mind, it is indeed prudent to assume that supermax facilities and SHUs contain a disproportionate number of individuals from economically disadvantaged backgrounds. Thus extant correctional practices, including solitary confinement, engender and reinforce "a very real and perhaps intentioned sense of social and economic immobility among the disadvantaged, particularly African-Americans and women" (Bersot & Arrigo, 2011, p. 240).[58]

A Psychological Jurisprudence Approach

As we have documented, the existing and relevant empirical literature suggests that solitary confinement, particularly for protracted periods of time, is injurious to the physical and mental health of inmates. As such, it is worthwhile to consider "whether something more, or something better can (and should) be done for all parties" impacted by violence and the criminal justice system's current response to such harm (Arrigo et al., 2011, p. 150).[59] One avenue for change that is consistent with this normative reformist agenda is found in the philosophy of psychological jurisprudence (PJ).

PJ emerged from the law-psychology-justice perspective of forensic behavioral science research and practice.[60] As theory, PJ considers how extant systemic strategies intended to address crime can be made fair and dignified, salubrious and healing, and just and reparative for *all* affected individuals. This critical attention to collectivist recovery stems from the recognition that injury is communally experienced and that the nearest possibility for overcoming (and transforming) pain or loss is shared responsibility for either or both. This is responsibility that extends from those who offend to those who are offended, from those who manage and treat victimizers and victims to those who observe the unfolding of it all (e.g., legislators, educators, adjudicators).

The normative footing of psychological jurisprudence draws attention to the ways in which current laws and policies increase or fail to increase prospects for human well-being and societal welfare. To accomplish this Aristotelian or virtue-guided objective, PJ employs three distinct practices: commonsense justice, therapeutic jurisprudence, and restorative justice.[61]

Commonsense justice asserts that the "black letter of the law" is limited in its ability to meet the needs of individuals involved in legal conflicts. As such, proponents of this practice contend that the reasoning of "everyday citizens" (i.e., jury members), including their notions of what is fair and just, should play an integral role in the legal decision-making process (Finkel, Harre, & Lopez, 2001, p. 2). Clearly, this PJ-sourced practice could enhance the possibility for legal outcomes that would have positive impacts on the dignity, healing, and restoration of offenders, victims, and the community to which they are bound. However, commonsense justice principally examines the role of jury decision-making, rendering its significance of limited utility for this chapter's focus on the use of solitary confinement as a correctional intervention.

Therapeutic jurisprudence (TJ) seeks to identify where and how the law, when guided by psychology, can function as a healing agent.[62] In a very practical sense, TJ relies on the tools of the behavioral and social sciences so that it can then "study the extent to which a legal rule or practice promotes the psychological and physical well-being of the people it affects" (Slobogin, 2005, p. 196).[63] Those who advocate a TJ approach assert that the law, as it is currently administered, is a social force that inflicts considerable harm on individuals, particularly those who are most vulnerable to its power (e.g., racial and ethnic minorities, females, the economically disadvantaged, and the psychiatrically disordered).[64] However, when guided by psychological principles, the law possesses the potential to serve as a healing agent capable of producing healthy outcomes for *all* parties affected by its reach. In recent years, the practice of TJ has been increasingly informed by fields related to psychology, including psychiatry, criminology, and social work, in order to more comprehensively understand how the law can operate more therapeutically.[65]

To achieve resolutions that enhance the well-being of each individual, TJ proponents assert that an ethic of care should be employed.[66] Grounded in the belief that care is inherent in human beings, this approach is "a longing for goodness that arises out of the experience or memory of being cared for" (Flinders, 2001, p. 211). According to Noddings (2002), extending virtues such as sympathy, compassion, tolerance, and benevolence to others should inform our sense of justice. Indeed, as she asserted earlier (Noddings, 1998):

> Ethical caring does have to be summoned. The "I ought" arises but encounters conflict: An inner voice grumbles, "I ought but I don't want to," or "why should I respond?" or "This guy deserves to suffer, so why should I help?" On these occasions we need not turn to a principle; more effectively we turn to ourselves as carers. (p. 187)

Cultivating this habit of care—a practice to be exercised in which one intentionally and indiscriminately beckons an intrinsic regard for another's well-being—is integral to more fully and deeply addressing the unmet or unresolved needs of troubled or even dangerous incarcerates. Indeed, as other investigators have explained, historically these are individuals who have been harmed or otherwise damaged (e.g., racial and ethnic minorities, women, the poor, and the psychiatrically disordered) by prevailing governmental policies and entrenched public sentiment.[67] Further, an ethic of care makes the prospect of responding in a therapeutic manner to even the most recalcitrant of offenders (i.e., those deemed the "worst of the worst") that much more realizable.[68]

Restorative justice (RJ) endeavors to repair the harm experienced by all individuals affected by violence.[69] As practiced, RJ provides an opportunity for each party to engage in a reparative dialogue intended to "heal the relationship between the offender and victim and to reinstate the moral equilibrium of a community" (Arrigo et al., 2011, p. 151).[70] In this way, each aggrieved party has the opportunity to express a sense of responsibility, understanding, and forgiveness. This dialogical exchange helps make possible a genuinely transformative resolution that is as gratifying for all participants as it is healing by all participants.[71]

Although most RJ efforts have been employed within court-ordered or community-based settings, some have been implemented in correctional programming settings. According to Swanson (2009), RJ within penal facilities achieves the following:

> It implies a degree of overt power sharing that can be very different from the expectations of many [correctional] staff. It challenges the stereotyped perception that prisoners are not capable of exercising such personal power; it challenges that assumption that they remain in the role of offender through denial, rather than break out from it through becoming responsible citizens. It also challenges the separation between staff and prisoners that is often a psychological survival necessity in systems of coercion and overload of numbers. (p. 35)

Indeed, perhaps what makes RJ as practice so compelling is that it holds the potential to replace "the 'tough guy' image with honesty, understanding, kindness, and caring" (Swanson, 2009, p. 37).

While a number of penal facilities have created restorative justice programs for inmates, some commentators assert that the very nature of these institutions hinders or wholly prevents life-changing outcomes from occurring.[72] As Van Ness and Heetderks Strong (2006) explained:

> Force is used or threatened to keep prisoners from escaping and to control their movement in prison. Furthermore, life among prisoners is typically characterized by threatened or actual use of violence. Such realities work against efforts to instill in prisoners a strong value for peaceful conflict resolution. (p. 319)

Further, Robert and Peters (2003) asserted that incorporating RJ programs in correctional environs serves only to legitimize punitive incarceration. Such practices, they said, "distract the public and policymakers from the bankruptcy of prisons" (p. 116). Nevertheless, we maintain that the use of RJ to promote communal recovery among those affected by violence does warrant consideration. This is especially the case when, as with TJ, restorative justice is guided by an ethic of care.

Recommendations for Reform: Moving Beyond What We Know

The extant research on the mental health effects of solitary confinement for prisoners suggests a number of recommendations for reform of supermax prisons and segregation units.[73] Human Rights Watch (2000) generated several key recommendations for reform as well. Accordingly, the comments that follow incorporate insights from these respective proposals. In addition, some commentary is offered regarding how such changes, when guided by a PJ approach, could effectively attend to the needs of all parties implicated in the practice of solitary confinement.

Chief among the recommendations for reform is that prisoners with current or prior histories of psychiatric disorders should be excluded from correctional isolation. Prisoners whose dangerous or disruptive behavior stems from mental illness would be more appropriately managed in a secure unit specifically designed to provide treatment to psychiatrically disordered offenders, as prisoners with past histories of such illnesses are vulnerable to psychological deterioration in solitary confinement.

Central to this reform is TJ. As praxis, TJ encourages legal decision-makers to assume more of a "judge-as-counselor" position that allows them to "know the defendant, consider her or his life circumstances and motives, and take these into consideration when making a ruling" (Williams & Arrigo, 2008, p. 265).[74] Likewise, penal policymakers and administrators, as well as correctional mental health professionals responsible for delineating how and for whom solitary confinement is employed, are encouraged to embrace a similar role. In doing so, each of these decision-makers has the opportunity to perceive prisoners as human beings—persons who are far more than simply the crime, however heinous, that they most assuredly have committed.

Further, a care-minded TJ approach facilitates a more balanced assessment of convict needs, particularly among those who suffer from psychiatric disorders. Along these lines, isolated prisoners should be examined, physically and mentally, as needed through one-on-one time with correctional health care professionals. In addition, incarcerates should be afforded privacy, particularly when meeting with mental health professionals. If these men or women believe that their conversations with trained professionals are monitored by correctional staff or overheard by other prisoners, they will be less inclined to disclose any problems that they may be experiencing.

A second important recommendation is that staff abuses of convicts in supermax facilities and segregation units should be strictly prohibited. Many researchers have suggested that the adverse psychological consequences of solitary confinement are significantly related to the way prisoners are treated by correctional personnel.[75] Indeed, both TJ and RJ offer promising opportunities for changes in the ways that penal personnel are trained to oversee and interact with isolated prisoners. At the core of these reforms is the notion that prison staff should be "encouraged to consider that their principal purpose is not so much to exact control over inmates, as much as it is to advance (or ascertain) the therapeutic potential of correctional law and policy" (Bersot & Arrigo, 2011, p. 252).

Guided by the principles of care, a TJ approach also requires that the needs of those who work within supermax facilities and SHUs be considered. Indeed, the extant literature indicates that prison workers frequently suffer from a similar kind of dissonance and disillusionment that many inmates experience.[76] Although they may feel compelled to enforce order within penal facilities, staff "can remain aloof only with great difficulty, for [they possess] few of those devices which normally serve to maintain social distance between the rulers and the ruled" (Sykes, 1958, p. 54).

When conflict arises between staff and segregated prisoners, RJ provides occasions for each party to engage in a candid exchange intended to increase understanding so that a mutually satisfying resolution can be reached. Expressing grievances is critical to defusing conflicts that arise within the ever-hostile prison milieu. In this way, isolated prisoners are actively exposed to meaningful dialogue with others. This practice also presents correctional staff with routine opportunities to cultivate a sense of care for those whom they are charged with overseeing.

A third recommendation for reform is that the SHU maintain humane physical conditions of confinement, mindful of that which is therapeutic. Prisoners should be housed in cells that are clean, well ventilated, and provide some exposure to natural light. Incarcerates should be allowed to control the artificial light in their own cells. Segregated inmates should never be isolated behind solid steel cell doors. Convicts in secure housing units should have access to personal belongings, including reading materials. Furthermore, prisoners should be given sufficient space for engaging in physical and mental health-enhancing exercise, and they should be permitted to use recreational equipment. Indeed, each of these care-inspired changes provides inmates in solitary confinement with a greater sense of dignity and autonomy—conditions that are critical to their physical and psychological well-being.

A fourth recommendation is that prisoners should be offered opportunities for normal and ongoing social interaction. It is extremely important that SHU convicts be allowed some prospect for congregate activity, such as dining, exercise, educational programming, or religious services, with other prisoners. This regular social contact enables prisoners to engage in reality testing, which is critical for maintaining mental health. Indeed, as Haney (2009) commented:

> Because so much of our individual identity is socially constructed and maintained, the virtually complete loss of genuine forms of social contact and the absence of routine and recurring opportunities to ground thoughts and feelings in recognizable human contexts is not only painful but also personally destabilizing. This is precisely why long-term isolated prisoners are literally at risk of losing their grasp on who they are, of how and why they are connected to a larger social world. (p. 16)

Additionally, prisoners should be permitted (and encouraged) to have frequent contact with their families or other visitors under conditions that facilitate communication. Regular visits with family members are therapeutic and central to preparing offenders to make a successful transition from prison to the community after they are released.

Although the foregoing recommendations offer sound strategies for immediately improving the conditions of solitary confinement, interring *any prisoner* for *any period of time* in correctional isolation remains a grave concern for a number of researchers and human rights activists. Indeed, because isolation strikes at the very core of what many believe is an essential need of human well-being—social experience—a growing number of social scientists and civil liberties advocates are demanding an end to its use. As an early commentator on the importance of social interaction in the development of the self noted,

> The self . . . is essentially a social structure and it arises in social experience. After a self has arisen, it in a certain sense provides for itself its social experiences, and so we can conceive of an absolutely solitary self. But it is impossible to conceive of a self arising outside of social experience. When it has arisen we can think of a person in solitary confinement for the rest of his life, but who still has himself as a companion, and is able to think and to converse with himself as he had communicated with others. . . . This process of abstraction cannot be carried on indefinitely. (Mead, 1934, p. 135)

As such, the final recommendation is that the use of penal solitude should be abolished.

Care asks that we consider the needs of all individuals—offenders, victims, and the communities of which they are a part, as well as judges, policy-makers, correctional administrators, and staff—affected by and implicated in harm. An ethic of care compels us to consider, then, whether placing inmates—particularly those who suffer from preexisting mental health conditions—in extreme solitude is the most therapeutic and just response imaginable for a humane and civil society. As we have noted elsewhere, sustaining such a practice, particularly when acknowledging the assorted debilitating mental health effects that follow from its use, is nothing short of "madness for one and for all" (Arrigo et al., 2011, p. ix). Rather than turn to injurious policies and practices like solitary confinement, TJ and RJ provide critical opportunities for each of us to summon an inherent regard for the well-being of one another. As we contend, these two PJ-sourced and care-infused approaches help make healing and transformation that much more likely for *all* who are affected by harm.

Summary and Final Thoughts

Short- and long-term solitary confinement of convicts for disciplinary or administrative purposes has become an increasingly popular means of controlling prisoner populations in the United States. This trend is evidenced by the proliferation of supermax facilities and isolation units throughout the nation.[77] The SHU allows administrators to exert almost total dominion over incarcerates deemed dangerous or dissident in the prison population. These units are also politically popular, as public fear of crime leads to increasingly punitive crime control policies. However, the use of supermaximum security units remains constitutionally suspect. The near complete social isolation and lack of stimulation accompanying segregation raise serious civil rights questions.

In this chapter, we have principally discussed the mental health impact of solitary confinement on inmates completing their prison sentences at supermaximum security units. As we argued, long-term isolation can have emotionally devastating consequences for convicts. The impact of short-term segregation, although reported as less traumatic in the empirical literature, nonetheless remains a source of some debate and serious concern. Moreover, the psychological effects of solitary confinement are related in part to the duration and conditions of the isolation. Prisoners with preexisting mental illnesses are especially vulnerable to the destructive psychological effects of segregated housing. The lack of adequate medical and psychiatric care—in prisons in general and in supermaximum facilities and isolation units in particular—compounds these problems. Additionally, convicts in solitary confinement are uniquely susceptible to physical and verbal abuse by staff. These hostile conditions increase the risk that prisoners will suffer emotionally crippling effects from punitive and administrative isolation.

We have also discussed the effects of race, gender, and class on the decision to place incarcerates in solitary confinement. Researchers have demonstrated that poor minority convicts are more likely to be placed in compulsory isolation than their nonminority counterparts. Furthermore, women are uniquely vulnerable to the traumatizing effects of correctional solitude.

Mindful of the destructive effects that stem from unremitting isolation, as delineated in the current literature, we presented a number of recommendations. These change initiatives were guided by current reformist proposals and informed by the theory and practice of psychological jurisprudence, involving care-minded therapeutic jurisprudence and community-centered restorative justice. Our recommendations consisted of the following: excluding mentally disordered convicts from supermax facilities and secure housing units; strictly prohibiting abusive treatment of prisoners by staff; providing humane physical conditions of internment; allowing prisoners opportunities for meaningful and routine social interaction; and abolishing the use of solitary confinement for *all* incarcerates serving time in correctional facilities.

Future research would do well to focus on identifying feasible and humane alternatives to the utilization of isolation as a penal management tool. Strategies should be pursued that more effectively meet the assorted needs of not only prisoners, but also their victims, those who treat and manage both of them, and the communities to which they all are tethered. Although there are several challenges to overcome in this process, moving toward an approach that more fully honors and affirms each person's dignity, healing, and restoration through care-minded responses to violence and harm warrants further scrutiny. Along these lines, PJ's core practices of therapeutic jurisprudence and restorative justice signal a novel reformist direction in corrections, including issues such as solitary confinement, that grows prospects for human justice and social well-being for, by, and about one and all.

Notes

1. See Foucault, 1975; Rhodes, 2004; Shalev, 2011.

2. See Cockburn, 2001; Toch, 2003; Shalev, 2008, 2009a, 2009b. We note the distinction between "disciplinary" and "administrative" segregation as discussed in the literature (e.g., Blanchette, 2001; Haney, 2006; Roberts & Gebotys, 2001; *Sandin v. Conner*, 1995; Zinger & Wichmann, 1999; Zinger, Wichmann, & Andrews, 2001). However, the thrust of this chapter emphasizes the psychological effects stemming from solitary confinement *generally*, regardless of its correctional form, particularly for those confined in a supermax prison. Admittedly, the conditions of confinement, the attitude and behavior of the staff, and the experiences and outlook of inmates may be quite different (e.g., Bonta & Gendreau, 1990). Nonetheless, "isolation research supports the notion that greater levels of deprivation contribute to more psychological and emotional problems" (Pizarro & Stenius, 2004, p. 255; see also Toch, 2001). This position obtains whether for the purpose of protective custody or punishment (Haney, 2006; Kupers, 1999; Miller, 1994).

3. See Reiman, 2005; Simon, 2009.

4. See Haney, 2006; Rhodes, 2004; Shalev, 2009a, 2009b.

5. E.g., Arrigo, Bersot, & Sellers, 2011; Bersot & Arrigo, 2010; Kupers, 1999; Metzner & Fellner, 2010; Ross & Richards, 2003; Shalev, 2011; Toch, 1977. For a thorough examination of the prevailing case law addressing inmate mental health, solitary confinement, and the Eighth Amendment's prohibition of cruel and unusual punishment, see Arrigo et al., 2011, and Bersot & Arrigo, 2010.

6. E.g., Haney, 2003; Kurki & Morris, 2001; Metzner & Fellner, 2010; Miller, 1994; Shalev, 2008, 2009a, 2009b, 2011.

7. E.g., Mears & Watson, 2006.

8. See Grassian, 2006; Haney, 2003; Kupers, 1999; Rhodes, 2004; Shalev, 2008, 2009a, 2009b, 2011.

9. See Arrigo et al., 2011; Bersot & Arrigo, 2010; Mears & Watson, 2006; Shalev, 2009b.

10. See Arrigo et al., 2011; Bersot & Arrigo, 2010; King, 1999; Luise, 1989; Mears & Reisig, 2006; Miller, 1995.

11. See Johnston, 2009.

12. See Rogers, 1993.

13. See Kurki & Morris, 2001; Pizarro & Stenius, 2004.

14. See Grassian, 1983; Haney, 1993; King, 1999.

15. See Grassian, 1983; Shalev, 2008.

16. See Arrigo et al., 2011; Bersot & Arrigo, 2010; Mears, 2005; Shalev, 2009b.

17. See Mears & Reisig, 2006.

18. See Pizarro & Stenius, 2004; Richards, 2008.

19. See King, 1999.

20. See Committee to End the Marion Lockdown, 1992; Richards, 2008.

21. See Kurki & Morris, 2001.

22. See Kurki & Morris, 2001.

23. See Shalev, 2008.

24. See also Haney, 2003; Kupers, 2008; Shalev, 2009b; Toch, 2003.

25. See Bersot & Arrigo, 2010; Committee to End the Marion Lockdown, 1992; Human Rights Watch, 2000; Shalev, 2011.

26. See Haney, 2003; Kupers, 2008; Shalev, 2008, 2009a, 2009b, 2011.

27. See Cockburn, 2001; Mears & Watson, 2006.

28. See Mears & Reisig, 2006.

29. See Mears & Reisig, 2006.

30. See Jackson, 2001; Pizarro & Stenius, 2004.

31. See Haney, 2003.

32. See Human Rights Watch, 2000.

33. Contributing to this position is the fact that much of the isolation research examining the psychological consequences of short-term segregation emphasizes administrative confinement only. The absence of studies focused specifically on short-term segregation for disciplinary or punitive purposes represents a serious deficiency in the literature and a significant limitation to the present inquiry.

34. See Haney, 2006.

35. See Zinger & Wichmann, 1999.

36. Overall, methodological and assessment concerns here cluster around five key issues: (1) the failure to administer pretests; (2) the failure to review an inmate's presegregation psychological or behavioral record, or both; (3) the failure to disaggregate those who volunteer to be placed in solitary confinement from those who do not; (4) relying on and generalizing from small sample sizes; and (5) drawing inferences from isolated inmates with special circumstances (e.g., those that file class-action lawsuits for their treatment while segregated in control units) (Pizarro & Stenius, 2004). These concerns can lead to erroneous evaluative findings, making it difficult, if not impossible, to explain and predict accurately the psychological effects of solitary confinement.

37. See Haney & Lynch, 1997; Toch, 2001.

38. See *Jones'El v. Berge*, 2001; *Madrid v Gomez*, 1995.

39. See Haney, 2006; Haney & Lynch, 1997; Kupers, 2008; Shalev, 2008, 2009a, 2009b.

40. E.g., Grassian, 1983, 2006; Grassian & Friedman, 1986; Haney, 2003, 2006; Jackson, 2001; Shalev, 2008, 2009a.

41. See Haney, 2003.

42. However, evidence in support of the negative consequences of solitary confinement, even the most extreme, rests principally on case study data, testimonials, availability heuristics, and anecdotal reporting. Scientifically speaking, these data represent "weak" evidence necessitating validation through sound quasiexperimental designs. Complicating the procurement of such evidence-based analyses is the highly politicized nature of the U.S. prison system generally. Regrettably, this condition makes any assessment of the iatrogenic effects of solitary confinement very unlikely.

43. Certainly the pathological behavior exhibited by those in solitary confinement could well have existed in much less severe lockup conditions or even "on the street." Indeed, the importation and psychological "deep freeze" theories of Thomas, Peterson, and Zingraff (1978) and Zamble and Porporino (1988) aptly make this point. In short, the behavior of incarcerates may have less to do with the conditions of confinement than with their personality makeup and their coping mechanisms, which are themselves longstanding character traits. Empirical research on the psychological effects of solitary confinement has yet to systematically account for these potential confounds. For a thoughtful analysis examining the complexities of prison adjustment in general, mindful of various individual, environmental, and interactive effects, see Wright (1991); and in relation to supermax facilities in particular, see Mears and Watson (2006).

44. See Haney, 2003.

45. See also Haney, 2003; Kupers, 1999.

46. Admittedly, Grassian's research findings could be questioned on the basis of several response bias artifacts, especially given the small sample size. However, more recent clinically oriented studies provide some support for Grassian's overall findings (see, e.g., Toch, 2001, 2003, especially in relation to supermax facilities).

47. See Jackson, 2001; Suedfeld, 1974; Suedfeld, Ramirez, Deaton, & Baker-Brown, 1982; Zinger et al., 2001.

48. It is worth noting, however, that the classic sensory deprivation (SD) literature reports that the dramatic effects of extreme SD—as a pure form of solitary confinement—have yet to be replicated due to response bias on the part of the researchers (e.g., Zubeck, 1969). The lack of replication studies focused on an acute and chronic stimulus-reduced environment (i.e., no light, no sound, and no sensation) within the SD literature raises questions about the validity of those findings that point to the harmful effects of SD in a prison-based solitary confinement setting.

49. See Casella, 2010; Grassian, 2010; Shalev & Lloyd, 2011.

50. See Cockburn, 2001; Grassian, 2006.

51. See Fellner, 2006; Haney, 2003, 2006; Human Rights Watch, 1997; Jackson, 2001; McCorkle, 1995.

52. See McCorkle, 1995.

53. See Haney 2003; Kurki & Morris, 2001; Shalev 2009b.

54. See Mears & Watson, 2006.

55. See Mears, 2005; Mears & Reisig, 2006.

56. See McCorkle, 1995; Shaylor, 1998.

57. See also Fagan & Meares, 2008; Reiman, 2005; Rhodes, 2004.

58. See also Fagan & Meares, 2008; Herivel & Wright, 2003; Reiman, 2005.

59. See also Bersot & Arrigo, 2010; Sellers & Arrigo, 2009.

60. See Arrigo & Bersot, 2013; see also Arrigo, 2004, 2011.

61. See Arrigo et al., 2011; see also Bersot & Arrigo, 2010; Sellers & Arrigo, 2009.

62. See Wexler, 2008; Winick & Wexler, 2006.

63. See also Schma, Kjervik, & Petrucci, 2005; Wexler, 2008.

64. See Winick & Wexler, 2006.

65. See Wexler, 2008.

66. See Winick & Wexler, 2006.

67. See Kupers, 1999; Rhodes, 2004; Shalev, 2009b.

68. See Polizzi & Draper, 2009.

69. See Sullivan & Tifft, 2005.

70. See also Sullivan & Tifft, 2005; Van Ness & Heetderks Strong, 2006.

71. See Bazemore & Boba, 2007; Umbreit, Coates, & Armour, 2006.

72. See Robert & Peters, 2003; Van Ness & Heetderks Strong, 2006.

73. See Haney, 2003; Haney & Lynch, 1997; Mears & Watson, 2006; Shalev, 2008, 2009a, 2009b; Toch, 2001, 2003.

74. See also Wexler, 2008; Winick & Wexler, 2006.

75. See Bonta & Gendreau, 1995; Polizzi & Draper, 2009; Rogers, 1993; Suedfeld et al., 1982.

76. See Banks, 2009; Rhodes, 2004.

77. See Kurki & Morris, 2001; Mears & Reisig, 2006; Pizarro & Stenius, 2004; Shalev, 2008, 2009a, 2009b.

PART III

International Perspectives on Solitary Confinement

When first I was put in prison some people advised me to try and forget who I was. It was ruinous advice. It is only by realizing what I am that I have found comfort of any kind. Now I am advised by others to try on my release to forget that I have been in a prison at all. I know that would be equally fatal. It would mean that I would always be haunted by an intolerable sense of disgrace, and that those things that are meant for me as much as for anybody else—the beauty of the sun and the moon, the pageant of the seasons, the music of daybreak and the silence of great nights, the rain falling through the leaves, or the dew creeping over the grass and making it silver—would all be tainted for me, and lose their healing power, and their power of communicating joy. To regret one's own experiences is to arrest one's own development. To deny one's own experiences is to put a lie into the lips of one's own life. It is no less than a denial of the soul.

—Oscar Wilde, *"The Picture of Dorian Gray" and Other Writings*

| 11 |

Doing Hard Time in the United Kingdom

David Honeywell

Between 1984 and 1985, I was serving a 30-month youth custody prison sentence in North East England's Durham Prison, one of the most famous old penal institutions in the United Kingdom. It has been the home of some of Britain's most infamous criminals over the years, including Rose West, Myra Hindley, the Kray twins, Frankie Fraser, and John McVicar. It is also the resting place of a number of men and women executed and buried on its grounds.

Like most of the prisoners at Durham, I was fascinated by the prison's past and some of the infamous villains who had been incarcerated there, such as McVicar. I wanted to read his biography (McVicar, 1979),[1] but the prison authorities banned it, and if anyone was caught with the book, it was confiscated. It was said that this was because, apart from his infamous escape from Durham's E wing in 1968, which embarrassed the authorities, he "slagged off" (insulted) the prison and the "screws" (guards), many of whom were still working at Durham when I was a prisoner there.

My first job in Durham was working as a cleaner in the "search tank," where prisoners were frisked before going over to reception. This job was a real easy number, just doing a bit of sweeping and polishing for a few hours a day. The screw in charge of me remembered McVicar and had a reputation of being a nasty piece of work, but he was all right with me. He told me McVicar was a real handful but very intelligent. Someone eventually did manage to smuggle McVicar's book in to me by tearing off the front page. But when one of the screws "sussed" (discovered) it, the book was removed and put in my property for when I was released. However, I noticed it had mysteriously vanished when that day arrived. I was inspired by McVicar's educational achievements during his time in prison. It really made me want to do the same as he had, and when I was released in 1985, I tried to follow his example.

My First Stay at Durham Prison

I was dreading my 30 months ahead, while other men just took it as an occupational hazard, eager to get on the wing and see all their buddies. After being processed, signing for our property, getting a bath, and exchanging our clothes for our new prison attire, we were taken to our cells. My new clothes consisted of two blue T-shirts, two blue-and-white-striped shirts, an ill-fitting pair of half-mast blue denims, and hard black shoes that had been worn by hundreds of others before me and would give you blisters, if not cripple your feet. We were then each given a plastic mug, knife, fork and spoon, toothbrush, tooth powder, some White Windsor soap, two towels, two blankets, two pillowcases, and two sheets.

By the time we were processed and taken to our cells, it was usually quite late because we had spent all day at court, so by the time we'd gone through the prison reception ordeal, the day was over. Once we were on D wing, we

Figure 11.1. Exterior of Durham Prison. Courtesy of the *Northern Echo*

were allowed a free reception letter and some money to buy a few items or toiletries. We were also entitled to a reception visit, which was an extra visit you could request where your friends or family could come and see you as soon as they could get there. In the "tuck shop" (inmate store), which was the old gallows, I bought a half ounce of Golden Virginia tobacco, a box of matches, some Rizla cigarette papers, and a penny chew. We were then led up the steep metal stairs to the second landing, called "the twos," where the first man was let into his cell. Eventually, we reached the third landing, "the threes," where my cell was situated.

Reality hit me as my door was unlocked and I looked into this tiny, cold, dark room. I entered what was now to become my new home. The door slammed behind with a deafening sound that echoed across the whole landing. There was a single blue hospital bed with a striped mattress and a single pillow. I threw all of my bedding onto it and absorbed my new surroundings. In the corner was a triangular table with a blue top, with another small table next to it to have my meals on. The cell window was so high that I couldn't reach it without standing on the table. But when I sat on the wooden chair and gazed up toward it, I could see the stars, which made me wish I could just freely stand out there in the cold night air.

The cell had a single lightbulb, which I couldn't turn on because the switch was on the other side of the door. At 10 P.M. was lights-out, and we were plunged into total darkness. Then I was alone in the dark with only my thoughts, and like replaying a video, my mind drifted back and recalled the day's events, which now seemed to be a far distant memory.

It was difficult to get to sleep. Every so often I could hear the spyhole cover move slightly, as a screw would take a peek to make sure all was well. Thinking of my family, I felt a deep sadness inside me that they were so far away and I would not be able to get close to them for quite a while. I started to realize that I would not have my mother's home cooking to look forward to for a long time, and I wouldn't be able to watch late films with her like we used to do. I thought about how she was now alone in that house back in Middlesbrough. She told me years later how, just after I was sent down, she went over to a café and bought a coffee, which lasted an hour as she stared into space, numbed with shock. Her son, who had always been such a good kid in the past, was now an inmate at one of the most notorious prisons in the country.

The First Morning

I must have drifted off to sleep, because suddenly a bright light glaring in my face woke me as the screws stomped along the landings, switching on the cell lights and peeping through our spyholes. It was morning and time to get up. As I forced myself out of bed and onto the icy floor on this cold winter's day, I could hear the loud, piercing echoes of screws shouting to one another. "All ready on the twos, Mr. Pendlworth?" "All ready on the twos, sir!" came the response. "All ready on the threes, Mr. Stevens?" "All ready on the threes, sir!" Then the order followed: "Okay, unlock!"

The doors were unlocked and left slightly ajar. I popped my head out and could see lines of men wearing blue T-shirts and blue denims, sleepily dragging themselves along the landing at 6:30 A.M. I saw that they were all carrying plastic chamber pots to slop out their human waste that had accumulated through the night, bowls to collect water to wash their grubby hands and faces, and white plastic jugs to carry drinking water. In those days, we didn't have toilets and washbasins in the cells, so we had to use those plastic chamber pots as toilets. Three times a day, we were unlocked to dispose of their contents in the daily ritual known as "slop out," when we emptied our chamber pots into a toilet down the hall and the bowls of dirty water into large sinks situated in the recess area.

Tempers were frayed, as it was far too early in the morning to be suddenly woken by a bright light and a bang on the door, followed by the screw bellowing, "Slop out!" There was one toilet in the recess area at the foot of each landing, and if you could get there before someone else beat you to it, you made the most of it. I had never thought using a toilet could be such a luxury, but it was at times like these that we realized how much we'd taken everything in life for granted. The disadvantage of the toilet, though, was that the door was only waist high, so while everyone was crammed in the packed recess slopping out, they could see you sitting on the "throne." The prisoners had sort of a mutual respect among each other, though. Whenever you had to use the chamber pot in the cell, your cellmate would read a newspaper or, if lying on his bed, turn and face the wall to give you some privacy. The cells didn't have toilets in those days because Durham dated from the Victorian era and wasn't originally designed to have toilets.

Some of the prisoners couldn't stomach the stench of their waste festering at the foot of the bed and would try to persuade a screw to let them use the toilet in the recess area. But because some power-mad screws wouldn't allow it, these prisoners would do their business on a newspaper, fold it up like a parcel, and sling it through the bars. Then some other poor mug would end up having to scoop it up the next day. If someone had bad guts and desperately needed to go, he would plead with the screws. Then some of the guards who were OK would allow them to use the toilet, but some just wouldn't. Sometimes when I was coming back from a visit or work, I would see rows of fallen "tallies" (metal number plates) where prisoners had pressed their buzzers to get the attention of the screws, who were standing at one end of the landing ignoring them all.

As the morning ritual unfolded, once we'd collected our water and slopped out, a screw would come around with a wooden box, which had all our individually named razor blades inside. The paper wrapped around the razor blades had our names on it, because we used the same blade every morning until it was replaced with a new one at the end of the week. You always had to be clean-shaven unless you made a formal application and were granted permission to grow facial hair, which was officially known as "changing your appearance." Shortly afterward, the screw would collect the razor blades, but while we were waiting for him to come back, we quickly used this period to split our matches into four so they would last longer. It was quite a skill to be able to slice a match into four parts while making sure the sulphur remained intact.

Slopping out was allegedly abolished in England and Wales by 1996 and scheduled to end in Scotland by 1999. But the abolishment was delayed because of budget restraints, and by 2004, prisoners in five of Scotland's 16 prisons still had to slop out. In 2007, when slopping out ended in Her Majesty's (HM) Young Offenders Institution Polmont, this left HM Prison Peterhead as the last prison where prisoners did not have access to proper sanitation. First opened in 1888, it was closed in 2013. For all that time, the cells had no electricity or plumbing. Until recently, 300 prisoners there used chemical toilets because of the difficulty of installing modern plumbing in the prison's granite structure.

The Prisoners

As my first eventful day in Durham continued, to my relief, I saw some familiar faces from Low Newton Prison, where I had been sent to await trial in 1983. Elvis, with whom I had shared a cell in Low Newton, was "banged up" (prison slang for celled) nearby, and a couple of others were there as well. They all looked as though reality was just kicking in for them too.

As I walked down the flights of metal stairs for breakfast, I saw what looked like a female prisoner strutting along the landing like a model on a catwalk. He had a certain rapport with the screws and other prisoners, and all you could hear was "Laura!" "Laura!" echoing from all directions. Laura was the first transsexual I had ever seen, and from what I was seeing, he was one very popular prisoner. He was going through a whole sex change, apparently, using hormone medication and so on. You could see he loved all the attention he received as much as everyone enjoyed having such a great character around to brighten up the long, dull days. On the big shower day, Laura had to have a bath segregated from the rest of us. I was told it was because of his body changes and that he would get excited being around us; prison gossip is even worse than gossip "on the out." He was always in and out of prison for soliciting on a regular basis, but he hadn't been released long when, one day, while gazing through my cell window, I saw him being escorted back in again by a screw. Someone shouted from his cell window, "What you in for Laura?" "Murder!" he replied. He was charged with murdering his father but was eventually acquitted.

Laura was a regular face in the prison, and it would have been difficult to distinguish him from a real woman had we not known who he was. Every Sunday morning, the chapel was packed with everyone wanting a glimpse of Laura, who basked in all the attention he was getting. Well, I very much doubt they were all in chapel because they'd all suddenly seen the light. It was also an extra hour out of our cells. On my last day before being released, I waved across to Laura's cell to say good-bye. Years later, I heard that Laura had died of AIDS in Newcastle.

One day, Dr. David Jenkins led the chapel service and received a rapturous applause from us all because of his outspokenness. Bishop Jenkins was known for his willingness to speak his mind. After leaving office in 1994, he continued to voice his opinions, such as in a BBC interview in 2003. Then in 2005, he became one of the first clergymen in the Church of England to bless a civil partnership between two homosexual men, one of whom was a vicar. In 2006, he was banned from preaching in some of his local churches after reportedly "swearing" in a sermon. The words used were "bloody" and "damn," but he was a huge hit with cons, that's for sure.

Prison doesn't have a particular type of person as one might expect. Prisoners come in all shapes and sizes, nationalities, ages, and backgrounds. There were murderers, shoplifters, rapists, persons who refused to pay for the license required in the United Kingdom to watch television, and some who preferred spending six weeks a year in prison to paying child support. It was a real mixed bag of people. The place was full of characters, some of whom scared me and fascinated me at the same time. There was one ruthless, well-known villain who was loud and as large as life. He was able to walk around as he pleased, and the screws never challenged him. He would go berserk at night hammering on his cell door, releasing his pent-up anger, but was never "nicked" (caught for doing something wrong and subsequently punished) for it.

As I got to the breakfast "queue" (line), a huge bloke who was as "camp" (homosexual) as they come was eyeing up the new young prisoners. He was in charge of the cleaners, who also served food to prisoners alongside some of the screws. There was old Albert, who had spent his lifetime in and out of the place since his first sentence of seven years for stealing a shirt from a store. He was about 72 years old and would always run up to you and "natter away" (chatter or talk) as you walked along. You'd see him every day walking along D wing picking up "dog-ends" (butts) off the floor, which he'd collect until he had enough to make a new cigarette.

Albert was respected by the screws because of his age, the fact he was harmless, and because they'd known him for so long. We all loved characters. He eventually died in the prison, which may sound sad, but he was among people he regarded as family. There was also a well-known tramp that would deliberately get sent back to prison by smashing a window or something as soon as he was released. Toward Christmas, a lot of homeless people would do the same. He saw the prison as his home, and it was better than his living conditions on the streets. This is one of the most tragic things about some of these prisoners' lives. Some of them would rather be in prison than in their alternative living arrangements. It wasn't necessarily because they were shirking responsibility, as many would think. In many cases, it was because of mental illness or an inability to cope with the outside world, and for some, because prison life was a damn sight better than their home life. This doesn't mean that prison was easy; it was just that their home lives were so tragic that prison was a better alternative. One elderly prisoner, who also died in prison, named the "governor" (prison warden) as his next of kin.

Meals

As we shuffled along the queue for our breakfast, we picked up a metal silver tray that had different sections: a circular one for your mug, another partition for your knife and fork, then two square sections for your main course and pudding. There were several long tables behind which stood a line of inmate cleaners and screws wearing white coats, who slopped food from huge pans onto the prisoner's trays. We each got two dollops of porridge that was so thick you could have used it to cement the cracks in your cell walls, along with a scoop of sugar that we saved in a jar as a sort of luxury for when we had our tea at suppertime. We also got a boiled egg with four slices of bread and a round knob of butter. At the far end of the cafeteria line were two large urns with coffee and tea.

Mealtimes were always the highlights of our day. Lunch would consist of something like chicken or vegetable pie, mash (creamed potatoes) and gravy, with "duff" (pudding) such as sponge and custard. At tea time, around 4:30 P.M., we were served a lighter meal, with perhaps chips (fried potatoes) and ham and a different piece of fruit each day. On weekends, we got large homemade cookies, which were delicious. Each night around 9 P.M., a screw and a kitchen orderly would come around with a tea urn on top of a trolley and a tray of cookies left over from earlier.

Once we'd all taken our food to our cells, we were locked in; then after lunch, our doors were unlocked so we could put our trays outside the cells for the cleaners to collect on a trolley. Then the whole prison would go silent for about an hour and a half while everyone "took 40 winks." Sometimes you could hear a pin drop, apart from the distant sound of soft music coming from transistor radios around the prison. At about 2 P.M., you would hear doors being unlocked for those who had to go back to work and for some who had visitors.

The Cockroaches

Durham Prison was loaded with cockroaches because of the lack of proper sanitation. The building was more than 170 years old and had housed prisoners for many decades. We ate our food in our cells among the cockroaches and human waste. I was usually on the top bunk, where my head was near the ventilator through which the cockroaches crawled into our cell, so I blocked all the holes up, but they still crawled underneath the cell door. Sometimes you would move a towel or book and there'd be one there. Sometimes they appeared in our food. I remember seeing the familiar long antennae peeping through my mashed potatoes, and another time I ate what I thought was a black chip, but then realized it was in fact half a cockroach.

Our Days in the Prison

Something that stood out was how everything echoed so loudly through the prison. Slamming gates and cell doors resonated across the whole building, and when you were in your cell, you could hear the screw's boots squeak as they stomped along the rattling metal landings. During visiting hours, you'd listen carefully, hoping that their footsteps would get closer and you'd be unlocked because a visitor had come to see you. You would hear them gradually getting closer to your door, then there would be a brief pause outside as your identity card was checked, then the sound of the keys turning in the keyhole. Our identity cards, which were outside the cell in a wooden slot, were different colors: white for Protestants and red for Catholics. The card displayed the prisoner's name, religion, prison number, sentence, and dietary requirements, if there were any.

Every evening, we were unlocked to socialize during what was known as "association." We were allowed about two hours starting around 6 P.M., when we could leave our cell doors open and mingle with one another, play pool, and watch television. We were "banged up" again about 8 P.M.

Once a week, our laundry was changed. We got fresh sheets, pillowcases, and clothing and were also allowed a shower. We collected our bedding from the cleaners, who were always supervised by a screw. Then we all congregated at the huge communal shower room and handed over our dirty clothes to a screw on reception in exchange for fresh clothing, which we then placed in a basket for after we'd finished showering.

Moves to Different Cells

During my time in Durham, I had several moves to different cells, my first one being on A wing, which was the young prisoner (YP) wing. YPs all wore green denim jackets, whereas the over-21-year-old prisoners, known as "the cons," wore blue denim jackets. We weren't allowed to mingle with the cons. We had to congregate together and go to the gym at different times, shower at different times, and all live on the same landing. The cell here was like an icebox. I just sat in it all day with a blanket wrapped around me.

I could see the women's E wing situated on H block, from where McVicar had escaped. The women convicts played their music loud enough for us to hear, and they'd wave across and shout to us. I can remember one day the reggae sounds of Bob Marley coming from one of their cell windows, filling the air. And for the short amount of time it lasted, the music took us beyond the prison walls, making us forget where we were. One of the female prisoners there at the time was Judith Ward, now known for being a victim of "unsafe convictions." She was convicted of bombing Euston Station in 1973 and the National Defense College and the M62 (the superhighway that connects Liverpool to Leeds) coach bombings in 1974. "Unsafe convictions" means a person was found guilty because the evidence was wrong or the witnesses didn't tell the truth. After a judge ruled her convictions unsafe, Judith Ward had her convictions quashed and was released from prison in 1992. The bombings were blamed on the Provisional Irish Republican Army.

Later I was moved to another cell, where I had a cellmate called Jonesy who really loved himself. He made my life miserable, so I asked to be moved to another cell, which was located next to the old gallows. One day in the gym, Jonesy was taunting me in front of his mates, so I threatened him. But as with all bullies, he backed down and left me alone.

Workshops

After working in the search tank, I ended up in one of the workshop sewing mailbags for the Royal Mail at the rate of 2 pence a bag. Those who didn't work were given an allowance of £1.13 per week. Some of the other workshops produced goal nets for football clubs and camouflage nets for the army. Our workshop used sewing machines, whereas the other mailbag shop hand-sewed them. I wasn't interested in this work at all; I just sat there and did nothing. The one and only female screw in the prison supervised this workshop, and she made some of the men look like pussycats. She sat perched high on a chair at the head of the room, overlooking four rows of prisoners who were all machining away earning their pittance of pay. One day, she had me escorted back to my cell after noticing I hadn't even attempted to sew a single stitch. She had actually done me a great favor.

The Old Gallows

My next cell was situated close to the old gallows, callously referred to by the screws as "the topping shed." It was now the "tuck shop" where we bought our tobacco and other supplies. Durham was one of the few prisons to retain a permanent gallows. It was housed at the end of D wing, which was built in 1925, and had two condemned cells, one immediately adjacent to the gallows and one separated from the execution chamber by a corridor that led to the exercise yard. The main condemned cell was formed from three standard cells combined into one and contained a toilet and washbasin. There was a small lobby between the cell and the gallows room. A mortuary was available in the yard adjoining the ground floor of the execution chamber. Parts of the execution block still remain to this day, although the condemned cell has been removed and the pit covered over; this area is now used for storage.

During my time in Durham Prison and before, there have been many accounts of paranormal activity and people scared senseless, myself included. The gallows was situated on the first landing, "the ones," which was the ground-floor landing. You could see the old trapdoor above as we walked in to queue. Outside was a steel pedal on which the screw used to keep his foot to prevent the trapdoors from opening too soon, should there be a last-minute reprieve for the condemned prisoner. I could see directly into the cell where prisoners used to spend the final night before execution. The cell was still there and we could see inside it, but what used to be the door on the other side was now bricked up.

In the early 1990s, when the prison was being modernized, the graves of some of those executed were disturbed, including that of Mary Ann Cotton. A pair of female shoes belonging to her was found along with her bones. Several bodies were removed, including Cotton's, and all were later cremated. All of the inmates hanged in the 20th century were buried alongside the prison hospital wall, with only a broad arrow and the date of execution carved into the wall to mark the location of each grave. The original instructions regarding the burial of executed inmates stated that the only clothing an inmate should be buried in was a prison-issue shirt. The body was to be placed into a pine box and covered with quicklime, and holes were to be bored into the box before burial.

Given the prison's sinister history, then, it would seem rather silly to tamper with the unknown. But boredom was the biggest problem in prison, so you had to try to alleviate this somehow. One night, my cellmate, Tim, and I foolishly decided to make our own Ouija board. Tim had a lot of experience with this sort of thing, although it was a really stupid idea that turned into a terrifying ordeal. It resulted in tables shaking, screams from inside the cell, objects randomly tipping over, and some very peculiar disembodied sounds. I never touched a Ouija board again. Those were the longest three sleepless nights I have ever had. I have always had an interest in the paranormal, but you should never play with things you don't understand. I was relieved, though, that we didn't tell the screws what we had done.

Education Classes

We had a Scottish screw in charge of us called Mr. Assenti, who had a "firm but fair" attitude. There were always some screws that just wanted to make prisoners' lives miserable, but you tried to avoid them as much as possible. After two weeks of sewing mailbags, my brain was so numbed that I tried to get something different to do. So I asked one of the nicer screws, Mr. Coates, if I could get another job.

A few days later, a small slip of paper was pushed under my cell door, telling me I was to attend education classes the next day. This would drive me on to knuckle down to the studying that McVicar's book had inspired me to do. But it was not until many years later that I actually made some real educational achievements. Classes consisted of basic learning skills to earn accredited qualifications. It was in prison that I passed my first ever exam, which took place in a cell and for which I gained a Royal Society of Arts (RSA) English language qualification. My exam results arrived after I'd been released and made my mother very proud. My mother used to tell me that when she left the prison after visiting me, she'd see students sitting in their classrooms at Durham University and wished I was one those students instead of being in prison.

Castington Prison

In the summer of 1984, I was shipped out to Castington Young Offenders Institution in Northumberland, situated next to Acklington's Category C adult prison. I detested it. A lot of the other YPs acted like children. I think my short but memorable stint in the British Army must have helped me grow up a bit, because I always seemed to have an older head than a lot of the others.

It was only a month before my 21st birthday, after which they could no longer hold me in a young offenders prison, so it was a pointless transfer in the first place. I'd have to be moved back to Durham once I was 21 anyway. That suited me fine, though, because Durham, even with all its downsides, was where I preferred to be. Even though in Castington, we had toilets and washbasins in our cells, a nice dining hall in which to have our meals, and jobs, I just couldn't stand the place. I wanted to get out of there as soon as possible. On the positive side of things, it had an excellent gym, and we were allowed to run around the inside of the fence where there was a path.

Violence and Lack of Maturity

Castington Prison was subject to a hostage crisis in 1997, when two inmates held a prison officer hostage for 19 hours. During the disturbance, inmates lit at least two small fires at the prison. Then in 2001, the institution was involved in more controversy when the Prison Reform Trust named it the most violent detention center in England. Various improvements to the regime and facilities at Castington were implemented over the next few years, with positive results. In 2005, the chief inspector of prisons declared the prison a safe, respectful, and purposeful environment.

During my stay, fires were lit every night and cells were smashed up. It was a world away from Durham. Young offenders lack maturity, so violence is even more spontaneous than in adult prisons. Young prisoners are still entering adulthood and want to prove themselves, so bullying was more rife among the ones who wanted to gain fearsome reputations. I just wanted to be back with the mature convicts.

Medical Treatment at Castington Prison

It was a stifling summer, one of the hottest I can remember. The overpowering heat from the sun would sometimes beam through the cell windows, yet we weren't allowed to hang up a cover or blanket to block out the direct sunlight. We couldn't escape it, and I developed a terrible migraine headache. It felt as though someone were sticking a sharp object through my eye socket. The pain was excruciating, but I couldn't leave the cell or hide from the direct rays of the scorching sun. I eventually became so ill I started vomiting.

Finally one Sunday, unable to suffer the pain anymore, I rang the bell and requested to see the doctor. I was warned that if the doctor had to come out to see me specially, I'd be confined to my cell for three days, because it was Sunday and a great inconvenience for him. But I was in too much pain to care. When he eventually turned up, he prescribed a few aspirin tablets and had me sent back to my cell. I was then punished for being unwell and causing such an inconvenience, but it was normal to be treated with contempt by the prison medical team and civilian staff. The mentality of these fools was to confine me for three days to my cell, where I was in constant pain from the direct sunlight for even longer periods of time. At least before then, I could go to the dining hall for my meals to escape it for a short time, whereas now I was having all my meals brought to me.

Prison medical care for inmates was diabolical. Rude, uncaring people ran the prison medical center. I despised the prison civilian medical staff. I reviled no prison officer or other member of staff as much as these people. If you were on medication, it was slammed down in front of you when you went to collect it. You could see the hate on their faces as they spoke to you like dirt.

Aspirin water, which was one or two aspirins crushed into water, was the answer to everything. Prisoners were given aspirin water for every type of ailment, even for some of the most serious injuries. I remember a prisoner once being given aspirin water after he broke his arm. During my time in prison in the 1990s, when I returned for another offense, some of my gums became infected, causing painful toothache, but so bad was the health care that my teeth were left to rot until I was released, at which point I had to have several removed.

Return to Durham Prison

When I turned 21, they transferred me back to Durham. After Castington, I looked forward to returning to Durham Prison. I got a job in the kitchen, which is usually one of the most popular jobs in any prison. The kitchen in Durham was infested with cockroaches, as were the cells and the rest of the prison. If you moved a bag of flour, you would suddenly see swarms of them scuttling across the kitchen floor. But the job brought with it certain privileges, such as extra portions of food and more than one shower a week with more changes of clothing. We always wore white T-shirts instead of the usual blue ones, and the screws always wore white coats.

As in most prisons, the screws who worked every day with prisoners, whatever the work was, tended to develop better relationships with prisoners than those who only worked on the "landings" (cellblocks). The "work screws" used to treat their prisoner sidekicks more like workmates, which led them to develop a rapport and mutual respect. Prisoners and prison officers in the workplace had a different kind of relationship and interaction than on the landings.

Applying for Parole

Several months earlier, I had applied to be considered for parole. The term "jam roll" is English prison slang for parole where a prisoner is released into the community to serve the remainder of his sentence. In criminal justice systems, parole is the supervised release of a prisoner before the completion of his sentence in prison. This differs from amnesty or commutation of sentence, in that parolees are still considered to be serving their sentences and may be returned to prison if they violate the conditions of their parole.

One day while lying on my bed, I could hear several prisoners talking outside while waiting to be let into their cells. Whenever you came back from work or a visit, a screw escorted you back to the landing. You would then walk to your cell and wait for the landing screw to come along and open the door to let you in. If there were no screws around, one of us would have to go to the office and ask to be let in. I didn't like to do this, because the screws' office was a place of hostility. Whenever you needed to go to the office for anything, there were usually half a dozen screws sitting around doing nothing. It felt quite intimidating at times, as they would just glare at you while you were trying to talk to the wing officer, the principal officer on D wing (the principal officer was in charge of the wing, and the senior officer was the next rank down). The wing officer was completely unapproachable and always appeared on the verge of a nervous breakdown. He used to sit at his desk with his bright red face looking as though he were about to explode at any moment. His blood pressure must have been sky-high.

It was about 4 P.M., as the lads had just finished work. A sheet of paper suddenly slid under my door, which I recognized by the logo at the top of the page as being from the Home Office. I knew it was my parole answer so, bracing myself for bad news, I anxiously read down the page until I saw "a panel of the parole board considered your case on 19 August 1984 and found you suitable for release on parole license from 4 September 1984." Nowadays, you're actually summoned to the office to see the wing officer, who presents you with the paper and discusses your conditions with you. But holding this letter in my hand that listed my parole conditions with a recommended date of release was all I needed, and the feeling inside was one of elation. I had butterflies, my adrenaline was pumping, and my mind was racing.

I had been in prison for only 10 months, but it had seemed like years. It had been my first time in prison for any length of time, and the prison environment was so far removed from any kind of reality. But it wasn't just the length of time I'd spent in prison that made me feel so isolated from the outside world; it was also the total absence of anything remotely associated with normality. Prison is an artificial environment with a false community and abnormal behavior, where mountains are made out of molehills and you view things from a totally different perspective than you would outside.

It soon got around the prison grapevine that my parole had come through. Someone I'd worked with in the mailbag workshop, a Liverpudlian I knew only as "Scouse," shouted through my cell door, "I heard you got your parole, mate!" "Yeah!" I shouted back. "Well done, mate," he said. Each day then became longer than usual, because once you are given a parole date, you're urging your release day on, as it's only days away. This is referred to as being "gate happy."

The day before my release, I was taken to reception to check my property and sign for it. I noticed that McVicar's book had mysteriously vanished from my property, and nobody had a clue what I was talking about. But at least I could buy another copy when I got home. Once I'd signed for my property, ready for the following day's release, I knew my parole hadn't been a mistake or a dream; I was actually on my way home. But even though it was official, I couldn't help but think that something would go wrong somehow. I became a bit paranoid, thinking, "What if someone starts trouble with me—someone who is jealous that I'm getting out?" I remember wondering if I should stay in my cell for the next few days in case anything happened to me and my parole got revoked before I was even released. But it never happened, and I was unlocked early that morning and told to be ready in 10 minutes. They didn't have to hurry me; I had been ready for hours. I used those 10 minutes to say good-bye to Scouse and some of the others.

Your release day is an exciting experience; you're on "cloud nine." There's no point trying to get any sleep the night before, because you won't manage it. I took breakfast in the reception area that morning while my paperwork was being prepared. Everyone makes sure he eats his breakfast before being released, even if he is too excited to have an appetite, because superstition says that if you don't eat it, you come back to finish it. One of the other inmates got into an argument with one of the screws behind the desk for some reason and was sent back to his cell. This made me feel very worried that this could happen on my release day. I kept my head down and my mouth shut and just went with the flow.

We were handed long, brown cardboard boxes with our names and numbers on them, containing the clothes we had been wearing when we came to prison. We were then told to go and get changed in some cubicles. Prisoners were always given the clothes they were wearing when they were brought in, unless they had served a long time and their body weight had changed considerably, in which case they could claim for a clothing grant. One of the prisoners, a huge black guy who was well over 6 feet tall and massively built, was arrested at Christmas wearing a Santa Claus costume, so he had to travel home dressed as Santa. He was forced to sit on public transport in his red-and-white suit, with a big hood and big black boots, in the middle of a hot summer's day on what must have been a very long journey.

After we had changed into our clothes, we were handed our property. It was nice to be able to hold my wallet and handle money again. It made me feel like a proper person again, because we didn't handle money while in prison. We were given a week's social security money and a green form to take to the Job Centre, where we then signed on for unemployment benefits. My ultimate feeling of excitement was when standing anxiously waiting in line at the gate, listening for my name to be called out by the screw reading from his list.

Getting Out of Durham Prison

As each person's name was called out, the screw would open the door for him to step out. When my name came, I stepped out and was immediately hit by the fresh air and smell of flowers. The air seemed different outside. Within the prison grounds, it's a dull gray air with a dead ambience. Another lad also from Middlesbrough was released with me, so we tagged along together. I got a chance to see the beautiful surroundings of Durham City as we walked toward the train station, soaking in every moment. Back in Middlesbrough, I couldn't wait to see my mother, who had stood by me all the way.

I was given instructions to go meet my new probation officer, Russell, who was quite new to his work and around the same age as me. Each week, I visited him to talk through what I'd been up to. But my euphoria was short-lived, as once again I became restless and bored with everything in my life. There were times I would turn up for my appointments under the influence of alcohol.

Recalled to Durham Prison

I was continually drifting, unsure what do with my life. I was drinking too much and being erratic. My parole license was supposed to last for 10 months. Unfortunately, my probation officer was concerned about me, as well as the safety of others, so he contacted the Home Office. After I had spent only six months on the street, the Home Office recalled me back to prison.

One evening around 7:30 P.M., while I was getting ready for a night out, I heard a knock at the door. When I moved the curtains and looked out the window, I could see a police sergeant. I knew why the police had come. They were unaware of why they had been sent to arrest me, but I knew my parole had been revoked. I was taken back to Durham Prison to complete another pointless four months.

Back at Durham, I went through the same old rigmarole of reception, and this time I was taken to D wing, where I shared a cell with two others. Most of the cells had three men sharing the 9-by-5-foot space. I tried to talk to a couple of screws about why I was back there to see if it could be appealed against, but it was falling on deaf ears.

Shortly after being back, I was transferred to C wing, which was a sort of privileged wing. It had a dartboard, pool table, and the usual television room. Some of the "cons" played chess and dominoes. It was smaller than the main D wing landing, which was massive. Prisoners had to be selected for C wing. It was where the red-band trustees, most being less violent offenders and short-termers, were housed. I don't know why I was taken to C wing, but it was probably because I was only there for four months. Going back to Durham

Prison had a bad psychological effect on me, though. I was so stressed because of the shock of being recalled. As part of the reception process, the day after I was recalled, I was taken to the see the governor (prison warden), who told me that they would be releasing me again on license as soon as possible, as they felt I didn't need to be there. This naturally lifted my spirits enormously.

My new cell was opposite the main gate, and at night, you could hear the pub goers leaving the local boozer. I hated my cellmate and he hated me, but it wasn't long to endure. I knocked about with some good guys, such as "Fingers," who at some point in his life had had some of his fingers chopped off. He was a fellow bodybuilder, so we used to chat about that and the benefits of training. Also within my close circle of friends was a chap named Andy, who was the manager of a North East England 1980s chart band. A few doors away lived a red band named Steve, who was a former soldier in the Army Intelligence Corps.

Red bands are trustee prisoners with extra privileges, and they were all housed on C wing. One of the best jobs in the prison that red bands could do was working in the officer's mess. I couldn't get over how different C wing and the prisoners there were compared with the others, but like Castington, this privileged environment nauseated me too. I always hated to see groveling and "sucking up." I preferred to be with the majority, where we were all in the same boat. I didn't ask to go on C wing.

Returning to Education Classes at Durham Prison

I took up my education classes from where I'd left off and started studying English language. The teachers who worked at the prison were always very approachable and easygoing, but it was common to get schoolboy crushes on some of them. After being deprived of female company for so long, it's easy to cling onto anything that touches the heart. It is very false, though, as is the whole prison environment. It's all in the mind, but it can bring out the more sensitive side of a man. One of my fellow prisoners did have an affair with a teacher, and the last I heard, they got married on his release. The interaction with the teachers made prison life a lot easier. We spent most of our days with them, so we developed a good rapport and bond. They made us feel like human beings by calling us by our first names or Mr. So-and-So. Some of the screws disapproved of this familiarity and objected to it, but thankfully, our liberal-thinking teachers had their own way of doing things. It was always a nice little victory to get one over on the screws as well.

It was at this stage of my sentence that I decided to work toward my first-ever exam. When exam day arrived and the cell door opened, a screw stood there with one of the teachers, named Debbie, ready to take me to an empty cell on the "ones," where I was to sit my exam. I flew through the questions in the hour I was given, but I still had to wait until I was unlocked. After the exam, I felt as though I'd achieved something for the first time in my life, so I went back to my cell and lay down on my bed to reflect.

The governor had mentioned to me when I was recalled that I would be released on license again, so I was so "chuffed" (pleased or happy) that I was getting out four weeks early. The day before my early release day, I was taken down to reception to check my property, so this confirmed in my mind that I was going home again. Excited to be going out, I was then taken to the wing office to see the principal officer, who told me that they'd made a mistake and I wasn't being released after all. He apologized, and although I had only four weeks left to do, it had a bad effect on me psychologically, because I had built my hopes up. So high were my feelings of anxiety that while I was eating my lunch, my nose suddenly started to bleed into my soup.

Completion of Sentence

I was fed up with cockroaches in the cell, I didn't get along with my cellmate, whom I thought was a bit of a dope, and I had just had a nasty shock, so I wasn't in the mood for anything. But my sentence wasn't for much longer, after all; it was only four weeks away, on July 25, 1985, and that's what kept me going. As the weeks passed, I was getting gate-happy again. Then finally, my latest date of release arrived. This was the release date when the sentence ended permanently, unlike parole, where you're technically serving your sentence in the community and can be sent back anytime, as I was. Some prisoners refused parole for this very reason, preferring to complete their sentences inside. Some felt that the controlling aspect of parole on their lives wasn't worth the stress. At least once you've completed your sentence, you didn't have to be supervised, abide by any rules set down by the Home Office, or attend weekly appointments with a probation officer.

Back home in Middlesbrough, I started leading a fairly stable lifestyle. I was keen on fitness and weight training, going to the local sports hall several times a week and doing long-distance running. I found exercise, running in particular, very helpful for my mental as well as physical health. I remember when I was first released from prison being too weak to run. It took several weeks of my mother's home cooking to get me back to normal.

Note

1. John McVicar grew up in East London, where he was a chess champion and scholarship schoolboy, but he turned to crime as a 16-year-old in the mid-1950s. He quickly racked up a number of jail sentences. Then at age 26, he escaped from an eight-year stretch in prison. On recapture, he received an extra 15 years.

In 1968, he escaped from Durham Prison's special wing, and for more than two years, he was hunted down as public enemy number one. Yet during that time, at the height of his infamy, he took an intellectual look at himself and, on the basis of that self-examination, decided that he would not escape if he were returned to prison nor return to crime after he was released. When he was recaptured, he hardly did anything except study. He achieved an external degree from London University, and after his release in 1978, he continued a postgraduate thesis at Leicester University. He then went on to establish himself as a reputable journalist and broadcaster.

| 12 |

Solitary Confinement and Convict Segregation in French Prisons

Martine Herzog-Evans

French public opinion has been analyzed as being much less tough on crime than that in many other countries. France is said to be in the least repressive quarter of the 60 countries that take part in the International Crime Survey.[1] If French public opinion is now becoming tougher on crime as a result of increasingly punitive penal policies,[2] future research such as the EURO-JUSTIS project will be able to tell us more about it.[3] The French people are still unlikely to accept the U.S. style of high-security regimes applying to a large number of prisoners or to let the authorities deal with inmates in an excessively harsh way. Given the current policy changes, could France nonetheless make a historical U-turn and again create high-security prisons? As I discuss in this chapter, it may be *partly* heading that way.

Former French president Nicolas Sarkozy had built his career on a "tough on crime" stance. At the time this chapter was being completed, he was returning to this old tune during the precampaign for the presidential elections of 2012, which he eventually lost. However, politicians can only go so far. France has a rather strong left wing, and this also contributes to the ambivalence of the French public and to its relative moderation. During his five years as president of France, and five years as minister of interior before that, Sarkozy had managed to change the French penal landscape considerably.[4] French prisons used to be more on a par with Foucault's descriptions.[5] However, before Sarkozy came to power, they had undergone a series of changes and opened up to the community. Since his inauguration, the Prison Administration (PA) led this institution toward a more U.S. sort of governance. Underpinning all this was an all too familiar shift away from traditional rehabilitation and back to an antiquated concept of prison and inmate management and control that emphasizes security. The history of solitary confinement in French prisons has followed these ups and downs.

From Traditional Management to Disciplinary Governance

The French prison system is now reverting to its origins. However, during the 1990s, it opened up to the community and underwent several modern reforms, and one hopes that this will prevent it from returning to the dangerous excesses of the past.

Pre-1990s: Traditional Prisons

French prisons of the 1940s and even the 1960s looked surprisingly like those of the 19th century.[6] The prison regime may have improved slightly, but it remained extremely strict. For instance, until 1969, disciplinary solitary confinement could last up to 90 days. Until 1972, prisoners who were thus punished were fed only dry bread and water just one day out of two. The prison regime was entirely based on discipline, but in a nonregulated way. For all its decisions, even of a disciplinary nature, the PA enjoyed total discretion. No judicial review existed, and prison walls were impenetrable. Inmates were deprived of most things that an ordinary citizen would take for granted. French prisoners only gained access to newspapers and the radio in 1975, to contact visits in 1983, and to television in 1985. Prison gear vanished completely in 1983 for all prisoners. Until the early 1980s, guards were typically uneducated and untrained rough men who more often than not used violence on inmates.

Such a situation was made possible as the community, politicians, and the courts had comfortably retreated from trying to control prison authorities and institutions. The legal system allowed prisons to self-determine what legal rules would regulate them.[7] This was for two reasons. First, in the French constitutional context, the executive branch can create decrees in specific domains that are separate from those that require laws. Previous interpretation of the Constitution had attributed competence to the executive and not to the legislative branch for prison matters. Second, politicians were afraid that the electorate would interpret time spent on reforming prison conditions as taking care of wicked prisoners while the poor hardworking French citizens were neglected.

In other words, prisons themselves ordinarily generated prison law virtually on their own, with historical exceptions when the French population suddenly paid attention to its prisons. This occurred in 1945, when people who resisted the Nazi occupation of France were incarcerated during the war and thus, having experienced prison conditions themselves, forced the prisons to accept changes; again after the turmoil of 1968, when revolutionaries who had been jailed started to politicize their fellow prisoners and obtained two reforms, the decrees of 1972 and 1975; and yet again after the election of a socialist president in 1981, resulting in the decrees of 1983 and 1985.

The history of solitary confinement in France thus must be seen through these lenses. Yet to fully understand its background, one must go a little farther back in time.[8] At the end of the 19th century, France was strongly influenced by the American use of solitary confinement as an ordinary prison regime for all.[9] An 1875 act made such a regime mandatory in all French prison settings. Still, France never went full scale with this reform, as it proved too costly.[10] Only some French prisons were affected by the 1875 reform, while the others kept their traditional overcrowded and more social environment. Gradually, solitary confinement receded as a normal regime. In 1957, a penal procedure code (PPC) was adopted, and all prison decrees were codified. The decrees stated that offenders would be alone in their cells at night but would share common activities during the day. In practice, however, overcrowding often meant that they also had to share their cells at night.

In 1972, after three years of post-1968 prison riots fueled by the politicization of inmates orchestrated by incarcerated young revolutionaries, the PA felt the need for new management and control tools. After decades and even centuries of using solely the stick, it added the carrot by creating remission for good behavior in the decree of 1972.

The years 1972 to 1975 also marked the first application of the concept of prison classification. Three types of prisons were created, which still exist to this day. *Maisons d'arrêt* [remand prisons] were for remand prisoners and those sentenced to short imprisonment, which meant less than one year then, two years today. In maisons d'arrêt, the prison regime was confinement at all times except during the rare activities offered to prisoners. In practice, though, extreme and chronic overcrowding has never allowed for the application of this rule. Today overcrowding is so extreme that some prisoners have to sleep on mattresses on the floor, and solitary confinement would probably appear to most inmates to be an impossible dream.[11] *Centres de detention* [detention centers] were medium-security prisons for nondisruptive prisoners or those sentenced to average-length custody sentences of longer than two years. In these prisons, prisoners were alone in their cells at night, but their doors would be opened during the days, and numerous activities were offered to them. *Maisons centrales* [central prisons] were maximum-security prisons for disruptive prisoners or those sentenced to long-term custody. They were supposed to be more security-oriented and to offer fewer activities than in centres de detention but a lot more than in maisons d'arrêt. Things were about to change again in the 1990s, however.

The 1990s: Opening Up to the Community and Law Regulation

By the end of the 1980s and for most of the 1990s, French prisons underwent drastic changes.[12] First, like their European counterparts,[13] they fully opened up to the community. Prisons hired real public servant teachers, hospital doctors, sports leaders, and so on, instead of underqualified prison contractors. The PA opened up to many third-sector agencies and charities that would come and help with such things as education, health, family links, and reentry. It even allowed the press access for interviews, photos, and films of prison staff and prisoners. Prison research became possible at long last. Sociologists and academics in other related fields obtained permission to investigate and work within the prisons relatively easily.[14]

During this period, everyday conditions in the prisons significantly improved. Convicts in both centres de detention and maisons centrales (respectively, medium- and maximum-security prisons) were allowed to make phone calls, and instead of the meager provisions of the PPC, which permitted one call a month, inmates soon were able to make calls as often as they could afford it.[15]

Another radical change concerned the recruiting and training of prison governors, or wardens,[16] and even more dramatically, of prison guards.[17] Prison governors from then on were at least master's degree graduates, and more often than not "master two" (i.e., having a fifth-year university diploma); some of them even had PhDs. Prison guards typically had a minimum of the French high school diploma, the baccalaureate, with many of them having a bachelor's degree or higher from a university. Their training at the National Penitentiary School (ENAP) improved considerably, consisting of four months at the ENAP and four months of internship. Consequently, guard-on-prisoner violence virtually disappeared, and guards were more prepared to accept better prison conditions for inmates and to submit to the rule of law. Many prisons, however, remained antique, unclean, and terribly overcrowded, as two parliamentary reports showed in 2000,[18] with the Senate calling it a "humiliation for the Republic."

Another dramatic change, a legal revolution, occurred at the time. It would have a direct influence on the choices made regarding solitary confinement and inmate classification. Before it did, albeit having being tailored by the PA itself, the rules that existed in the PPC were still deemed a bother in the field and hence were more often than not either violated or contradicted in sub-decree notes sent by the Paris central administration to its staff. At the time, administrative courts, competent with prison matters, did not control any of prison authorities' decisions. In 1932, the Conseil d'Etat [Council of State], the highest administrative court, ruled that disciplinary confinement could not be challenged in court;[19] in 1967, it ruled in the same way pertaining to administrative solitary confinement.[20] However, this was about to drastically change.

There were several reasons for this. First, the administrative courts, originally a Napoleonic invention intended to protect administrations from citizens' legal challenges, and which indeed were very friendly to the cause of administrations for most of their existence, started to significantly change throughout the 1990s. This evolution resulted in great part from the pressing influence of the European Human Rights Court, which had elaborated throughout the years a series of human rights guidelines applying to prisons.[21] Gradually, administrative courts started to overrule prison decisions and to play a larger role in monitoring the prison system.[22]

Improvement of the administrative courts' control over solitary confinement in prisons was progressive. Up until 2009, disciplinary confinement could last up to 45 days in a degraded, cold, and often nauseating solitary cell in a special unit of the prison called the "disciplinary unit." Things began to change with the *Marie* case on April 27, 1995.[23] The Conseil d'Etat ruled that from then on, disciplinary confinement could be challenged in court. However, it took several more years for the Conseil d'Etat to accept that administrative solitary confinement was not, as the PA had claimed, a mere organizational tool with no consequences for the inmate, other than being in a separate unit, and to recognize that it was in fact used as a disciplinary tool with more severe consequences than those of the disciplinary cell, since it could last for years. In *Remli*, the Conseil d'Etat ruled that these decisions could also be challenged in court.[24]

The PA was considerably annoyed at this. Not only could it no longer use any solitary confinement tool with total freedom, but also, because of a new law of April 12, 2000, both disciplinary and administrative confinement would have to be decided in the presence of the inmate, who could be, for the first time in history, assisted by an attorney. Meanwhile, many other decisions in which the PA exerted control over inmates, such as regarding visitation permits, prisoner transfers, and body searches, also became challengeable in court.

Parallel to this, and exercising a constructive competition with the administrative courts, a one-man or one-woman court, the *juge de l'application des peines* (JAP) [judge for implementation of sentences and reentry] had been pronouncing changes in prison release measures, such as conditional release and prison leave, since the 1950s, but these decisions could not be appealed. Two laws, enacted on June 15, 2000, and March 9, 2004, made such appeals possible.[25] They also imposed adversarial debates for most of the JAP decision-making.

Both of these acts were made possible by a significant circumstantial change in 2000. In January of that year, Dr. Véronique Vasseur, a general practitioner who had worked in the well-known Paris prison of La Santé (meaning "health" in English), published a book that attracted a great deal of attention from the media because, in the course of her activity at La Santé, she had met several incarcerated politicians, and in a rather unprofessional way, she revealed sensational secrets about their suicide attempts and depression. In spite—or rather, because—of this, and since at the time the media had no more compelling subject such as elections, tsunamis, or wars to cover, focus on prison conditions continued throughout the following weeks and even months. The news, talk shows, and documentaries, be they on the more commercial channels or the French equivalent of BBC (which often aired more intellectual public television programming), revealed to an increasingly shocked French public photos and videos of prison conditions, displaying rats and cockroaches, soggy showers and minuscule courtyards, sordid disciplinary cells and double or even triple bunk beds lining both sides of cells that were originally built for two inmates.

As Charles de Gaulle once famously put it, French people are exceptionally versatile when it comes to their prisons. They can get inflamed one day over so-called four-star prisons, and the very next day, when proved wrong, feel disgusted and ashamed that the "homeland of human rights" can contain such squalid jails. The latter opinion was voiced in 2000.

Unfortunately, the former point of view reappeared post September 11, 2001, and was the trigger for a decade of "tough-on-crime" discourses and reforms. France was ripe for this return to the tough-on-crime approach for the same reasons as the United States and England, as aptly described in Garland (2001).[26] This approach also halted an earlier governmental attempt to ameliorate prison conditions and regulations. September 11 enabled Nicolas Sarkozy to skyrocket through the political ranks all the way up to the presidential palace of the Elysées. His arrival at the Ministry of the Interior in 2002 marked the start of a U-turn in prison governance. He wanted not only to "discipline and punish" (Foucault, 1975), but also to control what happened in the field, and for this he relied on a traditionally Napoleonic centralist administration system, which had always given de facto superiority to the executive over all powers. From then on, penal policies were tougher on offenders through all steps of the penal process, from the investigation to trial, and then to sentence implementation and prison regime. Meanwhile, because of the increasing court control exercised over prison decisions and, in particular, solitary confinement, the PA felt the need for more control tools.

From High-Security Prisons to Disciplinary Confinement

Throughout its history, France has known various forms of solitary confinement,[27] some of which still exist to this day.[28] "Disciplinary confinement" can be pronounced when an inmate is sanctioned by the authorities and placed in a disciplinary cell. Until the 2009 Prison Act, an inmate could be made to stay in a disciplinary cell for a maximum of 45 days, setting France apart from other European countries, where the average length of time was only two weeks.[29] Today the maximum is 30 days for violent offenses and 20 days for other violations of prison rules. With reforms made in the decree of 1996 and the act of April 1, 2000, the procedure whereby the decision is made has consistently improved. Such a decision is now made by the prison governor or his substitute as part of a commission also including a prison chief and a citizen, after a hearing during which the convict is assisted by an attorney and, if needed, a translator. Appeal is possible by referring the case first to the regional director, then to the administrative court.

A second form is "administrative confinement," which is pronounced by the prison governor for the first six months; then, for periods exceeding six months, by the regional director, his superior; and for periods exceeding a year, by the central PA in Paris, their superior. Ultimately, it is thus the Ministry of Justice that takes responsibility for years-long confinement. For remand prisoners (those in local jails), the investigating judge makes the decision. He can also pronounce a third type of confinement, "communication prohibition," which totally prohibits prisoner communication with both other inmates and the free world. In this case, the prisoner is confined to a solitary cell for a maximum of 20 days and cannot communicate by visits, phone calls, or even letters with his family and other outside contacts. This chapter essentially deals with administrative confinement, which, because of its potentially endless duration, is by far the most coercive of all forms of confinements existing in French prisons. Prior to 1982, administrative confinement was rare and essentially was applied to only a few prisoners who needed protection from the rest of the prison population, the equivalent of what is called protective custody in U.S. prisons.

In 1955, France had created *quartiers de haute sécurité* (QHS) [high-security units or prisons]. For disruptive inmates, the PA used only disciplinary confinement; for dangerous, politicized, or rebellious inmates, essentially those capable of escaping, it used QHS. In QHS, as in today's American special housing unit or segregated housing unit (SHU) or supermax, everything is aimed at keeping prisoners under control. However, these prisons were first and foremost meant to prevent prison escape. In the 1950s to 1980s, they were not used for masses of inmates. In any case, it soon became apparent that

QHS were a failure. First, they were ridiculously unsuccessful at preventing prison escapes. Not only was it possible to escape from these prisons, but such escapes were much more violent because convicts could not merely "take the French leave" by using their intelligence or thanks to prison guards being negligent. Second, it soon became apparent that putting hardcore and disruptive prisoners in the same prison, even if they spent the most of their time alone, created a brewing stew of potential violence and mayhem.[30] Indeed, there were soon riots and other upheavals in these prisons, and some famous convicts managed to escape from high-security confinement, including "public enemy number one" Jacques Mesrine,[31] making a mockery of these so-called escape-proof prisons.

Human rights activists also pointed out that the conditions in these prisons were appalling and that they failed pitifully at reforming inmates because of a total lack of rehabilitative activities, which was part and parcel of the solitary confinement logic. However, real rehabilitative efforts and activities did not occur in most French prisons before the 1980s. By the time President François Mitterrand was elected in 1981, it was clear that QHS were doomed. After inaugurating his presidency with the highly symbolic abolition of the death penalty, Mitterrand and his government went on to improve prison conditions, allowing contact visits and abolishing prison gear in 1983 and introducing television in 1985.[32] By the end of the 1980s, prisoners were allowed to use phone booths.[33] It was during this same movement that, in 1982, QHS were abolished. In doing so, President Mitterrand and his government acted according to their electoral platform. Government officials had also read human rights activists' reports and pamphlets, and they paid attention to former inmates' descriptions of the severe conditions in QHS and analysis of their patent failure.[34]

Unfortunately, the PA immediately found a way out of this: it recycled administrative confinement and immediately filled confinement units with the very same prisoners it had previously sent to QHS.[35] Instead of having a whole prison or unit devoted to solitary confinement, it now used individually based administrative confinement decisions. Later, with the progress of fair trial in the case of disciplinary procedure, administrative confinement became an even more important tool for the PA when it did not want to be bothered by the rule of law nor have the courts interfere—which they did not, until 2003. The PA also felt the need for a more long-lasting and thus more damaging inmate management measure.

In practice, as in other countries, solitary confinement has not actually been used exclusively to segregate high-profile, dangerous prisoners who make the headlines with their out-of-the-ordinary violent crimes, as the PA suggested when it tried to justify this harsh measure.[36] Those who are involuntary placed in administrative confinement are typically rebels or inmates with enough charisma or networks to rally their fellow detainees, along with terrorists and people at risk of escaping. The PA thereby chooses to use this disciplinary tool to address "penitentiary dangerousness" as opposed to "criminological dangerousness."[37] So although QHS were discredited and in 1982 were abolished by President Mitterrand, for the next two decades administrative confinement became the tool of choice to tame these organized or strong personalities.[38] Where confinement in a disciplinary cell failed or was deemed insufficient, solitary confinement was used and often coupled with repeated—sometimes frantic—prison transfers.

Another PA argument in defense of this measure, voiced in particular during court cases challenging solitary confinement, is that it is in no way afflictive, as it takes place in an ordinary cell. What is thus implied is that it is in no way as uncomfortable as a squalid disciplinary cell, and it is true that inmates do reside in a solitary confinement unit with cells that are like all the others. The PA also implies that confined prisoners are actually better off than regular inmates, as they can enjoy being alone in their cells rather than having to endure overcrowding. There is some truth in this argument as well. But as in the ancient Greek myth of Scylla and Charybdis, just because one is a monster, this does not disqualify another as such. Overcrowding is unquestionably afflictive. Still, humans are social creatures, and they are usually worse off when they are alone for very long periods of time. Such is the intrinsic and acute pain attached to solitary confinement. Not only are convicts detained in one-person cells, but they also are not allowed to have any contact with the rest of the inmates, including others residing in solitary confinement. The one exception is prisoners who request solitary confinement because they fear for their own safety.

To ensure the enforcement of this no-contact rule, confined inmates go to a solitary "promenade." For the same reason, they cannot access regular prison activities such as work, training, schooling, or sports. Their only activity takes place within the cell. They can access the library at certain hours, but always alone. In other words, for those who are allegedly the most dangerous of all, the PA is virtually abandoning its core mission of rehabilitation and resocialization, as stated in both Article 707 of the PPC and Article 2 of the 2009 Prison Act. Thus the PA puts the community as a whole at risk, since its disciplinary decisions result in eventually releasing unchanged or, more likely, hardened convicts back onto the streets.

The PA also argues that prisoners are entitled to visits, an element that was decisive in the *Ramirez Sanchez* case. However, as we have seen, administrative solitary confinement is often coupled with repeated prison transfers, sending those inmates far from their families, which limits the amount of visits they can receive. In any case, these occasional visits are not sufficient to alleviate the pain associated with either long-term or solitary confinement. And indeed, this measure can last indefinitely, as there is no strict legal maximum for it, and convicts who are placed in these units thus can stay there for years.

Clearly, when the PA places a prisoner in one of these units for years, this is done with the aim of mentally breaking him or her. The French form of solitary confinement is unfortunately as dangerous and destructive for human mental health (Pedron, 1995, pp. 35–36)[39] as are its American supermax or other confinement or segregation counterparts,[40] and indeed, it "press[es] the outer borders of what most humans can psychologically tolerate" (*Madrid v. Gomez*, 1995). In addition, solitary confinement has adverse consequences, such as leading to greater chances of reoffending (Lovell & Johnson, 2003). It can thus be said that "inside safety is the enemy of outside safety."

The only hope for these inmates is a judicial review by administrative courts, which have made things much harder for the PA over the last several years. After the *Remli* ruling in 2003, whereby the Conseil d'Etat had showed it intended to control individuals, it then went on to annul a decree regulating administrative solitary confinement, as a law should have been passed and not a simple decree. The Conseil d'Etat referred to Articles 3 and 8 of the European Human Rights Convention,[41] along with the UN International Covenant on Civil and Political Rights of 1966, the UN Convention on the Rights of the Child, and French constitutional rules,[42] thereby importantly showing that France was ready to submit to all international regulations concerning prison law.

To be honest, the European Human Rights Court long remained rather understanding when it came to solitary confinement; it usually ruled that it did not violate Article 3 of the HER Convention,[43] unless the offender had been submitted to additional terrible duress.[44] Such was not the case for the terrorist nicknamed Carlos, who was detained in France, as he received more than 100 visits from his lawyer and had access to certain—albeit solitary—activities.[45] In 2009, however, France was held in breach of Article 3 in the case of M. Khider, a person with mental problems and thus more vulnerable, who had been placed in solitary confinement for several years, was transferred numerous times, and was made to submit to multiple body searches.[46]

As a result of this jurisprudence, during the early years of 2000, administrative solitary confinement suddenly became much less attractive as a management tool for the PA, which could not enjoy the same decisional discretion it had for the previous decades. Typically, though, it soon found another way of controlling troublesome convicts. This time, it aimed for large-scale control.

Today: From Disciplinary Confinement of a Few to the Classification of All

As soon as the *Remli* case had been definitely ruled in 2003, preceded in 2002 by an identical decision of the Administrative Court of Appeal of Paris, the PA decided to generalize a system that was new in France and had been experimental in one prison since 1999: "inmate classification." Rather than dealing with a handful of problematic prisoners on an individual basis with administrative solitary confinement or disciplinary sanctions, the PA decided to control the entire prison population by separating "no trouble" and "trouble" inmates.

Legally, though, it would not necessarily be a straightforward path. According to the Council of Europe's European Prison Rules (EPR), adopted in 2006, states should not use classification for a large number of prisoners. In the commentary to the rules (n° 51.5), it was explained that if classification could be useful in certain circumstances, there currently was a serious risk, given the manner in which it was implemented in Western world countries, that too many inmates would be subjected to high-security measures, which was naturally not necessary. Additionally, in its general report in 2001, the Torture Prevention Committee had deplored the fact that classification presented the risk of depriving those inmates who were placed in the "strict" unit of useful activities.

This time the PA could claim that other countries did it too, such as its close neighbor England (see Livingstone, Owen, & Macdonald, 2008, section 4.01). But just as it had done for two decades with solitary confinement, the PA tried to justify classification by claiming that in this day and age, it had to control very difficult prisoners: young offenders from the volatile ghettos, mentally ill prisoners, unpredictable inmates—in short, convicts who could, without any warning sign, become dangerously violent. However, in the exact same manner as with confinement, but on a much larger scale, the PA actually classified in the stricter unit prisoners who had been insolent to staff, who would not agree with a decision that had been made, who they feared (often based on presumptions or hearsay) were too charismatic, and so on.[47] In other words, those who caused menial troubles for staff were classified as "trouble" inmates. In all these instances, either the prisoner had committed no disciplinary offense or the PA preferred classification to the exasperating disciplinary procedure wherein it would have to establish proof, an attorney would argue in favor of reasonable doubt, the administrative courts would have the last word, and the measure at stake would have to have a finite length.

As usual, the prison administration wanted free rein to discipline without control. Typically, the new system reduced human interaction among offenders, with cell doors being closed during the day, and inmates could be in the strict regime for endless periods of time, since, as with solitary confinement, it was easier to enter a strict unit than to be released from it. Additionally, those residing in the strict unit had significantly reduced access to reinsertion and rehabilitation activities. Thus the PA again had placed its own internal needs before the needs of the community as a whole and distanced itself considerably from the much more humane approach of the EPR. In particular, Rule 51.2 advocated a "dynamic security provided by an alert staff who know the prisoners," and Rule 50 stated that prison staff should "be encouraged to communicate with the prisoners" concerning matters like good order, rather than use authoritarian methods.

Also archetypal, the legal basis for what is now known as *régimes différenciés* [differentiated regimes] originally was a sad reminder of the long gone pre-1990s era. No law or even a decree was passed for such a liberticidal system, which affected all prisoners detained in centres de detention. In short, neither the legislator nor the government was consulted in order to arbitrate concerning this radical shift. Once again deciding on its own, the PA looked for a subdecree, which on principle cannot be opposed to citizens (that is, they cannot be blamed for not complying with it), and found a 1990 *circulaire* [circular] that, in line with the penology of the time, had allowed the creation of a more open regime in centres de detention. Not only did this not constitute a valid legal ground for differentiated regimes, but also the PA was actually interpreting the circulaire in the opposite sense to its real meaning, as this would mean a stricter regime, not a softer one.

Still, the PA knew it could not endlessly sustain its new system on such a weak legal basis. In the course of the groundwork for the Prison Act of 2009 and during the parliamentary debate, it intensely lobbied senators and members of Parliament, arguing that it needed to be able to classify without fear of judicial review. The reason for this was that several administrative court rulings had previously allowed judicial review and actually annulled several allocations of inmates into a strict unit.[48] Luckily, unlike with the rest of the Prison Act, which had been entirely drafted by the PA and reinforced, in large part, a disciplinary governance shift,[49] legislators did fight this one battle and denied the PA its astonishing request. In 2011, the Conseil d'Etat confirmed that judicial control would be exercised on placement of prisoners in differentiated regimes.[50] However, it refused to go so far as to state that the PA would have to abide by some form of fair trial. At this point, the future does not look very bright.

What Does the Future Hold?

The PA has definitely won a war with the creation of differentiated regimes. It is currently drafting the decree required to implement the Prison Act of 2009, which has given it totally free rein to determine how differentiated regimes will be generalized to all types of prisons and what regulations will apply to these. Surprisingly, whereas all the other decrees were published in December 2010, the PA is still withholding this last decisive one.

It is thus difficult to foresee whether and how it will apply to maisons d'arrêt, which are overcrowded and where the regime has always been strict. With maisons centrales, implementing differentiated regimes is a serious concern in terms of human rights and criminological outcomes. Maisons centrales hold prisoners who serve the longest sentences, including lifers. Possibly preempting the future generalization of differentiated regimes, in 2003 the PA decided to lock all cell doors during the day, thereby locking up prisoners 22 to 24 hours in their cells with no activity.

Importantly, this first step in the path toward differentiated regimes was taken at the same time that other reforms were also differentiating the rules governing release of long-term prisoners. Whereas short-term prisoners were now benefiting from early release in order to free up prison space,[51] conversely, for long-term prisoners, reforms made it increasingly harder to obtain early release and virtually replaced it with mandatory forms of supervision called "safety measures" imposed on ex-offenders who had completed their sentences.[52] These reforms have already created a severely compromised atmosphere in maisons centrales. No doubt the extension of differentiated regimes to maisons centrales will further deteriorate the already damaged atmosphere of these prisons, which in turn will create more risk for both convicts and prison personnel, and this will consequently feed the discourse that prisoners are dangerous and unmanageable.

Already, institutional voices are saying that the next step forward is to specialize not just prison units (cellblocks), but prisons themselves. The logical progression from there is to have separate prisons with different types of prisoners: sexual offenders, old offenders, violent offenders, short-term prisoners, and so on. And from there it seems likely that France will return to the use of QHS (supermax) or a new equivalent. Indeed, a law was passed on March 27, 2012, that promised a return to the classification of prisons, ranging from low- to high-security ones. However, this law was voted in by Parliament at the very end of President Nicolas Sarkozy's term in 2012. One might have imagined that a socialist government would rescind this policy. Quite the contrary, Christiane Taubira, President François Hollande's socialist minister of justice, has recently announced that she would follow through with Sarkozy's plan.

Notes

1. See Mayhew & Van Kesteren, 2002; Cavadino & Dignan, 2006.
2. See the 2010 student poll at http://herzog-evans.com under "Editorial."
3. See Jackson et al., 2011.
4. See Danet, 2006.
5. See Foucault, 1975.
6. See Faugeron & Le Boulaire, 1991; Perrot, 1980.
7. See Herzog-Evans, 1998; Péchillon, 1999.
8. See Zysberg, 1990.
9. See Shalev, 2009a, 2009b.
10. See Petit, 1990; Badinter, 1992.
11. Some go so far as to commit disciplinary offenses so that they will be sent for a few days to a disciplinary cell, where, albeit in squalid conditions, they can at least gain a short respite from promiscuity.
12. See Herzog-Evans, 1998.
13. See De Schutter & Kaminski, 2002.
14. E.g., Chauvenet, Orlic, & Benguigui, 1992; Combessie, 1996.
15. See Herzog-Evans, 1998.
16. See Ministry of Justice, 1998.
17. See Froment, 1998; Hertrich and Faugeron, 1987.
18. See Senate, 2000; National Assembly, 2000.
19. See CE, 28 juill. 1932, Bruneaux, *Rec. CE*, p. 316.
20. See CE, 8 déc. 1967, Kanayakis, *Rec. CE*, p. 475.
21. See Céré, 2003; Dünkel & Snacken, 2004; Van Zyl Smit & Snacken, 2009.
22. See Herzog-Evans, 2012–2013b.
23. See CE, 27 avr. 1995, Marie, *RFD adm.* 1995, p. 379, concl. Frydman—P. Couvrat, « Le Contrôle du juge sur les sanctions disciplinaires du milieu pénitentiaire », *RSC* 1995, chron. p. 381—M. Herzog-Evans, « Droit commun pour les détenus », *RSC* 1995, chron. p. 62—F. Moderne, « Le Point de vue du publiciste », *RFD adm.* 1995, p. 822—J.-P. Céré « Le Point de vue du pénaliste », *RFD adm.* 1995, p. 826; *D.* 1995, p. 381, note Belloubet-Frier; *JCP* 1995, n° 22426, note Lascombe et Bernard—v. A. Otekpo, *LPA* 4 août 1995, p. 28.
24. See CE, 30 juill. 2003, Remli, *D.* 2003, jur. p. 2331, note M. Herzog-Evans; *AJ pénal* 2003, n°2, p. 74, obs. P. Remillieux; *AJDA* 2003, p. 2090, note D. Costa; *Dr. Pénal*, 2004, Comm. 43, obs. Maron.
25. See Janas, 2010; Herzog-Evans, 2012–2013a.
26. See also Danet, 2006.
27. See Seyler, 1990.
28. See Herzog-Evans, 2012–2013b.
29. See Darbeda, 1993.
30. For a discussion of this issue in more modern times, see Snacken, 2005.
31. Mesrine (1936–1979) was a famous French criminal known for robbing banks, kidnapping, and escaping from prison. He did prison time in the United States, Canada, and France. He claimed to have killed more than 40 people, including

a number of police officers. He escaped from several so-called escape-proof maximum-security prisons, including Saint-Vincent-de-Paul in Montreal (1972) and La Santé in Paris (1978). See Schofield, 1981.

32. See Favard, 1986.

33. See Herzog-Evans, 2000.

34. In particular, government officials read the writings of ex-convict Knobelpiess (1980).

35. See Seyler, 1990.

36. For a discussion of how U.S. prisons use solitary confinement to punish ordinary prisoners, see Shalev, 2009a.

37. See Mbanzoulou, 2010.

38. See Seyler, 1990; Herzog-Evans, 2001.

39. See also Choquet, 1983; Danet, 1996; Faucher, 1999.

40. See Luise, 1989; Grassian, 1983; Walters, Callaghan, & Newman, 1963; Arrigo & Bullock, 2008; Richards, 2008.

41. Article 3 is an absolute stipulation, with no exception, limit, or reserve. It states that "no one shall be subjected to torture or to inhuman or degrading treatment or punishment" (see, e.g., Van Zyl Smit & Snacken, 2009; Foster, 2011). Article 8 § 1 states that "everyone has the right to respect for his private and family life, his home and his correspondence" (Herzog-Evans, 2000). However, § 2 allows for interferences with the exercise of the rights mentioned in § 1, by a public authority under strict conditions, "as in accordance with the law" and only when it "is necessary in a democratic society in the interests of national security, public safety or the economic well-being of the country, for the prevention of disorder or crime, for the protection of health or morals, or for the protection of the rights and freedoms of others."

42. CE 31 oct. 2008, D. 2009. 134, note M. Herzog-Evans; *AJ pénal* 2008. 500, obs. E. Péchillon; AJDA 2008. 2092, et 2389, obs. E. Geffray et S.-J. Liéber; RFDA 2009. 73, obs. M. Guyomar, D 2009, pan., 1680, obs. E. Péchillon, *Dr. pénal* 2009, p. 37 s. note A. Maron et M. Haas.

43. EHR Com., 8 July 1976, *Ensslin Baader and Raspe v. F.R.G., DR* 14/64; EHR Com, 16 Dec. 1982, *Kricher and Miller, DR* 34/25; EHR Com, 9 July 1991, EHR Com *Treholt v. Norway, DR* 71/168; EHRct, *Ilascu and others v. Moldova and Russia*, 8 July 2004, applic. n° 49787/99; *Öcalan c. Turkey*, 12 May 2005, applic. n° 46221/99.

44. EHRct, *Lorsé and al. v. Netherlands*, 4 Feb. 2003, applic. n° 52750/99.

45. EHRct, *Ramirez Sanchez v. France*, 27 Jan. 2005, applic. n° 59450/00.

46. EHRct, (Great Chamber), *Khider v. France*, 9 July 2009, applic. n° 39364/05.

47. See Cliquenois, 2009.

48. TA Bordeaux, 14 mai 2009 n° 0704553, *AJ pénal* 2009, p. 323, obs. M. Herzog-Evans; CAA Bordeaux, 18 nov. 2008, n° 07BX01485, *D.* 2009, pan. p. 1378, obs. E. Péchillon; TA Nantes, 26 juill. 2007, n° 066227, *AJ pénal* 2007, p. 495, obs. M. Herzog-Evans, C.A.A. Nantes, 21 fev. 2008, n° 07NT02832, unpublished.

49. For a detailed discussion, see Herzog-Evans, 2010a.

50. CE 28 mars 2011, n° 316977, *AJ pénal* 2011, obs. G. Cliquenois et M. Herzog-Evans.

51. See Janas, 2010; Herzog-Evans, 2009.

52. See Herzog-Evans, 2010b.

|13|

Israeli Maximum-Security Prisons

Lior Gideon, Dror Walk, and Tomer Carmel

The Israel Prison Service (IPS) is an organization that defines itself as a security-oriented organization with a defined mission to serve social needs as an arm of the Israeli criminal justice system. Consequently, its mandate is to control sentenced offenders in an appropriate manner while securing inmates' dignity, providing them with their basic needs, and exposing them to rehabilitative interventions in order to prepare them for reentry and reintegration, as can be seen in this formal mission statement from the Ministry of Public Security (2006):

> The Israel Prison Service is the national detention authority of Israel. Beyond putting criminals behind bars, the Israel Prison Service also fulfills a social mission within the criminal justice system. In brief, its mission is to enhance offenders' potential for successful integration into society while ensuring them a safe, secure, and appropriate incarceration environment.
>
> This includes respecting their dignity and accommodating their basic needs, as well as providing them with rehabilitative services in collaboration with other government agencies and community organizations.

The Israel Prison Service (IPS) underwent some major change and growth between 2003 and 2012, when it assumed incarceration responsibility for those inmates who had been under the jurisdiction of the Israel Police (these would be equivalent to jail inmates in the United States) and Israel Defense Forces (mainly Palestinians charged with threats to national security or involved in terror activities). This change is reflected by dramatic growth of the inmate population, from 10,900 in 2003 to 20,100 at the beginning of 2013 (see Figure 13.1). This growth is attributed to the new populations of preindictment detainees, infiltrators, and terrorists. While the number of post-trial inmates has grown by 14.3%, this is still less than the anticipated change based on the natural growth in the population of Israel during this period (17.4%).[1]

As a result, the IPS inmate population in January 2013 consisted of 20,100 inmates—males, females, and juveniles—including those charged with terror and threat to national security. Of these, 4,800 were sentenced for terror- and national security–related crimes; 2,700 were African infiltrators (illegal immigrants and asylum seekers; and 12,600 were criminal prisoners, of whom 3,700 were on remand or awaiting trial (e.g., pretrial).

Currently, the Israel Prison Service manages 30 facilities, of which six are designated to house individuals charged with terror-related activities, and another three to house illegal immigrants and asylum seekers. The remaining 21 facilities are for those charged with or suspected of other criminal offenses. Of these, two house women and adolescents, six are reserved for adult male pre-trial detainees, 12 are designated for sentenced male offenders, and one

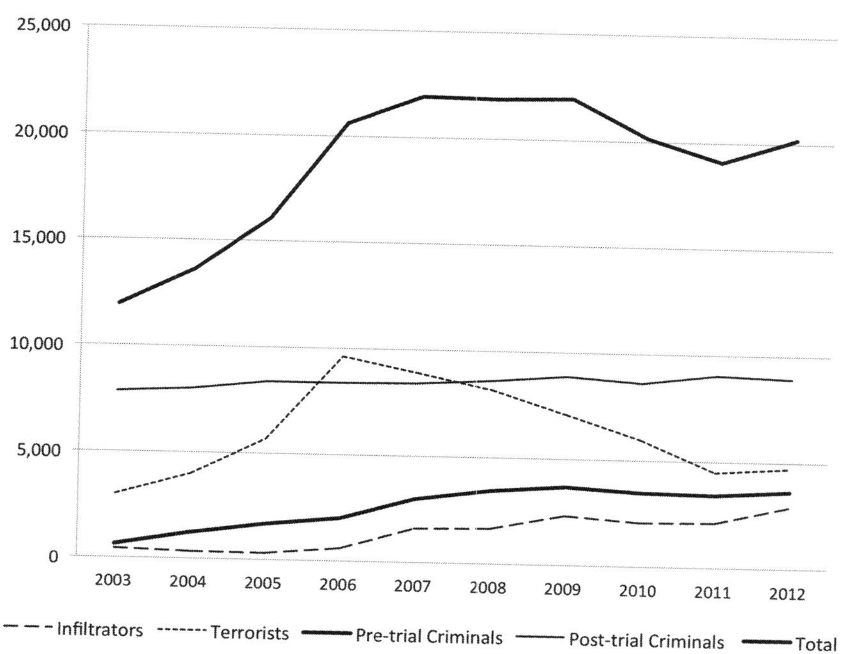

Figure 13.1. Trends in the number of IPS inmates between 2003 and 2012. Courtesy of the Israel Prison Service

is used as the IPS Hospital. There are only four maximum-security facilities, which currently house 2,385 inmates, and eight medium-security facilities with additional 4,911 inmates. At the time of this writing, the IPS does not have any minimum-security facilities.

This chapter focuses on the four maximum-security facilities (MSFs) governed by the IPS. Only 100 inmates currently incarcerated in the IPS are held in segregation blocks, which are a variation of the American super-maximum security facilities (SMSFs). We characterize and discuss both MSFs and SMSFs, while comparing them with medium-security facilities in the IPS. In addition, we offer some insight into the rationale and mode of operation of these facilities and describe how they serve the aims of punishment in Jewish culture and reflect the beliefs of Israeli society.

Inmates in Israeli Maximum-Security Facilities

The punitive philosophy behind the utilitarian approach to dealing with offenders seeks to stop them from committing more crimes by limiting their freedom. The ultimate goal of incarceration is to protect society while also protecting the safety and well-being of the inmates and prison staff. As such, MSFs are reserved for those prisoners who are considered at high risk to attempt an escape from prison, to commit crimes while incarcerated, or to harm others and are designed to closely monitor any movement and prevent escapes at all cost. Hence, these facilities represent "the ultimate punishment that custodians can inflict rather than the common fate of man in custody" (Sykes, 1958, p. 7). Accordingly, only a small percentage of the most dangerous and violent inmates are admitted to an MSF.[2] At times, MSFs will also serve as a solution for individual inmates who require extra protection from other inmates because of the nature of their crimes. This approach further received attention in the early 1990s, when Feeley and Simon (1992) introduced the concept of "new penology," which they defined as the management of groups or subgroups of offenders based on their actuarial risk to society, thus emphasizing the aspects of control and surveillance of prisoners, leaving little room for the idea of rehabilitation and the corresponding reintegration upon release.

From the very first day of incarceration, different measures to retain and control individual prisoners exist in any correctional institution. The type of segregation within a prison is determined by the prisoner's need for protection, as well as by the institution's need to protect its staff members and other inmates and to secure the orderly running of the institution.[3] The IPS set its security levels to meet these needs while emphasizing escape prevention to maintain public safety. This is done in several ways:

- Infrastructure. MSFs have more protection layers than other facilities, including walls, fences, and dogs, and blocks and cells are built using thicker walls and more solid construction (see Figure 13.2).
- Technologies. MSFs implement a wide variety of inspection technologies, such as closed-circuit television and inspected doors.
- Control of inmates' movement. Inmates in MSFs are restricted to their cells more often than those in medium-security prisons, and their movements inside the wing and in the prison compound are strictly monitored by the prison staff.

Since the year 2000, only three attempts to escape Israeli MSFs were made, and none succeeded.

Upon being sentenced, convicted offenders are scheduled to be screened and assessed in order to determine their risk and needs. This assessment is done by the Diagnosis and Classification Committee (DCC). Assigning the level of security—medium or maximum/supermax—is determined during this process, and risk of escape plays a major role in the decision. Risk of escape usually is assessed according to the length of sentence. In Israel, a sentence of seven years or more automatically accords a prisoner the status of high risk and consequently makes him a high priority to be transferred

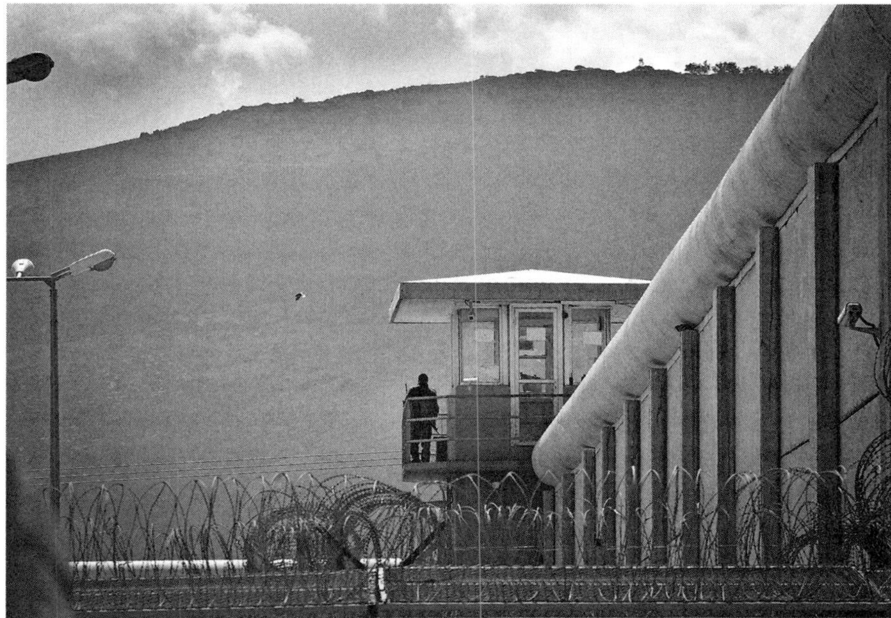

Figure 13.2. Perimeter of an Israeli MSF. Courtesy of the Israel Prison Service

to a maximum-security facility.[4] More than 90% of inmates sentenced for seven or more years are individuals charged with murder, assault (severe cases), drug trafficking, or sex offenses, making them classical archetypes of high-risk offenders suitable for maximum-security facilities.[5]

Other important considerations in determining the suitable level of security are risk of violence, risk of committing new crimes while incarcerated and during furlough,[6] risk of violating prison regulations and rules, and being identified as senior gang members. Moreover, when there are no accommodations in close-to-home medium-security facilities, many low-risk inmates may prefer to be housed in a nearby MSF rather than in a lower-security facility farther away. IPS regards the continuous connection between inmates and their families and the community to have a vital role in rehabilitation and later reentry, and thus the DCC considers such preferences positively.

In addition to the criteria set by the DCC, other operational and intelligence considerations exist, and they may complicate the standard classification process. For example, information about rivalries between offenders, gang affiliation, and previous criminal history can play a major role in risk assessment and the definition of the security level desired for the prisoner. Such considerations often require the DCC to make exceptions and deviate from the standard procedure, thus resulting in lower-risk offenders being placed in maximum-security facilities. In fact, such practice has become fairly common to ensure the safety of inmates by diverting specific prisoners away from their enemies already housed in medium-security facilities. About one-third of the maximum-security classifications made are based on such considerations.

Paradoxically, among all those inmates who are housed in MSFs, those deemed high-risk may actually require less care and attention from prison staff. Those who were diverted to MSFs for a host of other reasons not directly related to their actual level of risk often pose more challenges. This is somewhat baffling and requires further discussion into the differences between those assigned to medium-security and maximum-security facilities. The mere distinction between high-risk and low-risk offenders may not always translate into potential trouble and disturbance.[7]

Comparisons Between Maximum- and Medium-Security Inmates

The offense types of the majority of MSF inmates are distinctly different from those of prisoners housed in medium-security facilities, as can be seen in Table 13.1. Since the major criterion for MSF assignment is length of imprisonment, it's not surprising that many of them were sentenced for major crimes. Specifically, the main difference between these two groups is that a much larger number of MSF prisoners were charged with murder, manslaughter, or sex offenses; the numbers are fairly close in both types of facilities for drugs, assault, or property crimes.

Table 13.1. Percentage of Inmates with Major Offense Types by Distribution to Maximum- and Medium-Security Facilities

Offense Type	Maximum-Security (n = 2,385)	Medium-Security (n = 4,911)
Murder and manslaughter	33.2	8.4
Sex	18.8	11.3
Drugs	13.2	15.1
Assault	34.9	30.8
Property	41.2	43.1

Note: Totals equal more than 100% because many inmates have multiple charges. For example, an offender can be charged with both possession of narcotics and an assault.

Another way to examine how these groups differ is to examine the distribution of multiple-offense inmates. Table 13.2 presents the distribution of inmates in both kinds of facilities with the three most severe types of offenses: murder or manslaughter, assault, and sex offenses.

Table 13.2. Percentage of Inmates with the Most Severe Offense Types in Maximum- and Medium-Security Facilities

Number of Severe Offenses	Maximum-Security (n = 2,385)	Medium-Security (n = 4,911)
0	31.5	55.9
1	50.6	38.0
2	17.3	5.9
3	0.6	0.2
Total	100.0	100.0

It's clear that there are significantly more inmates in maximum-security facilities with one or more severe offenses (68.5%) than in medium-security facilities (44.1%), and the percentage of inmates with two or more severe offenses in MSFs is almost triple that found in the medium-security facilities. However, the fact that almost one-third of the inmates in maximum-security facilities do not have any severe offenses suggests the mixed nature of this group, as explained earlier.

In regard to previous arrests and incarcerations, those sentenced to Israeli MSFs are characterized by overall fewer entries than those serving their sentences in medium-security facilities: 2.5 times (standard deviation [SD] = 3.2) and 3.3 times (SD = 3.5), respectively. Furthermore, MSFs house significantly more first-timers (35.2%) than can be found among medium-security inmates (21.1%). This also accounts for the differences in sentence lengths between maximum- and medium-security facility inmates, as shown in Figure 13.3. The median sentence term is 7.0 years for maximum-security and 2.1 years for medium-security inmates. However, maximum-security inmates that are sentenced for shorter terms are not rare: 15.8% of these inmates are sentenced for less than two years (compared with 37.1% of the medium-security inmates).

The religious and ethnic distribution between the two facility types, detailed in Table 13.3, is almost identical. The current inmate population includes 13% foreign nationals in MSFs and 18% in medium-security facilities. No major difference is observed in the mean age of those incarcerated in the two types of facilities: the mean age is 37.3 (SD = 12.2) for maximum-security inmates and 35.7 (SD = 12.3) for medium-security inmates.

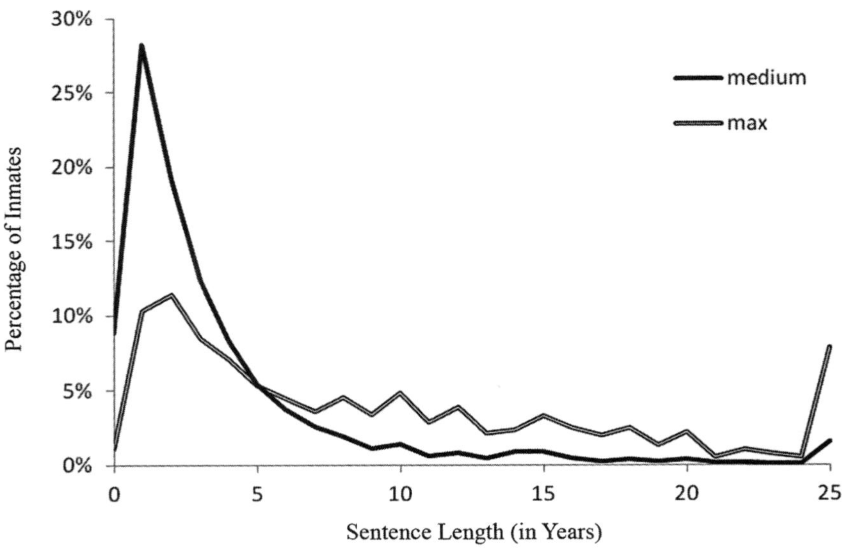

Figure 13.3. Distribution of sentence lengths for maximum- and medium-security inmates. Courtesy of the Israel Prison Service

Table 13.3. Percentage of Religious and Ethnic Groups in Maximum- and Medium-Security Facilities

Religious/Ethnic Group	Maximum-Security (n = 2,385)	Medium-Security (n = 4,911)
Jewish	50.2	49.2
Muslim	43.6	45.2
Christian	3.8	3.9
Druze	1.7	1.2
Other	0.7	0.5
Total	100.0	100.0

The Role of Furloughs in Maximum-Security Facilities

The role of furloughs among the incarcerated is well documented in the research literature.[8] Although it received some negative attention in the United States during the second half of the 1980s, a wealth of evidence shows that almost all inmates on furloughs do return to the facilities on time,[9] and that furloughs do more good than harm. For example, LeClair (1978) reported that participation in the Home Furlough Program led to improved reintegration experiences and a significant reduction in recidivism rates among Massachusetts inmates. In a later study that followed inmates released from the Massachusetts prison system for 11 years, LeClair and Guarino-Ghezzi (1991) found more support for their argument that furloughs provide consistent positive impact in lowering recidivism. Hallinan (2003) further argued that furloughs have the ability to reduce stress, improve inmates' conduct,[10] and promote rehabilitation and successful reintegration.

For an outsider observing maximum-security inmates in Israel, such practice may come as a surprise. After all, these are inmates classified as high-risk, and accordingly, the system invests great effort to prevent their escapes, and yet some enjoy the freedom to pass outside the walls with permission and return on time. According to prison laws and regulations in Israel, IPS officials can grant a furlough of up to 96 hours to an inmate who meets specific standards, at their discretion. The following terms should be met for an inmate to receive a furlough: police approval has been obtained for home visit eligibility (meaning low risk of criminal activity while away); the inmate has already served more than a quarter of his term; and the inmate has exhibited good behavior and participated in a rehabilitation program.

Current IPS data show that 13.9% of maximum-security inmates visit their families, compared with 9.9% of medium-security inmates. This difference can be attributed to the fact that there are more inmates with short-term incarceration sentences in medium-security facilities than in MSFs. Since inmates do not become eligible for furlough until after their fourth month in prison, very short-term inmates cannot earn this privilege. Moreover, inmates usually arrive in prison following up to nine months of in-trial detention. Staff must know a prisoner thoroughly before approving his first furlough, but many medium-security inmates are released before this can occur.

Management of Maximum-Security Facilities and Inmates

In the United States, maximum-security facilities are custodial institutions reserved for adult male and female prisoners who are thought to require extremely close supervision and control.[11] As such, they represent social systems in which an attempt is made to create and maintain total or almost total social control. This is done by means of detailed regulations extending into every area of the individual's life, constant surveillance, and concentration of power in the hands of the administration and guards. Accordingly, U.S. MSFs are not considered to have a rehabilitative component and are perceived as totalitarian institutions aimed at punishing the inmates while isolating them from society. Indeed, most maximum-security facilities around the world do not serve the goals of rehabilitation and do little to prepare the incarcerated individual for reentry and successful reintegration. If anything, maximum-security and supermaximum (supermax) facilities are achieving the opposite goal. Sherman (1993) described what he called the "defiance theory," stating that punishments that are perceived to be unjust, unfair, and excessive, and violate basic rights, can result in a backfire effect, causing prisoners to become more defiant and rebellious, which in turn increases future criminal behavior and recidivism.

The operation and management of maximum-security facilities in Israel is based on a significantly different philosophy. The IPS does not differentiate between the goals of maximum-security and medium-security facilities. Instead, the administration has created a hierarchy of cellblocks (or blocks, for short), perceives the cell as a miniature supporting community, prevents prisoner idleness, and implements reward systems, such as the furlough privilege, to encourage good behavior. In many ways, this innovative correctional philosophy is guided by the Jewish religion.

Judaism's Approach to Crime and Incarceration

IPS chief rabbi, Colonel Yekutiel Yehuda Visner

Immediately after the flood, God said in his heart, "I will not again curse the ground any more for man's sake; for the imagination of man's heart is evil from his youth" (Genesis 8:21). Judaism acknowledges that sin is part of humanity. The human being as composed of flesh and blood is liable to make wrong, as King Solomon phrased it, "For there is not a righteous man upon earth, that doeth good, and sinneth not" (Ecclesiastes 7:20). Yet since he is a rational creature and has moral judgment, the individual is responsible over his activities. This responsibility is total and comprehensive, as the Mishnah says, An "individual is always liable whether he acts inadvertently or willfully, whether awake or asleep" (Baba Kamma 2:6).

Above all, Judaism perceives the human being as the crown of the creation, made in the image of God. Thus, even if he is made wrong, an individual deserves dignity, even before correction. In light of these principles, Judaism believes in human being correction and entire world correction. As Rabbi Nachman of Breslev phrased it, "If you believe that it can get spoiled, you must believe it can be corrected."

Judaism acknowledges the fragility of societal being and asserts that society has to defend itself from unwanted behavior of its members—using enforcement and sanctions. The Talmud says, "Just as among fish of the sea, the greater swallow up the smaller ones, so with men, were it not for fear of the government, men would swallow each other alive. This is just what we learnt: R. Hanina, the Deputy High Priest, said: Pray for the welfare of the government, for were it not for the fear thereof, men would swallow each other alive" (Avoda Zara 4a).

The first time prison appeared in the Bible was the story of Joseph in Egypt. Joseph was a Hebrew slave who was incarcerated after being falsely accused by his Egyptian master of sleeping with his master's wife (see Genesis 39). From here we can realize the existence of such an institution in the ancient world: "And Joseph's master took him, and put him into the prison, the place where the king's prisoners were bound; and he was there in the prison" (Genesis 39:20).

However, Judaism never mentioned incarceration as a sanction method. The Rashar Hirsch, a German scholar in the 19th century, phrases it clearly: "Incarceration sanctions, with the loss of hope and corruption of morality situated behind the wall, with family grief and sigh—have no room in the Torah of God. There is no place for prison castles in the Kingdom of the Torah" (the Rashar Hirsch, Parashat Mishpatim). This approach is expressed by the Lubavitcher Rebbe, Rabbi Menachem Mendel Schneerson, in his letter to Israeli Supreme Court Judge Gad Frumkin: "The laws of our holy Torah differ from the other nations' Laws, in fact that we completely miss the prison sanction. . . . According to the Torah there is no room for revenge but for correction" (Igrot Kodesh, Vol. 9, 199).

Although the Torah opposes incarceration, it enables the use of pre-trial arrest. This was the case when the Israeli man blasphemed the Name of Lord: "And the son of the Israelitish woman blasphemed the Name, and cursed; and they brought him unto Moses. And his mother's name was Shelomith, the daughter of Dibri, of the tribe of Dan. And they put him in ward, that it might be declared unto them at the mouth of the LORD" (Leviticus 24:11–12). The Rashar; only, and that for a short term, according to procedures (the Rashar Hirsch, Parashat Mishpatim).

Block Hierarchy

Inmates in Israeli maximum-security facilities have the ability to gradually improve the conditions of their incarceration sentence. Each inmate can move between three block types according to his behavior and compliance with facility rules. There are three major block types: beginners, advanced, and drug-free. Every block type has its unique characteristics, rules, and privileges, and accordingly, it symbolizes the prisoners' level of compliance and progress in the rehabilitation process. The higher on the hierarchy the block is, the more privileges the inmates enjoy. For example, beginners block inmates may enjoy only three hours a day in the courtyard and have restricted accessibility to telephone. Additionally, they are not allowed to participate in education and employment programs that are held outside the block. Advanced block inmates enjoy more hours a day outside their cells and thus are eligible for education and employment opportunities. Drug-free block inmates are out of their cells during most hours of the day, excluding inmate counts; are able to take part in education and employment programs; and have the much desirable privilege of open family visits, where the inmate can interact freely with his family without any barriers separating them.

Prisoners progress through the block hierarchy according to how well they adjust to the prison environment. Most inmates begin their term of incarceration at the beginners block and can move to the advanced and drug-free blocks once they prove themselves as stable, well behaved, and ready to function according to the standards required by the more advanced block types. Indeed, sometimes non–drug users or "normative" inmates may be assigned directly to such blocks, although the majority of prisoners start in the beginners block.

Ilan, Jew: Sentenced Three and a Half Years for Drug Offense

I am 26 years old, have served so far one and a half years, and have another two years until release. I started my term in the beginners block. It was a jungle. I saw a prisoner stabbed, a prisoner burned by fire. I don't mix with other prisoners because I don't want to get caught up in any trouble. The groups I did with the social workers and education officers gave me breathing space; the moment you see someone from outside, it helps you keep your sanity. Visits from my family are very important to me. Sometimes people on the block bother me, they speak in a bad way, they play power games—that's the way it works—but in order to get permission to go out on home leave, I've got to forget about my ego and not respond, because I prefer freedom.

Using such a graduated placement practice achieves two goals. First, it enables the administration to separate problematic inmates while leaving other prisoners to develop a routine of living, work, and education. Second, it serves as a preventive and compliance measure for those in the higher status block, who know that if they violate the rules, they might be downgraded and transferred to a lower-level block where their movement will be restricted again and their life will be more difficult, control-wise. In many ways, such practice helps prepare the inmate for eventual release from prison and reentry

Figure 13.4. View from the inside of a block in one of Israel's MSFs.
Courtesy of the Israel Prison Service

into society. It also provides the prisoner with a valuable opportunity to reflect on the consequences of his behavior while developing accountability. This gradual process presents a man with an opportunity to reflect on his behavior, which greatly affect his chances of early release from prison.

The Cell as a Community

U.S. maximum-security prisons confine large numbers of prisoners in isolation cells. Typically, in most American maximum-security prisons, men are basically left to their own devices in terms of support and are thus at a higher risk of depression and anxiety. This can contribute to high rates of violence and suicide in prison. In comparison, IPS administration recognizes that prisoners have already been deprived of freedom and removed from society, and isolation from human interaction adds an unnecessary punishment. In order to address these issues and reduce the additional and unnecessary pains of incarceration in MSFs, IPS developed its own innovative system.

An MSF consists of several blocks with several cells, which are the smallest residential units in the prison. Prison staff assigns inmates to cells in a way that will reduce conflict and tension. This goal is achieved by first considering how well each candidate inmate fits into the cell's miniature community, a task conducted by the intelligence officer. The prisoners are also allowed to hold communal activities inside the cell, such as food preparation, canteen purchases, TV watching, and other recreational activities.

In addition, the cell functions as a support group in which mentally strong inmates are coupled with weaker inmates who are at high risk of self-harm, to assist, support, and observe while providing guidance through the prison adjustment process. Such practice was developed several years ago to include a formal function of inmates as supporters ("shadows") to help weaker inmates survive their time behind bars. To that extent, inmates are carefully selected and trained by the prison therapeutic staff and receive constant guidance through the process. In addition, the supporters receive monetary compensation.

The smooth operation of each cell is a top priority for prison staff and guards. Accordingly, if a new inmate is not welcome in his assigned cell, veteran cell inhabitants will talk to the prison officers and notify them that a particular inmate is unwelcome. Then the prison staff will find another cell to house that inmate in an effort to avoid unnecessary incidents and violence. As a result, guards are rarely required to intervene and take control over problematic inmates in their cells. Relevant to this point is the issue of the number of inmates in a given cell. The IPS wished to meet international standards of block density and cell capacity of two beds, so during the 1990s, a new prison was built with two-bed cells. However, within a short time, prisoners began complaining about this arrangement. They claimed that in the two-bed cells, when conflict arose, nobody was there to calm the situation down and help reach a compromise. In response to this, a third bed was added to each of the cells, and the inmates were satisfied, although cells became highly condensed. In fact, prisoners and prison staff agree that a six-inmate cell provides the optimal environment.

It's not surprising that cells are often composed of inmates of the same ethnic group: native Jews, immigrant Jews from Russia and other countries, or Arabs. However, this social arrangement was directed to benefit the group members and rarely serves to promote intergroup conflict. It appears that in times of tension between Israel and its Arab neighbors, reasonable relationships between Jews and Arabs has been preserved within the cells.

Such practice created small communities within the cells and many times resulted in cell affiliation that is so strong that sometimes inmates refuse to advance to a higher block so that they will not have to leave their cell community. In such cases, the staff role is to talk with the prisoner in an attempt to convince him of the long-term benefit over the immediate inconvenience. The transition to another block or facility can be forced on the inmate, but this is regarded as destructive to the rehabilitation process and therefore is uncommon.

Preventing Prisoner Idleness

The daily routine of maximum-security inmates is not different from that of medium-security inmates. Cells are open at 7 A.M. and lockdown is at 10 P.M., depending on block type. During their time out of the blocks, the majority of prisoners are engaged in various activities, such as being employed in one of the prison industries, taking part in education programs offered at education centers inside the prison perimeter, being engaged in religious studies, or taking part in a therapeutic group. Prison staff makes significant efforts to prevent idleness and motivate prisoners to take an active part in the various activities the facility has to offer. Past experience demonstrates that once inmates have joined an activity, they tend to persevere, which in turn reduces disciplinary incidents and contributes to the inmate's ability to progress through the block hierarchy. This may also contribute to increased eligibility for additional privileges, including a better chance of early release from prison into the community.

Some of the typical activities spread over the daily routine are education classes, ranging from basic literary skill acquisition to the equivalent of 12th grade and GED programs; anger management workshops; gym; bibliotherapy groups, which use books, poetry, and writing as therapy; and inmates' block meetings. Besides the obvious utility of this schedule for the inmate, it also leaves little time for prisoners to become involved in undesirable activities and incidents. Overall, periods of idleness are infrequent, as the majority of prisoners keep active. A well-known saying among prison staff in IPS is "Make them busy or they will make you busy."

Omar, Bedouin: Life Sentence for Murder During Robbery

I'm 35 years old, Bedouin, and have seven brothers and sisters. I'm the oldest. The financial situation at home was always tough, and from the age of 10, I started to work and help my parents. After the army, I worked as a truck driver for five years with my uncle. The wage I earned was not enough for me or for my two children. Two of my friends put it into my head to go and do a robbery with them, steal money from the supermarket. For over a month they persuaded me, every day, until in the end I gave in and went with them.

In prison, I got used to Russians, Jews, Druze—I don't have any fear, because I'm a straightforward guy, so nothing to be scared of. Outside, I never went to pray even though I was a believer. Inside, I started to pray; it relaxes me, I sleep well when I pray. My parents and everyone else come to visit me; my dad is like a friend. It was only when I came into prison that I started to realize how much my dad loves me. I wasn't like everybody else when I was a child. I didn't have toys like everyone else because of the financial situation at home, and there wasn't even enough money to keep me at school.

When I was arrested, I wanted to change from inside, but I didn't know how. The problem really started when my son asked me, "Why are you in prison?" and I didn't know how to answer him. I turned to ask the social worker, and she told me that I've got to do parents group, which I then requested from the education officer. In the course, the instructor told me to tell him the truth. There are days when I say to myself that if I had never entered prison, then I wouldn't know what I know today. If I hadn't come to prison, then I wouldn't have the skills I have today.

Currently, more than 70% of all inmates in ISP MSFs participate in programs of employment, education, or religious studies. Inmates that do not participate in such activities include active drug addicts,[12] those that are radically antisocial, and hostile inmates. Most inmates participate because they simply prefer activity over idleness, but in recent years another motivation was created. The Israeli court system approved IPS policy in which prisoners may earn furlough eligibility through participation in therapeutic programs. Moreover, the Release Committee, which can deduct one-third of the sentence, looks favorably on those inmates who used their term of incarceration to better themselves by being engaged in the various employment, education, and therapeutic activities.[13]

Ziad, Arab: Life Sentence Commuted to Thirty Years for Murder

Ziad is 31 years old, and this is his first time in prison. His criminal background consists mainly of stealing property from his hometown, with no history of drug use. He was convicted of a family honor murder. Following an offer from the education officer, he decided to study and enlisted in a beginners class. From there he got a high school equivalency diploma and now works as a teaching assistant in the education center. According to Ziad:

> My whole turnaround in prison was through education, and following all the positive feedback and the certificates I got, the daily contact with the education team, people who are warm and normative, and the appreciation I was shown, it gave me a springboard from which to start to make the change in my life. In prison, I'm completing everything that only now I understand was lacking on the outside, and this is something that I'm trying to show to all the other prisoners.

The Reward System

IPS inmates have much to lose. Implementing a reward system of "carrot and stick" is one of the main practices that guide prisoner management. It is up to the facility warden to decide how to reward the inmates under his or her custody. Many tend to follow the written punitive law and offer some leniency policies to reward those who demonstrate compliance with the prison rules and regulations. Specifically, wardens have the prerogative to grant various privileges, beyond what is stated in the law, and to take them away as means of discipline if the inmate does not comply with the rules and regulations. For example, according to IPS regulations, inmates are entitled to one 30-minute family visit every two months, during which the inmate is kept separate from his visitors by a barrier to prevent contact. The prison warden is authorized to reward inmates with up to two contact visits a month, with more family members and for longer periods of time, if the inmates conform to prison regulations. This act benefits both inmate and administration.

Other privileges that can be used as rewards are frequent access to canteen purchasing, possession of private authorized articles and belongings, more frequent telephone calls, and conjugal visits. This wide range of discretion, which is well regulated through IPS ordinances and guidelines, serves as a tool to influence inmates' behavior. Using such practices is more frequent in maximum-security than in medium-security facilities.

Avi, Jew: Sentenced to Fifteen Years for Arms Dealing

Avi is 34 years old, married, and a father of four children. Both he and his wider family are well known and appreciated among the Jerusalem criminal underworld. In the past, he used soft drugs. When he came into prison, he immediately started to try to use his powers to obtain hardened criminal status, but he quickly realized that it complicated his situation and prevented him from obtaining privileges such as visits and conjugal rights. As Avi described it:

> At first, making the change was all about just being seen, meeting my own interests and getting the prison administration to like me, but afterwards I started to enjoy the idea, and after a meeting with a volunteer in the education center, the idea came up of joining the Prisoner Mutual Support Project, and I found a place in which I could obtain a position of respect amongst the prisoners and staff, but in a positive way. What started as being a self-serving interest to obtain a position of power actually became something positive. Despite everything, I still don't always have the full faith of the staff, and from time to time my home visits get suspended whilst reports lodged against me are being checked out by intelligence.

Using such an approach to control inmates' behavior is also beneficial to the rehabilitation process. Leaning on behavioral approaches, modifying inmates' behavior through rewards was documented as a motivational method for therapy and treatment in the late 1960s.[14] This practice motivates inmates to take responsibility for their own actions and behavior and to develop accountability. It teaches them to rely on themselves and not solely on the group,[15] as well as to become a wiser and more conscientious decision-maker. Consequently, it is not rare to see prisoners requesting to be removed from their gang affiliation just so they can be integrated into the prison rewards system. They want more family visits, home furloughs, conjugal visits, and early release. Not long ago, prisoners used to adhere to the "convict code" and followed a very strict "moral" classification to judge newcomers. For example, sex offenders were targeted for violent attacks, and inmates were willing to pay the high price of attacking them. Today things are different. As one prison warden put it, "Today our inmates are much more pragmatists than ideologists."

Multiple Roles of Prison Staff

The roles of correctional officers may be challenging. Prison guards are often required to carry out difficult tasks that may involve regaining control over violent inmates, handcuffing, restraining, and conducting frisk searches. On the other hand, prison staff also includes social workers, education officers, teachers, and other therapeutic personnel. While such occupational distinction exists in many prisons around the world, the IPS aims to create some ideological overlap between the two.

IPS correctional officers are trained to maintain security and order, while at the same time to act as "field therapists." They are trained to notice how much tension the inmates are experiencing, to spot signs of distress and depression, and to react accordingly. Beginning with basic training, trainees are taught to attempt to resolve conflicts, reduce tensions, and achieve compliance without the need to resort to force. These lessons are reinforced further during the various stages of on-the-job training. For example, twice a year, every officer is trained to monitor inmates who are at risk of suicide. Before each holiday season—a period that is considered to be highly sensitive—officers are instructed to be more vigilant, and cases of individual inmates who are considered to be at risk are discussed during staff meetings.

This complicated professional identity is not easily implemented, and officers sometimes complain about being too much of a social worker. For example, Gideon, Shoham, and Weisburd (2010), in a study that aimed to examine the Israeli prison as a therapeutic milieu, interviewed a correctional guard who expressed the following: "I joined the prison system to be a guard, as I always had this aggression in me and I was always looking for action.

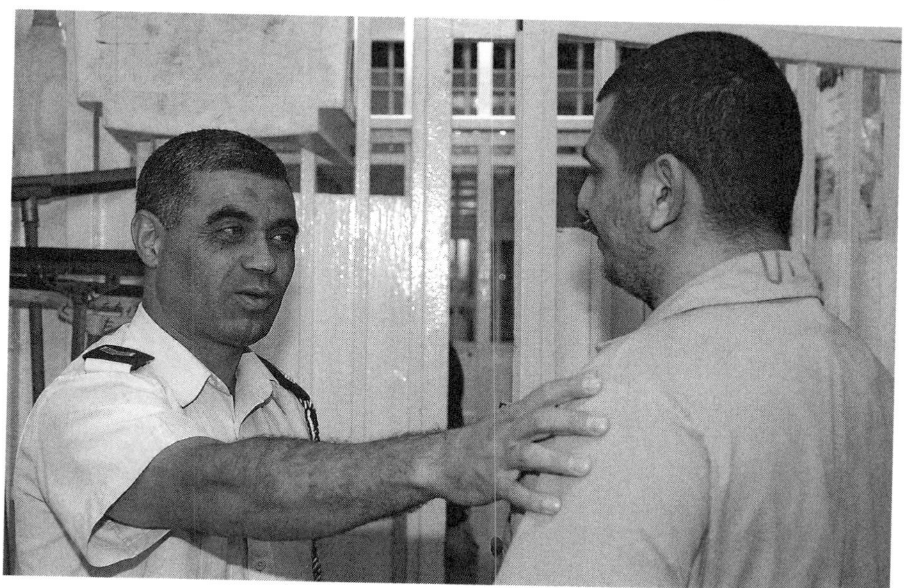

Figure 13.5. Friendly gesture exchanged between a guard and an inmate. Courtesy of the Israel Prison Service

Now I see that this is not the case. I have to listen and talk to inmates, try to understand them. . . . I feel like a social worker." However, it seems that the younger generation of guards accepts this new role. Such versatility has become common in Israeli maximum-security prisons, where officers feel comfortable about comforting and encouraging inmates.

Comparing the Results of the U.S. versus Israeli Systems

Israel has a significantly lower recidivism rate than the United States. During the last decade, the rate of recidivism for Israeli prisoners was a little over 40%, as measured by reincarceration within five years from release. Today few if any high-security prisons in the United States allow contact visits with family, conjugal visits, or furloughs. No U.S. prisons pay inmates to help other inmates or encourage community-style cellblock living. American prison sentences tend to be much longer than in Israel. Most U.S. prison systems, both federal and state, require prisoners serve 85% of their sentences, with few to no opportunities for early release. American prison management relies much more on the stick, including segregation of prisoners in long-term solitary confinement in high-security cellblocks or supermax penitentiaries. Israel, on the other hand, has not forgotten the carrot.

The harsh prison practices under the ideas of the "new penology" in the United States create serious impediments to successful prisoner rehabilitation and, following completion of sentence, reintegration back into normative society. The American approach tends to rely on punishing prisoners with solitary confinement and is thus not conducive of a more humanitarian approach that seeks to eventually reintegrate offenders back into society. It is counterproductive for all sides in the equation—prisoners, prison staff, and community—as such practices are causing more harm than good. Accordingly, the approach to punish and incarcerate is portrayed as unjust and discriminatory.

The Israeli experience presented in this chapter offers a slightly different approach rooted in the principles of Judaism. According to Judaism, all individuals deserve dignity, even when punished. It is within this religious tradition that IPS operates its prisons, and MSFs are no different. Most prisoners in Israel are sentenced to short periods of incarceration compared with those given for similar offenses in the United States. The leading assumption is that any length of imprisonment harms the individual offender and his family.[16] Prisons in Israel aim to serve a much broader goal: to restore the peace. To that extent, IPS invests in offering prisoners alternatives and venues to change their behavior and rehabilitate their lives while planning for when the time comes for them to reenter society.

Nevertheless, the goal of reforming prisoners is in itself far from clear, and when agreement can be reached on this point, the means to achieve it remain uncertain at best, as Sykes (1958) argued more than five decades ago. More recent studies also confirm such difficulty.[17] Many scholars agree that prison is not an adequate place for rehabilitation.[18] Scores of articles, chapters, and books have been written about the best practices for rehabilitating prisoners and how to better reintegrate them upon release.[19] Yet the practice of incarceration and MSFs exist, and it seems that they are here to stay for many more years to come.

IPS officials have worked hard to maintain the idea of rehabilitation as a main goal. From the early stages of screening and intake through the gradual advancement through the block system, prisoners are encouraged to develop accountability and in return be rewarded with various privileges. The majority of inmates choose to be involved in employment, education, religion studies, and therapy as vehicles of change, while improving their chances of early release. These program opportunities enable most prisoners to maintain some control and direction over their lives and to better the conditions of their incarceration and sentence, thus posing less of an assault on individual dignity. Further, the practice of furloughs available to MSF inmates helps them maintain their connections with family and the community. The relatively low recidivism rate for prisoners released from Israeli prisons suggests that these practices are not only humane but utilitarian as well. Such low rates are evidence that redemption is possible and lives can be changed even in the harshest of places, as in a maximum-security prison.

Notes

1. As of August 19, 2013, Wikipedia gave the following details on the demographics of Israel:

> The demography of Israel is monitored by the Israel Central Bureau of Statistics. The State of Israel has a population of approximately 8,012,400 inhabitants as of 31 March 2013. 75.4 percent of them are Jewish (about 6,037,700 individuals), 20.6 percent are Arabs (about 1,656,600 individuals), while the remaining 4 percent (about 318,100 individuals) are defined as "others" (family members of Jewish immigrants who are not registered at the Ministry of Interior as Jews, non-Arab Christians, non-Arab Muslims and residents who do not have an ethnic or religious classification). (http://en.wikipedia.org/wiki/Demographics_of_Israel)

2. See Seiter, 2012.
3. See Miller & McCoy, 2013.
4. Most incarcerated offenders in Israel are sentenced to much shorter terms. The median sentence for terms started in 2012 was 12.2 months.

5. Less than 20% of drug offenders are sentenced for more than seven years, and 30% of them are incarcerated in MSFs.

6. Furloughs are aimed at strengthening family ties and are a privilege afforded to those inmates who proved themselves in prison and are considered at low risk of criminal activity by the police.

7. Usually, the high-risk offenders are more experienced and therefore tend to be more cooperative with prison rules and regulations and with staff instructions, so that they may enjoy some privileges that will make their long stays in prison somewhat more comfortable. The fact that they don't need to build a reputation anymore also helps. On the other hand, low-risk inmates are sentenced for shorter periods, so the leverage on them is smaller. They also probably haven't been in prison for long enough to establish themselves, and thus many tend to be more "wild."

8. See LeClair 1978; LeClair & Guarino-Ghezzi, 1991; Cheliotis, 2012.

9. See Carlson & Simon-Garrett, 2008.

10. More violence occurs in MSFs (8.4 events per 100 inmates per year) than in medium-security facilities (6.3 events per 100 inmates per year).

11. See Sykes, 1958.

12. Some active drug addicts receive methadone treatment, while others that wish to participate in programs may be transferred to a specific facility and certain blocks to participate in an intensive rehabilitation program (see Gideon, Shoham, & Weisburd, 2010).

13. Section 9 of the Israeli Conditional Release from Prison Law 5761-2001 states,

> In deciding on inmate's eligibility for conditional release, the committee will consider the expected and potential risk to public safety, including the safety of the family, victim and the safety of the state of Israel; it will also consider the rehabilitative prospects of the individual and his conduct while incarcerated; to that extent, the committee will take into account, among other things, the following: (6)a. good behavior during the period of incarceration; (6)b. the inmate's positive attitude and values toward work and the steps taken by him toward rehabilitation. (p. 5, 4th Amendment from 2004, translated from the Hebrew)

14. See Ayllon & Azrin, 1968.

15. However, there are merits to the group. The group can reward the individual inmate in various ways, in particular when the definitions of compliance are more favorable. After all, this is what Narcotics Anonymous and Alcoholics Anonymous are all about.

16. See Shoham & Shavitt, 1990.

17. See Andrews et al., 1990; Wozner, 1998.

18. See Ortmann, 2000; Gideon, Shoham, & Weisburd, 2010.

19. See, e.g., Petersilia, 2003; Drucker, 2011; Gideon, 2011, 2013; Sung & Gideon, 2011.

Conclusion: Rethinking Prisons in the 21st Century

Stephen C. Richards

The Marion experiment was a failure on at least three levels. First, it directly contributed to the death or serious deterioration of hundreds of human beings. Second, the Federal Bureau of Prisons compounded the problems created at USP Marion by building more supermax prisons (ADX Florence) and high-security cellblocks to confine thousands of prisoners in similarly brutal squalor. Third, the experiment was replicated when Marion became the model for numerous new prisons constructed by the states and other advanced industrial countries. George F. Will (2013) concluded much the same when he wrote, "The first supermax began functioning in Marion, Ill., in 1983. By the beginning of this century there were more than 60 around the nation, and solitary-confinement facilities were in most maximum-security prisons." He noted that "tens of thousands of American prison inmates are kept in protracted solitary confinement that arguably constitutes torture and probably violates the Eighth Amendment prohibition of 'cruel and unusual punishments.'"

Austin and Irwin (2001) wrote regarding prison that "it's about time." Going one step farther, I argue that prison is about both time and space. The longer people are in prison and the more severe the environment, the harder and tougher they become and the more difficulty they will have if and when they are eventually released to rejoin free society.[1] The U.S. prison system has developed different institutions to separate diverse populations of prisoners:

supermax and maximum-, medium-, and minimum-security prisons. The prisoners are classified by length of sentence and expected adjustment to imprisonment. The federal prison system classifies prisoners into security levels from one (minimum low) to six (maximum high).

Many convicts do not passively comply with long prison sentences. They respond in diverse ways, some developing and displaying active defiance, others going mad or committing suicide. Most struggle as best they can not to become a compliant slave. If an inmate is to survive as an individual, someone more than a number, without drifting into madness, he will become a hardened convict. Because prisoners are human, they do not adjust gently to the artificial world they are forced to occupy. They resist imprisonment any way they can, depending on who they are, the time to be served, and the conditions of confinement they encounter in different prisons.

Some even develop remarkable routines to pass the years. In the penitentiary, men pass the years running, lifting weights, reading books, attending religious services, working in the kitchen, teaching classes, tutoring other men, finding ways to serve the community, and working suicide watch. The old cons teach the new how to do time by developing a daily routine that helps them retain or regain their dignity and self-esteem. A number of the convict authors of chapters in this book completed undergraduate and graduate degrees while in prison. For example, I earned a bachelor's degree in U.S. federal prison, Greg Newbold a master's degree in New Zealand federal prison, Seth Ferranti both bachelor's and master's degrees in U.S. federal prison, and Jon Marc Taylor bachelor's and master's degrees as well as a doctorate in state prison. Still, this small collection of authors does not represent the norm. As with all prisoners, despite their educational accomplishments, their nemesis was the difficulty of doing time in a given space.

Time and Space

Prison is all about time and space. While it is difficult to generalize about men and women incarcerated, I suggest this much we know. When prisoners first go to prison, they are simply inmates with a number and typically try to go along with the dictates of the regime. Although a few young men and women act out and are escorted to the hole, most fall into line as best they can. They read the prison inmate handbook rules and regulations, attempt to obey the guards when given direct orders, and hope that if they don't make any trouble, they will somehow survive intact without serious alterations to their personas. Interned in their first state or federal prison, they make a few friends, adjust to the noise and bad food, and then breathe a bit easier. These inmates think they can "do their own time."

The real reckoning comes later, when they are confronted with the reality of time and space. If they find themselves in a maximum-security penitentiary, it means they have a serious sentence of 10 years or more. In ways most unexpected, the penitentiary does its damage. Two or three years in, most inmates become convicts. It may not occur all at once, but over time there's a metamorphosis that transforms the relatively compliant inmate into an angry and resistant convict. While doing time, inmates come to see their suffering as injustice. They must become convicts to handle the longer sentences.

"Johnny 99"

Convicts know the Bruce Springsteen song "Johnny 99." The song is about an unemployed man who loses his home to the bank, gets drunk, and kills a night clerk at a motel. In court, he is represented by a public defender and gets sentenced to 99 years. Prisons receive these men and women, most of them what we call "straight Johns and Janes." They are not real criminals, just victims of sad events, where a life for a life is the punishment.

Typically, many of them are adolescents or young adults, and they arrive at prison angry, confused, and scared to death. Unable to adjust to the daily regimen of "general population" cellblocks, they go straight to the hole. No psychiatric intervention or therapy is offered. You can hear them screaming, banging the cell door, as they begin 99 years alone in segregation. If they do not quiet down, eventually the screws will silence them with clubs, restraints, gas, shock batons, or heavy meds. If they are lucky, they may survive their first encounter with solitary confinement without physical or mental damage. Eventually, a veteran convict will teach them the ways of the penitentiary.

Convict Authors in This Book

All of the ex-convict and convict authors who wrote chapters in this book were sentenced to considerable time in prison. I was sentenced to nine years in U.S. federal prison. Greg Newbold served over seven years in New Zealand. Jon Marc Taylor has been in state prisons for more than 32 years, including time in Indiana and Missouri. Seth Ferranti has completed 21 years of a 25-year sentence in federal prison. In and out of prison most of his adult life, Eugene Dey has spent much of the past 30 years doing time in different prisons in California. Brian Edward Malnes served nearly 10 years in federal and state prisons. Gregory J. McMaster has served more than 34 years of two concurrent life sentences, including 15 years in maximum-security prisons in the United States, before being extradited to Canada. David Honeywell served a 30-month youth custody sentence, and then a 10-year and later a five-year adult sentence in the United Kingdom.

At the time of this writing, I am a professor in the United States, while Newbold is a professor in New Zealand. McMaster is still in prison in Canada. Taylor is in prison in Missouri. Ferranti is scheduled for release from federal prison in 2015. Malnes is a doctoral student in the United States, while Honeywell is a freelance journalist and doctoral student in the United Kingdom, and Dey was recently released from prison in California. All of these accomplished authors comprehend how time twists inmates into convicts.

The Militarization of American Law Enforcement

In the United States, the criminal justice system has become militarized, with police chiefs in uniforms with stars on their epaulets and medals on their chests. Police and corrections officers display military-style ranks: Captains and lieutenants have bars on their shirt collars, while sergeants and corporals wear stripes on their sleeves. Both law enforcement and corrections recruit military combat veterans who may easily transition from the battlefield to law enforcement, exchanging one uniform for another. The police, especially in big cities, train officers in military-style operations and procedures, including the use of heavy infantry fire power and armored vehicles.

The militarization of prisons includes the warehousing of more than two million prisoners. In some states, there is no longer any policy of therapeutic intervention as correctional management. Instead, prisons detain the "enemy." Corrections are impossible when federal and state prison employees are trained to see inmates as enemy "prisoners of war."

The United States has waged wars against crime, drugs, and now terrorism. These wars have led to dramatic increases in the nation's prison populations that cannot be sustained without creating a police state, and they threaten the very social and economic fabric of our society. Abroad, they have contributed to U.S. military operations across the globe that will eventually bankrupt the nation. At home, they are evidence of the "internal colonial" state that has given up on full employment.

Needed Reforms

We must reduce the number of people in prison, reduce the length of sentences they do, and improve prison conditions, or we risk losing our leadership role in the community of nations. We cannot continue to keep millions of people in prison and hundreds of thousands in solitary confinement without becoming an outlaw nation existing beyond the pale of human decency.

The fact is that the courts in the United States have sentenced children, women, and men to ridiculous sentences that exceed any logical standards for a civilized society. In turn, these sentences—20, 30, 40, 99 years and more—have resulted in more maximum-security prisons, and then more solitary confinement units and supermax prisons. Yes, some prisoners have been convicted of terrible crimes, with victims murdered or injured. Nevertheless, a civilized society cannot be based on wars that lock people in cages and boxes for decades of slow, deliberate torture.

A civilized society builds a social fabric from education, employment, and civic duty. We must find a way to temper our retribution and show mercy for even the worst offenders. I suggest we begin by passing a federal law eliminating the death penalty and limiting all sentences to 20 years total for crimes of violence and 10 years total for nonviolent offenses. Most prisoners would serve less than the total 20 or 10 years in prison, with the balance on parole.

Reducing the length of prison sentences will reduce the prison population. In turn, this provides prison administrators with an opportunity to end the warehousing of millions of people and return to a focus on prison programs, including vocational and higher education. The idea would be to "do corrections." This means hiring more college-educated teachers, social workers, and corrections workers that are well trained and paid to organize and manage prisoner programs and activities that help convicts complete their sentences with dignity, leading to a dramatic reduction in recidivism. Doing corrections requires ending the military model and renaming correctional officers as correctional workers, well-educated social workers that specialize in working with prisoners.

I suggest we also need federal laws to "ban the box" that felons are required to check on employment applications, make it illegal to ask any questions about criminal records during job interviews, and limit all access to criminal records to only law enforcement, courts, and government oversight. We should protect the privacy of criminal records much like we already do for medical records. The public should not have easy access to criminal records on the Internet. This would give former prisoners a fair opportunity to find housing and employment upon return to free society.

Given shorter sentences of 10 years or less, most prisoners do their time with few problems if treated with consideration for their needs and future potential. The problem comes when political actors ignore social science, make bad decisions, and adopt "war on crime" legislation that creates a criminal class, felony ghettos, and supermax prisons. A properly designed criminal justice system, predicated on smart sentencing and humane prison programming, would not need to lock down tens of thousands of men and women prisoners in long-term solitary segregation.

American criminal justice administrators and academics need to begin serious study of the more humane prison practices of other advanced industrialized nations,[2] such as Denmark, Finland, France, Germany, Israel, the Netherlands, Norway, Sweden, and the United Kingdom. We can learn a lot from Israel, which has short sentences for even violent offenders and terrorists, community cells, conjugal visits, and home furloughs. Closer to home, we could learn a lot from Canada, which is also known to have humane prisons compared with those in the United States.

We need a federal law in the United States that prohibits torture, including long-term solitary confinement. No child, woman, or man should ever be locked down in solitary for more than seven days. After one week in solitary, the inmate should be moved to a four- to eight-person "community cell." The prisoners must first accept the new prisoner into their cell and then assume responsibility for his or her care. These cells might also be called transitional or structured living environments, as in Canada. As designed, they are a more humane alternative to solitary confinement, as they may be used to remove inmates from the general population and discipline them for violations of prison rules through loss of privileges, without the damage of complete isolation. Ideally, the community cell provides a quiet place where prisoners can find support to more peacefully do the time they have been assigned. After doing a few days in solitary, prisoners should serve the balance of disciplinary punishment in these larger cells, and then be returned to general population.

No judge or warden should have the legal authority to torture prisoners with months or years in solitary confinement. As discussed in the chapters in this volume and the many academic studies cited, long-term solitary confinement serves no legitimate correctional purpose.

Shedding Light on Prisons

Most U.S. prison systems do not welcome the press inside. Prison authorities do not want the press interviewing maximum-security prisoners. Over the last 40 years, since the beginning of the dramatic increase in prison populations, prison sentences, and the building of supermax prisons and solitary confinement units, correctional authorities have also limited access to academic researchers, and few new studies of high-security prisons have been authorized. Given the documentation provided by the authors in this book, the reasons are obvious.

As a democratic society, we need to open U.S. prisons to the press, academic research, and international inspection. This should include confidential and anonymous interviews of prisoners, without the supervision or surveillance of prison staff. Prisoner allegations of abuse that can be substantiated by witnesses or physical evidence should be thoroughly investigated by Congress and the U.S. Department of Justice. The call for investigations has already begun. Criminal charges and civil complaints should be litigated as needed. Prison administrators and staff that are alleged to have broken the law should be indicted and prosecuted.

I also suggest that the legislators that vote on crime bills, court officials that hand down sentences, prison administrators that order convicts into segregation, and academics that write criminal justice policy recommendations need to get a real education. I propose a science experiment where 100 brave volunteers, including politicians, judges, wardens, academics, and reporters, spend 30 days in solitary confinement.[3] They should sign consent forms to protect prison authorities from being sued and be assigned randomly to the holes of different maximum-security or supermax penitentiaries, without notice given to their keepers. They would be allowed to terminate confinement at any time. My guess is that few would last 30 days. Provided they survive the ordeal, they would then be interviewed and their responses recorded. Maybe when their stories are reported in mass media, the torture would finally end.

At the very least, if we are to conduct any meaningful evaluation research on supermax and long-term solitary confinement, the study needs to begin with face-to-face open-ended interviews of the prisoners. The Convict Criminology group includes numerous research criminologists that experienced many months in solitary confinement. Evidence-based policy needs to be based on research conducted by these former prisoners that are now professors. They are the researchers the prisoners will trust with frank and honest replies.

A Last Word: The Dilemma of Prison Reform

A dramatic change in public opinion will have to occur before we are able to reduce the length of prison sentences, the number of people in prison, and the use of solitary confinement. Unfortunately, I think academic criminology has been ineffective at educating the public and supporting humane reforms, although a few academics have become "public criminologists" whose ideas have been shared with a wider audience through books and even Hollywood movies.

Public criminologists must find the courage to help give voice to the men and women who live and die in cages. Both academics and prison employees can help educate the public about the need for more humane public policy concerning prisoners. This can be accomplished through writing letters to the editors of newspapers, speaking on radio and television programs, publishing books like this, and producing movies that take people inside prisons. The authors of the chapters in part two (Minor and Baumgardner; Stevens; Bickel; Immarigeon; Arrigo and Bersot) and part three (Honeywell; Herzog-Evans; Gideon, Walk, and Carmel) have made their contributions in this volume.

One example worth remembering is Tom Murton (1928–1990), who earned a doctorate in criminology from the University of California–Berkeley in 1968. Murton began his career in corrections by opening five prisons when Alaska was granted statehood in 1959. He taught criminology at Southern Illinois University before he was hired in 1967 to be the warden at Tucker and Cummins Prison Farms in Arkansas. Robert Redford played the part of Murton in the 1980 film *Brubaker*, which was a critical and commercial success. The movie helped educate the public about the use of torture and murder at the Arkansas prisons.

Murton submitted a 67-page report to Governor Winthrop Rockefeller, detailing the conditions he found at the two prison farms. He wrote that inmates were routinely tortured. This included flogging them, beating them with clubs, inserting needles under their fingernails, crushing their testicles with pliers, and applying electricity to their genitals (Trippett, 1980; also Woodward, updated March 6, 2014).

Prisoners later led Murton to some 200 graves scattered across the fields on the prison farm outside the barracks. The convicts had been buried in 4-foot wooden boxes. They dug up and exhumed a few bodies, to find corpses that had been beheaded and had the legs sawed off. Witnesses explained that when escaped prisoners were recaptured, they were routinely murdered and buried. Governor Rockefeller ordered that no more bodies be disinterred, and Murton was fired, less than a year after being hired.

Murton's experience in Arkansas was discussed in detail in two books: *Accomplices to the Crime: The Arkansas Prison Scandal*, coauthored with Joe Hyams (1969), and *The Dilemma of Prison Reform* (1976). After the statements he gave to the press and the publication of his first book, he was never again employed in prisons. Returning to academia, he worked as a professor of criminology at the University of Minnesota from 1971 to 1979 and at the University of Central Oklahoma and Oklahoma State University in the 1980s.

The dilemma of prison reform is that politicians and prison bureaucrats do not want the public to know what is happening in American prisons. Instead, they conceal the truth by silencing prisoners, whether in solitary cells or secret graves. The public needs to know what prisoners think about long-term solitary confinement, because eventually most of these children, men, and women will be released from prison to once again live among us. Films like *Brubaker* (1980) and *The Shawshank Redemption* (1994) present a complex reality and contribute to a public conversation about inhumane prisons that suggests prisons need to be open to the press and academic researchers. It is hoped that a civilized society will eventually end the brutal and criminal treatment of prisoners.

Notes

1. See Richards, 1998, 2009a; Richards & Jones, 1997, 2004; Ross & Richards, 2009.
2. See Ross, 2013.
3. See Mears, 2013.

References

Contributors

Index

References

Abbott, J. H. (1981). *In the belly of the beast: Letters from prison*. New York, NY: Random House.

Abbott, J. H., & Zack, N. (1987). *My return*. Buffalo, NY: Prometheus Books.

Abramsky, S. (2002). Return of the madhouse. *The American Prospect* (February 11), 26–29.

Ahn-Redding, H. (2007). *The "million dollar inmate": The financial and social burden of nonviolent offenders*. Lanham, MD: Rowman & Littlefield.

American Friends Service Committee. (1971). *Struggle for justice*. New York, NY: Hill & Wang.

———. (1993). *Lessons of Marion: The failure of a maximum security prison: A history and analysis, with voices of prisoners*. A. Prete (Ed.). Philadelphia, PA: American Friends Service Committee Criminal Justice Program. (Original work published 1985)

———. (2011). Women in prison: A fact sheet. *Women's Human Rights Program*. Retrieved December 15, 2011, from http://www.prisonpolicy.org/scans/women_prison.pdf.

Andrews, D. A., Zinger, I., Hoge, R. D., Bonta, J., Gendreau, P., & Cullen, F. T. (1990). Does correctional treatment work? Clinically relevant and psychologically informed meta-analysis. *Criminology, 28*, 369–404.

Annin, P. (1998, July 13). Inside the new Alcatraz. *Newsweek*, p. 35.

Anonymous. (2009). Some barriers detained migrant women face. *Social Justice, 36*(2), 104–105.

Antonaccio, O., & Tittle, C. R. (2008). Morality, self control, and crime. *Criminology, 46*(2), 479–511.

Arrigo, B. A. (Ed.). (2004). *Psychological jurisprudence: Critical explorations in law, crime, and society.* Albany, NY: SUNY Press.

———. (2011). Forensic psychiatry and clinical criminology: On risk, captivity, and harm. *International Journal of Offender Therapy and Comparative Criminology, 55*(3): 347–349.

Arrigo, B. A., & Bersot, H. Y. (2013). Behavioral forensic science: An overview. In J. A. Siegel, P. K. Saukko, & G. C. Knupper (Eds.), *Encyclopedia of forensic sciences* (2nd ed.) (pp. 159–163). San Diego, CA: Academic Press.

Arrigo, B. A., Bersot, H. Y., & Sellers, B. G. (2011). *The ethics of total confinement: A critique of madness, citizenship, and social justice.* London, UK: Oxford University Press.

Arrigo, B., & Bullock, J. (2008). The psychological effects of solitary confinement on prisoners in supermax units: Reviewing what we know and recommending what should change. *International Journal Therapy and Comparative Criminology, 52,* 622–640.

Associated Press. (2010, April 26). Court to hear appeal in guard's sexual assault. Retrieved July 11, 2014, from http://www.ohioprisonwatch.org/2010/05/court-to-hear-appeal-in-guards-sexual.html#more.

Austin, J., Bruce, M. A., Carroll, L., McCall, P. L., & Richards, S. C. (2001). The use of incarceration in the United States: ASC National Policy Committee white paper. *Critical Criminology, 10*(1), 17–41.

Austin, J., & Irwin, J. (2001). *It's about time: America's imprisonment binge.* Belmont, CA: Wadsworth.

Ayllon, T., & Azrin, N. (1968). *The token economy: A motivational system for therapy and rehabilitation.* East Norwalk, CT: Appleton-Century-Crofts.

Badinter, R. (1992). *La prison républicaine* [The republican prison]. Paris: Fayard.

Baillargeon, J., Hoge, S. K., & Penn, J. V. (2010). Addressing the challenge of community reentry among released inmates with serious mental illness. *American Journal of Community Psychology, 46*(3–4), 361–375.

Banks, C. (2009). *Criminal justice ethics: Theory and practice* (2nd ed.). Thousand Oaks, CA: Sage Publications.

Barker, V. (2009). *The politics of imprisonment: How the democratic process shapes the way America punishes offenders.* New York, NY: Oxford University Press.

Baumgardner, M. (2011). *Supermax confinement: A descriptive and theoretical inquiry* (Unpublished master's thesis). Eastern Kentucky University, Richmond, Kentucky.

Bazemore, G., & Boba, R. (2007). Doing good to make good: Community theory for practice in a restorative justice civic engagement reentry model. *Journal of Offender Rehabilitation, 46*(1/2), 25–56.

Beck, V. S., Richards, S. C., & Elrod, P. (2008). Prison visits: On the outside looking in. *Journal of Prisoners on Prisons, 17*(1), 91–105.

Bell v. Wolfish, 441 U.S. 520 (1979).

Benjamin, T. B., & Lux, K. (1977). Solitary Confinement as Psychological Punishment. *California Western Law Review, 13*, 265.

Bergin, T. (2013). *The evidence enigma: Correctional boot camps and other failures in research-based policymaking.* Burlington, VT: Ashgate.

Bersot, H. Y., & Arrigo, B. A. (2010). Inmate mental health, solitary confinement, and cruel and unusual punishment: An ethical and justice policy inquiry. *Journal of Theoretical and Philosophical Criminology, 2*(3), 1–82.

———. (2011). The ethics of mechanical restraints in prisons and jails: A preliminary inquiry from psychological jurisprudence. *Journal of Forensic Psychology Practice Special Double Issue, 11*(2–3), 232–265.

Bickel, C. (2010). From child to captive: Constructing captivity in a juvenile institution. *Western Criminology Review, 11*(1), 37–49.

Blanchette, K. (2001). Characteristics of administratively segregated offenders in federal corrections. *Canadian Journal of Criminology, 43*(1), 131–144.

Bonta, J., & Gendreau, P. (1990). Reexamining the cruel and unusual punishment of prison life. *Law and Human Behavior, 14*(4), 347–372.

———. (1995). Reexamining the cruel and unusual punishment of prison life. In T. J. Flanagan (Ed.), *Long-term imprisonment: Policy, science, and correctional practice* (pp. 75–94). Thousand Oaks, CA: Sage Publications.

Bosworth, M. (2002). *The U.S. federal prison system*. Thousand Oaks, CA: Sage.

———. (Ed.). (2005). *Encyclopedia of prisons and correctional facilities*. (Vols. 1–2). Thousand Oaks, CA: Sage Publications.

———. (2010). *Explaining U.S. imprisonment*. Los Angeles, CA: Sage.

Bourdieu, P. (1977). *Outline of a theory of practice*. New York, NY: Cambridge University Press.

Briggs, C. S., Sundt, J. I., & Castellano, T. C. (2003). The effects of supermaximum security prisons on aggregate levels of institutional violence. *Criminology, 41*(4), 301–336.

Brown, M. (2009). *The culture of punishment: Prison, society, and spectacle.* New York, NY: New York University Press.

Buchanan, K. S. (2007). Impunity: Sexual abuse in women's prisons. *Harvard Civil Rights–Civil Liberties Law Review, 42*, 45–87.

Bureau of Justice Statistics. (2010). State court processing: Violent felons in large urban communities: 2006. *Office of Justice Programs*. NCJ 228944. Washington, DC: U.S. Department of Justice. Retrieved

December 20, 2001, from http://bjs.ojp.usdoj.gov/content/pub/pdf/fdluc06.pdf.

———. (2011a). Prisoners in 2009. *Office of Justice Programs*. NCJ 231675. Washington, DC: U.S. Department of Justice. Retrieved December 21, 2011, from http://bjs.ojp.usdoj.gov/content/pub/pdf/p09.pdf.

———. (2011b). Federal Justice Statistics 2009. *Office of Justice Programs*. NCJ 233464. Retrieved December 21, 2011, from http://www.bjs.gov/content/pub/pdf/fjs09st.pdf.

Butler, H. D., Griffin III, O. H., & Johnson, W. W. (2013). What makes you the "worst of the worst"? An examination of state policies defining super-maximum confinement. *Criminal Justice Policy Review, 24*(6), 676–694.

Byrne, J. M., & Hummer, D. (2008). The nature and extent of prison violence. In J. M. Byrne, D. Hummer, & F. S. Taxman (Eds.), *The culture of prison violence* (pp. 12–26). Boston, MA: Allyn and Bacon.

California Department of Corrections and Rehabilitation. (2011). Weekly report of population: Reports. Retrieved December 6, 2011, from http://www.cdcr.ca.gov.

Canzi, C. (2010, January 5). Abuses exposed at Fluvanna Correctional Center. *Charlottesville News and Arts*, Issue 22:05.

Carlson, N. A., Hess, K. M., & Orthmann, C. M. H. (1999). *Corrections in the 21st century: A practical approach*. Belmont, CA: Wadsworth.

Carlson, P. M., & Simon-Garrett, J. (2008). *Prison and jail administration: Practice and theory* (2nd ed.). Sudbury, MA: Jones and Bartlett.

Casella, J. (2010, December 4). ACLU and experts slam findings of Colorado DOC report on solitary confinement. *Solitary Watch*. Retrieved January 1, 2014, from http://solitarywatch.com/2010/12/04/aclu-and-experts-slam-findings-of-colorado-doc-report-on-solitary-confinement/.

Casella, J., & Ridgeway, J. (2010, May 3). Woman prisoner sent to solitary for reporting rape by guard. *Solitary Watch*. Retrieved October 23, 2011, from http://solitarywatch.com/2010/05/03/woman-prisoner-sent-to-solitary-for-reporting-rape-by-guard/.

———. (2011a, April 23). Report from panel discussion on prison isolation units. *Solitary Watch*. Retrieved October 23, 2011, from http://solitarywatch.com/2011/04/23/report-from-panel-discussion-on-prison-isolation-units/.

———. (2011b, June 28). Voices from solitary: On solitary confinement and finding humanity. *Solitary Watch*. Retrieved October 23, 2011, from http://solitarywatch.com/2011/06/28/voices-from-solitary-on-solitary-confinement-and-finding-humanity/.

Cavadino, M., & Dignan, J. (2006). *Penal systems: A comparative approach*. London: Sage.

CBC News. (2010). Ashley Smith, 19, prison inmate commits suicide by hanging herself in her cell as guards watched. Retrieved December 6, 2011, from http://www.youtube.com/watch?v=tP-k47rIlyA&feature=related.

Cecil, D. K., McHale, J., Strozier, A., & Pietsch, J. (2008). Female inmates, family caregivers, and young children's adjustment: A research agenda and implications for corrections programming. *Journal of Criminal Justice, 36*(6), 513–521.

Center for Constitutional Rights. (2011). CMUs: The federal prison system's experiment in social isolation. Retrieved December 8, 2011, from http://ccrjustice.org/cmu-factsheet.

Center for Juvenile and Criminal Justice. (2007, May 1). California Juvenile Justice Reentry Partnership. Retrieved July from http://www.cjcj.org/news/5911.

Céré, J.-P. (2003). *Panarama européen de la prison* [European prison panorama]. Paris: L'Harmattan.

Chambers, R. (1998, July 17). Writer heads to Missouri to search for justice. *Richmond Indiana News Times.*

Chauvenet, A., Orlic, F., & Benguigui, G. (1992). *Le personnel de surveillance des prisons. Essai de sociologie du travail* [Prison staff. An essay in sociology of work]. Paris: Centre d'études des mouvements sociaux.

Cheliotis, L. K. (2012). Suffering at the hands of the state: Conditions of imprisonment and prisoner health in contemporary Greece. *European Journal of Criminology, 9*(1), 3–22.

Choquet, J.-P. (1983). La suppression des QHS [The deletion of high security wings]. *Revue pénitentiaire*: 33s.

Clear, T. R. (1994). *Harm in American penology: Offenders, victims, and their communities.* Albany, NY: State University of New York Press.

Cliquenois, G. (2009). *La réduction des risques et la responsabilisation dans la prise de décision en établissement pénitentiaire* [Accountability and risks in prison decision-making]. (Unpublished Sociology Ph.D. thesis, Ecole des Hautes Etudes en Sciences Sociales, Paris).

Cockburn, A. (2001, July 15). Commentary: Insane in the SHU box. *Los Angeles Times*, p. M5.

Collins, W. E. (2004). Supermax prisons and the Constitution: Liability concerns in the extended control unit. *National Institute of Corrections*. Retrieved December 9, 2011, from http://static.nicic.gov/Library/019835.pdf.

Combessie, P. (1996). *Prison des villes et des campagnes* [Prisons of cities and countryside]. Paris: Ed. de l'Atelier.

Committee to End the Marion Lockdown. (1992). From Alcatraz to Marion to Florence: Control Unit Prisons in the United States. Retrieved July 20, 2014, from http://people.umass.edu/~kastor/ceml_articles/cu_in_us.html.

Correctional Forum. (2007). Supermax. *The Blog of the Pennsylvania Prison Society*. Retrieved December 6, 2011, from http://prisonsociety.typepad.com/blog/mental_health/.

Corrothers, H., Alexander, M. E., Carlson, N. A., & Quinlan, M. J. (1994). Issues, past and present. In J. W. Roberts (Ed.), *Escaping prison myths: Selected topics in the history of federal corrections* (pp. 175–188). Washington, DC: American University Press.

Cuellar, J. P. (2007). In re Superior Court for the State of California, Lassen County #CCW2225.

Cullen, F. T., & Jonson, C. L. (2012). *Correctional theory: Context and consequences*. Los Angeles: Sage.

Danet, J. (1996). La notion d'état de santé et la détention en Europe [The notion of health and detention in Europe]. *Revue de sciences criminelle et de droit pénal comparé,* 49–80.

———. (2006). *Justice pénale, le tournant* [Criminal justice, turning]. Paris: Folio-Le Monde Actuel.

Darbeda, P. (1993). L'Action disciplinaire en détention: Un panorama européen [Prison disciplinary procedures: A European panorama]. *Revue de sciences criminelle et de droit pénal comparé,* 808–815.

Davis, A., De-Groot, A., & Shaylor, C. (1998). Symposium: Women in prison. *New England Journal on Criminal & Civil Confinement, 24*(2), 339–453.

De Giorgi, A. (2006). *Re-thinking the political economy of punishment: Perspectives on post-Fordism and penal politics*. New York, NY: Oxford University Press.

Denisovitch, I. (1992a, January). In praise of the reformatory lockdown: For my protection, of course. *Indianapolis Recorder*.

———. (1992b, March). Catch-22 at the reformatory: Correctional administrators: The new oxymoron? *Indianapolis Recorder*.

———. (1992c, May). The top-ten reasons for the lockdown at Pendleton. *Indianapolis Recorder*.

———. (1992d, June). Where's a reporter when you need one? *Indiana Defender*.

De Schutter, O., & Kaminski, D. (Eds.). (2002). *L'institution du droit pénitentiaire*. Paris-Bruxells: Bruylant-LGDJ.

Dey, E. (2005a, January 31). Death penalty alternative. *The Sacramento Bee*.

———. (2005b, June 16). Free speech lockdown. *San Francisco Bay View*.

———. (2005c, June 29) Sobriety behind bars. *The North Bay Bohemian*.

———. (2006a, May 24). The real hep C virus. *Metro Silicon Valley*.

———. (2006b, November 29). Civil death. *The North Bohemian*.

———. (2007a). Cauldron. PEN American Center, Honorable Mention, Nonfiction.

———. (2007b, December 13). Lockdown blues. *Sacramento News & Review*.

———. (2007c). A requiem for Freddy. PEN American Center, Honorable Mention, Nonfiction. Retrieved July 13, 2014, from http://www.pen.org/nonfiction-essay/requiem-freddy.

———. (2008a). Correctional asylums of the 21st Century. *Journal of Prisoners on Prisons*, 17, 2, 28–30.

———. (2008b, June 27). Don't just lock 'em. *Sacramento News & Review.*

———. (2008c). Frontline reflections of a drug war journalist. PEN American Center, Third Place, Nonfiction.

———. (2008d). In re Superior Court for the State of California, Lassen County #CCW2396.

———. (2009). Prison tours as a research tool in the golden gulag. *Journal of Prisoners on Prisons, 18*(1&2), 119–125.

———. (2010a). Grey goose. *J Journal: New Writing on Justice, 3*(2) 25–29.

———. (2010b, May 19). Soapbox: Health care for elderly inmates costly. *The Salinas Californian.*

———. (2011a). Cauldron of solitude. *Journal of Prisoners on Prisons, 20*(2), 35–46.

———. (2011b, March 24). Segregation = survival: Prison officials tell us integrate or else. But it's far too dangerous. *Sacramento News & Review.*

Dowker, F., & Good, G. (1993). Proliferation of control unit prisons in the United States. *Journal of Prisoners on Prisons, 4*(2), 95–110.

Drucker, E. (2011). *A plague of prisons: The epidemiology of mass incarceration in America.* New York, NY: The New Press

Duff, R. D., & Garland, D. (Eds.). (1995). *A reader on punishment.* New York. Oxford University Press.

Dünkel, F., & Snacken S. (2004). *Prisons en Europe* [European prisons]. Paris: L'Harmattan.

Dunne, B. (1993). Dungeon Marion: An instrument of oppression. *Journal of Prisoners on Prisons, 4*(2), 51–94.

Durkheim, E. (1964). *The division of labor in society.* New York, NY: Free Press. (Original work published 1893)

Earley, P. (1993). *Hot house: Life inside Leavenworth prison.* New York, NY: Bantam.

Editor. (1998a). Missouri prisoner is being persecuted for his editorial and legislative activism! *Cry Justice Journal,* #19.

———. (1998b, June). Persecution of an inmate activist. *Jusiticia.*

Fagan, J., & Meares, T. L. (2008). Punishment, deterrence, and social control: The paradox of punishment in minority communities. *The Ohio State Journal of Criminal Law,* 6, 173–229.

Faucher, D. (1999). *Éthique médicale en milieu carcéral: Suivi des personnes détenues en quartier d'isolement* [Medical ethics in a prison setting: caring for inmates placed in solitary confinement]. Dissertation, University René Diderot, Paris.

Faugeron, C., & Le Boulaire, J. M. (1991). *Prisons et peines de prison, éléments de construction d'une théorie* [Prisons and custodial sentences. Elaboration of a theoretical framework]. Vaucresson CESDIP, Études et données pénales.

Favard, J. (1986). La télévision dans les prisons [Television in prison]. *Revue de sciences criminelles et de droit pénal comparé*, 903s.

Feeley, M. M., & Rubin, E. L. (1999). *Judicial policy making and the modern state: How the courts reformed America's prisons*. New York, NY: Cambridge University Press.

Feeley, M. M., & Simon, J. (1992). The new penology: Notes on the emerging strategy of corrections and its implications. *Criminology, 30*(4), 449–474.

Fellner, J. (2006). A corrections quandary: Mental illness and prison rules. *Harvard Civil Rights & Civil Liberties Law Review, 41*(2), 391–415.

Finkel, N., Harre, R. & Lopez, J. R. (2001). Commonsense morality across cultures: Notions of fairness, justice, honor, and equity. *Discourse Studies, 3*(1), 5–27.

Fleisher, M. S. (1989). *Warehousing violence*. Newbury Park, CA: Sage.

Flinders, D. J. (2001). Nel Noddings. In J. A. Palmer (Ed.), *Fifty modern thinkers on education: From Piaget to the present* (pp. 210–215). London, UK: Routledge.

Ford, J. (2009). Corrections and mental health information needs of women in prison with mental health needs. Retrieved July 20, 2014, from http://community.nicic.gov/blogs/mentalhealth/archive/2011/08/26/information-needs-of-women-in-prison-with-mental-health-needs.aspx.

Foster, S. (2011). *Human rights and civil liberties*. Harlow, UK: Pearson.

Foucault, M. (1975). *Surveiller et punir: Naissance de la prison* [Discipline and punish: The birth of the prison]. Paris: Gallimard.

———. (1979). *Discipline & punish: The birth of the prison*. New York, NY: Vintage. (Original work published 1975)

Fraser, D. A., Mosley, V. R., Thornion, W. C., Belknap, P. H. & Rogers, R. A. (1984). Recent legal developments. *Criminal Justice Review, 9*(1), 47–52.

French, S. A., & Gendreau, P. (2006). Reducing prison misconduct: What works! *Criminal Justice and Behavior, 33*(2), 185–218.

Friedlander, H. (1995). *The origins of Nazi genocide: From euthanasia to the final solution*. Chapel Hill, NC: University of North Carolina Press.

Froment, J.-C. (1998). *La république des surveillants de prison. Ambiguïtés et paradoxes d'une politique pénitentiaire (1958–1998)* [The republic of correctional officers. Ambiguity and paradoxes of prison policies (1958–1998)]. Paris: LGDJ.

Gaes, G. G., & Goldberg, A. L. (2005). Prison rape: A critical review of the literature, executive summary. *National Criminal Justice Reference Service*. U.S. Department of Justice. Retrieved December 15, 2011, from https://www.ncjrs.gov/App/Publications/abstract.aspx?ID=234861.

Garland, D. (1990). *Punishment and modern society: A study in social theory.* Chicago, IL: University of Chicago Press.

———. (2001). *The culture of control: Crime and social order in contemporary society.* Chicago, IL: University of Chicago Press.

Gaucher, B. (1999). Inside looking out: Writers in prison. *Journal of Prisoners on Prisons, 10*(1&2), 14–31.

Gawande, A. (2010). Hellhole: Is this torture? *Long Term View, 7*(2), 20–33.

Giddens, A. (1991). *Modernity and self-identity: Self and society in the late modern age.* Stanford, CA: Stanford University Press.

Gideon, L. (2011). Correction in an era of reentry. In L. Gideon & H.-E. Sung (Eds.), *Rethinking corrections: Rehabilitation, reentry, and reintegration* (pp. 1–18). Thousand Oaks, CA: Sage.

———. (2013). Special needs offenders. In L. Gideon (Ed.), *Special needs offenders in correctional institutions* (pp. 1–20). Thousand Oaks, CA: Sage.

Gideon, L., Shoham, E., & Weisburd, D. L. (2010). Changing prison into a therapeutic milieu: Evidence from the Israeli National Rehabilitation Center for Prisoners. *The Prison Journal, 90*(2), 179–202.

Goffman, E. (1961). *Asylums: Essays on the social situation of mental patients and other inmates.* New York, NY: Doubleday.

Goode, E. (2014, March 15). After 20 hours in solitary, Colorado's prisons chief wins praise. *The New York Times*, A16.

Gordon, B. (1995). Let prisoners graduate first. *World & I, 10*(3), 93.

Gottschalk, M. (2006). *The prison and the gallows: The politics of mass incarceration in America.* New York, NY: Cambridge University Press.

Grassian, S. (1983). Psychopathological effects of solitary confinement. *American Journal of Psychiatry, 140*(11), 1450–1454.

———. (2006). Psychiatric effects of solitary confinement. *Washington University Journal of Law and Public Policy, 22*, 325–350.

———. (2010, November 15). "Fatal flaws" in the Colorado solitary confinement study. *Solitary Watch*. Retrieved January 1, 2014, from http://solitarywatch.com/2010/11/15/fatal-flaws-in-the-colorado-solitary-confinement-study/.

Grassian, S., & Friedman, N. (1986). Effects of sensory deprivation in psychiatric seclusion and solitary confinement. *International Journal of Law and Psychiatry, 8*(1), 49–65.

Greene, S. (2010, November 7). Questioning study that showed inmates in solitary get better. *The Denver Post*. Retrieved January 1, 2014, from http://www.denverpost.com/fdcp?1289216236539.

———. (2013, July 8). Tom Clements death: Prison officials acknowledge chief's death tied to solitary confinement policies. *The Colorado Independent.* Retrieved July 23, 2014, from http://www.huffingtonpost.com/2013/07/08/tom-clements-solitary-con_n_3564019.html#slide=more287578.

Grey, Stephen. (2007). *Ghost plane: The true story of the CIA rendition and torture program.* New York, NY: St. Martin's Griffin.

Griffin, E. (1993). Breaking men's minds: Behavior control and human experimentation at the federal prison in Marion, Illinois. *Journal of Prisoners on Prisons, 4*(2), 17–28.

Hallinan, J. T. (2003). *Going up the river: Travels in a prison nation.* New York, NY: Random House.

Hamm, M. S. (1991). The abandoned ones: A history of the Oakdale and Atlanta prison riots. In G. Barak (Ed.), *Crimes by the capitalist state* (pp. 145–180). Albany, NY: SUNY Press.

———. (1995). *The abandoned ones.* Boston, MA: Northeastern University Press.

———. (1997). *Apocalypse in Oklahoma: Waco and Ruby Ridge revenged.* Boston, MA: Northeastern University Press.

Hamm, M. S., Coupez, T., Hoze, F. E., & Weinstein, C. (1994). The myth of humane imprisonment: A critical analysis of severe discipline in U.S. maximum security prisons, 1945–1990. In M. Braswell, R. Montgomery Jr., & L. X. Lobardo (Eds.), *Prison violence in America* (2d ed.) (pp. 167–200). Cincinnati, OH: Anderson.

Haney, C. (1993). "Infamous punishment": The psychological consequences of isolation. *The National Prison Project Journal, 8*(2), 3–7, 21.

———. (2003). Mental health issues in long-term solitary and "supermax" confinement. *Crime & Delinquency, 49,* 124–156.

———. (2006). *Reforming punishment: Psychological limits to the pains of imprisonment.* Washington, DC: American Psychological Association.

———. (2009). The social psychology of isolation: Why solitary confinement is psychologically harmful. *Prison Service Journal, 181*(1), 12–20.

Haney, C., & Lynch, M. (1997). Regulating prisons of the future: A psychological analysis of supermax and solitary confinement. *New York University Review of Law and Social Change, 23*(4), 477–570.

Haney, C., & Zimbardo, P. (1998). The past and the future of U.S. prison policy: Twenty-five years after the Stanford prison experiment. *American Psychologist, 53*(7), 709–727.

Hanif, N. M. (2008). Prison's spoilt identities: Racially structured realities within and beyond. *Current Issues in Criminal Justice, 20*(2), 243–264.

Harrington, S. P. M. (1997). Caging the crazy: Supermax confinement under attack. *The Humanist* (January–February), 14–19.

Hassine, V. (2011). *Life without parole: Living and dying in prison today.* London: Oxford University Press.

Hayes, L. (2004). Juvenile suicide in confinement: A national survey. Baltimore, MD: National Center on Institutions and Corrections.

Henman, G. (1988). Inside Marion: Warden Gary Henman talks about BOP's (Bureau of Prisons') most secure prison. *Corrections Today, 50*(4), 92–94, 96–101, 155.

Herivel, T., & Wright, P. (2003). *Prison nation: The warehousing of America's poor.* London, UK: Routledge.

Hertrich, V., & Faugeron, C. (1987). Les Elèves surveillants de 1968 à 1986: Données statistiques [Correctional officer trainees from 1968 to 1986. Statistical data]. CESDIP, *Etudes et données pénales, n° 52*. Vaucresson: Center for Sociological Research on Law and Criminal Justice Institutions (CESDIP).

Herzog-Evans, M. (1998). *La Gestion du comportement du détenu. Essai de droit pénitentiaire* [Managing inmates' behavior. Essay in prison law]. Paris: L'Harmattan.

———. (2000). *L'Intimité du détenu et de ses proches en droit comparé* [Prisoners and their significant others' intimacy in comparative law]. Paris: L'Harmattan.

———. (2001). Les Sanctions pénitentiaires occultes [Occult prison sanctions]. In *Mélanges P. Couvrat*. Paris: PUF: 471–487.

———. (2009). Application des peines: la prétendue « bonne partie » de la loi pénitentiaire [Sentences' implementation: The so-called "good part" of the prison law]. *Actualité juridique pénal.* December: 483–490.

———. (2010a). Loi pénitentiaire n° 2009–1436 du 24 novembre 2009: changement de paradigme pénologique et toute puissance administrative [The prison act no. 2009-1436 of November 24, 2009: Paradigmatic changes in penology and administrative omnipotence]. *Recueil Dalloz*, p. 31.

———. (2010b). Safety measures in France. In M. Herzog-Evans (Ed.), *Transnational Criminology Manual* (Vol. 3) (pp. 423–438). Nijmegen, Netherlands: Wolf Legal Publishers.

———. (2012–2013a). *Droit de l'exécution des peines* [Law enforcement of penalties] (4th ed.), Paris: Dalloz.

———. (2012–2013b). *Droit pénitentiaire* [Prison law]. Paris: Dalloz.

Hill, G., & Hill, K. (n.d.). Solitary confinement. In *The People's Law Dictionary*. Retrieved December 6, 2011, from http://dictionary.law.com.

Hirsch, A. J. (1992). The rise of the penitentiary: Prisons and punishment in early America. New Haven, CT: Yale University Press.

Hucklebury, C. (1999). Writing on the walls: It isn't just graffitti [*sic*]. *Journal of Prisoners on Prisons, 10*(1&2), 32–39.

Human Rights Watch. (1997). *Human Rights Watch world report*. New York, NY: Human Rights Watch.

———. (2000). *Out of sight: Supermaximum security confinement in the United States*. Retrieved January 1, 2014, from http://www.hrw.org/reports/2000/supermax/.

———. (2009). *No equal justice: The Prison Litigation Reform Act in the United States*. New York, NY: Human Rights Watch.

Id, D. (2011, April 21). Isolation units in U.S. prisons panel discussion, San Francisco, 4/5/11: photo and audio. *San Francisco Bay Area Independent Media Center*. Retrieved December 8, 2011, from http://www.indybay.org/newsitems/2011/04/21/18677734.php.

Illinois Department of Corrections. (2011). Annual Report 2010. *Illinois Department of Corrections*. Retrieved October 25, 2011, from http://www.idoc.state.il.us/.

Immarigeon, R. (1992). "Marionization" of American prisons. *National Prison Project Journal, 7*, 4.

Inderbitzin, M. (2007). A look from the inside: Balancing custody and treatment in a juvenile maximum-security facility. *International Journal of Offender Therapy and Comparative Criminology, 51*, 348–362.

In re Medley, 134 U.S. 160 (1890).

Inviting Convicts to College Program. (2014). *University of Wisconsin–Oshkosh, Department of Criminal Justice*. Retrieved January 1, 2014, from http://www.uwosh.edu/criminaljustice/internships.

Irwin, J. (1970). *The felon*. Berkeley, CA: University of California Press.

———. (1980). *Prisons in turmoil*. Boston, MA: Little, Brown.

———. (1985a). *The jail*. Berkeley, CA: University of California Press.

———. (1985b.) The return of the bogeyman. Keynote Address at the American Society of Criminology Annual Meeting, San Diego, CA.

———. (2005). *The warehouse prison: Disposal of the new dangerous class*. Los Angeles, CA: Roxbury Publishing.

———. (2009). *Lifer: Seeking redemption in prison*. New York, NY: Routledge.

Irwin, J., & Cressey, D. (1962). Thieves, convicts, and the inmate culture. *Social Problems, 2*, 142–155.

Jackson, J., Bradford, B., Hough, M., Kuha, J., Stares, S., Widdop, S., . . . Galev, T. (2011). Developing European indicators of trust in justice. *European Journal of Criminology, 8*(4), 267–285.

Jackson, M. (2001). The psychological effects of administrative segregation. *Canadian Journal of Criminology, 43*(1), 109–116.

Jacobs, J. B. (1983). *New perspectives on prisons and imprisonment*. Ithaca, NY: Cornell University Press.

Janas, M. (2010). Les dispositions relatives au prononcé et à l'application des peines de la loi n° 2009–1436 du 24 novembre 2009 dite loi pénitentiaire [The rules pertaining to sentencing and sentences' implementation in the act no. 2009-1436 of November 24, 2009]. *Droit Pénal*, janv., pp. 7–13.

Johnson, K. (2010, June 14). States start reducing solitary confinement to help budgets. *USA Today*. Retrieved January 1, 2014, from http://www.usatoday.com/news/nation/2010-06-13-solitary-confinement-being-cut_N.htm.

Johnston, N. (2009). Evolving function: Early use of imprisonment as punishment. *Criminology & Penology, 89*(1), 10S–34S.Johnson, R. (2005). Brave new prisons: The growing social isolation of modern penal institutions. In A. Liebling & S. Maruna (Eds.), *The effects of imprisonment* (pp. 255–284). Cullompton, UK: Willan Publishing.

Jones, R. S., Ross, J. I., Richards, S. C., & Murphy, D. S. (2009). The first dime: A decade of Convict Criminology. *The Prison Journal, 89*(2), 151–171.

Jones'El v. Berge, 164 F. Supp. 2d 1096 (2001).

Just Detention International. (2009). Truths about sexual abuse in U.S. detention facilities. *Just Detention International*. Retrieved December 9, 2011, from http://www.justdetention.org/en/factsheets/Truth_vWeb.pdf.

Keve, P. W. (1991). *Prison and the American conscience: A history of U.S. federal corrections*. Carbondale, IL: Southern Illinois University Press.

King, R. D. (1999). The rise and rise of supermax: An American solution in search of a problem? *Punishment and Society, 1*, 163–168.

Klebe, K. J. (2010). Long-term solitary confinement's impact on psychological well-being: The Colorado study. Symposium presented at the annual meeting of the American Psychological Association, San Diego, CA.

Knobelpiess, R. (1980). *QHS: Quartier de haute sécurité* [High security wings]. Paris: Stock.

Krisberg, B. (2003). *General corrections review of the California Youth Authority*. Oakland, CA: National Council on Crime and Delinquency.

———. (2005). *Juvenile justice: Redeeming our children*. Thousand Oaks, CA: Sage Publications.

Kupers, T. (1999). *Prison madness: The mental health crisis behind bars and what we must do about it*. San Francisco, CA: Jossey-Bass.

———. (2008). What to do with survivors? Coping with the long-term effects of isolated confinement. *Criminal Justice and Behavior, 35*(8), 1005–1016.

Kupers, T. A., Dronet, T., Winter, M., Austin, J., Kelly, L., Cartier, W., . . . McBride, J. (2009). Beyond supermax administrative segregation: Mississippi's experience rethinking prison classification and creating alternative mental health programs. *Criminal Justice and Behavior OnlineFirst*. Retrieved December 15, 2011, from http://www.aclu.org/files/images/asset_upload_file359_41136.pdf.

Kurki, L., & Morris, N. (2001). The purposes, practices, and problems of supermax prisons. *Crime and Justice: A Review of Research, 28*, 385–424.

Landis, B. (2005). Rape and sexual assault of women in prison, nationally and in Oregon. Retrieved October 22, 2011, from http://www.law.uoregon.edu/faculty/cforell/docs/prisonrape.pdf.

LeClair, D. P. (1978). Home furlough program effects on rates of recidivism. *Criminal Justice and Behavior, 5*(3), 249–258.

LeClair, D. P., & Guarino-Ghezzi, S. (1991). Does incapacitation guarantee public safety? Lessons from the Massachusetts furlough and prerelease programs. *Justice Quarterly, 8*(1), 9–36.

Leder, D. (1996). It's our Christian duty to educate prisoners. *U.S. Catholic, 61*, 12–16.

Lenza, M. (2011). The critical role of ethnography and autoethnographic research: Validating voices of prisoners and former prisoners within postmodern theories and methods. In I. O. Ekunwe & R. S. Jones (Eds.), *Global Perspectives on Reentry* (pp. 146–172). Tampere, Finland: Tampere University Press.

Levasseur, R. L. (1998). Trouble coming every day: ADX, one year later. In D. Burton-Rose, with D. Pens & P. Wright (Eds.), *The celling of America: An inside look at the U.S. prison industry* (pp. 206–211). Monroe, ME: Common Courage Press.

Levasseur, R. L., & Burton-Rose, D. (1998). From USP Marion to ADX Florence (and back again): The fire inside. In D. Burton-Rose, with D. Pens & P. Wright (Eds.), *The celling of America: An inside look at the U.S. prison industry* (pp. 200–205). Monroe, ME: Common Courage Press.

Lippke, R. L. (2004). Against supermax. *Journal of Applied Philosophy, 21*(2), 109–124.

Lipton, D., Martinson, R., & Wilks, J. (1975). The effectiveness of correctional treatment: A survey of treatment studies. Westport, CT: Praeger.

Livingstone, S., Owen, T., & Macdonald, A. (2008). *Prison law* (4th ed.). Oxford: Oxford University Press.

Lockwood, D. (1980). *Prison sexual violence*. New York, NY: Elsevier.

Lovell, D. (2008). Patterns of disturbed behavior in a supermax population. *Criminal Justice and Behavior, 35*(8), 985–1004.

Lovell, D., & Johnson C. (2003). *Felony and violent recidivism among supermax prisoners in Washington state: A pilot study*. (Unpublished report.) Seattle, WA: Department of Psychosocial and Community Health, University of Washington.

Luise, M. A. (1989). Solitary confinement: Legal and psychological considerations. *New England Journal on Criminal and Civil Confinement, 15*(2), 301–324.

Lynch, M. (2013). The social psychology of mass imprisonment. In J. Simon & R. Sparks (Eds.), *The Sage handbook of punishment and society* (pp. 242–259). Los Angeles, CA: Sage.

MacKinnon, C. A. (1989). *Toward a feminist theory of state*. Cambridge, MA: Harvard University Press.

Madrid v. Gomez, 889 F. Supp. 1146, 9617277v2. US 9th Circuit Court of Appeals (ND CA 1995).

Mann, C. D., & Cronan, J. P. (2002). Forecasting sexual abuse in prison: The prison subculture of masculinity as a backdrop for deliberate indifference. *Journal of Criminal Law and Criminology, 92*, 127–185.

Marks, A. (1997, March 20). One inmate's push to restore education. *The Christian Science Monitor*.

Martinson, R. (1972, April 1). Paradox of prison reform. *The New Republic, 166*, 6, 15, 29.

———. (1974, Spring). What works? Questions and answers about prison reform. *The Public Interest*, 22–54.

———. (1979). New findings, new views: A note of caution regarding sentencing reform. *Hofstra Law Review, 7*:242–258.

Massing, M. (2001, April 22). Everybody wants one. *The New York Times*. Retrieved January 18, 2013, from http://www.nytimes.com/books/01/04/22/reviews/010422.22massint.html.

Mayhew, P., & Van Kesteren, J. (2002). Cross-national attitudes to punishment. In M. Hough & J. V. Roberts (Eds.), *Changing attitudes to punishment, public opinion, crime and justice* (pp. 63–92). Cullompton, UK: Willan Publishing.

Mbanzoulou, P. (2010). Dangerousness: La dangerosité [Dangerousness: Dangerousness]. In M. Herzog-Evans (Ed.), *Transnational criminology manual* (Vol. 1) (pp. 109–123). Nijmegen, Netherlands: Wolf Legal Publishers.

McCorkle, R. C. (1995). Gender, psychopathology, and institutional behavior: A comparison of male and female mentally ill prison inmates. *Journal of Criminal Justice, 23*(1), 53–61.

McMaster, G. J. (1999a). Hole time. *Journal of Prisoners on Prisons, 10*(182), 87–97.

———. (1999b). Maximum ink. *Journal of Prisoners on Prisons, 10*(1&2), 46–52.

McVicar, J. (1979). *McVicar by Himself.* London: Arrow.

Mead, G. H. (1934). *Mind, self and society.* Chicago, IL: University of Chicago Press.

Mears, D. P. (2005). A critical look at supermax prisons. *Corrections Compendium, 30*(6–7), 45–49.

———. (2008). Supermax prisons: The policy and the evidence. *Criminology & Public Policy, 12*(4), 681–719.

———. (2013). An assessment of supermax prisons using an evaluation research framework. *The Prison Journal, 88*, 43–68.

Mears, D. P., & Bales, W. D. (2009). Supermax incarceration and recidivism. *Criminology, 47*(4), 1131–1166.

Mears, D. P., Mancini, C., Beaver, K. M., & Gertz, M. (2009). Housing for the "worst of the worst" inmates: Public support for supermax prisons. *Crime & Delinquency, 59*(4), 587–615.

Mears, D. P., & Reisig, M. D. (2006). The theory and practice of supermax prisons. *Punishment & Society, 8*, 33–57.

Mears, D. P., & Watson, J. (2006). Towards a fair and balance assessment of supermax prisons. *Justice Quarterly, 23*(2), 232–270.

Metzner, J. L. & Fellner, J. (2010). Solitary confinement and mental illness in U.S. prisons: A challenge for medical ethics. *The Journal of the American Academy of Psychiatry and the Law, 38*(1), 104–108.

Miller, H. A. (1994). Reexamining psychological distress in the current conditions of segregation. *Journal of Correctional Health Care, 1*(1), 39–53.

Miller, H. A., & McCoy, L. (2013). Special needs offenders in correctional institutions: Inmates under protective custody. In L. Gideon (Ed.), *Special needs offenders in correctional institutions* (pp. 259–284). Thousand Oaks, CA: Sage.

Miller, J. (1991). *Last one over the wall: The Massachusetts experiment in closing reform schools.* Columbus, OH: Ohio State University Press.

Miller, N. (1995). International protection of the rights of prisoners: Is solitary confinement a violation of international standards? *California Western International Law Journal, 26*, 139–172.

Ministry of Justice (Ministère de la Justice). (1998). *Etre chef d'établissement pénitentiaire en 2010. Réflexion prospective* [Being a prison in 2010. Prospective analysis]. Travaux et Documents n° 56, 1998. Paris: Ministère de la Justice, Direction de l'administration pénitentiaire.

Ministry of Public Security. (2006). *Israel Prison Service mission statement.* Retrieved January 1, 2014, from http://mops.gov.il/English/CorrectionsENG/Pages/IPS.aspx.

Minor, K. I., Wallace, L. H., & Parson, J. S. (2008). *Protective custody.* In P. M.

Carlson & J. S. Garrett (Eds.), *Prison and jail administration: Practice and theory* (2nd ed.) (pp. 321–336). Boston, MA: Jones and Bartlett.

Minor, K. I., Wells, J. B., & Soderstrom, I. R. (2003). Corrections and the courts. In J. Whitehead, J. Pollock, & M. Braswell (Eds.), *Exploring corrections in America* (pp. 60–107). Cincinnati, OH: Anderson.

Mitford, J. (1973). *Kind and usual punishment: The prison business.* New York, NY: Alfred A. Knopf.

Mobley, A. (2003). Convict Criminology: The two-legged data dilemma. In J. L. Ross & S. C. Richards (Eds.), *Convict Criminology* (pp. 209–226). Belmont, CA: Wadsworth.

Morris, N., & Rothman, D. J. (Eds.). (1995). *The Oxford history of the prison: The practice of punishment in western society.* New York, NY: Oxford University Press.

Moshenberg, D. (2010, January 8). What is left: Solitary confinement. *Women In and Beyond the Global.* Retrieved December 9, 2011, from http://www.womeninandbeyond.org/?p=599.

Murphy, D. S. (2003). Aspirin ain't gonna help the kind of pain I'm in: Health care in the Federal Bureau of Prisons. In J. L. Ross & S. C. Richards (Eds.), *Convict Criminology* (pp. 247–266). Belmont, CA: Wadsworth.

Murphy, D. S., Fuleihan, B., Richards, S. C., & Jones, R. S. (2010). The electronic "scarlet letter": Criminal backgrounding and a perpetual spoiled identity. *Journal of Offender Rehabilitation, 50*(3), 101–118.

Murton, T. (1976). *The dilemma of prison reform.* New York, NY: Holt, Rinehart and Winston.

Murton, T., & Hyams, J. (1969). *Accomplices to the crime: The Arkansas prison scandal.* New York, NY: Grove Press.

National Assembly (Assemblée Nationale). (2000). *La France face à ses prisons, rapp. de la comm. enquête sur la situation dans les prisons françaises*, t. I, *Rapport*, et t. II, *Auditions*, doc. adm. n° 2521, AN. Paris: Assemblée Nationale.

National Institute of Corrections. (1997). *Supermax housing: A survey of current practices, special issues in corrections.* Longmont, CO: National Institute of Corrections Information Center.

———. (2011). Corrections & mental health. *National Institute of Corrections.* U.S. Department of Justice. Retrieved December 6, 2011, from http://nicic.gov/Library/024961.

National Prison Rape Elimination Commission. (2009). National Prison Rape Elimination Commission report. Retrieved December 20, 2011, from https://www.ncjrs.gov/pdffiles1/226680.pdf.

Neal, D. (2003). *Supermax prisons: Beyond the rock.* Lanham, MD: American Correctional Association.

New York Department of Correctional Services. (2011). Under custody report. New York Department of Correctional Services. Retrieved December 6, 2011, from http://www.doccs.ny.gov/Research/Reports/2013/UnderCustody_Report_2012.pdf.

Newbold, G., Ross, J. I., Jones, R. S., Richards, S. C., & Lenza, M. (2014). Prison research from the inside: The role of convict auto-ethnography. *Qualitative Inquiry, 20*(4), 439–448.

Noddings, N. (1998). Perspectives from feminist philosophy. *Educational Researcher, 27*, 5, 17–18.

———. (2002). Starting at home: Caring and social policy. Berkeley, CA: University of California Press.

Ohio Prison Watch. (2010, May 1). Court to hear appeal in guard's sexual assault. Retrieved July 11, 2014, from http://www.ohioprisonwatch.org/2010/05/court-to-hear-appeal-in-guards-sexual.html#more.

O'Keefe, M. (2005). Analysis of Colorado's Administrative Segregation. Retrieved February 23, 2010 from http://www.doc.state.co.us.

———. (2008). Administrative segregation from within: A corrections perspective. *The Prison Journal, 88*, 123–143.

O'Keefe, M. L., Klebe, K. J., Stucker, A., Sturm, K., & Leggett, W. (2010). *One year longitudinal study of the psychological effects of administrative segregation.* Colorado Springs, CO: Colorado Department of Corrections. Retrieved May 21, 2014, from https://www.ncjrs.gov/pdffiles1/nij/grants/232973.pdf.

Ortmann, R. (2000). The effectiveness of social therapy in prison: A randomized experiment. *Crime & Delinquency, 46*(2), 214–232.

Padfield, N., van Zyl Smit, D., & Dünkel F. (Eds.). (2010). *Release from prison: European policy and practice.* Cullompton, UK: Willan Publishing.

Papen, M. K. (2011). Senate Memorial 40, 50th Legislature, state of New Mexico. Retrieved December 9, 2011, from http://www.nmlegis.gov/sessions.

Parenti, C. (1999). *Lockdown America: Police and prisons in the age of crisis.* New York, NY: Verso.

Péchillon, É. (1999). *Sécurité et droit du service public pénitentiaire* [Safety and prison public service law]. Paris: LGDJ.

Pedron, P. (1995). *La Prison et les droits de l'Homme* [Prison and human rights]. Paris: LGDJ.

Peltier, L. (1999). *Prison writings: My life is my sundance.* New York, NY: St. Martin's Press.

Pens, D. (1998). Federal prisons erupt. In D. Burton-Rose, with D. Pens & P. Wright (Eds.), *The celling of America: An inside look at the U.S. prison industry* (pp. 244–249). Monroe, ME: Common Courage Press.

Perkinson, R. (1994). Shackled justice: Florence Federal Penitentiary and the new politics of punishment. *Social Justice, 21*(3), 117–132.

Perrot, M. (1980). *L'impossible prison* [The impossible prison]. Paris: Le Seuil.

Petersilia, J. (2003). *When prisoners come home: Parole and prisoner reentry.* New York, NY: Oxford University Press.

Petit, J.-G. (1990). *Ces peines obscures. La prison pénale en France (1780–1875).* Paris: Fayard.

Piché, J. (2008). Editor's introduction: Barriers to knowing inside: Education in prisons and education on prisons. *Journal of Prisoners on Prisons, 17*(1), 4–17.

Piller, C. (2010, August 1). The public eye: California prisoners' rights often trampled. *The Sacramento Bee.*

Piven, F. F., & Cloward, R. A. (1971). *Regulating the poor: The functions of public welfare.* New York, NY: Vintage.

Pizarro, J. M., & Narag, R. E. (2008). Supermax prisons: What we know, what we do not know, and where we are going. *The Prison Journal, 88*, 23–42.

Pizarro, J., & Stenius, V. M. K. (2004). Supermax prisons: Their rise, current practices, and effects on prisoners. *The Prison Journal, 84*(2), 248–264.

Pizarro, J. M., Stenius, V. M. K., & Pratt, T. C. (2006). Supermax prisons: Myths, realities, and the politics of punishment in American society. *Criminal Justice Policy Review, 17*, 6–21.

Polizzi, D., & Draper, M. (Eds.). (2009). *Transforming corrections: Humanistic approaches to corrections and offender treatment.* Durham, NC: Carolina Academic Press.

Poole, E. D., & Regoli, R. M. (1980). Race, institutional rule breaking, and disciplinary response: A study of discretionary decision making in prison. *Law and Society Review, 14*(4), 931–946.

Pratt, J. (2013). Punishment and "the civilizing process." In J. Simon & R. Sparks (Eds.), *The Sage handbook of punishment and society* (pp. 90–113). Los Angeles, CA: Sage.

Prendergast, A. (2010). Articles by Alan Prendergast. Retrieved July 22, 2014, from https://www.prisonlegalnews.org/news/author/alan-prendergast.

Quigley, B. (2010, April 3). Not just Guantanamo: US torturing Muslim pre-trial detainee in NYC. *Huffington Post.* Retrieved May 15, 2014, from http://www.huffingtonpost.com/bill-quigley/not-just-guantanamo-us-to_b_524226.html.

Raemisch, R. (2014, February 20). My night in solitary. *The New York Times*, A25.

Raine, R. D. (1993). USP Marion's version of Orwell's 1984 and beyond. *Journal of Prisoners on Prisons, 4*(2), 29–45.

Ramirez, J. (1983). Race and the apprehension of inmate misconduct. *Journal of Criminal Justice, 11*(4), 413–427.

Reich, A. (2010). *Hidden truth: Young men navigating lives in and out of juvenile prison.* Berkeley, CA: University of California Press.

Reiman, J. (2005). *The rich get richer and the poor get prison: Ideology, class and criminal justice* (7th ed.). Boston, MA: Allyn and Bacon.

Rhodes, L. (2004). *Total confinement: Madness and reason in the maximum security prison*. Berkley, CA: University of California Press.

———. (2005). Pathological effects of the supermaximum prison. *American Journal of Public Health, 95*(10), 1692–1695.

———. (2009). Supermax prisons and the trajectory of exception. *Studies in Law, Politics, and Society, 47,* 193–218.

Rhodes, L. A., & Lovell, D. (2011). Is "adaptation" the right question? Addressing the larger context of administrative segregation: Commentary on one year longitudinal study of the psychological effects of administrative segregation. Washington, DC: National Institute of Corrections. Retrieved July 22, 2014, from http://community.nicic.gov/blogs/mentalhealth/archive/2011/06/21/is-adaptation-the-right-question-addressing-the-larger-context-of-administrative-segregation.aspx.

Rhodes v. Chapman, 452 U.S. 337 (1981).

Richards, S. C. (1990). Sociological penetration of the American gulag. *Wisconsin Sociologist, 2*(4), 18–28.

———. (1995a). *The structure of prison release: An extended case study of prison release, work release, and parole*. New York, NY: McGraw-Hill.

———. (1995b). *The sociological significance of tattoos*. New York, NY: McGraw-Hill.

———. (1998). Critical and radical perspectives on community punishment: Lessons from the darkness. In J. I. Ross (Ed.), *Cutting the edge: Current perspectives in radical/critical criminology and criminal justice* (1st ed.) (pp. 122–144). New York, NY: Praeger.

———. (2003). My journey through the Federal Bureau of Prisons. In J. I. Ross & S. C. Richards (Eds.), *Convict Criminology* (pp. 120–149). Belmont, CA: Wadsworth.

———. (2004a). Born illegal. In R. Berger & R. Quinney (Eds.), *Storytelling sociology: Narrative as social inquiry* (pp. 183–193). Boulder, CO: Lynne Rienner Publishers.

———. (2004b). Penitentiary dreams: Books will take you anywhere you want to go. *Journal of Prisoners on Prisons, 13,* 60–73.

———. (2005a). United States Penitentiary Leavenworth. In M. Bosworth (Ed.), *Encyclopedia of prisons and correctional facilities* (pp. 538–540). Thousand Oaks, CA: Sage.

———. (2005b). United States Penitentiary Marion. In M. Bosworth (Ed.), *Encyclopedia of prisons and correctional facilities* (pp. 569–573). Thousand Oaks, CA: Sage.

———. (2008). USP Marion: The first federal supermax. *The Prison Journal, 88*(1), 6–22.

———. (2009a). A convict perspective on community punishment: Further lessons from the darkness of prison. In J. I. Ross (Ed.), *Cutting the edge: Current perspectives in radical/critical criminology and criminal justice* (2nd ed.) (pp. 122–144.). Edison, NJ: Transaction.

———. (2009b). John Irwin. In K. Hayward, S. Maruna, & J. Mooney (Eds.), *Fifty key thinkers in criminology* (pp. 173–178). London: Routledge.

———. (2013a). I fell from the sky: Convict becomes professor. *Euro Vista: Probation and Community Justice, 3*(1), 1–6.

———. (2013b). The new school of convict criminology thrives and matures. *Critical Criminology: An International Journal, 21*(1), 257–271.

Richards, S. C., Austin, J., Owen, B., & Ross, J. I. (2010a). In memory of John Irwin. *Justice Policy Journal, 7*(2), 1–5.

———. (2010b, Spring). In memory of John Irwin, *The Critical Criminologist.*

———. (2010c). In memoriam: John Irwin. *The Criminologist: The Official Newsletter of the American Society of Criminology, 35*(2), 30.

Richards, S. C., & Jones, R. S. (1997). Perpetual incarceration machine: Structural impediments to post-prison success. *The Journal of Contemporary Criminal Justice, 13*(1), 4–22.

———. (2004). Beating the perpetual incarceration machine. In S. Maruna & R. Immarigeon (Eds.), *After crime and punishment: Pathways to offender reintegration* (pp. 201–232). London: Willan Publishers.

Richards, S. C., & Lenza, M. (2012). *Journal of Prisoners on Prisons: A Special Issue Commemorating the 15th Anniversary of Convict Criminology, 21*(1&2), 1–202. Toronto, Canada: University of Toronto Press.

Richards, S. C., Lenza, M., Newbold, G., Jones, R. S., Murphy, D., & Grigsby, R. (2010). Prison as seen by Convict Criminologists. In M. Herzog-Evans (Ed.), *Transnational criminology manual* (Vol. 3) (pp. 343–360). Nijmegen, Netherlands: Wolf Legal Publishers.

Richards, S. C., & Ross, J. I. (2001). The new school of Convict Criminology. *Social Justice, 28*(1), 177–190.

———. (2003a). Conclusion: An invitation to the criminology/criminal justice community. In J. I. Ross & S. C. Richards (Eds.), *Convict Criminology* (pp. 347–353). Belmont, CA: Wadsworth.

———. (2003b). Convict perspective on the classification of prisoners. *Criminology & Public Policy, 2*(2), 243–252.

———. (2003c). Ex-convict professors doing prison research. In *The state of corrections: 2002 proceedings ACA Annual Conferences* (pp. 163–168). Lanham, MD: American Correctional Association.

———. (2004). The new school of Convict Criminology. *Journal of Prisoners on Prisons, 13*, 11–26.

———. (2005). Convict Criminology. In M. Bosworth (Ed.), *Encyclopedia of prisons and correctional facilities* (pp. 169–175). Thousand Oaks, CA: Sage.

———. (2009). Convict perspective on the classification of prisoners. *Criminology & Public Policy, 2*(2), 243–252. Reprinted in M. Stohr, A. Walsh, & C. Hemmens (Eds.), *Corrections: A reader* (pp. 113–119). Thousand Oaks, CA: Sage.

Richards, S, C., Ross, J. I., & Jones, R. S. (2008). Convict Criminology. In G. Barak (Ed.), *Battleground: Criminal justice* (pp. 106–115). Westport, CN: Greenwood.

Richards, S. C., Ross, J. I., Newbold, G., Lenza, M., Jones, R. S., Murphy, D. S., & Grigsby, R. S. (2011). Convict Criminology: Prisoner re-entry policy recommendations. In I. O. Ekunwe & R. S. Jones (Eds.), *Global perspectives on re-entry* (pp. 198–222). Tampere, Finland: University of Tampere Press.

Richards, S. C., Terry, C. M., & Murphy, D. S. (2002). Lady hacks and gentlemen convicts. In L. F. Alarid & P. Cromwell (Eds.), *Contemporary correctional perspectives: Academic, practitioner, and prisoner* (pp. 207–216). Los Angeles, CA: Roxbury.

Ridgeway, J., & Casella, J. (2011, October 6). Federal judge rules 28 years in solitary confinement not "extreme," dismisses Silverstein case. *Solitary Watch*. Retrieved October 23, 2011, from http://solitarywatch.com/2011/10/06/federal-judge-rules-28-years-in-solitary-confinement-not-extreme-dismisses-silverstein-case/.

Riveland, C. (1999). Supermax prisons: Overview and general considerations. *National Institute of Corrections*. Retrieved December 9, 2011, from http://static.nicic.gov/Library/014937.pdf.

Robert, L., & Peters, T. (2003). How restorative justice is able to transcend the prison walls: A discussion of the "restorative detention" project. In E. Weitkamp & H. J. Kerner (Eds.), *Restorative justice in context* (pp. 95–122). Dover, UK: Willan Publishing.

Roberts, J. V., & Gebotys, R.J. (2001). Prisoners of isolation: Research on the effects of administrative segregation. *Canadian Journal of Criminology, 43*(1), 85–97.

Roberts, J. V., & Jackson, M. (1991). Boats against the current: A note on the effects of imprisonment. *Law and Human Behavior, 15*(5), 557–562.

Roberts, J. W. (1994). *Escaping prison myths: Selected topics in the history of federal corrections*. Washington, DC: American University Press.

Rodriguez, D. (2006). *Forced passages: Imprisoned radical intellectuals and the U.S. prison regime*. Minneapolis, MN: University of Minnesota Press.

Rodriguez, S. (2011, September 8). "A form of torture": Testimony of Laura Magnani on solitary confinement. *Solitary Watch*. Retrieved October 26, 2011, from http://solitarywatch.com/2011/09/08/a-form-of-torture-testimony-of-laura-magnani-on-solitary-confinement.

Rogers, R. (1993). Solitary confinement. *International Journal of Offender Therapy and Comparative Criminology, 37*(4), 339–349.

Rose, C. D., Beck, V., & Richards, S. C. (2010). The mass incarceration movement in the USA. In M. Herzog-Evans (Ed.), *Transnational criminology manual* (Vol. 2) (pp. 533–551). Nijmegen, Netherlands: Wolf Legal Publishers.

Ross, J. I. (2007). Supermax prisons. *Social Science and Public Policy, 44*, 60–64.

———. (2013). *The globalization of supermax prisons*. New Brunswick, NJ: Rutgers University Press.

Ross, J. I., & Richards, S. C. (2002). *Behind bars: Surviving prison*. New York, NY: Alpha/Penguin Group.

——— (Eds.). (2003). *Convict Criminology*. Belmont, CA: Wadsworth.

———. (2009). *Beyond bars: Rejoining society after prison*. New York, NY: Alpha/Penguin Group.

Ross, J. I., Richards, S. C., Newbold, G., Jones, R. S., Lenza, M., Murphy, D. S., . . . Curry, G. D. (2010). Knocking on the ivory tower's door: The experience of ex-convicts applying for tenure-track university positions. *Journal of Criminal Justice Education, 21*(3), 1–19.

Ross, J. I., Richards, S. C., Newbold, G., Lenza, M., & Grigsby, R. S. (2012). Convict Criminology. In W. DeKeseredy & M. Dragiewicz (Eds.), *The Routledge handbook of critical criminology* (pp. 160–171). London: Routledge.

Rothman, D. J. (1971). *The discovery of the asylum: Social order and disorder in the new republic*. Boston, MA: Little, Brown.

———. (1980). *Conscience and convenience: The asylum and its alternatives in progressive America*. Boston, MA: Little, Brown.

Rotman, E. (1995). The failure of reform: United States, 1865–1965. In N. Morris & D. J. Rothman (Eds.), *The Oxford history of the prison: The practice of punishment in Western society* (pp. 169–197). New York, NY: Oxford University Press.

Sandin v. Conner, 115 S. Ct. 2293 (1995).

Scharff-Smith, P. (2006). The effects of solitary confinement on prison inmates: A brief history and review of the literature. *Crime and Justice, 34*, 441–528.

Schma, W., Kjervik, D., & Petrucci, C. (2005). Therapeutic jurisprudence: Using the law to improve the public's health. *Journal of Law, Medicine, & Ethics, 33*(4), 59–63.

Schofield, C. (1980). *Mesrine: The life and death of a supercrook*. New York, NY: Penguin Books.

Schofield, C. (1981). *Mesrine*. New York, NY: Penguin Books.

Seamons, K. (2011). UN: Solitary confinement amounts to torture, isolation longer than 15 days should be banned, says lead investigator. Retrieved July 11, 2014, from http://www.newser.com/story/131398/un-solitary-confinement-amounts-to-torture.html.

Sedlak, A., & McPherson, K. (May 2010). Conditions of confinement: Findings from the survey of youth in residential placement. Washington, DC: Office of Juvenile Justice and Delinquency Prevention.

Seiter, R. P. (2012). *Correctional administration: Integrating theory and practice* (2nd ed.). Saddle River, NJ: Prentice Hall.

Sellers, B. G., & Arrigo, B. A. (2009). Developmental maturity, adjudicative competence, and adolescent transfer: An ethical and justice policy inquiry. *Journal of Criminal Law and Criminology, 99*(2), 435–488.

Selman, D., & Leighton, P. (2010). *Punishment for sale: Private prisons, big business, and the incarceration binge.* Boulder, CO: Rowman & Littlefield.

Senate (Sénat). (2000). *Prisons: Une humiliation pour la République* [Prisons: A humiliation for the Republic]. French Senate, Report no. 449. Paris: Sénat.

Seyler, M. (1990). L'isolement en prison. L'un et le multiple [Solitary confinement. Unique and multiple]. *Études et données pénales, n° 60.* Paris: Center for Sociological Research on Law and Criminal Justice Institutions (CESDIP).

Shakur, A. (2006). *Assata: An autobiography.* Chicago, IL: Lawrence Hill & Co.

Shalev, S. (2008). *A sourcebook on solitary confinement.* London, UK: Manheim Center for Criminology.

———. (2009a). Inside supermax. *Prison Service Journal, 181*(1), 21–25.

———. (2009b). *Supermax: Controlling risk through solitary confinement.* Devon, UK: Willan Publishing.

———. (2011). Solitary confinement and supermax prisons: A human rights and ethical analysis. *Journal of Forensic Psychology Practice Special Double Issue, 11*(2–3), 151–183.

Shalev, S., & Lloyd, M. (2011). Though this be method, yet there is madness in't: Commentary on one year longitudinal study of the psychological effects of administrative segregation. *Corrections & mental health: An update of the National Institute of Corrections.* Retrieved January 1, 2014, from http://community.nicic.gov/blogs/mentalhealth/archive/2011/06/21/though-this-be-method-yet-there-is-madness-in-t-commentary-on-one-year-longitudinal-study-of-the-psychological-effects-of-administrative-segregation.aspx.

Shaylor, C. (1998). "It's like living in a black hole": Women of color and solitary confinement in the prison industrial complex. *New England Journal of Criminal and Civil Confinement, 24*(2), 385–416.

Shelden, R. (2008). *Controlling the dangerous classes: A history of criminal justice.* Boston, MA: Allyn and Bacon.

Sherman, L.W. (1993). Defiance, deterrence, and irrelevance: A theory of the criminal sanction. *Journal of Research in Crime and Delinquency, 30*(4), 445–473.

Sherrets, S., & LeBel, J. (2011, March). Final report of review of due process procedures in Special Management Units at the Maine State Prison and the Maine Correctional Center. Retrieved July 22, 2014, from http://www.maineprisoneradvocacy.org/FinalReport_MaineSMUdueprocessprocedures.pdf.

Shoham, S. G., & Shavitt, G. (1990). *Crimes and punishments: An introduction to [Israeli] penology* (2nd ed.). Tel-Aviv, Israel: Am-Oved [*In Hebrew*].

Silberman, M. (1995). *A world of violence: Corrections in America.* Belmont, CA: Wadsworth.

Simon, J. (2009). *Governing through crime: How the war on crime transformed American democracy and created a culture of fear.* New York, NY: Oxford University Press.

———. (2013). Punishment and the political technologies of the body. In J. Simon & R. Sparks (Eds.), *The Sage handbook of punishment and society* (pp. 60–89). Los Angeles, CA: Sage.

Simon, J., & Sparks, R. (2013). Punishment and society: The emergence of an academic field. In J. Simon & R. Sparks (Eds.), *The Sage handbook of punishment and society* (pp. 1–20). Los Angeles, CA: Sage.

Skinner, B. F. (1953). *Science and human behavior.* New York, NY: The Free Press.

Slobogin, C. (2005). *Minding justice: Laws that deprive people with mental disability of life and liberty.* Cambridge, MA: Harvard University Press.

Smith, P. (2008). *Punishment and culture.* Chicago: University of Chicago Press.

Snacken, S. (2005). Forms of violence and regimes in prison: Report of research in Belgian prison. In A. Liebling & S. Maruna (Eds.), *The effects of imprisonment* (pp. 306–339). Cullompton. UK: Willan Publishing.

Solzhenitsyn, A. (1973). *The gulag archipelago: Book I–II.* New York, NY: Harper & Row.

———. (1975). *The gulag archipelago: Book III–IV.* New York, NY: Harper & Row.

———. (1978). *The gulag archipelago: Book V–VII.* New York, NY: Harper & Row.

Sourcebook of Criminal Justice Statistics. (2009). Hispanic and female prisoners under sentence of death. Table 6.83.2009. Retrieved October 25, 2011, from http://www.albany.edu/sourcebook/pdf/t6832009.pdf.

Stannow, L. (2010, April 20). More must be done to prevent prison rape. *The News Tribune.* Retrieved December 9, 2011, from http://www.justdetention.org/en/jdinews/2010/main.aspx.

Stevens, D. J. (1994). The depth of imprisonment and prisonization: Levels of security and prisoners' anticipation of future violence. *The Howard Journal of Criminal Justice, 33*(2), 137–157.

———. (1997). Violence begets violence: Study shows that strict enforcement of custody rules causes more disciplinary problems than it resolves. *Corrections Compendium: The National Journal for Corrections, 22*(12), 1–3.

———. (1998a). The impact of time-served and regime on prisoners' anticipation of crime: Female prisonization effects. *The Howard Journal of Criminal Justice, 37*(2), 188–205.

———. (1998b). *Inside the mind of a serial rapist.* Baltimore, MD: Austin Winfield.

———. (1999). Interviews with women convicted of murder: Battered women syndrome revisited. *International Review of Victimology, 6*, 117–135.

———. (2000). Origins and effects of prison drugs gangs in North Carolina. In D. J. Stevens (Ed.), *Corrections perspective* (pp. 50–54). Madison, WI: Coursewise Publishing.

———. (2005). The history of prisons: Continental Europe and England. In *The Encyclopedia of Criminology*. New York, NY: Routledge/Taylor & Francis.

———. (2006). *Applied community corrections: An applied approach.* Upper Saddle River, NJ: Prentice Hall.

———. (2010). *The media and criminal justice: CSI effect*. Sudbury, MA: Jones and Bartlett Publishers.

———. (2011). Wicked women: A journey of super predators. Bloomington, IN: IUniverse.

———. (2012). Imprisoning sexual offenders. In C. Kaltefleiter, M. Nagel, & A. Nocella, (Eds.), Prison abolition: Unchaining ourselves from U.S. imperialism. Binghamton, NY: Arissa Media Group.

Stopmax Voices. (2008, June 27). Solitary confinement testimonials: Testimony from women's control unit in FLA. Retrieved December 6, 2011, from http://www.stopmaxvoices.blogspot.com/.

Suedfeld, P. (1974). Solitary confinement in the correctional setting: Goals, problems, and suggestions. *Corrective and Social Psychiatry and Journal of Behavior Technology, Methods and Therapy, 20*(3), 10–20.

Suedfeld, P., Ramirez, C., Deaton, J., & Baker-Brown, G. (1982). Reactions and attributes of prisoners in solitary confinement. *Criminal Justice and Behavior, 9*(3), 303–340.

Suedfeld, P., & Roy, C. (1975). Using Social Isolation to Change the Behavior of Disruptive Inmates. *International Journal of Offender Therapy and Comparative Criminology, 19*(1), 90–99.

Sullivan, D., & Tifft, L. (2005). *Restorative justice: Healing the foundations of our everyday lives* (2nd ed.). Monsey, NY: Criminal Justice Press.

Sundt, J. L., Castellano, T. C., & Briggs, C. S. (2008). The socio-political context of prison violence and its control: A case study of supermax in Illinois. *The Prison Journal, 88*, 94–122.

Sung, H. E., & Gideon, L. (2011). Major rehabilitative approaches. In L. Gideon & H. E. Sung (Eds.), *Rethinking corrections: Rehabilitation, reentry, and reintegration* (pp. 71–96). Thousand Oaks, CA: Sage Publishers.

Swanson, C. G. (2009). *Restorative justice in a prison community: Or everything I didn't learn in kindergarten I learned in prison*. Lanham, MD: Lexington Books.

Sykes, G. M. (1958). *Society of captives: A study of maximum-security prison*. Princeton, NJ: Princeton University Press.

Talvi, S. J. A. (2007). *Women behind bars: The crisis of women in the U.S. prison system*. Emeryville, CA: Seal Press.

Tannenbaum, F. (1938). *Crime and the community*. Boston, MA: Ginn.

Taylor, J. M. (1994, August 24). There ought to be a law, but not this crime bill. *The New York Times*.

———. (1995a). It's criminal to deny Pell grants to prisoners. *World & I, 10*, 88–92.

———. (1995b, March 17). Prisoner takers prison figures apart. *Catholic Missourian*.

———. (1996a, February). How many times do we have to pay? *Catholic Missourian*.

———. (1996b, July 8). A view from inside prison walls. *St. Louis Post-Dispatch*.

———. (1997a, January). Calling for sheepskins. *Cry Justice Journal*.

———. (1997b, February 19). College tuitions subsidize prisoners. *Columbia Missourian*.

———. (1997c, March). Dialing for diplomas, Part I. *Justicia*.

———. (1997d, March 17). State's philosophy on crime hard on education. *Springfield News-Leader*.

———. (1997e, April). Dialing for diplomas, Part II. *Justicia*.

———. (1997f, May 15). Bait and switch: More prisons "fight crime" as statistics drop. *Southeast Missourian*.

———. (1997g, May 20). Recovery symposium helps inmates. *Columbia Missourian*.

———. (1997h, June 11). Missouri doesn't need more prisons. *Columbia Missourian*.

———. (1997i, November). Civil disabilities of convicted felons: A state-by-state survey. *Prison Legal News*.

———. (1998a). The unity walk. *Journal of Prisoners on Prisons, 9*(2), 70–80.

———. (1998b, March). More on Texas training tape. *Justicia*.

———. (1998c, May). The balloon. *Fortune News*.

———. (1999–2000). Prison scriptorium aids blind. *Fortune News*, p. 6.

Terry, C. M. (1997). The function of humor for prison inmates. *Journal of Contemporary Criminal Justice, 13*(1), 23–40.

Thomas, C., Peterson, D., & Zingraff, R. (1978). Structural and social psychological correlates of prisonization. *Criminology, 16*(3), 383–393.

Thompson, A. C. (2009). What happens behind closed doors: The difficulty in eliminating rape in prison. *New England Journal of Criminal and Civil Confinement, 35*, 119.

Thornhill, R., & Palmer, C. T. (2000). *A natural history of rape: Biological bases of sexual coercion*. Boston, MA: Massachusetts Institute of Technology Press.

Toch, H. (1977). *Living in prison*. New York, NY: Free Press.

———. (1992). *Living in prison: The ecology of survival*. Washington, DC: American Psychological Association.

———. (2001). The future of supermax confinement. *The Prison Journal, 81*(3), 376–388.

———. (2003). The contemporary relevance of early experiments with supermax reform. *The Prison Journal, 83*(2), 221–228.

Tonry, M. (2011). *Punishing race: A continuing American dilemma*. New York, NY: Oxford University Press.

Trippett, F. (1980, May 5). U.S. prisons: Myth vs. mayhem. *Time Magazine*.

Torry, J. (2010, April 26). Supreme Court will hear sexual-assault case involving Ohio prison. Columbus Dispatch. Retrieved December 8, 2011, from http://www.dispatch.com/content/stories/local/2010/04/26/assault-case.html.

Umbreit, M. S., Coates, R. B., & Armour, M. (2006). *Victims of severe violence in mediated dialogue with offenders: The impact of the first multi-site study in the U.S. International Review of Victimology, 13*(1), 27–48.

United Nations. (1990). United Nations rules for the protection of juveniles deprived of their liberty. Retrieved May 18, 2014, from http://www.un.org/documents/ga/res/45/a45r113.htm.

U.S. Department of Justice. (2006). The nation's federal criminal justice caseload grew substantially during ten-year period. *Office of Justice Programs*. Washington, DC: U.S. Department of Justice. Retrieved December 21, 2011, from http://ojp.gov/newsroom/pressreleases/2006/BJS08302006.htm.

Useem, B., & Piehl, A. M. (2008). *Prison state: The challenge of mass incarceration*. Cambridge: Cambridge University Press.

Van Ness, D., & Heetderks Strong, K. (2006). *Restoring justice: An introduction to restorative justice*. Cincinnati, OH: Lexis Nexis/Anderson.

Van Zyl Smit, D., & Snacken, S. (2009). *Principles of european law and policy: Penology and human rights*. Oxford: Oxford University Press.

Vasseur, V. (2000). *Médecin-chef à la prison de la santé* [Chief medical doctor in the prison of La Santé]. Paris: Le cherche midi éditeur.

Wacquant, L. (2009). *Punishing the poor: The neoliberal government of social insecurity*. Durham, NC: Duke University Press.

———. (2010a). Class, race & hyperincarceration in revanchist America. *Daedalus, 139*(3), 74–90.

———. (2010b). Crafting the neoliberal state: Workfare, prisonfare, and social insecurity. *Sociological Forum, 25*, 197–220.

Walker, S. (2006). *Sense and nonsense about crime and drugs* (6th ed.). Belmont, CA: Wadsworth.

Walters, R. H., Callaghan, E., & Newman, A. F. (1963). Effects of solitary confinement on prisoners. *American Journal of Psychiatry, 119*, 771–773.

Ward, D. A. (1987). Control strategies for problem prisoners in American penal systems. In A. E. Bottoms & R. Light (Eds.), *Problems of long-term imprisonment* (pp. 75–95). Brookfield, VT: Gower.

———. (1994). Alcatraz and Marion: Confinement in super maximum custody." In J. W. Roberts (Ed.), *Escaping prison myths: Selected topics in the history of federal corrections* (pp. 81–94). Washington, DC: American University Press.

Ward, D. A., with Kassebaum, G. G. (2009). Alcatraz: The gangster years. Berkeley, CA: University of California Press.

Ward, D. A., & Werlich, T. G. (2003). Alcatraz and Marion: Evaluating super-maximum custody. *Punishment and Society, 5*, 53–75.

Welch, M. (2009). Guantanamo Bay as a Foucauldian phenomenon: An analysis of penal discourse, technologies, and resistance. *The Prison Journal, 89*, 3–20.

West, C. (2004). *Democracy matters: Winning the fight against imperialism*. New York, NY: Penguin.

Western, B. (2006). *Punishment and inequality in America*. New York, NY: Russell Sage Foundation.

Wexler, D. B. (2008). Two decades of therapeutic jurisprudence. *Tuoro Law Review, 24*(1), 17–29.

Wilkinson v. Austin, 544 U.S. 74 (2005).

Will, G. F. (2013, February 20). When solitude is torture. *The Washington Post*. Retrieved March 1, 2013, from http://www.washingtonpost.com/opinions/george-will-the-torture-of-solitary-confinement/2013/02/20/ae115d74-7ac9-11e2-9a75-dab0201670da_story.html.

Williams, C. R., & Arrigo, B. A. (2008). *Ethics, crime, and criminal justice*. Upper Saddle River, NJ: Pearson Prentice Hall.

Wilson, C., Goodwin, S., & Beck, K. (2002). Rape attitude and behavior and their relationship to moral development. *Psychiatry, Psychology and Law, 9*(1), 85–95.

Wilson, S. D. (1993). Warrior's fast. *Journal of Prisoners on Prisons, 4*(2), 47–49.

Wilson, W. J. (1987). *The truly disadvantaged: The inner city, the underclass and public policy.* Chicago, IL: University of Chicago Press.

Wilson v. Seiter, 501 U.S. 294 (1991).

Winick, B. J., & Wexler, D. B. (2006). The use of therapeutic jurisprudence in law school clinical education: Transforming the criminal law clinic. *Clinical Law Review, 13*, 605–632.

Wolff, N., Jing, S., & Siegel, J. A. (2009). Patterns of victimization among male and female inmates: Evidence of an enduring legacy. *Violence & Victims*, 24(4). 469–484. women & the law. Retrieved October 22, 2011, from http://www.law.uoregon.edu/faculty/cforell/docs/prisonrape.pdf.

Wolff, N. & Shi, J. (2011). Patterns of victimization and feelings of safety inside prison: The experience of male and female inmates. *Crime & Delinquency, 57*(1), 29–55.

Wooden, K. (2000). *Weeping in the playtime of others: America's incarcerated children*. Columbus, OH: Ohio State University Press. (Original work published 1976)

Woodward, C. E. (2014). Thomas Orhelius Murton (1928–1990). The encyclopedia of Arkansas history & culture. Retrieved July 12, 2014, from http://www.encyclopediaofarkansas.net/encyclopedia/entry-detail.aspx?entryID=7697.

Wozner, Y. (1998). Rehabilitation efforts in the Israeli Prison Service. In R. R. Friedman (Ed.), *Crime and criminal justice in Israel* (pp. 337–355). Albany, NY: State University of New York Press.

Wright, K. N. (1991). A study of individual, environmental, and interactive effectives in explaining adjustment in prison, *Justice Quarterly, 18*, 2, 217–242.

Yeager, M. (2011). Frank Tannenbaum: The making of a Convict Criminologist. *The Prison Journal, 9*(2), 177–197.

Zamble, E., & Porporino, F. J. (1988). Coping behavior and adaptation in prison inmates. New York, NY: Springer-Verlag.

Zinger, I., & Wichmann, C. G. (1999). *The psychological effects of 60 days in administrative segregation.* Research Report R-#85. Ottawa, ON: Correctional Services of Canada.

Zinger, I., Wichmann, C., & Andrews, D. A. (2001). The psychological effects of 60 days in administrative segregation. *Canadian Journal of Criminology, 43*(1), 47–83.

Zubeck, J. P. (1969). *Sensory deprivation: Fifteen years of research.* New York, NY: Appleton-Century-Crofts.

Zysberg, A. (1990). *Histoire des galères, bagnes et prisons: XIIIe–XXe siècles* [A history of the galleys, penal colonies and prisons: 13th–20th centuries]. Paris: Privat.

Contributors

Stephen C. Richards is a professor of criminal justice at the University of Wisconsin–Oshkosh. In 1983, he was convicted of conspiracy to distribute marijuana and sentenced to nine years. He did time in nine federal prisons, including U.S. penitentiaries, federal correctional institutions, and federal prison camps. Richards serves on the boards of directors of the federal and Wisconsin chapters of Citizens United for Rehabilitation of Errants, known as FedCURE and WisconsinCURE. He coordinated volunteers for prison visitation and support at federal prisons from 1994 to 2004. Since then, he has supervised student interns teaching college-level courses inside Wisconsin prisons. He has been interviewed by CNN, MSNBC, ABC, NBC, and *60 Minutes* on CBS, among many other media outlets.

Richards's writings include nearly 100 published works, among them books, journal articles, and book chapters. Of his five previous books, the most recent are *Behind Bars: Surviving Prison* (2002), *Convict Criminology* (2003), and *Beyond Bars: Rejoining Society after Prison* (2009), all coauthored with Jeffrey Ian Ross. Richards is a Soros Senior Justice Fellow, he is a former member of the American Society of Criminology's national policy committee and was named the 2012 critical criminologist of the year, and he is the lead organizer of the Convict Criminology Group (http://www.convictcriminology.org/index.html).

Bruce A. Arrigo is a professor of criminology, law, and society within the Department of Criminal Justice and Criminology at the University of North Carolina–Charlotte. In the College of Liberal Arts and Sciences, he holds additional faculty appointments in the Psychology Department and the Public Policy Program. In the College of Health and Human Services, he holds an appointment in the Department of Public Health Sciences. He has authored more than 150 peer-reviewed journal articles, law reviews, book chapters, and academic essays. He is also the author, coauthor, editor, or coeditor of 29 volumes. Selected recent books include *Psychological Jurisprudence* (2004), *Theory, Justice, and Social Change* (2005), *Philosophy, Crime, and Criminology* (2006), *The Terrorist Identity* (2007), *Revolution in Penology: Rethinking the Society of Captives* (2009), and *The Ethics of Total Confinement: A Critique of Madness, Citizenship, and Social Justice* (2011). Recent textbooks he coauthored include *Ethics, Crime, and Criminal Justice* (2nd edition, 2012), and *Introduction to Forensic Psychology* (3rd edition, 2012).

Marisa M. Baumgardner is a doctoral student at Bowling Green State University. She worked as a youth counselor at a juvenile residential facility in Kentucky, and earned a master of science degree in corrections and juvenile justice at Eastern Kentucky University. During her graduate studies, Baumgardner became interested in prison culture, especially supermax confinement. Her unpublished thesis, *Supermax Confinement: A Descriptive and Theoretical Inquiry* (2011), is an attempt to understand the theory behind the rise of supermax confinement.

Heather Y. Bersot is a criminal justice researcher and consultant with a master of science degree in criminal justice from the University of North Carolina–Charlotte. Prior to undertaking graduate studies, she served as coordinator of a juvenile justice diversion program for the Administrative Office of the Courts. Her peer-reviewed articles have appeared in the *Journal of Theoretical and Philosophical Criminology*, the *Journal of Forensic Psychology Practice*, and *Contemporary Drug Problems*. Bersot served as managing editor of the *Journal of Forensic Psychology Practice* in 2008–2009 and as coeditor of the journal's *Special Double Issue* in 2011. She coauthored the book *The Ethics of Total Confinement: A Critique of Madness, Citizenship, and Social Justice* (2011) and coedited *The Routledge Handbook of International Crime and Justice Studies* (2013). Her research interests include ethics, solitary confinement, justice studies, corrections, and penology.

Christopher Bickel is an assistant professor of sociology at California State University–San Marcos. He is both an academic and a prison rights activist.

Aside from researching juvenile institutions, he has taught sociology inside a federal penitentiary and worked with the formerly incarcerated in drug rehabilitation centers, sober living homes, and a halfway house. He is also the founder of the Continuation to College program, which teaches critical thinking and the sociological imagination to students at a continuation high school.

Tomer Carmel is a major in the Israel Prison Service (IPS) and a doctoral student in the School of Psychological Sciences at Tel Aviv University. In 2009, after almost a decade of researching cognitive processes, he joined the IPS research unit, where he serves as a research officer. He uses computational models and advanced statistics to investigate inmates' behavior inside prison, as well as after reentry into the community. His main interests are inmate violence in prisons, both against each other and against staff, and criminal behavior throughout the lifespan of "career" criminals.

Eugene Dey has been in and out of prison since 1984. He was sentenced to a 25-to-life sentence. In 2013, he was released from prison, due to a change in California law. He has published in academic journals and newspapers. By using higher-education certifications in alcohol and drug studies as an educational foundation, Dey and a cohort of "qualified offenders" are developing programming models that adhere to evidence-based principles. While adapting his previously published journal article as a chapter for this book, he was incarcerated at the correctional training facility in Soledad, California.

Seth Ferranti was convicted of running a continuing criminal enterprise in 1991 and sentenced to 304 months in prison at the age of 22. He has served more than 21 years in seven different facilities and is scheduled for release in 2014. Using Pell grants and his parents' help, Seth completed a master's degree through California State University in 2010. When he gets out of prison, he hopes to enroll in a doctorate program and continue his studies in the field of cultural criminology. He has had five books published to date: *Prison Stories* (2005); *Street Legends*, volumes 1 and 2 (2008, 2010); *The Supreme Team* (2012); and *The Prison Writings of Seth Ferranti* (2012).

Lior Gideon is a professor at John Jay College of Criminal Justice in New York. He specializes in evaluation of corrections-based programs and focuses his research on rehabilitation, reentry, and reintegration issues, especially offenders' perceptions of their needs. His research interests also involve international and comparative corrections-related public opinion surveys and their effect on policy. Gideon has written or edited several books on these topics, including *Substance Abusing Inmates: Experiences of Recovering Drug*

Addicts on Their Way Back Home (2010), *Rethinking Corrections: Rehabilitation, Reentry, and Reintegration* (with Hung-En Sung, 2011), and *Special Needs Offenders in Correctional Institutions* (2013). Gideon has also published two methodology books and is currently working on another volume, tentatively titled *Correctional Management and the Law.* In addition, he is the co-chief editor for a Springer Open Access journal titled *Health and Justice.* His other works have been published in *The Prison Journal, International Journal of Offender Therapy and Comparative Criminology, Asian Journal of Criminology, Social Science Quarterly, International Criminal Justice Review, Israeli Law Review*, and *Journal of Business Ethics*, to name a few.

Martine Herzog-Evans teaches law and criminology at Reims University, France. She also teaches at the Universities of Paris II and Bordeaux IV/National Prison Academy. She has published extensively (see http://herzog-evans.com). Her latest books are *Droit de l'exécution des peines* (*Sentences' Implementation and Probation Law*; 4th edition, 2012–2013); *Droit pénitentiaire* (*Prison Law*; 2nd edition, 2012–2013); *French reentry courts and rehabilitation: Mister Jourdain of desistance*, 2014; and *Réformer la probation française: Un défi à relever* (*Reforming French Probation: A Challenge*; 2013); and she edited *Offender release and supervision: The role of courts and the use of discretion* (forthcoming). Since the 1990s, she has fought for prisoners' rights via "legal guerrilla" and academic systemic analysis and has endeavored to create a systemic framework for prison law, a legal field that until then was rather unexplored in France.

David Honeywell is a criminology and sociology tutor, researcher, and guest lecturer in the United Kingdom. At age 20, in 1984, he was convicted of two attempted robberies, which resulted in a 30-month youth custody sentence in Durham Prison. Ten years later, he was sentenced to five years in prison for wounding with intent to cause grievous bodily harm; it was then he decided to halt his slide toward lifelong criminality. He started writing for magazines from prison and enrolled in a social sciences foundation course through the Open University. This experience qualified him, upon his release, to enroll at Northumbria University, in Newcastle upon Tyne, for two years' study before transferring to Teesside University. David is currently working toward a doctorate in sociology at the University of York, where he also teaches sociology and criminology to undergraduate students. His research is a study of ex-prisoners in higher education and their experiences of desistance, self-change, identity, and negotiation. In 2012, he published his story, *Never Ending Circles: The Autobiography of a Former Criminal Turned Criminologist*, and more recently, in 2014, *Deadly Encounters*, a memoir about his time spent with the Newcastle underworld.

Russ Immarigeon is an editor of *Offender Programs Report*, published by the Civic Research Institute (CRI). In years past, he edited the nationally distributed newsletter publications for the National Moratorium on Prison Construction, the American Civil Liberties Union's national prison project, the Victim Offender Mediation Association, and the International Community Corrections Association, as well as CRI publications about at-risk children and youth, community corrections, jail and prison management, and women and girls in the criminal justice system. He also has edited publications of New York's Statewide Youth Advocacy and the New York State Coalition on Criminal Justice, as well as four books: *After Crime & Punishment* (with Shadd Maruna, 2004); *Women and Girls in the Criminal Justice System: Policy Issues and Program Strategies*, volumes 1 and 2 (2006, 2011); and *Pathways to Prisoner Reentry* (with Larry Fehr, 2012).

Brian Edward Malnes, a doctoral student in English at the University of Louisiana–Lafayette, focuses on creative writing and poetry about the prison experience. In 1991, Malnes robbed a bank for the first time. His struggle with heroin and petty crimes led to nearly 10 years of imprisonment in both the federal and the Colorado prison systems. He has been out of prison since 2000. Malnes's writing is varied. He was a reporter for *The Denver Post*, and his poetry has appeared in *Portland Review*, *Blood Lotus*, and elsewhere. He has edited literary journals and written two books of poetry, *Seven Years' Bad Luck* and *Hollow Order*. A memoir, *Dark Like Never*, chronicles Malnes's bank robbery spree and imprisonment. Malnes's research interest is the eradication of social prejudice that follows the prisoner throughout his or her life. To this end, he has created a prisoner theory based not only on the experiences of the prisoner but also on the part played by humanity in systematically separating the prisoner, thus making him or her inhuman (www.prisonertheory.com).

Gregory J. McMaster has served more than 35 years of two concurrent life sentences, including 15 years in maximum-security prisons in the United States, before being extradited to Canada. He has won several writing awards, including first place in a contest sponsored by *Prison Life Magazine* (1995). He served as a contributing editor to the *Voices of Canadian Literacy* textbook (2002) and has been a regular contributor to the *Journal of Prisoners on Prisons*. Not restricting himself to the written word, he was the associate producer and American correspondent for the Canadian Prison Television Network (1993–1997), and he orchestrated several highly acclaimed television specials intended to educate the Canadian public about the realities of prison life. He has also been interviewed for numerous radio shows. As a jailhouse lawyer in Canada, he has set legal precedent for prisoners and the Canadian public with his successful litigations.

Kevin I. Minor is a professor of justice studies at Eastern Kentucky University. He has published extensively in the fields of adult corrections and juvenile justice and is presently conducting research on correctional staff issues, correctional law, as well as capital punishment and other extremist punishments. Minor's practitioner experience includes work at a state penitentiary and a juvenile institution.

Greg Newbold is a professor of sociology at the University of Canterbury, New Zealand. In the 1970s, he served a seven-and-a-half-year sentence for selling heroin and completed his master's degree while in maximum security. After his release in 1980, he read for his doctorate, which was awarded in 1987. Now regarded as one of New Zealand's leading criminologists, since 1980 he has written seven books and more than 70 articles and book chapters. He is frequently consulted by New Zealand courts and government agencies for expert advice on matters relating to criminal justice.

Dennis J. Stevens received a doctorate from Loyola University of Chicago in 1991. Currently he teaches criminology at the University of North Carolina–Charlotte and has taught at the University of Massachusetts–Boston. In addition to teaching traditional students, he has taught and counseled law enforcement and correctional officers at law academies such as the North Carolina Justice Academy and the Boston Police Academy and felons at maximum-custody penitentiaries such as Attica in New York, Eastern and NC Women's Institute in North Carolina, Stateville and Joliet near Chicago, and Massachusetts Correctional Institution–Framingham (for women). Stevens has published 17 textbooks, two novels, and almost 100 scholarly and popular literature articles. He has led intervention groups for sexually abusive parents in New York, North Carolina, and South Carolina and led group crisis sessions among New Orleans and Jefferson Parish officers after Hurricane Katrina. His website is crimeprofessor.com.

Jon Marc Taylor has been in prison for more than 32 years. While there, he earned a bachelor of science in history from Ball State University, a master of arts in executive development in public service with concentration in adult and community education at the same university, a certificate in criminal justice from the University of Alabama, and a doctorate in public administration from Kennedy-Western University. He is currently enrolled in a master of science criminal justice program at Southwest University. Taylor's own work and cowritten articles have been published in newspapers and many peer-reviewed academic journals. His numerous book chapters appear in scholarly anthologies and edited books. His book *Prisoners' Guerrilla Handbook to*

Correspondence Programs in the United States and Canada (2009) is now in its 3rd edition.

Dror Walk is a colonel in the Israel Prison Service (IPS). In 2009, he founded the IPS research unit and serves as its head. The unit carries out research on operational as well as correctional aspects of prison and inmates using advanced statistical methods. Walk's main interests are evaluation and cost-benefit analysis of correctional programs' effectiveness, and decision rule for surveillance of inmates with risk of suicide.

Index

Italicized page numbers refer to figures and tables.